New Challenges for Macroeconomic Policies

T0372507

Gilles Dufrénot

New Challenges for Macroeconomic Policies

Economic Growth, Sustainable Development,
Fiscal and Monetary Policies

Gilles Dufrénot
Sciences Po Aix
Aix-en-Provence, France

ISBN 978-3-031-15753-0   ISBN 978-3-031-15754-7   (eBook)
https://doi.org/10.1007/978-3-031-15754-7

This Palgrave Macmillan imprint is published by the registered company Springer Nature Switzerland AG
The registered company address is: Gewerbestrasse 11, 6330 Cham, Switzerland

I dedicate this book to my sister Thérèse

PREFACE

Macroeconomists' efforts to investigate a series of new phenomena have been considerable over the past decade. Theories and methods hitherto considered to be the backbone of reasoning are gradually being called into question, because they do not provide answers to new puzzles. Why don't current Phillips curves take into account financial inflation, that is, changes in the financial asset prices? Why should a central bank worry about controlling the real sector inflation when it is low? How should governments behave to reduce income and wealth inequalities? Why do macroeconomists continue to consider climate changes and countries' health situation as exogenous to economies? Has industrial capitalism come of age? Why have natural interest rates been falling for at least two decades? What about helicopter money? Is it not an appropriate way to settle public debts? Isn't it dangerous for governments to continue accumulating debt as they do today? Who will repay the debt? Are we going to reduce public debts as we did after the Second World War by using financial repression policies?

One of the reasons why macroeconomists sometimes lack the appropriate tools to assess the overall impact of new realities is because macroeconomics is not a "pure" hypothetico-deductive science, but also relies on inductive reasoning. One difficulty is to draw general conclusions from a set of specific observations. A number of the macroeconomic developments discussed in this book are new. Their theoretical interpretations are therefore based on hypotheses, conjectures that we must consider with caution, because the new theories are built in real time. Our view could evolve quickly. For example, the phenomenon of "secular stagnation" is sometimes interpreted as a decline in natural interest rates in industrial economies caused by a slowdown in productivity gains and demographic factors. But are we measuring productivity gains properly? Have we taken sufficient account of the contribution of digital capital since the 1990s (computers, software, telecommunications) to growth? Are we not simply in a phase of maturation of the innovations of the digital economy, which, if they spread rapidly through the economy in a few years, will radically modify potential growth trajectories upward?

It seems important to summarize here some thoughts on the new and fundamental problems facing macroeconomists. The aim is not to reject the usual ideas and models of economics that have been the subject of consensus up to now, but to glimpse some of their limits.

Macroeconomics is as a way of reading how economies function by studying how interactions between actors in society give rise to global phenomena, such as inflation, growth, trade between nations, global warming, pollution, interest rate movements on financial markets, financial crises, and so on. In their analytical tools and models, most macroeconomists use an approach common to other sciences (physical sciences, biology, psychology, etc.). They are primarily interested in the equilibrium state of functioning of economies subject to constraints. However, they do not agree among themselves on how to interpret situations of imbalances. Some view the damages that nations may experience (major crises, high unemployment rate, situations of hyperinflation or lasting deflation, etc.) as abnormal situations created by the undesired and unforeseeable action of shocks that disrupt economies up to the point of breaking the equilibria observed in normal times. Others consider that capitalism in its historical evolution itself creates endogenous mutations of economic systems. Finally, some economists consider that economic phenomena cannot be understood separately from other phenomena with which they interfere without being able to be dissociated: societal culture, geochemical and geophysical equilibria, and other living ecosystems. These different conceptions have always fueled debates among academics.

These debates extend beyond the academic sphere, when a major crisis occurs and policymakers have to make decisions. Sometimes they turn to economists to hear their point of view. This was the case during the 1929 crisis and the development of Keynesian macroeconomics, and then during the periods of stagflation of the 1970s and 1980s, which encouraged the development of more liberal theses—exemplified by the monetarists—suggesting less state interventionism. The 1990s and 2000s were the years of great moderation, with policymakers adopting ideas that seemed to have gained consensus among economists and that can be summarized in two premises.

The first premise is that the capitalist economies of the industrialized countries regulate themselves, unless major rigidities prevent them from moving naturally toward the right equilibria. So-called structural macroeconomic policies have therefore become important: reforms of labor and goods markets to ensure better regulation of production and employment through easier adjustments of wages, prices, capital movements, people, goods, and so on.

The second premise is that the regulation of the business cycle is carried out through a division of tasks between fiscal and monetary policies. Budgets are useful for mitigating the depth of recessions. But they must be used in a way that ensures medium-term equilibrium, which implies making savings during expansions. The economic literature has attributed fiscal problems to procyclical biases that lead to sustained deficits and high debt ratios. On the subject of debt, it must be sustainable, and if necessary rules are adopted to complement discretionary policies. On the monetary policy side, its management has been geared toward a flexible inflation targeting strategy. The independence of central banks from governments has become the norm, and the fight against inflation has been the main objective of central bankers, to which has been added financial stability in a financial capitalism that has expanded greatly.

If we look at theoretical models, macroeconomists have sought over the last 30 years to make the logic of their arguments more consistent with the reality of the data. This has resulted in a strong integration of the methodology of simulations and calibrations at the heart of theoretical models. Several advances illustrate this. DSGE (dynamic stochastic general equilibrium) models of the New-Keynesian synthesis, most often with microeconomic foundations, have gained importance. Greater attention has also been paid to the role of institutions in the regulation of capitalism (the contribution of post-Keynesian and Regulationist economists on the role of finance in capitalism has been decisive for a better understanding of the recent financial crises). Macroeconomic models whose logic is based on the observation of the limited rationality of economic actors have given rise to theories on the determination of macroeconomic equilibria and to a discipline known as behavioral macroeconomics. Finally, in order to facilitate the understanding of the conditions for policy success, macroeconomic policy evaluation programs and methodologies have become popular in academic circles.

What will macroeconomic theories be made of in the coming decades? Capitalism in the industrialized nations brings out new facts that must be analyzed in new ways. This book gives a sketch of the ideas that are starting to be developed.

A first major change is the evolution of topics that deserve a great attention. For a long time, the concern of macroeconomists was focused on short-term problems, notably growth, the regulation of business cycles, inflation, employment, trade between nations, and so on. The evidence now suggests that a better understanding of capitalism requires attention to the macroeconomics of structural change. Factors such as demography, savings, long movements of financial cycles, distribution of wealth within societies, and innovation systems impact unemployment, inflation, and growth.

A second major change is the succession of crises of different natures that we have been experiencing for several decades (the succession of climatic crises in the world that affect migratory movements, the financial crisis of 2008, the large-scale social crises fueled by the increase in poverty and inequalities, the recent pandemic crisis of Covid-19). A superficial analysis could lead one to interpret them as shocks exogenous to the economic system, but they rather reflect transformations endogenous to financial and globalized capitalism.

Let's take a few examples. Over the past decade, macroeconomists have been surprised by low inflation rates, despite the offensive monetary policies of central banks. But inflation has not disappeared. It has simply changed spheres. In fact, in the economies characterized by financial hypertrophy, one must distinguish between two types of inflation: real sector inflation and financial inflation. The two are inversely related. Friedman's maxim remains valid: inflation is everywhere and always a monetary phenomenon. The mass of liquidity that circulates in economies does not fuel consumer spending or over-investment, but a demand for financial assets. It would be wrong to think that the downward pressure that quantitative monetary policies exert on interest rates reduces the cost of bank credit and should thus encourage business investment. Indeed, the financial globalization of the 1990s has changed the management strategy of companies. Their value depends less on their net results than on their stock market valuation. From this point of view, it may be more attractive, even in the case of sustained growth, to buy back their own shares rather than invest.

Keeping the example of inflation, the low levels we have observed until the recent period are not only explained by a weakness in aggregate demand. The globalization of economies (a major structural change in the 1990s) and the weakening of institutional regulation in which states played an important role, has shattered the mechanisms that have long governed Phillips curves: the wage-price loop has been weakened and the entry of millions of workers from emerging countries into the global labor market has disconnected the links that existed between inflation and unemployment. If Phillips curves in some industrialized countries have become less steep, this is not necessarily due to econometric flaws. The most likely explanation comes from structural factors, such as globalization.

The behavior of public actors to tackle the recent crises, guided by a pragmatic concern—particularly in Anglo-Saxon countries—is giving rise to a body of jurisprudence from which new approaches to fiscal and monetary policies are derived.

First, the role of governments has evolved. They no longer intervene only in the regulation of business cycles. First, they appear to be the only ones able to correct the structural imbalances generated by financial and globalized capitalism (income and wealth inequalities, technological bias, rampant poverty). Second, in the face of unexpected and large-scale shocks, their role as income insurers has been emphasized (insurers of bank deposits during the 2008 crisis in the event of bank failure, insurers of wages and guarantors of bank loans to companies during the Covid-19 crisis). The corollary is that budget deficits and debt have risen sharply and are on an upward trajectory. Since we are dealing with crises whose causes are endogenous and structural, a legitimate question is how far to go in supporting economies? Not all macroeconomists agree on what should be done.

Some see the consequences for the public accounts and fear a difficult future when it comes to repaying the debts. Will governments be able to do this? Won't they have taken on so much debt that it will burden several generations to come? They would then devote their resources to servicing the debt rather than investing. Those who have these fears focus on the sustainability of the debt.

On the contrary, others call for a change of perspective. Those who see only debt sustainability act as if public finances were used for business cycle regulation. They also fear the future reaction of financial markets, which could lead to higher interest rates on public debts. But this type of reasoning forgets several things. First, what matters is not who finances, but who ultimately holds the debt. The central bankers, who are currently buying up public debt on a massive scale, are performing a public service. They are simply doing their job by injecting into the economies what modern monetary theory calls helicopter money. Secondly, interest rates are so low (close to zero, or even negative in some cases) that it is hard to see why governments should not take advantage of this to take on debt. Here too, they would be rendering a public service to society if they use this money to finance structural expenditure (social expenditure aimed at correcting inequalities, accelerating the ecological transition, reducing poverty).

In the field of economic policies, an important change concerns central banks. Quantitative monetary policies have replaced interest rate policies. Will it be necessary at some point to abandon these policies, to mop up some of the liquidity that has been provided to the financial markets, in order to hope for a return to interest rate policy? An initial answer could be yes. This would be the case, for example, if structural inflation were to rise again, in a context of slowing financial globalization, and where wage inflation would once again become a key to negotiations between employers and employees. But the answer could be no. No, because this withdrawal would provoke a financial crisis following the fall in financial asset prices, with heavier consequences for the real economy (in terms of unemployment, social costs, etc.). No, also if we think differently about the objectives to be assigned to monetary policy. Considering that the sustainability of public debts could be based in part on bank support for fiscal policies is no longer a taboo subject. Of course, this calls into question habits developed over the last three decades. The policy mix would no longer be characterized by total independence between central bankers and finance ministers. Central bankers would be assigned objectives other than the fight against real sector inflation.

The macroeconomic practices and theories of the twenty-first century are likely to be revolutionary, shaking up the modes of reasoning that were used during the long period of great moderation. These changes are imposed on us by the structural changes at work in the heart of capitalism. This book provides an overview of some of the ongoing changes in macroeconomic analysis that challenge current thinking. I try to be non-judgmental, taking on board different currents of thought and analysis (New-Keynesian macroeconomics, the Regulationist camp, post-Keynesian and neo-Cambridgian economists, neoclassical approaches, etc.). I believe macroeconomists should abandon the idea of constructing a unified and global framework of thought on events that necessarily call for different reading grids.

The book is intended for the following audience: any macroeconomist, academic or professional, wishing to know the recent developments of growth theories in industrialized economies; policymakers, in central banks, governments, international organizations wishing to have an overview of the new challenges of the policy mix; master's and doctoral students in macroeconomics and economic policy; non-economists interested in recent developments on sustainable growth, fight against inequalities, and ecological transition.

Marseille, France   Gilles Dufrénot
November 2022

ACKNOWLEDGMENTS

The ideas presented in this book owe much to discussions I have had with some colleagues, students, and economists in business and international organizations. All of us are trying to understand the changing world that is unfolding before our eyes. I am particularly grateful to some of the people who helped me open my mind to approaches other than those I was used to. Michel Aglietta is one of the brilliant minds I have met in my career. He has devoted most of his career to thinking about the transformations of capitalist economies. I thank him for having associated me with his reflections around different working groups where we discussed once a month for four years to sharpen our understanding of the changes in macroeconomics. Thanks to Marcel Aloy, Thomas Brand, Renaud Dutertre, Anne Faivre, and William Oman for discussions that helped me to better understand the role of macroeconomic policies. The work carried out with colleagues at the Banque de France, at the time of the Great Recession of 2008, and then of the European public debts, made it possible to see the changes in the orientation of macroeconomic policies. Thanks to Carine Bouthevillain, Bruno Cabrillac, Mariam Camarero, Caroline Clerc, Philippe Frouté, Jean-Baptiste Gossé, Sheheryar Malik, Tarik Mouakil, Laurent Paul, and Cecilio Tamarit for the hours spent together discussing and writing about new fields in macroeconomics. The Centre d'Etudes Prospectives et d'Informations Internationales (CEPII) and the Aix-Marseille School of Economics have provided an ideal setting for these discussions. I would like to thank some of my co-authors who have accepted to take the risk of writing on new macroeconomics topics: Fredj Jawadi, Guillaume Khayat, Meryem Rhouzlane, Etienne Vaccaro-Grange, and Alexandros Vardoulakis. I am grateful to my students, who are always happy to play the question-and-answer game of whether a particular theory or model accurately describes macroeconomic reality. Recent developments have provided us with many surprises. Finally, I thank my colleagues who accepted to read some chapters and make some comments. I especially express my gratitude to Céline Poilly and Frédéric Dufourt.

CONTENTS

LIST OF FIGURES

LIST OF TABLES

CHAPTER 1

Introduction

1.1 MACROECONOMIC POLICIES ARE FACING NEW CHALLENGES

Recent stylized facts on macroeconomics show profound changes in the functioning of capitalism over the last four decades. New doctrines are emerging. As Larry Summers writes in a Peterson Institute memo to US President Joe Biden, the challenges currently facing macroeconomic policies are very different from what they have been in the past.

This book reviews some of the new ideas that will form the basis of doctrines, economic policies, and reading grids on the evolution and future of growth in the industrialized economies over the next few decades. The attention of macroeconomists is now focusing on problems of structural change, whereas the debate and theories of the last 40 years have focused on short-term regulation, losing sight of medium-/long-term transformations. To introduce some of the changes underway, let us take some examples.

Example 1 During the years following the onset of inflation (from 1980), and until very recently (until the Great Financial Crisis [GFC] in 2008), central banks were assigned the task of monitoring inflation—or sometimes the general level of prices—to prevent it from rising too much or falling too much. To achieve this objective, the interest rate was the preferred instrument in a context of deregulation and liberalization of

© The Author(s), under exclusive license to Springer Nature Switzerland AG 2023
G. Dufrénot, *New Challenges for Macroeconomic Policies*,
https://doi.org/10.1007/978-3-031-15754-7_1

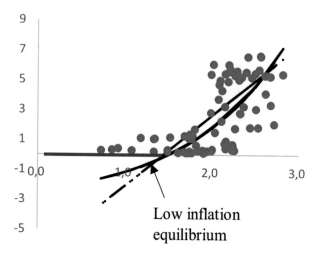

Fig. 1.1   Interest rate and inflation rate: United States: 1997–2017

financial markets. A simple presentation of the economic equilibrium in a monetary economy is the following. The macroeconomic equilibrium can be represented by the intersection of two curves. One is the Taylor rule (this "rule" explains that the nominal interest rate set by the central bank depends on the deviation of inflation from a target and the deviation of growth or the level of GDP from a target) and the Fisher relationship (this relationship defines the nominal interest rate as the real interest rate plus inflation expectations).

Figure 1.1 shows an illustration for the United States. The horizontal axis corresponds to inflation rate in % (source: OECD, excluding food and energy), while the vertical axis represents nominal short-term interest rate in % (source: OECD). The dotted line represents the zero barrier of the nominal short-term rate. The line with a positive slope describes a Fisher relationship obtained by regressing the nominal rate on the inflation rate. The convex curve is a non-linear Taylor rule estimated by the relation $R = Aexp(Binfl) - C$, where R is the nominal rate, infl is the inflation rate, and A, B, and C are real coefficients. The points of intersection show two stationary states, one of which, the left most, corresponds to a situation of secular stagnation.

According to the standard interpretation, the two points of intersection are "stationary" equilibria, that is, possible stationary states of the US economy during the period under study. Until very recently, a widespread idea was that, of the two equilibria, only one is viable, namely the one showing positive inflation and interest rates.

The study of the behavior of the economy is then carried out by "linearizing" the Taylor rule in the vicinity of the only viable equilibrium, which leads to the situation known as "divine coincidence," so called by Olivier Blanchard to emphasize that the mere fact of bringing the inflation rate to its target level allows the output gap of an economy to close. Before the GFC, we could not have imagined that the low equilibrium (low inflation and zero or negative interest rates) could correspond to a stable state of a real economy where it is "trapped" for a long time. We used to believe that central bankers and governments have the full range of tools at their disposal to pull any economy out of this "bad" equilibrium. When inflation was low, all the central banks would have to do was to lower their policy rate permanently to generate inflationary expectations by the private sector. Alternatively, a cut in the central bank's interest rate would stimulate demand and lead to a rise in inflation. In an article by the Fed of Saint Louis published shortly after the 2008 crisis, James Bullard wrote that massive quantitative monetary policies would be likely to take economies out of equilibrium with low interest rates and low inflation. However, a decade later, the situation has not changed (see Bullard 2010).

Second Example At the end of the Second World War, matching aggregate supply and demand was crucial to prevent economies from falling into depression. However, today the industrialized countries are undergoing two important changes. The first relates to the transition from "brown" to "green" economies. This should accelerate under the pressure of civil societies. The second concerns the disruptive innovations (robotics, automation, nanotechnologies, artificial intelligence, digital technology) that the development of the Internet, electronics, and new information and communication technologies in the 1990s and 2000s prepared for. The question of the value of productive capital in a period of transition from the capitalist regime is once again becoming important.

The *third example* concerns the Phillips curves. So far, it has been an instrument used by central banks to forecast inflation. However, these curves have become increasingly flat, at least since the last two decades. This observation leads two reactions. The first is to interpret this fact as an anomaly, because it does not fit economic theory. Some researchers look for explanatory variables that "re-slop" the curves in empirical works. And they conclude that the Philips curve has not "disappeared," since the slopes become significant again as soon as the problem of omitted variables is solved. An alternative reaction is that the theoretical framework used so far needs to be revised for several reasons. First, the domestic component of inflation has declined, following globalization and structural changes in the labor markets, notably the atomization of jobs. Second, the slope of the Phillips curve, that is, the response of inflation to the unemployment rate, has been modified under the influence of various factors, including the historical distortion of the functional distribution of income. Finally, inflation has not disappeared, but has shifted from the real sector to the financial sector. It is currently manifested by high asset prices (sometimes bubbles) in financial markets. Therefore, among the factors explaining inflation, financial variables will now need to be included because of the interdependencies between the real and financial cycles.

Our *last example* concerns the coordination of fiscal and monetary policies. The current context is very much reminiscent of the one that prevailed before the mid-1980s. There was monetary management of public debt, following the sharp rise in public debt ratios at the end of the Second World War. The British, American, Japanese, and other European countries' central banks intervened directly on the sovereign bond markets to keep interest rates low. France used its Treasury circuit to place its debt at low interest rates with the banking system. However, many academic economists, trained in the decades following the 1980s, still consider as the "norm" a situation in which central banks need only concern themselves with inflation, and in which governments are asked to respect a neutrality of fiscal policy (which leads, for example, to the assertion that strategies to combat the negative effects of Covid-19 through fiscal stimulus should be temporary). Moreover, during the last 30 years the norm has been a separation between central banks and governments' fiscal actions.

Policymakers, those in charge of applying fiscal and monetary policies, are currently conducting policies that are paving the way to the emergence of new approaches of policy mix (the combination of fiscal and monetary policies). For instance, in the industrialized countries, central banks are massively buying up public debts. The Japanese have even made legislative changes by assigning the Bank of Japan the objective of targeting the structure of interest rates to keep them at low levels (and ease the government refinancing in capital markets). Kenneth Rogoff considers that central bankers should deepen their policy of negative interest rates (by making them plunge to lower levels than they are at present, down to −3%!). On the fiscal policy side, more and more governments are being convinced of the need to take advantage of the configuration of negative rates to increase public spending. The reason is not only to stabilize the business cycle by cushioning falls in aggregate demand. Although this is one aspect of their strategy, massive spending is justified by the transitions that the economies are currently undergoing and that policies must accompany: transition linked to the disruptive innovations of Economy 2.0, ecological transition, social transition, and so on. Fiscal policy seems to be oriented toward supporting productivity and potential growth. And monetary policy supports the stability of the debt ratio, especially when the stock of public debt reaches high levels.

The structural change that industrialized economies are undergoing thus leads to the emergence of new ways of analyzing macroeconomic events. Research in macroeconomics owes much to the richness of the debates initiated in the United States by economists from the Peterson Institute and the American Economic Association (see, e.g., the work presented at the 2015 annual conference), to the work on productivity initiated in academic circles following Robert Gordon's work on the decline in productivity gains in the United States, the work initiated by Joseph Stiglitz and Thomas Piketty on the rise of inequalities, as well as research on the non-neutrality of finance on the real economy conducted at the Bank for International Settlements under the leadership of Claudio Borio. Let us also mention the work of Stiglitz and Greenwald on the economics of learning as a key factor in the growth of economies around the world.

Unfortunately, the diffusion of new ideas to academic circles is slow. Among researchers themselves. One of the explanations is undoubtedly that provided by Akerlof (2020) on how the objectives and methodologies of economic research have evolved over the last 30 years: a high degree of specialization leading to the development of increasingly complex tools to study simple phenomena, rather than the use of simple reasoning and methodologies to understand an increasingly complex economic reality. However, a few articles and books that can be understood by economists who are not specialists in macroeconomics have been published. Baldwin and Teulings (2014) have edited a book devoted to the causes and effects of secular stagnation. Blanchard (2018) explains the direction that macroeconomic models will take in the future. In France, Aglietta (2019), one of the founders of the theory of regulation, has recently edited a volume on the breaks in capitalism in which the challenges of twenty-first century macroeconomics are presented. In the academic field, let us mention some textbooks that question the approach of the models usually used to understand macroeconomic developments: Blanchard (2021) and Amighini et al. (2017).

The field of macroeconomics is today the subject of significant debate, with regard to both mainstream theories and those described as heterodox.

In the field of mainstream macroeconomics, let us mention a few examples of authors whose contributions influence the debates. Woodford, in his contribution to the Jackson Hole Economic symposium in 2012, revisited the question of monetary neutrality in a context of zero lower bounds, by restating the Wallace neutrality problem in a context of quantitative easing monetary policies (Methods of policy accommodation at the interest-rate lower bound, a Jackson Hole symposium on the changing policy landscape, August 30–September 1, 2012). Roger Farmer's work contributed to breaking with an approach to macroeconomics inherited from the old Classical-Keynesian synthesis, which described the economy as a Keynesian equilibrium in the short term (because of rigidities) and neoclassical in the long term. Farmer has brought back to the forefront the fact that the heart of macroeconomics is the presence of indeterminacy, multiples, and sunspots (see, e.g., Farmer 2010; Farmer and Platonov 2019; Farmer 2020, 2021). Another important change concerns the vision about the role of fiscal policy. This came to light with the zero interest rate regime. The idea that fiscal policy should be as neutral as possible is being challenged. The worst may even happen if governments embark on fiscal consolidation policies: due to hysteresis effects, economies may become permanently depressed, without quantitative policies being able to return to expansionary regimes. This change of course is expressed in several works, including Delong and Summers (2012).

Concerning the so-called heterodox macroeconomics—because it questions certain hypotheses of the neoclassical or New-Keynesian models—the succession of crises of various kinds (financial, economic, health) has given a renewed interest in changing paradigms. Important debates have taken place in three areas. The first area is the re-emergence of the institutional approach to analyze growth regimes and the dynamics of capitalist economies. What is called institutions goes beyond the standard governance-based approach as reflected, for example, in the World Bank's governance indicators (Polity, Country Policy and Institutional Assessment (CPIA), etc.) that serve as a reference. What matters here is the structuring of social and political relations, values, and cultural traits. This has a consequence on the vision of the actors and their behavior. These elements are not fixed in time, hence the central role of history in interpreting growth processes. The second area is monetary policy. A new so-called modern theory emphasizes the inseparable nature of monetary and fiscal instruments in the search for macroeconomic equilibrium (inflation and unemployment). This theory proposes a functional and neo-chartist reading of the monetary strategy adopted by central banks. Finally, a third area in which heterodox macroeconomics has invested is that of economic ecology. The change of perspective with respect to orthodox economics is radical in the theories of degrowth or post-growth economics. Even the proponents of a Green New Deal put forward the idea that monetary policy can massively support very expansive fiscal policies that will be useful for the ecological transition.

1.2 MAIN TOPICS DISCUSSED IN THE BOOK

This book has several objectives. First, we are interested in showing how different formulations of mainstream macroeconomic models, working especially with New-Keynesian assumptions, have provided more "space" for discussing policy alternatives and directions than the orthodox models that provide the intellectual framework on which New-Keynesian macroeconomic models have been built.

The second objective is to highlight some new approaches, in methods, models, and theoretical principles for understanding macroeconomics. For instance, one cannot study sustainable growth without a global approach, which implies giving up the idea that nature, environmental resources, social relations, geopolitics are constraints that economies must take into account. The objectives to be achieved are not only economic, since the other social and environmental ecosystems also have their own objectives that matter as much as the economic ones. In the same way, so far, we were sure of the validity of the idea of neutrality of fiscal and monetary policies. This is no longer the case, as soon as we understand that the objectives to be assigned to the policies are not "natural," but result from political and strategic choices.

Our third objective is to make the reader understand that, in a changing and increasingly complex world, macroeconomics is first and foremost an empirical science. It is empiricism that allows us to understand the changes and complexity that are taking place. Theories result more from "jurisprudence" than from first principles. The empirics always comes first. Theoretical frameworks are then used to tell stories, to propose mechanisms, to describe what is happening in a specific vision. This approach has allowed us to learn a lot over the last 30 years about various phenomena: the existence of financial cycles characterized by long waves, cyclical fluctuations and noisy dynamics; the presence of super-hysteresis phenomena; the existence of a saving glut phenomenon in firms (and not only at the level of global macroeconomic equilibria); the ambiguous relations between innovation and employment, the non-validity of traditional Phillips curves as soon as one takes into account globalization and financial asset prices as determinants of inflation, the secular decline of natural interest rates, and so on.

The book consists of two parts.

The first part, *Growth, macroeconomic imbalances and sustainable development*, discusses the following issues.

We start with some of the puzzles involved in understanding the drivers of growth in the midst of the fourth technological revolution. We explain why the standard accounting decomposition of growth does not allow us to understand everything about the role of technical progress. Technological breakthroughs have come with consequences that the macroeconomic production function cannot necessarily capture. We also try to understand some recent phenomena of growth dynamics: why has the accumulation of physical capital slowed down? Is there an exhaustion of productivity gains, and if so why? What are the impacts of demography on growth?

We then study a phenomenon that has become widespread, namely the high vulnerability of industrialized economies to various shocks that affect countries. This is reflected by a phenomenon of strong hysteresis. The 2008 Great Financial Crisis showed us that economies hit by a financial crisis can take more than a decade to shake off the adverse effects on the real economy. This has made obsolete one of the key references of macroeconomics over the last forty years, namely the usefulness of the Phillips curve to guide macroeconomic policies.

Part I also discusses issues related to sustainable growth. This approach includes dimensions other than production, including social, environmental, and epidemic aspects of macroeconomics.

Indeed, most of the theoretical growth models proposed in the literature since the beginning of the twentieth century have had one main objective, that is, understand the mechanisms for raising living standards in countries where the diffusion of innovations resulting from technological revolutions of the noneteenth and twentieth centuries were available for massive production to avoid the famines of yesteryear. The improvement of material life was thought to require an optimal allocation of resources between the factors of production. For many years growth theories were oriented toward optimal capital accumulation, functional income distribution, and policies to support medium- and long-term growth.

Today's concerns are different. First, poverty and inequality have leapt to the very heart of the world's richest nations. As a result, wealth can increase without a trickle-down effect. Second, capital that enables production is multiple: natural, human, physical, institutional. Some of its resources are not infinitely available. This is the case of the non-renewable energies that have been, until now, the basis of thermo-industrial growth. Moreover, the use of resources and the exploitation of raw materials of the subsoil (water and energy resources) can cause damages to the environment with negative feedback effects on economic activity. Likewise, massive production can sometimes "disrupt" ecosystems and the services they provide. In this context, the notion of sustainability is now at the heart of new growth paradigms. Macroeconomists' concern is no longer just a question of optimally allocating resources to the best jobs, but also of finding the right balance between increasing wealth and preserving ecosystems, environmental geophysical balances, and social balances.

Part II is titled *Financial, monetary and fiscal policies*. It presents some new challenges for macroeconomic policies. Up to the 2008 Great financial crisis, the focus was on economic stabilization, and the debates have long divided the advocates of neutrality (market self-regulation being considered optimal) and the proponents of more interventionism, particularly when shocks lead to large-scale unemployment (financial crises, health crises, natural disasters).

An important fact of the last three decades has been the long decline in interest rates in a context of financial globalization. Credit, real estate and stock market cycles now play a fundamental role in the economies. Understanding the causes of the fall in interest rates is important, especially since it has been accompanied by the emergence of a new regime of accumulation that is called *secular stagnation.*

Understanding the trend decline in interest rates leads to two types of interpretations. Some economists believe that macroeconomic equilibria are influenced by forces in the real economy: fall in aggregate demand, excess savings, and decline in productivity gains explain the so-called *natural* interest rates downward. The alternative reaction is to relate changes in the interest rates to determinants of profit rates in the medium-to-long term. We review several possible sources of this decline: the concentration of capital, a technology bias, financial globalization.

New social issues have emerged: the fight against inequality and precariousness, the need to restore medium-/long-term growth in economies, ecological transition and preventing the negative effects of epidemics on the economies. The succession of crises of various kinds has brought to light new individual and collective risks: the multiplication of pathologies linked to longer life expectancy after the age of 65, intermittent unemployment caused by the atomization of labor markets, and health and ecological risks. The objectives of economic policies need to go beyond the macroeconomic sphere. We present some current debates on how to conceive fiscal and monetary policies: unconventional monetary policies, Rogoff's recent proposal to "bury" interest rates in negative territory, proposals for the cancellation of sovereign debt by central banks, the use of the budget to slow the deceleration of productivity, fiscal policies as instruments for correcting inequalities, the new role of governments as insurers in the face of large-scale crises.

The last chapter of the book presents some ideas on heterodox macroeconomics about the causes of inflation, monetary policy and its interaction with fiscal policy, and the interaction between growth and ecology.

The topics analyzed in the book give an overview of major areas of discussions in growth and economic policies for the forthcoming decades. This book will be of interest to all people, economists and non-economists alike, interested in the new intellectual environment where structural changes are forcing us to think differently about long-term growth and economic policies. Academics will find in it a synthesis of new ideas on the macroeconomics of growth. The book is also aimed at a wider audience concerned with understanding the challenges of inclusive and sustainable growth in an era where our attention is captured by rising inequalities and the issue of ecological transition.

In addition, we have chosen to end each chapter by a presentation of the contributions of some economists—who are still alive—to the current debates.

The book focuses on industrialized countries. The macroeconomics of emerging and developing countries is a subject that deserves several volumes in its own right. For, where nations are looking for ways to develop in order to improve the living standards of their people, macroeconomists must be very ambitious in their reading of the world. Replicating what is done in rich countries is not enough. Sometimes the policies are even inappropriate. These discussions are beyond the scope of this book.

REFERENCES

Aglietta M (2019) Capitalisme, le temps des ruptures. Odile Jacob, Paris

Akerlof G (2020) Sins of omission and the practice of economics. J Econ Lit 58(2): 405–18

Amighini A, Blanchard O, Giavazzi F (2017) Macroeconomics: a European perspective 3rd edn. Pearson, Edinburgh

Baldwin R, Teulings C (eds) (2014) Secular stagnation: facts, causes and cures. CEPR Press eBook. Available via https://voxeu.org/content/secular-stagnation-facts-causes-and-cures

Blanchard O (2018) On the future of macroeconomics models. Oxf Rev Econ Pol 34(1–2):43–54

Blanchard O (2021) Macroeconomics, 8th edn. Pearson, Boston

Bullard J (2010) Seven faces of the "peril". Fed Res Bank of Saint-Louis Rev 92(5): 339–52

Delong JB, Summers LH (2012) Fiscal policy in a depressed economy. Brook Pap Econ Act, Spring

Farmer RE (2010) How the economy works: confidence, crashes and self-fulfilling prophecies. Oxford University Press, Oxford

Farmer RE (2020) The indeterminacy school in macroeconomics. Ox Res Enc Econ Fin.

Farmer RE (2021) The importance of beliefs in shaping macroeconomic outcomes. Ox Rev Econ Pol 36(3):675–711

Farmer RE, Platonov K (2019) Animal spirits in a monetary economy. Eur Econ Rev 115:60–75

Growth, Macroeconomic Imbalances, and Sustainable Development

Is There Any Evidence of a Deterioration of Production Capacities in the Advanced Economies?

The twentieth century was a century of industrialization. Many innovations of the late eighteenth and nineteenth centuries (automobile, iron and steel, electricity, rail and road infrastructures, maritime trade) reached their peak. The middle of the twentieth century saw the emergence of a knowledge-based economy (information and telecommunication technologies with the development of computers, electronics, and new telecommunications tools). The twenty-first century is characterized by what is often described as a fourth technological revolution artificial intelligence, automation, nanotechnologies, and digital revolution. Moreover, in the twenty-first century, as was the case in the twentieth century and before that in the nineteenth century, financial hypertrophy is continuing its development with an ever-increasing complexity of financial products and services and a growing gap between the stock market valuation of companies and the value of real GDP. Labor markets have also been transformed. Demographic dynamics are leading to an aging population in some industrialized countries, which poses difficulties in meeting certain social expenditures due to rising dependency ratios. Everywhere, work has become fragmented (fixed-term contracts, temporary work, outsourcing, off-shoring). The astonishing fact is the return of task-based work, outside the industrial sector. Do these phenomena, which signal the entry into a new growth regime, change the production capacity of capitalist economies?

This chapter is devoted to the study of some recent trends in the evolution of the so-called advanced economies' production capacity. The

G. Dufrénot, *New Challenges for Macroeconomic Policies*, https://doi.org/10.1007/978-3-031-15754-7_2

term "advanced" has long been a synonym for "industrialized", that is, countries with factories, large volumes of investment in physical capital and labor hours, as well as financial capital to sustain activity. These factors are considered as key engines of potential growth. Contrary to popular belief, rich countries are not de-industrializing, and the economies are not becoming virtual. On the contrary, the development of digital technology has as a counterpart an increase in material investments (data are stored on servers, fiber optics implies new physical infrastructures of millions of submarine and underground cables, robots require raw materials, and the information contained in the data circulates thanks to electronic chips). In addition, the development of the digital economy requires the extraction of millions of cubic meters of land (tantalum for cell phones, indium for flat screens, cobalt, silver, titanium, and beryllium for laptops, ferrous and non-ferrous metals) and therefore extraction infrastructures. Finally, in most advanced countries, working hours still contribute significantly to economic growth.

At first sight, we have no reason to believe that the production capacity of the advanced economies has decreased over time. How, then, can we explain a puzzle facing macroeconomists, that is, the decline in trend growth in these countries? Indeed, the data show that over the last three decades, potential growth has been declining. Does this happen because physical capital is also on a declining trend? Or because of the demographic changes that affect the functioning of the labor markets? Should we rather blame the decline in total factor productivity (TFP)?

2.1   Analysis of the Sources of Growth: The Challenges Raised by the Fourth Industrial Revolution

As we have just emphasized, during the beginning of the twenty-first century we are witnessing a technological breakthrough in various fields that affects not only productive processes but also modes of consumption and trade. One of its obvious manifestations is the extent of the digital economy. On a global level, about 45 million servers are connected to the Internet and mobilize 800 million network devices (e.g., routers, boxes). There are about 15 billion connected objects, and this number could reach 40 billion by 2025. The development of digital technology is expected to increase fivefold in the next few years, with its penetration rate covering only 54% of the world's population in 2021. Every hour ten billion emails are exchanged worldwide. The infrastructure of the digital sector is accounted for as digital capital (hardware and components, software and IT services, and telecommunication equipment). This capital produces digital services (e.g., e-commerce and digital marketing) and is used by all sectors of activity (agriculture, industry, and services). We need to keep these elements in mind when studying the sources of growth at the macroeconomic level.

2.1.1 ICT Investment and Growth Accounting Decomposition

A usual framework used to analyze the macroeconomic impact of ICT on economic growth is growth accounting decomposition. The growth rate of real GDP is described in terms of a production function (Cobb-Douglas or Translog) and requires assumptions to be made about the structure of markets (competitive or not), about the remuneration of factors of production, and about the distribution of value added between factors of production.

The growth accounting decomposition is based on the following equation that relates the growth rate of real GDP to those of several production inputs:

$$\Delta ln(Y_t) = \bar{s}_{kt} \Delta ln(K_t) + \bar{s}_{kt} ln(L_t) + TFP_t, \qquad (2.1)$$

where

- $\Delta x = x_t - x_{t-1}$,
- Y_t: value added in volume at time t,
- L_t: labor services (volume) at time t,
- K_t: capital services (volume) at time t,
- $\bar{s}_{Ft}, F = K, L$: share of factor F in value added.

These shares are defined as Divisia index, that is, $\bar{s}_{Ft} = 0.5(s_{Ft} + s_{Ft-1})$ and $\sum_F \bar{s}_{Ft} = 1$. The factor shares are defined as follows. Denoting P_{Ft} and P_{Yt} the factor input price and the price of the value added, we have $s_{Ft} = (P_{FT} F_t)/(P_{Yt} Y_t)$, $F = K, L$.

Total labor and capital can be decomposed into several categories when necessary.

Different types of labor consist of labor into educational attainment level, gender, age. It is also sometimes desirable to identify three sources of influences from labor to economic growth. First, the total number of hours worked. Second, the number of hours worked by certain categories of workers. Third, changes in the relative wages of different categories of workers. For example, a wage distortion in favor of the most skilled workers implies a higher share of their cost share, which has an impact on the labor composition effect. To show these different components, one usually considers the following decomposition:

$$\Delta ln(L_t) = \sum_l \bar{s}^l_{Lt} \Delta ln \left(\frac{H^l_t}{H_t} \right) + \Delta ln(H_t)), \qquad (2.2)$$

where $\bar{s}^l_{Lt}$ is a Divisia index corresponding to the nominal cost share of labor type l. H^l_t is the hours worked of labor type l, and H_t is the total hours worked at time t.

A similar decomposition can be made for capital, making a distinction between non-ICT and ICT capital services, and/or between tangible capital and intangible capital services. Divisia indexes are also used to compute the contribution of different types of capital to total capital services:

$$\Delta ln(K_t) = \sum_k \bar{s}^k_{Kt} \Delta ln(K^k_t), \qquad (2.3)$$

where K^k_t is capital services of asset type k and $\bar{s}^k_{Kt}$ is the nominal (Divisia) share of asset k.

Looking at the effects of ICT on growth from the KLEMS,[1] we can draw several conclusions.

Table 2.1 shows the decomposition of growth and the contributions of its factors over the period from 1995 to 2017. We choose five countries for illustration, that is, France, Germany, Japan, the United Kingdom, and the United States. In all these countries, primary factors (hours worked, tangible non-ICT capital, and total factor productivity (TFP) are the main direct contributors to growth. The contribution of new ICT (tangible capital) is not shown by the data, except in Japan (the numbers are small). In all countries except Germany, average growth declines from one sub-period to the next. A striking fact is also the decline in the contribution of tangible non-ICT capital services everywhere. In Japan,

---

[1] See Kirsten (2017) for a detailed presentation of this database.

Table 2.1 Growth accounting decomposition: 1995–2017

	France	Germany	Japan	United Kingdom	United States
Value added growth	6.44	5.93	3.15	8.72	6.27
Hours worked	**1.51**	0.26	−0.99	1.87	**0.91**
Labor composition	**1.36**	0.22	1.21	**0.86**	0.50
Tangible non-ICT capital services	**0.77**	**1.21**	**0.60**	**2.46**	**1.67**
Tangible ICT capital services	0.08	0.03	**0.81**	0.38	0.44
Non-tangible (software, databases) capital services	0.25	0.11	**0.32**	0.20	0.23
Non-tangible (R\& D) capital services	0.08	0.20	**0.36**	0.00	0.28
Non-tangible (other intellectual properties)	0.00	0.00	0.00	−0.05	0.06
Total factor productivity	**2.38**	**3.88**	**0.84**	**3.00**	**2.19**

Data source EU KLEMS database 2019
Numbers are in bold to show the main factors contributing to value added growth

France, and the United Kingdom, labor composition appears to be a key determinant of growth, and the contribution of hours worked has been almost systematically negative. In Japan, this phenomenon is linked to the consequences of the aging of the population on the labor market (early retirement of older workers and entry into the labor market of a younger, lower-paid population, which reduces the share of wages in value added).

The surprising fact in these observations is the low contribution of ICT capital services to growth (except in Japan), which gives rise to several interpretations by economists.[2] Is there any evidence of a new productivity paradox, as was observed in the mid-1980s at the height of the computer and electronics boom (a phenomenon known as Solow's productivity paradox)? One can answer that the impact of ICT is hidden in the aggregate statistics of growth decomposition. Indeed, some papers suggest the existence of a bias in the empirical literature leading researchers to underestimate the aggregate influence of ICT on growth by a ratio of 1 to 10! (see, among others, Polák 2017). Several reasons can be given to explain this bias.

First, some assumptions in the accounting framework may not be validated in reality. This is the case, for example, with the assumption of constant returns to scale. Indeed, a distinction must be made between the "social" marginal productivity of a factor at the macroeconomic level (the one retained in the production function) and the marginal productivity at the level of the firms that use the factor in question. Numerous econometric studies suggest that a fraction of the economies of scale linked to the production or use of ICTs within a firm is diffused outside the firm. The collective benefit is therefore greater than the individual benefit. Innovation experiences are transmitted through supply chains and modify organizational and coordination business processes. Innovations spread by imitation between companies according to their absorptive capacity. These interactions do not necessarily show up immediately in aggregate growth, although the impact on productivity gains at the sector level may be strong. The transition from productivity gains at the micro level to aggregate growth depends on several factors: the share of innovative firms (because the costs of adopting innovations require critical size), the degree of synchronization at the sector level of the organizational changes implied

---

[2] In a recent paper Cette et al. (2020) reach a similar conclusion for developed economies over a long period from 1960 to 2019.

by ICTs, the financial disincentives to investment in ICTs, and the capacity of firms to build business networks based on information technologies (see, among many authors, Cereola et al. 2012; Díaz-Chao et al. 2015). The sum of the shares of the different types of capital is therefore certainly greater than 1.

Second, the aggregate production function used in the growth accounting decomposition omits an important explanatory factor. In economies where digital technology is increasingly important, ICT producers and users use data as a raw material. This use takes place in a particular context: on the one hand, it gives rise to rents, and on the other hand, the market structure of this factor is not competitive. On the first aspect, digital companies claim several million, even billions of subscribers whose information they collect and exchange, at a very low cost. Billions of data and documents are stored on servers. Beyond the GAFAMs, the users of this data (e.g., freelance activity platforms) capture value. The rent is related to the remuneration received by digital companies by minimizing the cost of data acquisition. Because of this, the returns to scale of capital and labor could be decreasing. In this case, the weights used in the production function distort our view of ICT contributions to growth. On the second aspect, one of the characteristics of the sector is the preponderant weight of the GAFAMs in terms of markets and the asymmetry of information between data providers and users. The concentration of data makes it unlikely that the factors of production (data) are remunerated at their marginal cost (for a review of the arguments on these two aspects, see, e.g., Acquisti et al. 2016).

Another interpretation to the fact that digital capital gains are invisible in growth accounting decomposition is the following. The so-called TFP (Solow residual) incorporates not only true productivity gains but also a whole range of other sources of growth, including the indirect effects of digital capital: for example, the lower the cost of digital goods and services, the greater the diversification of goods and services offered. This residual also includes the rent of the digital sector.

All in all, the usual framework of growth accounting decomposition suffers from weaknesses that does not allow us to fully understand how the digital economy, and innovations in general, contributes to long-term growth. Based on endogenous growth models, the literature completes the growth decomposition equation with an equation where the TFP is endogenous and depends on capital and equipment related to ICT innovations. This is a way of capturing the indirect channels of ICT on growth, via their impact on TFP. However, as Stiglitz and Greenwald (2014) have shown, innovation processes depend on market structures (labor and goods market regulations and incentives). This implies the existence of circularity between the weights assigned to the different factors and the FPR and/or the productivity of labor and capital.

2.1.2   Some Alternatives to Growth Accounting Decomposition

There is a growing body of econometric work measuring the impact of the digital economy on growth using aggregate data. For a recent example see Stanley et al. (2018)'s meta-regression analysis. Is econometrics a good alternative to growth accounting decomposition? The latter faces several challenges which we briefly discuss: measurement problems, the identification of the diffusion and transmission channels of ICTs, and the issue of aggregation.

On the question of measurement, ICT investment is usually measured by bringing together three components, that is, computers and related hardware, telecommunication equipment, and software. However, these components have mainly characterized the birth of the digital economy during the 1990s, although they continue to play an important role. The new digital economy today includes the rise of big data, the development of artificial intelligence, robots, and the rise of the Internet use. If such variables are omitted, the impact of ICT on growth may be underestimated in the econometric equations. For this reason, some databases offer information on connectivity, use of Internet services, use of digital technology, and digital public services (the European Commission's DESI—Digital Economy and Society Index offers an index based on these indicators for the European countries. There is also an international version of this database called I-DESI). This type of base has the advantage of covering the aspects of the ongoing digitization of economies: mobile broadband, Internet use and advanced digital skills, citizens' use of online activities (communication, transactions, content), e-transactions, e-Government and e-Health, medical data exchange, online course, and big data. Using the DESI data, Fernández-Portillo et al. (2020) show that the indicators that seem to affect growth the most are Internet usage, e-commerce by SMEs, and the use of e-Government by administrations.

On the issue of identifying the sources of transmission and diffusion of innovations, we now have two literature that are expanding. The first is a voluminous literature (which began to develop in the mid-1980s) of micro-econometrics based on data on firms, sectors, and industries. The second literature is more concerned with macroeconomic models for calibrating and simulating the links between innovation and growth.

The main advantage of micro-econometric analyses is to broaden the channels through which ICT influences growth. This helps to identify the diffusion mechanisms of the digital economy at the firm and sector levels, not directly perceptible at an aggregate macroeconomic level (organizational routines, market selection processes, selection of the best technologies, effects on human capital, path dependence phenomena, etc.). For a survey of the literature, the interested reader can refer to Van Reenen et al. (2010), Koch and Windsperger (2017) and Vu et al. (2020).

There is also mounting interest in studying the impact of ICT, R&D, and innovation impacts on economic growth through the calibration and simulation of macroeconomic models. Some DSGE models take Romer's (1990) endogenous growth model as their theoretical framework of reference. They distinguish between intangible and tangible capital and prioritize labor according to several skill levels. They are New-Keynesian models that differentiate between constrained and unconstrained households, where firms in all sectors, including R&D, are in monopolistic competition and where knowledge is endogenous. In this type of model, the key parameter is the elasticity of domestic knowledge with respect to past international or domestic knowledge accumulation. Another interesting aspect is that the interaction between Schumpeterian innovations and price and wage rigidity has consequences for the endogenous decision of forms to innovate and is likely to push production frontiers. In addition to DSGE models, macro-econometric models of endogenous growth with innovations are also simulated. These models are based on aggregate production functions detailing the components of the digital economy (capital services in R&D, ICT, and externalities due to interactions between users and producers of ICT). The reader interested in these two fields of literature can refer to Di Comite and Kancs (2015), Hasumi et al. (2018) and Akcigit et al. (2022).

One issue that raises a major challenge for macroeconomists is the micro-macro transition for modeling the diffusion of technological innovations in order to investigate their impact on economic growth. This question can be addressed in several ways.

The first way is to look at it as a statistical measurement problem. The topics are then those studied by econometrics devoted to the aggregation of large panel data (see Pesaran and Chudik 2019 for a review of the different aspects of this issue). This requires careful consideration of the distributions of the microeconomic coefficients in the equations that describe the learning or evolution dynamics of ICT investments within each firm or sector. Moreover, the compositional effects linked to aggregation also depend on the share of innovation shocks that are common to firms/sectors and idiosyncratic shocks. One interesting point is that technical progress may spread rapidly at the micro level, within sectors or firms, but at the aggregate level it may result in a slow diffusion phenomenon, for example, because of spillover effects or because the share of laggards is larger than that of early adopters. This first approach is still in progress and should lead to further work in the future. Let us consider a simple example.

Suppose that the sources of growth are investigated using an econometric equation in which real GDP growth rate is explained by the growth rate of capital services (ICT and non-ICT), labor services, total factor productivity, and several control variables:

$$y_t = \alpha TFP_t + \beta k_{ICT,t} + \gamma k_{NICT,t} + \delta L_t + \omega X_t + \epsilon_t, \qquad (2.4)$$

where all variables are expressed as growth rates and $y, k_{ICT}, k_{INCT}, L,$ and X are respectively real GDP, ICT capital services, non-ICT capital services, labor services, and a vector of control variables. TFP is the total factor productivity and ϵ is an error term. The impact of ICT on GDP growth is related to the dynamics of this variable. We can therefore assume that $k_{ICT,t}$ is endogenous:

$$k_{ICT,t} = f(k_{ICT,t-1}, k_{ICT,t-2}, k_{ICT,t-3}, \ldots). \qquad (2.5)$$

The function f depends on the assumptions made on the distribution of ICT at the micro level. Let us assume that

$$ICT_{it} = \lambda_i ICT_{it-1} + F_t + \epsilon_{it}, \ i, = 1 \ldots, n, \ 0 \le \lambda_i \le 1, \qquad (2.6)$$

where $F_t \approx iid(0, \sigma_F^2)$ is a common sector ICT shock and $\epsilon_{it} \approx iid(0, \sigma_\epsilon^2)$ is an idiosyncratic shock. We assume that there are n individual firms or sectors. If the diffusion of ICT within each firm/sector is represented by a

Beta distribution

$$f(\lambda_i, a, b) = B^{-1}(a, b)\lambda_i^{a-1}(1 - \lambda_i)^{b-1}, \ a > 0, \ b > 0, \qquad (2.7)$$

with B the Beta function, then by considering the aggregate of the individual $ICT_{it}s$, we obtain:

$$ICT_t = n^{-1}\sum_{i=1}^{n} = A_t + B_t, \qquad (2.8)$$

where

$$A_t = n^{-1}\sum_{i=1}^{n} \epsilon_{it}/(1 - \lambda_i L), \qquad (2.9)$$

and

$$B_t = \sum_{k=0}^{\infty} \omega_k F_{t-k}, \ \omega_k = n^{-1}\sum_{i=1}^{n} \lambda_i^k. \qquad (2.10)$$

Assume that (a, b) is defined over the support $(-1, 1)$ and that $a = \omega/(1 - \omega)$, where ω is the mean of the distribution. Then, when $0.5 < b < 1$, we have $cov(B_t, B_{t-k}) \approx ck^{2d-1}$, where d is called a long-memory process. In such a situation, the function f in Eq. (2.5) characterizes a long-memory process, meaning that the diffusion of innovation at the aggregate level is very sluggish:

$$(1 - L)^d ICT_t = \epsilon_t, \ \epsilon_t \approx iid(0, \sigma_\epsilon^2). \qquad (2.11)$$

Another way of approaching the question of the micro/macro transition in the diffusion of technical progress is to characterize the distribution of innovations or ICTs across firms or industries. A standard assumption is that this distribution is described by bell-shaped curves. At the left end are firms that are laggards or recalcitrant to the adoption of innovations. At the right end are innovators, inventors, and those who are pioneers in the use of new technologies. The hump of the distribution describes majorities that may be close to laggards or on the contrary close to early adopters. From the distributions, we obtain cumulative distributions. These describe at an aggregate level how ICT/innovations spread in a country as a whole.

The literature on technology diffusion is dominated by three models: the S-shape model (with its theoretical background based on the Rogers' model), probit models, and density dependence models (for a survey, see Geroski 2000). The use of sigmoid curves is motivated by the idea of a diffusion in three phases: (1) introduction of a new technology with innovators and early adopters, (2) the new technology leads the largest benefit in terms of productivity and investment (a majority of firms/industries adopt it), and (3) a gradual exhaustion of the opportunity for applications. Such a diffusion process can be described by a cumulative S-shape equation:

$$\Delta ICT_\tau = \mu \left[ICT_\tau - f \right]^\alpha \left[M - ICT_\tau \right]^\beta , \ \mu, f, M, \alpha, \beta > 0. \qquad (2.12)$$

ICT increases and converges to M. It exhibits growth up to τ^* and then decelerates. α and β are used to capture the asymmetry between upswing and downswing phases. μ captures the transition between technological regimes, that is, the speed at which an economy develops a new technology. Equation (2.12) is known as a generalized Richards model (widely used in epidemiological literature). Note that τ is an index that may represent time or a couple (i, t) of (industry,time) if this equation is used on panel data.

A third aspect, little studied so far on the micro/macro transition, is the following. Asking the question of the aggregation of individual production functions supposes that one accepts the idea that ICT capital or innovations allow each firm, or each industry, to operate on its production possibilities frontier. Thus, digital inventions would aim to push the individual production frontier, either directly or indirectly via the effect on the TFP. However, this hypothesis—according to which firms produce by being on their production frontier—is not necessarily satisfied. It is possible that they are below this frontier and that digital innovations serve to close this gap. This means that at the aggregate level, even if we assign the same elasticities in the individual growth equations to all firms/industries in a sector, a country may not be on its production possibility frontier. It is therefore important to measure the gaps between the most innovative firms and the others, or between the potential level of output associated with technological innovations and the current situation of a firm and a country.

We take an example from Japanese industries. The exercise we are doing here can easily be replicated for other countries. We estimate the following model:

$$y_{it} = \lambda TFP_{it} + \alpha_{ICT} k_{it}^{ICT} + \alpha_{NICT} k_{it}^{NICT} + \alpha_{INT} k_{it}^{INT} + \beta L_{it} + \gamma X_t + V_{it} - U_{it},$$
(2.13)

$$TFP_{it} = a_0 k_t^{ICT} + a_1 k_t^{INT} + a_2 k_t^{soft} + a_3 k_t^{com} + a_4 k_{it}^{comp} + W_{it},$$
(2.14)

$$\mu_{it} = \kappa_1 k_{it}^{ICT} + \kappa_2 k_{it}^{INT} + \kappa_3 Z_t,$$
(2.15)

where
$V_{it} \approx iid(0, \sigma_V^2)$, $U_{it} \approx N^+(\mu_{it}, \sigma_U^2)$, $W_{it} \approx iid(0, \sigma_W^2)$,
$X_t = (hc_t, open_t, \Delta budg_t, \Delta credit_t)$,
$Z_t = (skill_t, internet_t, mobile_t, FSI_t)$.

Equation (2.13) is a stochastic frontier production equation. The growth rate of value added volume of sector i in year t (y_{it}) depends on the growth rates of ICT capital services, non-ICT capital and intangible capital (resp k_{it}^{ICT}, k_{it}^{NICT}, and k_{it}^{INT}), and the growth rate of labor services (L_{it}). Total productivity is aggregated (TFP_t), which allows to capture the spillover effects of the overall TFP on each sector. In addition, we add macroeconomic environment variables that may affect the sector growth rates, that is, the level of human capital in the country (hc_t), the degree of trade openness ($open_t$), changes in the government general lending/borrowing ($\Delta budg_t$), changes in credit to the private sector ($\Delta credit_t$).

In this equation, the residual term includes an inefficiency variable (the distance to the frontier U_{it}). This variable follows a truncated normal distribution with homoscedastic variance, and a mean (μ_{it}) that varies over time according to macroeconomic variables likely to limit or, on the contrary, to accentuate the distance to the production possibilities frontier (Eq. (2.15)): the sectors' growth rates of ICT and intangible capital services and other global indicators such as entrepreneurial skills ($skill_t$) proxied by the share of self-employment in total employment, indicators of use of Internet and mobile phones by the public ($internet_t$ and $mobile_t$). We also consider a financial stress indicator (FSI_t).

We assume that the growth rates of ICT capital and intangible capital have two effects on the growth rate of the sector's value added: a direct effect in Eq. (2.13) and an indirect effect through the effect on the

Table 2.2 Estimate of the frontier coefficients

	Coef.	Std. Err	z	Prob.
Productivity	0.39***	0.15	2.61	0.009
ICT capital	0.04**	0.02	2.29	0.02
NICT capital	0.30***	0.12	2.57	0.01
Intang. capital	−0.42***	0.09	−4.26	0.0
Labor	0.26***	0.07	3.79	0.0
Trade	0.44	3.91	0.11	0.91
Credit	−0.06	0.05	−1.31	0.19
Budget balance	−0.14	0.15	−0.98	0.33
Human capital	0.88	11.99	0.07	0.33
σ_U	36.99*	20.35	1.79	0.07
σ_V	2.56***	0.17	14.46	0.00

Note *, **, *** means significance at 10%, 5%, 1% level of confidence

sector's TFP growth rate in Eq. (2.14). Moreover, we consider that TFP_{it} growth rate depends on the growth rate of real investment in computing, communication, and software equipment.

Table 2.8 shows the list of industries selected from the KLEMS database. Our estimates cover the period from 1995 to 2017. Table 2.9 shows the source of the different variables used in the regressions (see the appendix). Equation (2.14) is first estimated by OLS (with robust standard errors), then the fitted values of the TFP are used to estimate the frontier and the deviation from the frontier (Eqs. (2.13) and (2.15)). The stochastic production frontier is estimated using Belotti et al. (2013)'s estimator.[3]

The estimated coefficients of the regression (2.14) show that the variables which have a significant impact on productivity are intangible capital and aggregate investment in software. The results in Table 2.2 show that ICT capital has a positive impact on productivity, while the coefficient on

---

[3] Our estimates have limitations. They could be improved by tackling more deeply some econometric issues, such as endogeneity, taking into account the dynamics or other problems related to the estimation of stochastic frontiers of production on panel data. Our goal is to show, despite these limitations, the issues raised by the simultaneous consideration of sector heterogeneity and aggregate data to assess the effect of ICT and intangible capital on production boundaries.

intangible capital is negative. This suggests the existence of substitutability between ICT investments and those related to other types of intangible capital (R&D, patents, brand, organizational, knowledge capital,...).

On the other hand, we find that ICT and non-ICT capital have complementary effects on the value-added growth frontier of sectors, as has labor.

Figure 2.1 and Table 2.11 in Appendix show the distribution of efficiency scores. The distribution is skewed with 90% of the observations having a score less than or equal to 37%.

An interesting point is to compare Figs. 2.1 and 2.2. In the latter, the distribution of the sectors' growth frontiers over time is quite symmetric, while the efficiency scores are very asymmetric with a majority of firms being far from their own frontier during the period under study. This suggests that the examination of frontiers to investigate the influence of different factors on growth, especially ICT and intangible capital, is not enough. Significant differences may exist between industries in terms of the gap at their frontier.

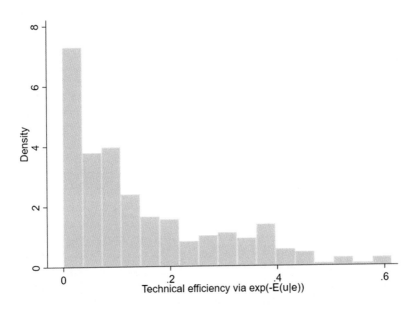

Fig. 2.1 Distribution of efficiency score across industries: Japan

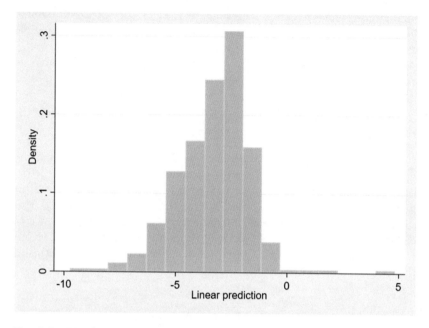

Fig. 2.2 Distribution of frontiers

Table 2.3 shows the marginal effects of changes in the variables in the Z vector on the inefficiency term in Eq. (2.15). Since these vary for each observation, we report here the results for different percentiles of the distribution of these marginal effects. The important information is provided by the sign of the coefficients. Higher investment in ICT capital, and in intangible capital in general, reduces the gap from the growth frontier. Similarly, the development of self-employment reduces this gap, as does the development of cell phone use. Higher financial stress in the country—that is, a destabilizing financial environment for firms—tends to increase the growth frontier gap.

One of the drawbacks of these regressions is that they assign the same coefficients to all sectors, whereas they are likely to be heterogeneous (in the quantities invested in ICT and intangibles, and in the impact of these investments on growth). We thus use another estimation technique that is better suited to take this heterogeneity into account. To keep things simple, since the variables in the vector X_{it} are not significant, we now consider

Table 2.3 Marginal effects on inefficiency

	Percentile	Mean	Lower	Upper
FSI	0.20	14.28	13.23	14.94
	0.50	20.87	19.74	21.99
	0.70	25.52	24.46	26.81
Internet	0.20	0.22	0.19	0.24
	0.50	0.47	0.42	0.53
	0.70	0.71	0.65	0.78
Mobile	0.20	−0.28	−0.35	−0.25
	0.50	−0.15	−0.16	−0.13
	0.70	−0.08	−0.10	−0.07
ICT capital	0.20	−0.01	−0.014	−0.011
	0.50	−0.006	−0.007	−0.005
	0.70	−0.0035	−0.004	−0.0032
Intang. capital	0.20	−0.48	−0.59	−0.42
	0.50	−0.25	−0.28	−0.22
	0.70	−0.14	−0.17	−0.13
Self	0.20	−2.65	−3.27	2,31
	0.50	−1.39	−1.54	−1.24
	0.70	−0.78	−0.96	−0.72

the following model to be estimated:

$$y_{it} = \lambda \, TFP_{it} + \alpha_{ICT} \, k_{it}^{ICT} + \alpha_{NICT} \, k_{it}^{NICT} + \alpha_{INT} \, k_{it}^{INT} + \beta \, L_{it} + \gamma \, Z_t + \epsilon_{it}, \tag{2.16}$$

where $\epsilon_{it} \approx iid(0, \sigma_\epsilon^2)$. In the vector Z, we introduce one by one the variables that seemed to influence the growth gaps in the preceding regressions. This is done to avoid colinearity. TFP is still the fitted values of total factor productivity obtained from the estimates of Eq. (2.14).

The quantile regression approach allows us to compare sectors over time by calculating the gap between low and high achievers. This is different from the OLS method. Instead of taking as a reference a set of sectors located around the conditional expectation of growth rates, the equation is estimated for different quantiles of the conditional distribution.

Let us define $\theta \in (0, 1)$ as the θth quantile of the endogenous variable $y_i t$ and gather the explanatory variables into a vector y_{it} (and similarly the coefficients are gathered in a vector β). A conditional quantile function is defined as:

$$Q_\theta(y_{it}|X_{it} = x_{it}) \equiv \inf\{y_{it} : F(y_{it}\ vert x_{it}) \geq \theta\}, \tag{2.17}$$

and the linear quantile regression model assumes:

$$Q_\theta(y_{it}|X_{it} = x_{it}) = x_{it}\beta(\theta). \tag{2.18}$$

$\beta(\theta)$ is a vector of quantile coefficients. Each component describes the marginal change in the θth quantile of $\{y_{it}\}$ following a marginal change in the components of X_{it}. A quantile estimation of the parameters is given by

$$\hat{\beta}(\theta) \in \arg\min_\beta \left[\frac{1}{nT} \sum_{t=1}^{T} \sum_{i=1}^{n} \rho_\theta(y_{it} - X_{it}'\beta) \right], \tag{2.19}$$

where ρ_θ in a symmetric absolute loss function is defined by

$$\rho_\theta(u) = (\theta - \mathbb{1}(u < 0))\ u, \quad 0 < \theta < 1. \tag{2.20}$$

For a detailed presentation of the inference of quantile regression, the reader can refer to Koenker (2005).

Figure 2.3 shows the evolution of the regression coefficients in the case where the Internet access variable is introduced in addition to the basic determinants (productivity, ICT and non-ICT capital, intangible capital, and labor). In addition to the estimated coefficients, the 95% confidence intervals are shown. The impact of productivity, ICT capital, and the Internet on growth is greater for higher achievers than for lower achievers. Indeed, the coefficients increase with the growth rate. As with the stochastic frontier regression, the negative effect of intangible capital is more pronounced as the growth rate increases. The impact of labor also decreases with growth rates.

We define the highest achievers as the observations corresponding to the top 10th percentile of the series (i.e., $\theta = 0.9$). To evaluate the gap of the other observations, we consider the following decomposition:

$$y_{it}(\theta) - y_{it}(0.9) = X_{it}'(\theta)\hat{\beta}(\theta) - X_{it}'(0.9)\hat{\beta}(0.9) \tag{2.21}$$
$$= -X_{it}'(0.9)\left[\hat{\beta}(0.9) - \hat{\beta}(\theta)\right]$$

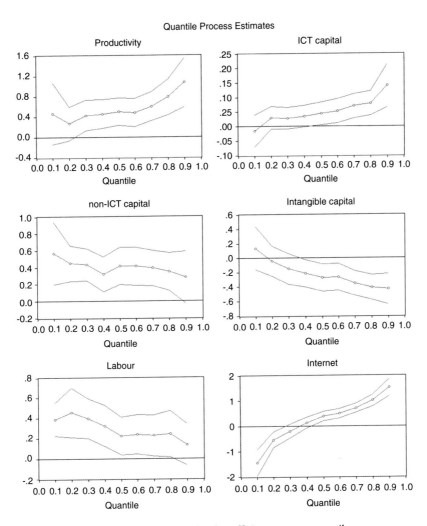

Fig. 2.3 Quantile regressions: graph of coefficients across quantiles

$$-\left[X'_{it}(0.9) - X'_{it}(\theta)\right]\hat{\beta}(\theta)$$
$$= A_{it}(\theta) + B_{it}(\theta), \ \theta \neq 0.9.$$

Once the coefficients are estimated, we calculate the percentile rank of the observations of $y_i t$. $X_{it}(\theta)$ denotes the values of exogenous variables for the observations classified in the θth percentile other than the 90% percentile. $\hat{\beta}(\theta)$ is the vector of estimates of the coefficients of covariates, for quantiles other than $\theta = 0.9$.

$A_{it}(\theta)$ describes the gap from the frontier due to differences in the performance of sectors in the way they use the factors that are determinants of their value-added growth. In other words, even if all industries had the same endowments—in terms of growth—as the countries/years with the highest growth, differences in growth rates could be observed because these endowments are less well used. $A_{it}(\theta)$ can be interpreted as a behavioral gap. $B_{it}(\theta)$ measures differences due to different factor endowments. In other words, with the same efficiency in the use of factors of production, differences in growth rates are explained by different Xs between sectors. $B_{it}(\theta)$ can be interpreted as an "endowment gap." In Table 2.4, we calculate, for each quantile, the averages of $A_{it}(\theta)$ and $B_{it}(\theta)$, as well as the contributions of each factor and each coefficient to these averages.

As seen in the table, the distance to the highest achievers (the observations in the top 10% of the value-added distribution) is negative. This means that the frontiers corresponding to the observations in the quantile classes $\theta < 0.9$ are some distance away from that of the highest achievers. The gap narrows as the quantiles get closer to $\theta = 0.9$. In the decomposition, it is the endowment gap that contributes most to explaining the distances between the frontiers. However, ICT capital stands out from the other factors. Indeed, the coefficients of the behavioral gap are positive and decrease with the quantiles, which may reflect a kind of law of diminishing returns in the influence of ICT on growth. Their contribution to growth is stronger, the further the frontier of a given sector is from the highest achievers, but the gains diminish as ICTs "push" the frontier toward the furthest frontier. The sectors further away from the highest frontier therefore benefit more—in terms of growth—than sectors close to that frontier. But a gap remains because the sectors in the highest quantiles have higher ICT endowments than the others.

Table 2.4 Quantile regressions: decomposition of frontier gaps

	Quantiles	q1	q2	q3	q4	q5	q6	q7	q8
Behavioral gap $A(\theta)$ contributions	Total (1)	−0.848	−1.009	−0.625	−0.346	−0.235	−0.342	−0.195	−0.033
	Productivity	−0.413	−0.549	−0.439	−0.419	−0.390	−0.402	−0.317	−0.196
	ICT capital	1.051	0.742	0.753	0.711	0.649	0.586	0.475	0.411
	NICT capital	−0.258	−0.151	−0.139	−0.038	−0.125	−0.121	−0.101	−0.063
	INTANG capital	−0.876	−0.601	−0.435	−0.337	−0.245	−0.260	−0.125	−0.037
	Labor	−0.352	−0.449	−0.365	−0.264	−0.123	−0.144	−0.127	−0.147
Endowment gap $B(\theta)$ contributions	Total (2)	−3.172	−1.837	−1.658	−1.332	−0.986	−0.815	−0.461	−0.161
	Productivity	−0.805	−0.221	−0.079	−0.037	−0.023	−0.026	0.216	0.344
	ICT capital	0.070	−0.027	−0.173	−0.206	−0.122	−0.184	−0.117	−0.140
	NICT capital	−1.042	−0.665	−0.397	−0.258	−0.077	0.030	0.157	0.279
	INTANG capital	−0.195	−0.013	−0.062	−0.185	−0.311	−0.322	−0.533	−0.483
	Labor	−1.200	−0.911	−0.947	−0.646	−0.454	−0.312	−0.184	−0.161
Frontier gap	Total (1) + (2)	−4.020	−2.846	−2.283	−1.678	−1.221	−1.157	−0.657	−0.194

2.1.3   New Theoretical Growth Models of Digital and Knowledge Economics

The literature is voluminous, and it is difficult to give an account in a few paragraphs of works that are in full expansion. We will refer the interested reader to some references for detailed presentations of theoretical models. Overall, the literature is divided into three parts.

The first remains in the tradition of neoclassical endogenous growth models, similar to the models of diffusion of innovations and R&D developed in the 1990s, the difference being that the specifications of the production functions (of goods and services, ideas) are enriched to take account of the role of the ICTs, robots, artificial intelligence, and so on. The main advantage is to capitalize on the research conducted in the literature on endogenous growth models, by enriching the hypotheses on how new innovations are created and diffused in the economies. For instance, a collective work such as that edited by Helpman (1998) is still relevant. It shows that macroeconomists were already interested in the role of radical, disruptive innovations such as those we are currently witnessing at the beginning of the twenty-first century.

A second strand of the literature aims to address the issue of the social returns to technological innovations, which are not necessarily internalized by firms. This second strand of literature has the advantage of analyzing long-term growth from technological "paradigms.' This leads to understand the importance of looking at global spillover effects, that is, the fact that the diffusion of technical progress takes place through channels involving not only firms and markets, but societies that are solidly embedded in social interdependence relationships. Historians have done a great deal of work on this awareness, producing new empirical evidence from long time series that have led to the following observation. Countries at the origin of advanced technologies are not necessarily those where technological revolutions significantly improve living standards and medium-term growth. The same reasoning applies to firms. It is fundamental to study how new technological paradigms lead to institutional and organizational changes and to the formation of new communities and learning modes. The development of knowledge-based economies depends on institutional, social, cultural, historical, geopolitical, and geographical contexts. And these contexts condition the behavior of economic agents. This implies shifting the focus to the social rate of returns of innovations, instead of simply focusing on their private return.

A third strand of the literature complements the previous one, but examines technological paradigm shifts at the firm level. Researchers investigate how new technological innovations change the business model of companies, modify their relations with stakeholders, and redefine their approaches, not only to production methods, but above all to their organization. This literature improves our understanding of what a company or a network of companies is in the era of the digital economy.

Each strand of the literature has its own research objectives.

For the first strand of literature, macroeconomists adopt an approach they have been used to since Kaldor in the 1960s, that is, to theoretically explain a number of stylized facts that seem to prevail in the new digital economy and in a context of new waves of innovations. These facts are summarized in Akcigit and Ates (2021):

1. the number of start-ups is decreasing (in advanced economies, fewer people are starting businesses, and the number of businesses that disappear exceeds the number of newly created businesses);
2. productivity gains are slowing down in industrialized countries;
3. the share of the wage bill in national income is on a downward trend, while the share of profits (or income accruing to the owners of capital) is increasing;
4. the degree of market concentration is increasing;
5. labor markets are less "fluid" (growth does not facilitate the reallocation of labor factors between different sectors);
6. differences in labor productivity are increasing between firms with the highest productivity and the others.

We can add another stylized fact: - inequalities in the personal distribution of income and wealth have increased over the last three decades.

The proposed theoretical models provide plausible explanations to these facts.

For the second strand of the literature, there is an incentive to study more rigorously how new technologies modify institutional structures, and social transformations that—because they are intimately intertwined with the economy—can have effects on GDP growth. The task is difficult, because it requires extensive expertise in history, organizational systems, sociology, economics, and knowledge of technological paradigms. The difficulty also arises from the fact that an ideal model would be based on trans-disciplinary approaches.

The third line of research is based on the idea that the basic link in the transmission of innovations to growth is the firm. It is therefore necessary to take a close look at how the digital economy and the new innovations of the twenty-first century affect the behavior of companies. We need to understand how ideas spread, how business actors organize themselves, and how business ecosystems are affected by inventions and their diffusion. This is a very promising line of research, because it involves revisiting, in the light of the new digital economy, the old theories of the firm: the firm as a place of information processing, creation and management of intangible resources, and a place where evolutionary processes explain the setting up of routines and learning phenomena for the diffusion of new ideas.

2.1.3.1 Models Which Belong to the Neoclassical and Schumpeter Traditions

During the last decade, a literature has grown up, aiming at extending the formal frameworks of the models proposed in the 1990s to study the endogenous characteristics of growth.

Akcigit and Ates (2021) propose a theoretical model where firms' markup is endogenous and depends on their technological gap and their decision to innovate or not. The growth equilibrium depends on the transmission flow between the firms at the frontier of innovations and the others (for a similar explanation, see Acemoglu and Akcigit 2012).

Other papers highlight the role of globalization on the market structure of innovations. Perla et al. (2021) show that by exporting, firms are encouraged to adopt their customers' best practices and innovations, which favors a rapid diffusion of productivity gains on a global scale, but also for the countries themselves. According to Sampson (2016), competition in the import market also drives firms to imitate best practices. This phenomenon is favored by Darwinian processes of firm selection, especially if the innovations of domestic firms are complementary to those of foreign firms. Recent models studying the links between innovation, trade, and growth show that, apart from the effects linked to the size of markets, a major ingredient that favors the diffusion of innovations is the distribution of technical progress among firms. For some papers along these lines of research, see Bloom et al. (2016), Buera and Lucas (2018) and Buera and Oberfield (2020).

Models linking innovation and inequalities are also gaining interest. For example, Moll et al. (2021) propose a theoretical framework in which technological innovations increase wage inequality through a mechanism of technological bias in favor of skilled workers and also generate inequality in the distribution of labor income because of a rent linked to the rate of return on assets representing innovative firms whose capital is held by rich agents. These two types of—functional—income inequalities lead to an unequal distribution of personal income. In a framework where households and workers are differentiated by the level of wealth and degree of qualification, the automation of tasks can imply inequalities through two mechanisms. The first is the increase in capital intensity that raises capital incomes and returns to wealth. The second is income stagnation, which increases income inequality for those agents who are in the bottom of income distribution. In this type of model, the returns to capital and wealth are endogenous and depend on the degree of automation in the technology used by the firms.

The stylized fact 6 is explained in theoretical models in which innovation equilibria depend on the interaction between innovations and their diffusion. In the new endogenous growth models, firms decide whether they want to innovate or whether they copy and imitate existing innovations. There is a cost, therefore, in both cases, and this cost depends on the distribution of the existing technology among the firms and on the rate at which the firms at the frontier innovate. See, among others, Benhabib et al. (2021), Känig et al. (2016), Känig et al. (2016) and Luttmer (2012).

A promising avenue of research concerns the effect of automation and artificial intelligence on economic growth, factor productivity, and the quantities of factors used (demand for capital and labor). A hot topic is whether there is substitutability between automation and labor input, whether any substitutability would only affect low-skilled workers, or whether it would also affect the most skilled workers. We will refer here to some papers among a growing literature.

Aghion et al. (2019) extend the standard neoclassical production function where automation changes the productivity of capital and labor. One of the interesting points of their paper is to show that, contrary to what one might think, automation does not necessarily improve the productivity of capital, because it has two effects: a capital augmenting effect and a capital depleting effect because a fixed amount of capital is used more thinly between various tasks. If the tasks are complementary factors in the production function, then the second effect dominates. Another interesting result is that growth based on a greater use of automated tasks can lead to a decrease in the contribution of the output of the most automated sectors to aggregate GDP.

To obtain these results, the authors consider the following production function:

$$Y_t = A_t F [B_t K_t, C_t L_t], \quad B_t = \beta_t^{(1-\rho)/\rho}, \quad C_t = (1 - \beta_t)^{(1-\rho)/\rho}, \quad (2.22)$$

where A_t is Hicks-neutral technical change, B_t is Solow-neutral technical progress and C_t is Harrod-neutral technical progress. ρ is a parameter that describes the degree of substitutability between capital and labor. In the economy there are automated tasks. A proportion β_t employs capital and a proportion $1 - \beta_t$ employs labor. When capital and labor are complements ($\rho < 0$), an increase in automation leads to a decrease in B_t (capital diluting effect) and an increase in C_t (labor-augmenting effect). When capital and labor are substitutable ($\rho > 0$), the augmenting effect of automation on capital dominates the diluting effect.

A necessary condition for automation to increase production is

$$\left[\frac{K_t}{\beta_t} \right]^\rho < \left[\frac{L_t}{1 - \beta_t} \right]^\rho, \quad (2.23)$$

where K_t/β_t denotes units of capital used in automated tasks and $L_t/(1 - \beta_t)$ denotes the units of labor used in non-automated tasks. When $\rho < 0$ output increases if the stock of capital allocated to each task exceeds the amount of labor allocated to each task.

The authors show that the ratio of automated to non-automated output is

$$R_t = \left[\frac{\beta_t}{1 - \beta_t} \right]^{1-\rho} \left[\frac{K_t}{L_t} \right]^\rho. \quad (2.24)$$

The first term on the right-hand side of the equality denotes the fraction of automated tasks in the economy. If capital and labor are complementary ($\rho < 0$), the evolution of the ratio depends on two effects. First, it decreases as capital intensity increases. On the other hand, it increases with the fraction of automated tasks. The share of GDP growth that goes to automated sectors increases as automation spreads to different sectors of the economy. But it is held back by the accumulation of capital (their relative price falls).

More sophisticated approaches have been proposed. For example, Acemoglu and Restrepo (2018) introduce two production functions, respectively, for sectors not employing automated technology and others using such technology. They consider that firms can decide either to automate already existing tasks or to discover new tasks to be performed to produce. They calculate an equilibrium level for the degree of automation of tasks and show that an increase in automation technology increases the share of capital in output and decreases the share of labor.

Other papers provide new avenues for research. For example, Bloom et al. (2020) question the idea that the production of new ideas generates exponential endogenous growth. They propose a framework to explain the diminishing returns in the production of new ideas. Jones (2021) discusses exciting opportunities for new area of future research where growth is interpreted from a semi-endogenous perspective—in the Romer sense—since the stock of knowledge, new ideas, and education attainment cannot go forever and is limited.

2.1.3.2 Hot Topics for Future Research

Without neglecting the rigor of theoretical models and the use of good quality data, the analyses devoted to the effects on the growth of the digitization of economies and the role of recent waves of innovation can be studied by extending the questions examined in the models of the neoclassical tradition. First, if it is true that the current new waves of innovation are the first phase of a new era of disruptive innovations (this idea is the basis of Schumpeterian optimism), one of the questions we should be concerned with is how they change the current growth regime to generate a new regime in the future. This can be done only by integrating into the models institutional changes, new types of economic and societal regulation, and long-term industrial structural changes. Such works are still lacking, with the exception of a few articles and seminal works.

Gordon (2016)'s book on the rise and fall of the American growth investigates the effects of innovations and productivity gains on the living standards (rather than just the growth) of Americans since 1870. This leads him to study the societal and institutional transformations that have been at the origin of both "great leaps forward" and headwinds to growth. The author does not share the optimism of the Schumpeterian but considers that innovations after 1970 are incremental. Not only are they confined to particular spheres, but they spread slowly. An interesting point is that the periods conducive to the rapid expansion of innovations are particular. According to the author, the second World War was the main source of acceleration in the growth of productivity gains during the 30 glorious years. According to him, the reasons for the current diminishing returns to productivity gains in the United States are non-economic, that is, demographic decline, the globalization of trade and financial flows that favors the concentration of capital, the erosion of human capital due to the high cost of higher education and health-care systems, and the inequalities that have led to the decline of the middle class. The Gordon approach should prompt comparative analyses of other industrialized countries: Germany, France, Japan, the United Kingdom, and others.

Stiglitz and Greenwald (2014) extend the topics of Schumpeterian and neoclassical models. Beyond innovation, what is at stake is the knowledge and learning society. Beyond growth, we need to be concerned about living standards and well-being. Looking at technological and knowledge systems, the interesting question is not so much what progress is being made, but why some societies are more learning and creative than others. Why does technical progress spread more rapidly in societies that have less knowledge than others? Why is it that while China has had very advanced technological knowledge for more than 800 years, industrial revolutions have taken place in Europe? Why do the returns on new knowledge seem to be decreasing in the United States, a country considered to be the technological frontier of the world? To investigate such questions, the societal, economic, and institutional contexts are important. The efficiency of an innovative and learning society is not necessarily measured by market price system or by the optimal allocation of resources. Government policies are fundamental to prevent factors that stifle growth: patent hold-ups, abuse of market dominance, appropriation of rents and inventions, financial distortions, and barrier-to-entry strategies in innovation markets. The contribution of the authors' book is to shift the focus from exclusively microeconomic agents to society. Knowledge and innovations are common goods. Their effects on growth and well-being can therefore be understood only if one investigates the social returns (or social value) of innovation externalities. For example, there may be an antinomy between private returns and social returns from innovations if patents protect the construction of new knowledge extending already existing knowledge. This kind of question is not trivial when it leads to compare the equilibrium of decentralized knowledge or decided by a social planner. In order to maximize knowledge, understood as a common good, how can we determine the share of new knowledge that must be protected by its inventor and the share that must be disclosed (companies benefiting from patent protection sometimes engage in fierce battles with their competitors to avoid any disclosure of their innovations?). The welfare function of the central planner must include the producer of the innovation and the future users/innovators. But according to which criteria and which weights? The question of the diffusion of innovations and their effects on economic growth—a social optimum—is therefore inseparable from the question of intellectual property, and therefore of patent systems.

An alternative to neoclassical and Schumpeterian models is Freeman-like approaches to studying the diffusion of innovations in capitalist economies. This approach relies on the examination of technological paradigms selected by societies and requires the combination of disciplines such as economics, sociology, history, and political science.

The first stage is to study how production and relationships between producers are reorganized. A rapidly growing literature today concerns the transformation of entrepreneurial ecosystems caused by the current waves of innovation. Some scientific journals publish groundbreaking articles on the subject, for example, *Cambridge Journal of Economics, Journal of Business Research, Journal of Management, Journal of Management Studies, Technology Analysis & Strategic Management,...*These works propose new concepts that endogenous growth models should take into account, for instance, Internet of everything (IOT), interest of people (IOP), networked business models (NBM). They are based on practical cases to theorize and measure the diffusion of knowledge and innovation flows between the actors of a firm: innovators, customers, competitors, shareholders, and so on. Such models lead us to revisit the theory of the firm. They favor mesoeconomic analyses, that is, they investigate value creation in the digital age from the perspective of the environment in which firms operate. An important lesson from this literature is that there is a wide variety of business models. The interested reader can refer to the following papers (among many others): the special issue of the *Journal of Management Studies*: corporate strategy and the theory of the firm in the digital age (2021, vol. 58, issue 7), Banalieva and Dhanaraj (2019), Burstöm et al. (2021), Cao and Shi (2021) Garzella et al. (2021), Kohtamäki et al. (2021), Langley et al. (2021) and Teece (2017).

The second step is to model the processes of emergence and convergence of new technological paradigms. This literature extends the models on technological paradigms that emerged in the 1990s. This involves identifying the factors that contribute to steering technological changes (science-push, institutions, sociological forces, etc.). The recent literature reveals over-promising conclusions, such as that new technological and economic paradigms do not always arise from disruptive innovations but can emerge from small incremental innovations (see for instance Pedota et al. 2021).

2.2   EVOLUTION OF THE FACTORS OF PRODUCTION: CAPITAL, LABOR, AND FACTOR PRODUCTIVITY

Beyond their contribution to growth, let us examine the evolution of the factors of growth themselves and their productivity. Indeed, we have the following two decompositions:

GDP growth rate = growth rate of labor productivity × growth rate of hours worked

Growth rate of labor productivity = growth rate of total factor productivity × growth rate of capital intensity.

How did TFP, capital intensity, and labor productivity change since the mid-1990s? We need to go back several decades, not just to the 2008 crisis, to detect possible structural transformations in the productive system of industrialized countries. The literature points to an exhaustion of productivity gains (slowdown in the growth rate of labor productivity and TFP). For a survey, see, for example, Bergeaud et al. (2016) and Crafts and O'Rourke (2013). Another well-established stylized fact is the fall in investment, especially corporate investment.

Figures 2.4, 2.5 and 2.6 show a downward trend in the growth rate of labor productivity, TFP, and capital intensity in the five countries. This phenomenon is general to advanced countries. The slowdown in productivity gains is a phenomenon that started before the 2008 financial crisis and has been observed since the end of the catch-up of the United States by Europe and Japan in the 1990s. These developments are now well documented so that we can speak of stylized facts (for international comparisons of productivity developments in industrialized countries, see, e.g., Bergeaud et al. 2016). We also recommend Gordon (2016) and Gordon (2018) for a specific analysis of the US case.

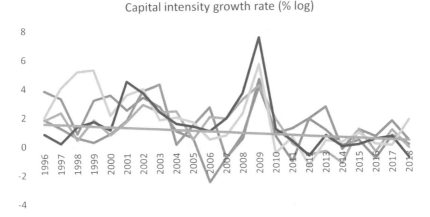

Fig. 2.4 Evolution of capital intensity

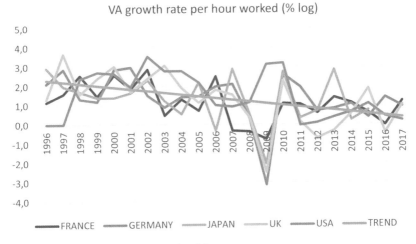

Fig. 2.5 Evolution of labor productivity

2.2.1 Why Are Productivity Gains Shrinking?

A first explanation for the gradual exhaustion of productivity gains is the following. The technological innovations of the second half of the

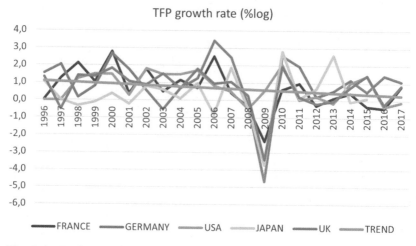

Fig. 2.6   Evolution of TFP

twentieth century were incremental. This contrasts with the earlier technological revolutions in the mid-nineteenth century onward that deeply transformed production and consumption activities. Innovations in electronics, computers, Internet, and telecommunications during the 1980s and 1990s raised productivity in the manufacturing and services sectors. However, these innovations cannot be compared to the invention of the steam engine or the incandescent light bulb. They have only paved the way for more disruptive innovations that are just starting now to emerge and spread: artificial intelligence, automation, robotization, digitization of economies, and big data. The latter are likely to radically change lifestyles in the coming years and decades (autonomous vehicles in the logistics and transportation sector, nanotechnologies in the medical sector, quantum computing for calculators, cryptography and computers, big data to feed artificial intelligence programs in many fields, etc.). We are not yet seeing the effects on overall factor productivity, because these innovations are at an early stage of their development. They have not yet found all their potential fields of application. According to some authors, the first visible effects on productivity will not be seen before 2030, within a decade (see, e.g., Saniee et al. 2018).

These questions fall within the field of the history of science and technology. Some studies emphasize that we are now at an inflection point, between two phases of emergence and diffusion of new innovations (see, e.g., Branstetter and Sichel 2017; Van Ark 2016).

A second explanation is that the technical progress embodied in capital and labor is too low to boost total factor productivity. This can be explained in several ways. First, new innovations are not disruptive enough. Many models of knowledge and new technology diffusion rely on a Schumpeterian vision of innovation processes. However, Christensen's seminal paper and empirical works suggest a completely different way in which innovating companies operate (see the collection of papers Christensen 1997). A disruptive innovation or technology—a source of rapid changes in TFP—is described by Christensen et al. (2015). Incumbent companies introduce higher-quality technologies, products, or services to satisfy segments of markets where profitability is higher. This opens opportunities for entrants to enter the less-profitable segments of the markets. Some of them enter a disruptive trajectory if, while improving their offering to the lowest segments of the markets, they also move up market (the segments with the highest profitability for them), thereby challenging the incumbents. So disruptive innovations originate in the low-end markets, not at the frontier! They begin at small scale, take time, are not necessarily triumphant. This explains why they can be overlooked by the incumbents and why shifts of the technological frontiers by the latter to maintain their position can be slow because the entrants use radically different business models than the existing ones and fringe knowledge redefine entire markets.

Another strand of the literature use frameworks of a "game" between leaders and followers. There is less creation of new innovations at the frontier since the costs of adopting new technologies can be high and therefore delay the diffusion of recent innovations. An explanation is that investment in R&D or adoption of new technologies is procyclical (see Anzoategui et al. 2019; Cette et al. 2015). As a result, when a major economic or financial crisis occurs, spending on such investments falls. But this depends on factors which have opposite effects: on the one side a cleansing effect that improves allocation efficiency when poorly performing firms are eliminated from the market during recessions; on the other side frictions in the credit market (the phenomena of moral hazard, adverse selection, and the policy of low interest rates contribute to the maintenance of poorly performing firms on the market). For an overview of some works on this topic, (see Ollivaud et al. 2016; Osotimehin and Pappadá 2017).

Analyzing the French case on firm data, Cette et al. (2017) find that there was no exhaustion of innovations in the firms located at the frontier (the most productive). But the dispersion between firms at the frontier and the less productive ones increased, implying a misallocation of production factors between firms (see also Andrews et al. 2015). This dispersion is sometimes due to the fact that the most innovative firms are also those that are the most globalized and therefore benefit from new ideas and techniques from outside financial institutions of varying qualities (see Gordon and Sayed 2019; Goldin et al. 2021; McGowan et al. 2017; Mokyr 2013).

Other factors related to demography are discussed below.

2.2.2   New Technologies and Employment

Do the new waves of technological innovation, the digitization of economies, and the automation of tasks create more employment in the industrialized economies? The literature on the race between machines and men is voluminous. We refer below to a selection of papers where the interested reader will find many other references (examples of survey papers are Deschacht 2021 and Lu and Zhou 2021). This issue is usually discussed from two perspectives. The first argument is based on the concept of technological bias and the second argument consists in linking technological progress and the wage share in total income.

Let us start with technological bias. A usual argument is that new technologies lead to distortions in the composition of jobs, with technology destroying lower-skilled jobs and increasing high-skilled jobs. However, empirical studies suggest that the reality is more complex. Each type of technology produces different consequences for employment and unemployment. Consider, for example, automation and automation. They had several effects. First, they caused a de-skilling of jobs reflected by the fact that, for a given level of skills, some workers today hold jobs that are less skilled than two or three decades ago. The reason is that automation replaces, for example, a whole series of jobs that require routine tasks and that required intermediate degrees of qualification. Second, they lead to a polarization of jobs, especially in cases where jobs—both high- and low-skilled—are complementary to the technology. For example, the automation of tasks on a production line is unlikely to reduce cleaning and building maintenance jobs. But it may lead to the disappearance of even highly qualified engineers, if a robot can do the same work as the engineers. The question of substitutability/complementarity between machines and humans is therefore raised for all levels of qualification. Autor (2019) highlights a phenomenon of de-skilling of jobs induced by technological innovations in urban labor markets in the United States. Dao et al. (2020) show that technological progress in developed countries has led to a decline in the labor share of middle-skilled workers, but that it has had very little effect on the work of high-skilled and low-skilled workers. The idea that learning by doing is a factor favorable to growth is a central mechanism of endogenous growth models. A question that has now become interesting concerns the trade-off between generalist of specialized skills. Learning by doing allows for the acquisition of job-specific skills. But specialization can also increase the degree of substitutability between technologies and jobs performed (see on this topic, a very interesting paper by Hanushek et al. (2017).

Let us consider now the issue of the effects of technical progress on the wage share in total income and therefore on aggregate employment.

An empirical study by Boskin and Lau (2000) shows that technical progress—which accounts for half of economic growth—has been neutral in the Solow sense, by increasing the productivity of tangible capital and human capital, based on data from the G7 countries covering the period after the Second World War. One cannot therefore say that it has been a source of increase in structural unemployment rates. But the authors show that the phases of slowing GDP per-capita growth since 1970 have been due to a fall in investment in these two types of capital.

Gregory et al. (2019) study the labor demand effects of routine-replacing technological change. Using European data, they highlight two effects. On the one hand, a substitution effect between factors leading to job losses. On the other hand, a complementarity effect leading to the appearance of new jobs. This second effect was, according to the authors, more important than the first between 1999 and 2010, which they explain by the fact that the digitization of economies induced a greater demand for new products and services (companies gained markets by benefiting from falling prices of these goods and services and high price elasticity of demand).

The digital economy and robotization can improve the creation of new jobs. This is the case, for example, in the e-commerce industry or in the automation industry (engineers are needed to write artificial intelligence programs, to build robots). Similarly, products ordered online open up new jobs in the logistics sector, deliveries). Caselli and Manning (2019) show that new technologies have mainly redistributive effects on the share of wages in income in the value added (it increases in sectors that are more intensive in new technologies, compared to other sectors).

In the future, the literature should focus on investigating some effects that have not yet been studied, that is, the consequences on the quality of jobs. This should lead to the development of growth models in which technical progress is endogenous in the sense of Harrod. Indeed, the gig economy leads to a return to piecework, to greater precariousness of workers—with a lower level of social protection. Remote work increases the risks of developing new pathological diseases—muscular-bone disorders— and reduces interactions between workers. The question of the effects of non-wage attributes, work intensity, working conditions, and jobs on workers' productivity opens a new field of research on the social return of technological progress on labor productivity growth. A labor-saving technology does not imply that it is necessarily labor-augmenting. There may be dilution effects on labor productivity.

At this stage, the conclusions of empirical work concerning the positive or negative effects of technological progress on employment are not convergent. However, many papers conclude that the short-term effects are negative, due to a number of phenomena: concentration of capital and rents for firms operating in a context of globalization, layoffs due to a phenomenon of substitutability between technology and labor, and an increase in capital intensity (for recent works, the interested reader can refer to Acemoglu and Restrepo 2018; Autor et al. 2020; Earnst et al. 2018).

2.2.3   What Are the Causes of the Trend Decline in Investment?

Table 2.5 shows the slowdown in the contribution to productivity growth of the capital intensity for different types of capital in five countries (France, Germany, Japan, United Kingdom, and United States), distinguishing between non-ICT capital, ICT capital, and tangible capital. The numbers are the increase/decrease in the contribution between two periods: 1996–2005 and 2006–2017. The contribution of the capital-labor ratio to growth since the mid-1990s has been primarily due to non-ICT capital (residential and non-residential investment, machinery and capital goods, transport). Germany and the United Kingdom differ from the other two countries, where ICT capital explains a large part of the decline in capital deepening.

Table 2.5 Slowdown in the contribution of K/L to economic growth

	Total	non-ICT	ICT	*Tangible*
France	0.07	0.08	0.01	−0.02
Germany	0.54	0.48	0.05	0.02
Japan	0.80	0.38	0.27	0.16
United Kingdom	0.53	0.38	0.09	0.05
United States	0.71	0.45	0.17	0.09

Note Data source: EU-KLEMS 2019 and Goldin et al. (2021)

A first investigation of the trend decline in the capital-labor ratio is to consider a long-run version of the accelerator theory by looking at whether there is a relationship between capital intensity and agents' expectations of the evolution of some variables related to long-term growth. Let us take the example of the United States. Using data from the Federal Reserve Bank of Philadelphia's survey of professional forecasters since 1992, we take the ten-year mean forecasts of real GDP growth, productivity growth, and stock returns, and look at their degree of correlation with the trend component of capital intensity. The latter is taken from the Penn World Table (PWT) 10.0, and the trend is calculated using a Christiano-Fitzgerald filter. As shown in Figs. 2.7, 2.8 and 2.9, there is a positive correlation between capital intensity and the long-term expectations of entrepreneurs, and for these three variables the correlation coefficients are 0.63, 0.62, and 0.52 respectively for growth, productivity, and stock market. Therefore, if the private sector expectations have been pessimistic about possible low long-term growth, weakening productivity gains, or negative financial shocks, this could explain the downward trend in the capital-labor ratio. Figure 2.10 shows the evolution over time of the first principal component of the forecast and the K/L ratio. It can be seen that both trajectories are oriented downward.

Another explanation is the following. The decline in the K/L ratio does not characterize reality, because capital is mis-measured. On the one hand, capital spending has declined in the manufacturing and industrial goods sectors. But on the other hand, investment in intangible or ICT capital has increased (due to increased services activities to industry). Given the current shortcomings of national accounting, the statistics show only part of the picture. Against this view, Haskel and Westlake (2018) argue

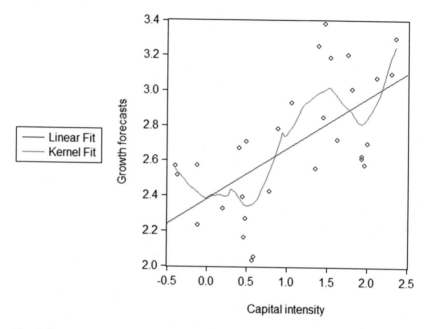

Fig. 2.7 Correlation between K/L ratio and growth forecasts in the United States over 1992–2020

that spending on intangible capital leads to high fixed costs that represent barriers to entry into a market and explain concentration phenomena. Since tangible and intangible capital are complementary, fixed costs can explain disinvestment due to high adjustment costs. This phenomenon is likely to occur because it is difficult to value tangible capital in the form of collateral with bankers. Caballero et al. (2017)'s and Duval et al. (2020)'s papers suggest that the risk premiums associated with these investments are high.

The rising cost of capital related to stock market valuations is another structural factor causing the downward trend in private investment. The importance of finance in investment decisions is reflected in the pressure exerted on firms by financial constraints linked to corporate governance through shareholder value. Corporates' financial constraint can be summarized by the following relationship:

$$ROE = ROCE + (ROCE - i) * (D/FP), \qquad (2.25)$$

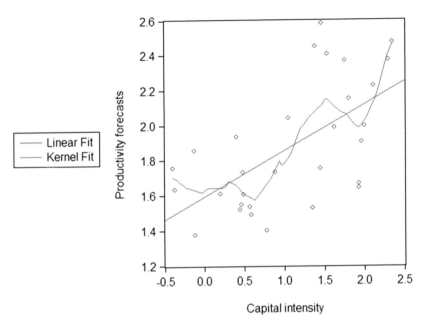

Fig. 2.8   Correlation between K/L ratio and productivity forecasts in the United States over 1992–2020

with

ROE: return on net assets (rate of return on equity required from shareholders),
$ROCE$: return on capital employed (measure of profitability of capital),
i: interest rate,
D: debt,
FP: shareholders' equity.

D/FP is debt leverage. Corporates seek to achieve a minimum level of ROE. For this purpose, they need to raise $ROCE$ as much as possible above the interest rate and maximize debt leverage. During bad times, shareholders are under pressure to continue to receive the same amounts of dividends. Therefore, the only way to maintain $ROCE$ is to lower the share of net income that remunerates the labor factor as well as self-financing of capital). The decrease in capital self-financing leads to a

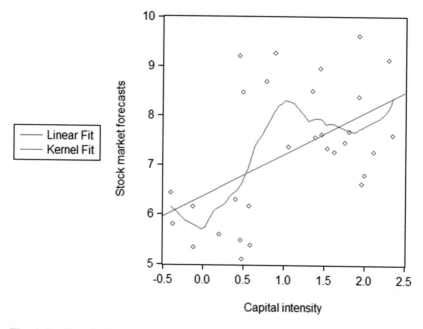

Fig. 2.9 Correlation between K/L ratio and stock market forecasts in the United States over 1992–2020

decrease in investment. As self-financing declines, equity capital decreases and companies are less likely to use debt leverage (the decline in bank loans is another constraint on investment). Moreover, during financial booms, private debt increases (Minsky moment), and the leverage effects come into full play. Since investment is fueled by debt, when financial cycles turn around, output gaps remain open for a very long time (balance sheet effects imply periods of deleveraging that can last a long time). The difficulty of output gaps to close quickly has consequences on medium/long-term growth. Long-term unemployment degrades human capital, and the prolonged decline in productive capacity leads to a depreciation of physical capital).

An additional factor of the downward trend of capital deepening is globalization. First, offshoring and outsourcing activities have reduced the attractiveness of domestic investment relative to foreign investment. Financial globalization has also changed corporate governance since the

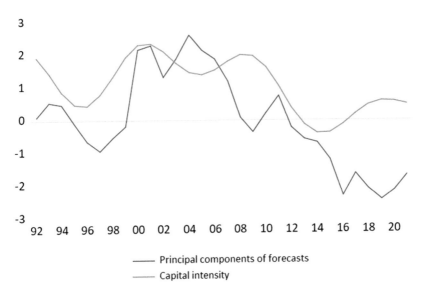

Fig. 2.10   Evolution of K/L and first principal component of forecasts

mid-1990s, which has had an impact on the trade-off between physical and financial investment. Globalization has changed the behavior of the demand for factors of production—and therefore for capital—by changing their relative prices. Second, when labor markets became global—with the arrival of millions of workers from emerging countries—the relative cost of labor fell. For the cost of capital, this is less obvious, because of the importance of shareholder financing.

2.2.4   Demography, Productivity, and Weakening Growth

The literature usually distinguishes three demographic regimes. In the Malthusian regime, birth rates are positively correlated with the rate of growth of GDP; there is virtually no technical progress, and GDP per capita stagnates. In the post-Malthusian regime, GDP per capita grows at a constant rate, and technical progress starts to accelerate. In the modern regime, the rate of population growth declines and depends inversely on GDP growth; the latter evolves at a constant rate, as does technical

Table 2.6   Fertility rates

	1990	2000	2010	2019/2020
France	1.78	1.89	3.03	1.88
Germany	1.45	1.38	1.39	1.6
United Kingdom	1.83	1.64	1.92	1.68
Japan	1.54	1.36	1.38	1.4
United States	2.08	2.06	1.97	1.77

Note Data source: INED

progress. A historical study of these three regimes for advanced countries has been made by Galor and Weill (1998). We focus here on the most recent two and three decades.

The dynamics of demographic factors are the result of three components: fertility rates, life expectancy at birth, and migration flows.

Table 2.6 shows the fertility rates of five industrialized countries taken as examples: France, Germany, the United Kingdom, Japan, and the United States. In these countries, the replacement rates are below the minimum threshold of 2.05, that is, 205 children per 100 women. This implies that the size of the population is decreasing. The factors are socioeconomic. There is an inverse correlation between fertility rates and standards of living, as parents prefer to focus on the quality of their children's human capital, rather than on the quantity. Another factor is the erosion of family policies over time (which has led to a decline in public support to families). In addition, the metamorphosis of labor markets around the world has led to a form of "precariousness" that has increased the uncertainty faced by new generations.

If we look at the average annual trends of life expectancy at birth, since 1980, we can see that it has increased in the vast majority of industrialized countries. Figure 2.11 shows this trend for the G7 countries. However, there are differences in levels between countries. Japan is the country with the highest historical life expectancy curve. Italy and France are catching up with this country, while the United States is falling behind (the improvement in life expectancy has slowed down considerably over the years, whereas it has continued to rise in the other countries). Table 2.7 shows that life expectancy at age 60 is lower in the United States than in the other countries. There are many reasons for these changes, but the one that

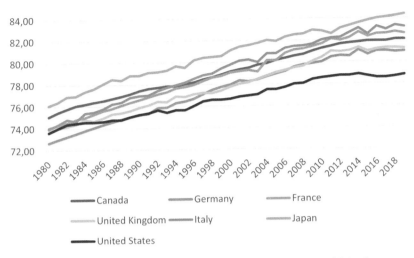

Fig. 2.11   Life expectancy at birth. Data source: WHO and World Bank

Table 2.7   Life expectancy in G7 countries

	Life expectancy at birth	Life expectancy at age 60
France	82.50	25.34
Germany	81.72	24.4
Italy	83.0	25.0
Japan	84.26	26.34
United Kingdom	81.4	24.13
United States	79.5	23.3
Canada	82.24	25.15

Note Data source: WHO and World Bank

seems to dominate is related to nutritional and epidemiological patterns. The countries with the lowest life expectancy are those where non-communicable diseases are progressing most rapidly (diabetes, cholesterol, heart disease, obesity, hypertension). See Tsugane (2021) for details.

Figure 2.12 shows net migrations since the early 1980s. They have increased weakly in France and Japan. Developments in Germany show several waves, with net migration increasing since 2007. After a steady increase, the United Kingdom shows a decline. The United States stands

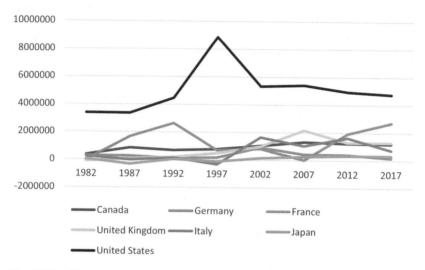

Fig. 2.12 Net migration. Data source: World Bank

out from the other countries. Although they have been declining since the mid-1980s, net migration levels are much higher than in other countries.

What are the effects of these developments on labor, productivity, and growth?

The case of the United States has been documented by Gordon (2018). The author shows that demographic factors activate forces that counteract the positive effects that innovations, patents, digitization, and robotization have on long-term growth. He establishes a link with the widening inequality gap. One problem in the United States is the gap in life expectancy according to income level and education level. Life expectancy at age 60 has declined for middle class and poor people but has increased for those in the top 15% of the income distribution. These developments are affecting the labor force participation rate, especially as other forces are at play. The retirement of the baby boom generation, coupled with the reduction in the number of jobs, is resulting in fewer hours worked. Moreover, it results in a decrease in intergenerational wealth transfers, which increases inequalities of opportunity. Gordon also shows that the quality of the labor force has deteriorated. The number of higher education graduates has fallen sharply because the costs of education are high and their increase has not been compensated by an increase in wages, which have stagnated. This stagnation is correlated with a phenomenon of de-skilling of jobs offered on the labor market. The indices of efficiency of the labor force and of the contribution of higher education to growth are declining. According to Gordon, these phenomena are ill-timed, because they occur at the wrong time: the IT revolution seems to have reached maturity since the mid-2000s, which has implied a decline in the demand for cognitive skills. Readers interested in comments on the arguments made by Gordon in his historical work on American capitalism can refer to Clark (2016).

Let us now consider the case of Japan. The situation in that country provides a glimpse of the developments to come in other industrialized countries with aging populations. To curb the mechanical decline of population aging on growth measured as a percentage of the working-age population, Japan has increased the proportion of its oldest active workers located in the 55–64 age category. Figure 2.13 shows the employment rate of this age group (compared with other OECD countries). It can be seen that their number is much higher than the average for OECD countries. This means that the labor force is being used more intensively. This development is accentuated by "incentive" mechanisms: lower retirement pensions and an increase in the retirement age that encourages

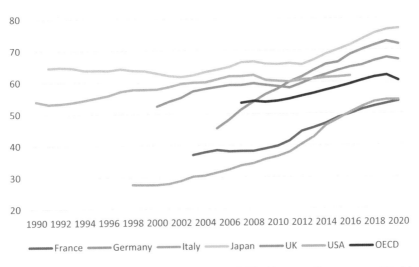

Fig. 2.13 Employment rate of workers aged 55–64 years. Data source: World Bank

older workers to remain in the workforce. In a context of increasing life expectancy after age 60, the main aim is to reduce the dependency ratio, which would have a negative effect on growth. This trend has been observed in all OECD countries since the late 1990s. But is this enough to slow the slowdown in overall productivity?

Empirical work suggests that the answer is no, whether in Japan, Europe, or the United States. One reason is that productivity per worker is correlated with age. Productivity peaks in the 40–49 age group and then declines. Over the past two decades, the increase in the number of workers in the 55+ age group has reduced total factor productivity by 0.1 percentage points in Europe (see Aiyar et al. 2016). In Japan, it has cost between 0.7 and 0.9 percentage points less productivity between 1990 and 2007 (see Liu and Westelius 2016). In the United States, two-thirds of the negative effects of the dependency ratio on growth explain the slowdown in productivity (see Maestas et al. 2016). These results corroborate the theoretical hypothesis of an inverted U-shaped relationship between worker age and TFP. This relationship is based on the assumption that, while older workers have a higher level of know-how and experience, younger workers have more skills for innovation (better physical health, speed of learning, greater creativity). Moreover, the increase in the age of the working population increases the demand for services in the health sector and in more labor-intensive sectors (which reduces overall productivity).

To go further, it would be interesting to look at the distribution of the labor force by age according to the size of firms and sectors of activity, and to reflect on the quality of the jobs held by older workers. Empirical and theoretical studies on this subject are still lacking.

2.3   CONCLUSION

Is there evidence of an erosion of the production capacities of industrialized countries? This question is prompted by an apparent paradox. On the one hand, these countries are experiencing a fourth technological revolution characterized by disruptive innovations that will change the quality of life of their inhabitants. On the other hand, their societies show signs of a deterioration in people's well-being: inequalities have exploded, work is undergoing metamorphoses that are driving the less educated away from the labor markets, and above all, the expected increasing returns to technical progress do not yet seem to be forthcoming. The challenge for theorists and empiricists of medium/long-term growth is therefore to analyze the role of AI, machine learning, digital economy, and automation as a historical phase in the development of capitalism, and to understand the driving forces behind them. This changes the work of researchers in several ways. The most important change is that they have to spend more time conceptualizing the production functions of economies: production of goods and services, but above all production of knowledge, production of innovations, and production of new organizational forms and business models due to the ongoing technological revolution. The second change is that we are seeing results that were previously inconceivable. For example, technical progress can generate dilution phenomena and cause factor productivity to fall instead of rising. Another element is that capital is heterogeneous (ICT, non-ICT, tangible, and intangible) and that national accounting still struggles to measure all contributions. Finally, demography is becoming a structuring factor of long-term growth, a phenomenon that has been captured exclusively through the number of hours worked or human capital. However, the dynamics of birth rate, migration, and life expectancy now condition the way in which technological innovations impact on growth trajectories.

PIONEERS IN THE FIELD

Daron Acemoglu

He has investigated the role of automation and artificial intelligence on growth and has worked on the issue of substitutability between IA and factors of production, particularly labor. His contributions lead us to question the links between the fourth technological revolution and unequal prosperity. The author shows that AI, machine learning, and various algorithms have reduced the quality of jobs, exacerbated inequalities in the functional and personal distribution of income, and reduced the standard of living of the least qualified workers. This observation applies at least to the United States, one of the countries considered to be the technological frontier of the world. His models highlight the dilution effects of innovations linked to automation, which, when developed excessively, entails high social costs that

(continued)

jeopardize productivity gains. Acemoglu's work shows that there are not necessarily direct links between innovations whose main goal is to reduce labor costs and those aimed at increasing productivity. According to him the question of the composition of innovations is crucial and should lead to technologies that are human-friendly. Hence the importance of governments guiding technical progress.

Philippe Aghion

His work focuses on the links between innovation and growth. He is one of the most convinced Schumpeterian economists of the beneficial role of new technologies for productivity, because of the incredible capacity of men to innovate. His models are based on the creative destruction hypothesis, which illustrates the fundamental mechanism of technological revolutions. The negative effects on workers' employability and wages are transitory, thanks to the possibility of retraining through investment in human capital throughout the working life. The author considers that governments play an important role during technological transitions. His work is based on the following conception of technical progress: all novelties are based on previous novelties (new technology improves older technologies), and this is possible only in a competitive environment. Technological discoveries generate rents only if firms adopt strategies that create barriers to entry in a sector. Governments must therefore accompany technical progress with market regulation policies that prevent the abuse of dominant positions. At the same time, they must guarantee the protection of property rights, especially patents.

Robert J Gordon

He can be considered a specialist in the long history of Western capitalism. His recent work on the American case highlights the perils of American growth and undermines the idea that a country considered to be the economic frontier of the world can experience long periods of prosperity and economic growth shared by all members of society. The author shows the slow erosion of productivity gains following an explosion of all forms of inequalities that characterize American society. The uninterrupted period of growth up to now is likely

(continued)

to come to an end in the forthcoming years because of numerous institutional and societal constraints: in addition to inequality, we should mention the burden of the public debt, the retirement of the baby boom generations, the erosion of human capital that has accelerated with the soaring cost of higher education, and the diminishing returns of new discoveries. One of the advantages of Gordon's historical approach to the role of innovations is that it does not lock us into a global history, but into a history that is relevant only when embedded in the realities of a country. In his work, the author draws our attention to the possibility of phases of possible decline in growth in the United States and its singularity. His approach differs from another one based on a leader-follower mechanism (e.g., the idea that all countries should follow the same declining trajectory of technical progress, on the grounds that the country at the frontier would experience difficulties associated with the diminishing returns to its innovations).

APPENDIX

See Tables 2.8, 2.9, 2.10 and 2.11.

Table 2.8   List of industries

Agriculture, forestry, and fishing

Mining and quarrying
Total manufacturing
Electricity, gas, steam, and air conditioning supply
Water supply, sewerage, waste management, and remediation activities
Construction
Wholesale and retail trade; repair of motor vehicles and motorcycles
Transportation and storage
Accommodation and food service activities
Information and communication
Financial and insurance activities
Real estate activities
Professional, scientific, technical, administrative, and support service activities
Public administration, defense, education, human health, and social work activities
Arts, entertainment, recreation; other services and service activities

Source: EU KLEMS database 2019 release. Japan: 1995–2015

Table 2.9 Definition of variables and sources

Variable	Definition	Sources	Transformation
y_{it}	Growth rate of value-added volume, %,	EU KLEMS	None
L_{it}	Labor services, volume indices, 2010=100	EU KLEMS	Δln
k_{it}^{ICT}	ICT capital services, volume indices, 2010=100	EU KLEMS	Δln
k_{it}^{NICT}	Non-ICT capital services, volume indices, 2010=100	EU KLEMS	Δln
k_{it}^{INT}	Intangible capital services, volume indices, 2010=100	EU KLEMS	Δln
hc_{it}	Human capital index, based on years of schooling and returns to education	Penn World 10.0	ln
TFP_{it}	TFP at constant national prices (2017=1)	Penn World 10.0	Δln
$skill_{it}$	Self-employment in total employment	World indicators of skills in employment—OECD	ln
k_{it}^{soft}	Real GFCF vol. index (2005=100.0)—Software	Japan World Klems	Δln
k_{it}^{comp}	Real GFCF vol. index (2005=100.0)—Computer	Japan World Klems	Δln
k_{it}^{com}	Real GFCF vol. index (2005=100.0)—Communication	Japan World Klems	Δln
$internet_{it}$	Access to internet per 100 inhabitants	World Development Indicators	ln
$mobile_{it}$	Access to mobile phones per 100 inhabitants	World Development Indicators	ln
fsi_{it}	Financial stress index—Japan	Asian Development Bank	None
$credit_{it}$	Domestic credit to private section (% GDP)	World Development Indicators	Δln
$open_{it}$	Trade (% GDP)	World Development Indicators	ln
$budg_{it}$	General Government net lending/borrowing (% GDP)	FRED database (Fed St Louis	none

Table 2.10   First step regression: the determinants of productivity

Dependent variable: productivity
Method: panel least squares

Sample: 1996 2015
Periods included: 20
Cross-sections included: 15
Total panel (balanced) observations: 300
White cross-section standard errors and covariance (d.f. corrected)

Variable	Coefficient	Std. Error	t-Statistic	Prob.
Constant	−2.25**	1.05	−2.13	0.03
ICT capital	−0.09	0.06	−1.42	0.15
Intang. capital	0.48*	0.27	1.74	0.08
Software	11.57*	6.65	1.73	0.08
Computer	21.22	13.45	1.57	0.11
Telecom	−2.31	7.18	−0.32	0.74
R-squared	0.082	Mean dependent var		−0.98
Adjusted R^2	0.06	S.D. dependent var		9.42
F-statistic	5.26	Durbin-Watson stat		1.839
(F-stat)	0.0001			

Note *,** means significance at 10%, 5%, 1% level of confidence

Table 2.11   Distribution of efficiency scores

	Percentile	*Lower*	*Upper*
10	0.0016	0.0003	0.005
20	0.014	0.007	0.03
30	0.04	0.029	0.061
40	0.072	0.06	0.08
50	0.094	0.08	0.111
60	0.13	0.108	0.151
70	0.185	0.149	0.221
80	0.27	0.22	0.31
90	0.37	0.347	0.39

Note this table shows the distribution of efficiency scores
Second column: percentiles
Third and fourth columns: 95% confidence interval lower and upper bound

REFERENCES

Acemoglu D, Akcigit U (2012) Intellectual property rights policy, competition and innovations. J Eur Econ Ass 10(1):1–42

Acemoglu D, Restrepo P (2018) The race between man and machine: implication of technology for growth, factor shares and employment. Am Econ Rev 108(6):1488–1542

Acquisti A, Taylor C, Wagman L (2016) The Economics of Privacy. J Econ Lit 54(2): 442–92

Aghion P, Jones BF, Jones CI (2019) Artificial intelligence and economic growth. In: Agrawal G, Goldfarb A (eds) The economics of artificial intelligence: an agenda. NBER, Chicago, pp 237–282

Aiyar S, Ebeke C, Shao X (2016) The impact of workforce aging on European productivity. IMF WP 16/238

Akcigit U, Ates ST (2021) Ten facts on declining business dynamism and lessons from endogenous growth theory. Am Econ Rev 13(1):257–298

Akcigit U, Benedetti F, Impullitti G, Licandro O, Sanchez-Martinez M (eds) (2022) Macroeconomic modelling of R&D and innovation policies, 2022, Palgrave Macmillan

Andrews D, Criscuolo C, Gal PN (2015) Frontier firms, technology diffusion and public policy: micro evidence from OECD countries. OCDE Working Paper 39

Anzoategui D, Comin D, Gertler M, Martinez J (2019) Endogenous technology adoption and R&D as sources of business cycle persistence. Am Econ J Macroecon 11(3):67–110

Autor DH (2019) Work of the past, work of the future. AEA Papers Proc 109:1–32

Autor DH, Dorn D, Katz LF, Patterson C, Reenen JV (2020) The fall of the labor share and the rise of superstar firms. Quat J Econ 135(2):645–709

Banalieva ER, Dhanaraj C (2019) Internalization theory for the digital economy. J Int Bus Stud 50:1372–1387

Belotti F, Daidone S, Ilardi G, Atella V (2013) Stochastic frontier analysis using Stata. Stata J 13(4):719–758

Benhabib J, Perla J, Tonetti C (2021) Reconciling models of diffusion and innovation: a theory of the productivity distribution and technology frontier. Econometrica 89(5):2261–2301

Bergeaud A, Cette G, Lecat R (2016) Productivity trends in advanced countries between 1890 and 2012. Rev Inc Wealth 62(3):420–444

Bloom N, Draca M, van Reenen J (2016) Trade induced technical change? The impact of Chinese imports and innovations, IT productivity. Rev Econ Stud 83(1):87–117

Bloom N, Jones CI, van Reenen J, Webb M (2020) Are ideas getting harder to find? Am Econ Rev 110(4):1104–1144

Boskin MJ, Lau LJ (2000) Generalized Solow-neutral technical progressand postwar economic growth. SIEPR Discussion Paper 00-12

Branstetter L, Sichel D (2017) The Case for an American productivity revival. Pet Inst Int Econ Policy Brief 17–26

Buera FJ, Lucas RE (2018) Ideas flows and economic growth. Ann Rev Econ 10:315–345

Buera FJ, Oberfield F (2020) The global diffusion of ideas. Econometrica 88:83–114

Burström T, Parida V, Lahti T, Wincent J (2021) AI-enabled business-model innovation and transformation in industrial ecosystems: a framework, model and outline for further research. J Bus Res 127:85–95

Caballero RJ, Farhi E, Gourinchas PO (2017) Rents, technical change, and risk premia accounting for secular trends in interest rates, returns on capital, earning yields, and factor shares. Am Econ Rev 107(5):614–20

Cao Z, Shi X (2021) A systematic literature review of entrepreneurial ecosystems in advanced and emerging economies. Sm Bus Econ 57:75–110

Caselli F, Manning A (2019) Robot arithmetic: new technology and wages. Am Econ Rev Insights 1(1): 1–12

Cereola SJ, Wier B, Strand Norman C (2012) Impact of top management team on firm performance in small and medium-sized enterprises adopting commercial open-source enterprise resource planning. Beh Inf Tech 31(9):889–907

Cette G, Dromel N, Lecat R, Paret AC (2015) Production factor returns: the role of factor utilization. Rev Econ Stat 97:134–143

Cette G, Corde S, Lecat R (2017) Stagnation of productivity in France: a legacy of the crisis or a structural slowdown?. Econ Stat 494:11–36

Cette G, Devillard A, Spiezia V (2020) Growth factors in developed countries: a 1960–2019 growth accounting decomposition. AMSE Working Paper

Christensen CM (1997) The innovator's dilemma: when new technologies cause great firms to fail. Harvard Business Review Press, Boston

Christensen CM, Raynor ME, McDonald R (2015) What is disruptive innovation? Harv Bus Rev Dec 44–53

Clark G (2016) Winter is coming: robert gordon and the future of economic growth. Am Econ Rev 106(5):68–71

Crafts N, O'Rourke K (2013) Twentieth century growth. CEPR Discussion Paper DP9633

Dao M, Das M, Koczan Z (2020) Technological progress and holowing-out of the middle-skilled labour share of income. Vox EU CEPR

Deschacht N (2021) The digital revolution and the labour economics of automation: a review. Robonomics: J Aut Econ, 1(8):8–8

Díaz-Chao Á, Sainz J, Torrent-Sellens J (2015) The competitiveness of small-network firms. J Bus Res 69(5):1769–1774

Di Comite F, Kancs D (2015) Macro-economic models for R&D and innovation policies. Publications Office of the European Union, Luxembourg

Dupont J, Guellec D, Oliveira Martins J (2011) OECD productivity growth in the 2000s: a descriptive analysis of the impact of sectoral effects and innovation. OECD J Econ Stud 2011(1):1–23

Duval R, Hong GH, Timmer Y (2020) Financial frictions and the great productivity slowdown. Rev Fin Stu 33(2):475–503

Earnst E, Merola R, Samaan D (2018) The economics of artificial intelligence: implications for the future of work. ILO Future of Work Research Paper Series No. 5

Fernández-Portillo A, Almodóvar-González M, Hernández-Mogollón R (2020) Impact of ICT development on economic growth. A study of OECD European union countries. Technol Soc 63:101420

Galor O, Weill DN (1998) Population, technology and growth: from the Mathusian regime to the demographic transition. NBER WP 6811

Garzella S, Fiorentino R, Caputo A, Lardo A (2021) Business model innovation in SMEs: the role of boundaries in the digital era. Tech Anal Strat Manag 33(1):31–43

Geroski P (2000) Models of technology dependence. Res Pol 29(4–5):603–625

Goldin I, Koutroumpis P, Lafond F, Winkler J (2021) Why is productivity slowing down? Oxf Mart Sch Working Paper Series n°2021-6

Gordon RJ (2016) The rise and fall of American growth: the US standard of living since the Civil War. Princeton University Press, Princeton

Gordon RJ (2018) Why has productivity slowed when innovation appears to be accelerating? NBER Working Paper n°24554

Gordon RJ, Sayed H (2019) The industry anatomy of the transatlantic productivity growth slowdown, NBER Working Paper 25703

Gregory T, Salomons A, Zierahn U (2019) Racing with or against the machine? Evidence from Europe," IZA Discussion Papers 12063

Hanushek EA, Schwerdt G, Woessmann L, Zhang L (2017) General education, vocational Education, and labour market outcomes over the lifecycle. J Hum Res 52(1):49–88

Haskel J, Westlake S (2018) Capitalism without capital: the rise of intangible economy. Princeton University Press, Princeton

Hasumi R, Hiboshi H, Nakamura D (2018) Trends, cycles and lost decades: decomposition from a DSGE model with endogenous growth. Jap World Econ 46(C):9–28

Helpman E (1998) General purpose technologies and growth. The MIT Press, Cambridge

Jones CI (2021) The past and future of economic growth: a semi-endogenous perspective. NBER WP 29126

Känig M, Loren J, Zilibotti F (2016) Innovations versus imitation and the evolution of productivity distribution. Econ 11(3):1053–1102

Kirsten J (2017) EU KLEMS growth and productivity accounts 2017 release: description of methodology and general notes. New York, The Conference Board

Koch T, Windsperger J (2017) Seeing through the network:competitive advantage in the digital economy. J Org Des, 6(1):1–30

Koenker R (2005) Quantile regression. Cambridge University Press, Cambridge

Kohtamäki M, Paris V, Oghazi P, Gebauer H, Bianes T (2021) Digital servitization business models in ecosystems: a theory of the firm. J Bus Res 104:380–392

Langley DJ, van Doorn J, Ng, ICL, Stieglit S, Lazovik A, Boonstra A (2021) The internet of everything: smart things and their impact on business models. J Bus Res 122:853–863

Liu Y, Westelius N (2016) The impact of demographics on productivity and inflation in Japan. IMF WP 16/237

Lu Y, Zhou Y (2021) A review on the economics of artificial intelligence. J Econ Surv 35:1045–1072

Lucchetti R, Sterlacchini A (2004) The impact of ICT among SMEs: evidence from an Italian survey. S Bus Econ 23(2):151–168

Luttmer EG (2012) Technology, diffusion and growth. J Econ Th 147:602–622

Maestas N, Mullen KJ, Powell D (2016) The Effect of population aging on economic growth, the labor Force and productivity. NBER WP 22452

McGowan MA, Andrews D, Millot V (2017) The walking dead?: Zombie firms and productivity performance in OECD countries. OECD Working Paper Series, 2017/4

Mokyr J (2013) Human capital, useful knowledge, and long-term economic growth. Econ Pol 30(3):251–272

Moll B, Rachel L, Restrepo P (2021) Uneven growth: automation's impact on income and wealth inequality. NBER WP 28440

Ollivaud P, Guillemette Y, Turner D (2016) Links between weak investment and the slowdown in productivity and potential output growth across the OECD. OECD Economic Department Working Papers, n° 1304

Osotimehin S, Pappadá F (2017) Credit frictions and the cleansing effect of recessions. Econ J 127(602):1153–1187

Pedota M, Grilli L, Piscitello L (2021) Technological paradigms and the power of convergence. Ind Corp Ch 30:1633–1654

Perla J, Toneti C, Waugh ME (2021) Equilibrium technology diffusion, trade and growth. Am Econ Rev 111(1):73–128

Pesaran MH, Chudik A (2019) Aggregation in large dynamic panels. J Econ 178(1):273–285

Polák P (2017) The productivity paradox: a meta-analysis. Inf Econ Pol 38:38–54

Sampson T (2016) Dynamic selection: an idea flows theory of entry, trade and growth. Quat J Econ 131(1):315–380

Saniee I, Kamat S, Prakash S, Weldon M (2018) Will productivity growth return in the new digital era? Bell Labs Tech J 22:1–18

Stanley TD, Doucouliagos H, Steel P (2018) Does ICT generate economic growth? A meta-regression analysis. J Econ Surv 32(3):705–726

Stiglitz J, Greenwald B (eds) (2014) Creating a learning society. A new approach to growth, development, and social progress. Columbia University Press, New York

Teece DJ (2017) Towards a capability theory of (innovative) firms: implications for management and policy. Camb J Econ 41(3):693–720

Tsugane S (2021) Why has Japan become the world's most long-lived country: insights from a food and nutrition perspective. Eur J Clin Nutr 75:921–928

Van Ark B (2016) The productivity paradox of the new digital economy. Int Prod Mon 31:1–18

Van Reenen J, Bloom N, Draca M, Kretschmer T, Sadun R (2010) The economic impact of ICT, centre for economic performance, London School of Economics Report

Vu K, Hanafizadeh P, Bohlin E (2020) ICT as a driver of economic growth: a survey of the literature and direction for future research. Tel Pol 44(2):101922

CHAPTER 3

Hysteresis, Inflation, and Secular Stagnation

In this chapter we discuss several topics that have fueled recent debates among macroeconomists. The first is what we might call the "super-hysteresis" of economic activity, that is, the existence of self-sustaining dynamics in GDP and growth in both the short and long run. The second phenomenon concerns the changes observed in the relationship between inflation and unemployment. The third topic is secular stagnation, a hypothesis that is hotly debated among macroeconomists. The following paragraphs summarize the main ideas presented in the chapter.

Hysteresis and Super-Hysteresis

The hysteresis of the unemployment rate has been discussed since the 1980s in the theoretical and empirical literature to explain that a shock creating a deviation of the unemployment rate from its natural level has permanent effects, because it influences the path of the natural rate itself. This observation was initially made for European countries and challenged an idea that had been accepted for decades: policies aiming at fighting unemployment should differentiate between cyclical and structural actions, because the factors determining the unemployment gap (rigidities and market imperfections) and the natural rate (structural factors) are not similar. For the original idea, see Blanchard and Summers (1986), Clark (1989), and the recent empirical evidence on OECD countries by Ball and Onken (2021).

G. Dufrénot, *New Challenges for Macroeconomic Policies*, https://doi.org/10.1007/978-3-031-15754-7_3

The reasons for the hysteresis of the unemployment rate have been investigated in an abundant literature. For example, longer unemployment spells degrade human capital. Extended spells of inactivity reduce the productivity of capital. Both phenomena can affect the economies' productive capacity in the medium term. In their original paper, Blanchard and Summers (1986) blamed institutional rigidities for the reduced responsiveness of wages to imbalances in European labor markets. Microeconomic models of unemployment theories have provided various explanations for the causes of labor market rigidities (insider-outsider theories, implicit contracts, efficiency wages, etc.). See Lindbeck and Snower (1988), among many others.

Galí (2015) recently investigated two other sources of the hysteresis of the unemployment rate. First, the wage mark-up (i.e., the wage indexation to past inflation) remains below the level desired by workers and unions for a long time (it follows a random walk process). This leads them to always push their wage claims upward in the hope of reaching the desired level. Secondly, the central bank does not have a fixed inflation target. The latter moves according to a dynamic that can be of the type of a random walk. This instability is transmitted to wage inflation and to the unemployment rate, and implies that the long-run Phillips curve is not vertical. There is then a long-run trade-off between inflation and unemployment. Other causes have been studied, such as the persistent effects of job losses and timing of entry into and exit from the labor markets.

Hysteresis effects in GDP have also been extensively investigated in the literature. The empirical evidence of the existence of non-stationary components in the level of GDP has been motivated by the presence of permanent demand shocks leading to permanent declines in employment and investment. This calls into question the supposed separation between demand shocks and supply shocks, on the grounds that the former would have no impact on the economies' production capacity in the long term (and therefore not on potential GDP). The current context of secular stagnation suggests that this view is false. Moreover, we have seen—in Chap. 2—that the financial cycle can have a lasting effect on GDP at frequencies exceeding that of the business cycle. Therefore, fluctuations in the business cycle are not only movements along a trend, but can also modify the trend itself.

Some theoretical explanations for these phenomena were provided by endogenous growth models during the 1990s. Temporary technological shocks can have permanent effects if they affect the stationary equilibrium output. The same phenomenon occurs when the business cycle affects $R\&D$ expenditure, or when human and capital accumulation drive long-term growth (see, e.g., Fátas 2000). For Schumpeterian economists, recessions can cause economies to bifurcate onto higher long-term trajectories. Indeed, during recessions, resources are reallocated to innovation and $R\&D$ activities, and the least efficient firms are eliminated from the markets. This improves efficiency and resource allocation and puts economies on higher growth trajectories once recessions are over. For a summary of all these models, see Cerra et al. (2020). Financial imbalances are another cause of the observed permanent losses in GDP. The literature on this topic is voluminous (see, e.g., Jordá et al. 2011; Reinhart and Rogoff 2014).

In the following sections, we highlight another phenomenon that is super-hysteresis. This concept introduced by Blanchard et al. (2015) means that shocks can lead to both long-run path changes, but also to changes in the slope of those paths.

The concept of hysteresis used throughout the sciences illustrates a situation where, in general, effects persist while their primary causes have disappeared. Changes in the causes modify the initial conditions. Systems with a high sensitivity to initial conditions exhibit hysteresis dynamics. This means that one cannot return to the prevailing situation observed before changes occur. Empirically, economists initially adopted a strict definition of the concept of hysteresis, by using random walk processes or I(1) series, that is, with no spontaneous mean-reverting dynamics. A looser view is to consider hysteresis as reflecting a situation where the effects persist long after the causes have occurred (even if they have not completely disappeared). This has led to the interpretation of the long-run components of GDP, not necessarily as permanent components, but as very persistent components. There can therefore be several forms of hysteresis for GDP: deterministic trends, unit roots, or structural breaks (i.e., endogenous regime shifts). Taking the example of three countries (the United States, the United Kingdom and Japan), we will see that GDP series, even over a recent period (since 1990), contain breaks that cause stalls in long-term GDP trajectories, that is, irreversible losses of potential GDP (potential being assimilated to the evolution of GDP in level over its trend). This phenomenon of stalling can be highlighted by modeling GDP as long-memory processes (ARFIMA models). The latter were first applied to GDP by Diebold and Rudebusch (1989). Diebold and Inoue (2001) have shown that they can be used to characterize systems with regime changes. We shall see that level GDP's have three properties: their long-run trajectory is subject to regime shifts that occur after large shocks hit the economies; they have a permanent component described by a unit root; and changes in long-run trajectories affect slopes, and hence long-run growth (potential growth). The combination of these three phenomena produces an undesirable consequence: the output gaps are also persistent, which means that the return to the levels of GDP observed before the stalls is very slow.

Changes in the Relationship Between Inflation and Unemployment

Does economic activity have an effect on inflation? The question is usually investigated by studying the behavior of aggregate supply, obtained by combining two concepts. On the one hand, Okun's law, which investigates the employment content of economic growth, and the links between unemployment gaps and the business cycle. On the other hand, the Phillips curve which links the inflation rate to the unemployment rate. A commonly accepted idea is that an economic recovery characterized by a large and sustained upturn in activity can, in the medium/long term, be synonymous with inflationary pressures. However, the reality can be surprising.

Indeed, the economic recessions caused by the 2008 Great Financial Crisis did not involve large-scale deflation or disinflation. The recoveries of the following years did not produce any inflationary boom either. The same observation was made during the recessions following the Covid-19 crisis in 2020, and then at the end of the sanitary crisis, when, with the exception of the United States, prices did not rise sharply. These phenomena have led macroeconomists to examine a hypothesis known as "missing disinflation" and "missing inflation".

A first explanation is that of hysteresis effects causing breaks in the inflation/unemployment relationship when a large negative shock (i.e., a crisis) hits the economies. In this case, economic recoveries do not describe mean-reverting phenomena to pre-crisis levels of GDP, growth or unemployment. Rather, one observes a recovery along lower trajectories. The reasons for this phenomenon are analyzed by the theories of secular stagnation. Endogenous transformations of the productive systems (slow-down of TFP, aging demography, persistent excess of net savings, impact of the financial cycle, fall in investment) can make the economies less resilient to negative shocks. It is then possible that not only will growth rates be lower, but also that the level of GDP itself will fall. An example of such a phenomenon is the lost decades of the Japanese economy between 1991 and 2001. A bursting of a bubble led to a prolonged recession and inflation at very low levels. In the presence of hysteresis, private sector agents form inflation expectations that remain anchored at low levels.

A second hypothesis for the fact that inflation is not necessarily responsive to activity is to be found in Okun's law. We need to look at whether the employment content of growth—or the response of the unemployment rate to the output gap—has changed over time. The degree of sensitivity of unemployment to the business cycle is conditioned by the behavior of firms (productivity, number of hours worked) and labor suppliers (participation rate). If the degree of sensitivity of the unemployment gap to the output gap decreases over time, then this implies that in the Phillips curve a good indicator to study the effects of market disequilibria is not the unemployment rate, but the capacity utilization rate or the output gap. And, even if we keep the unemployment rate variable, it must be instrumented by considering not only the output gap, but also productivity indicators, hours per employee and labor force participation rate.

A third hypothesis is that the influence of domestic imbalances is supplanted by globalization factors, that is, international prices and financial cycles. The stronger degree of integration of industrialized economies into international trade and the global strategies of crushing production costs have played a role in explaining the regular fall in domestic prices.

The Hypothesis of Secular Stagnation

This hypothesis is not a fantasy of heterodox economists, nor a heresy of macroeconomics. It is the subject of very serious studies by macroeconomists, after Lawrence Summers noted a number of empirical regularities characteristic of the dynamics of potential growth, inflation rates and the real rate of return to capital when we look at their evolution over the medium term: they have all been evolving on downward trajectories for several decades. If it is relevant to understand such phenomena, it is not so much to underline the decline of capitalist economies, as to highlight the existence of hysteresis effects that have been little known until now. Some economists call it "the missing recovery", when economies get stuck into low equilibria. Metaphorically speaking, one could say that the more altitude an airplane loses while flying in lower and lower air corridors, the more difficult it is to regain the original altitudes. The plane here is potential growth. The "flashing lights," or alarm signals, are not only the dynamics of trend inflation, but also the dynamics of the natural interest rate (the medium-term rate of return to capital).

Works on secular stagnation have made it possible to understand that there is no fixed "natural" medium-/long-term levels for unemployment, growth, or inflation. There are no stationary points around which the short-term variables would evolve. On the contrary, there are important path-dependence phenomena that prevent the achievement of stable steady states. We will see that there are several interpretations of this phenomenon.

The future of capitalist economies in the medium/long term may give rise to concern if one believes in the hypothesis of diminishing returns of productive ecosystems. The fear fades if one believes that this is a normal phenomenon of "wear and tear" in the use of the factors of production, but that it can be postponed, or even eliminated, thanks to technological progress. This is what Schumpeterian economists, and before them the endogenous growth theorists, firmly believe. But technological progress does not solve everything. One must examine the endogenous functioning of economies and understand the role of factors such as demographic phenomena, savings choices, investment decisions, the diffusion of technical progress in societies, and so on. The phenomenon of prolonged stagnation represents a situation where very strong hysteresis of macroeconomic variables, when economies suffer shocks and their effects keep them on low growth trajectories for a long time, sustainable recoveries are difficult to find and the factors that traditionally boost potential growth take time to manifest their beneficial effects.

The topic of secular stagnation is not new. Historically, it has resurfaced whenever economies have endured severe crises that seemed to last a long time.

It was during the 1930s to 1950s that the last debates on the subject were the most intense. The crisis of the 1930s pitted the "stagnationists" against the "conjuncturists." In the first group were economists such as Fisher, Hansen, Higgins, Kaldor, Kalecki, Robbins, Sweezy, and in the second group economists such as Burns, Haberler, Hayek, Keynes, Kuznets, Mitchell, Morgenstern, Pigou, Samuelson, Schumpeter, Tinbergen, and Yule.

The conjuncturists, whose ideas were widespread—especially in political decision-making circles—adopted a grid for reading crises as normal recessionary phases of a ten-year (sometimes longer) economic cycle. In addition to a better understanding of the formation of cycles, their discussions focused on ways to emerge from crises (technological innovations, pricing policies, increased public spending, combating runaway phases of financial cycles, etc.).

The stagnationists had a more historical approach and favored a medium-term perspective. They noted that the archetypal situations of secular stagnation were the occurrence of crises that repeated themselves in an approximate manner after brief periods of calm, as European countries or the United States had experienced in the nineteenth century: 1815, 1825, 1836–1837, 1857, 1867. These crises were to be understood as breaks inherent to the productive regimes of capitalism, which the countries had managed to overcome through strategies of extensive growth (notably the territorial invasions of other nations and the geographical extension of their markets and outlets, the exploitation of the discovery of new sources of raw materials and metals).[1]

They noted that the margins for extensive growth were more limited in the 1930s than in the nineteenth century and that countries had to tackle the core of the problem, that is, the elimination of the factors of under-accumulation of capital and deficient demand. They questioned the harmful role of the phenomenon of concentration of capital due to monopolies, restrictive migration policies in the United States in the midst of a period of slowing demographic growth, income inequalities that were the source of excess savings and insufficient aggregate demand, and the slowdown in the growth of wages in relation to that of profits. They advocated structural transformations for systemic change, rather than cyclical regulation policies.

Interestingly, many of the arguments raised by the stagnationists of the 1930s to 1950s can be found in the current debates. We have already mentioned some of them in the two previous chapters, presenting the analyses of Robert Gordon, the analysis of growth by the Schumpeterian, or the explanations for the prolonged fall in interest rates in the Summers/Mehrotra models. We continue these discussions here. Readers

---

[1] The reader may wonder whether the phenomenon of secular stagnation is unique to industrialized countries. In any case, it has been most discussed there for the following reason. It is a concept that is applied to characterize a growth regime of supposedly industrially mature economies, countries that are technologically advanced and have managed to achieve a high standard of living for their population for many decades. In these economies, the growth rates shown for the medium/long term are growth rates at cruising speed: the countries are no longer in a catch-up phase and have a regular growth rate that allows them to maintain a high standard of living. Secular stagnation occurs when, under the influence of external factors or factors endogenous to the capitalist regime, medium-/long-term growth trajectories begin to decline slowly. That is, potential growth rates slow down.

interested in the historical aspects of secular stagnation can refer to Backhouse and Boianovsky (2016).

3.1   HYSTERESIS AND SUPER-HYSTERESIS IN GDP DATA

To highlight these two properties in GDP series, we briefly present the concept of long memory using ARFIMA models. Then, we illustrate their use on three countries chosen as examples, that is, Japan, the United States, and the United Kingdom.

3.1.1   Long-Memory Processes: Definition

We present here only a few notions necessary for understanding the macroeconomic analysis. The reader interested in a detailed presentation can refer to Guégan (2005). A process often used by economists that belongs to the class of long-memory models is the ARMA fractionally integrated model: ARFIMA (autoregressive fractionally integrated moving average model).

We define $(X_t), t = 1, \ldots, T$, the sequence of aggregate output time series between times 1 and T. This sequence follows an $ARFIMA(p, d, q)$ process if its dynamics is described by the following equation:

$$\Phi_p(L)(1 - L)^d X_t = \Theta_q(L)\epsilon_t, \qquad (3.1)$$

(ϵ_t) is an ergodic process with mean 0 and variance σ_ϵ^2 and

$$\Phi_p(L) = 1 - \sum_{j=1}^{p} \phi_j L^j, \quad \Theta_q(L) = 1 - \sum_{k=1}^{q} \theta_k L^j, \quad L^j X_t = X_{t-j}. \quad (3.2)$$

d is a fractional (non-integer) parameter. The ARFIMA process is invertible and stationary if the roots of the characteristic polynomials $\Phi_p(L)$ and $\Theta_q(L)$ are outside the unit circle and if $|d| < 0.5$.

A moving average representation of the process allows to obtain a measure of persistent impacts of the shocks ϵ_t on (X_t):

$$\Delta X_t = A(L)\epsilon_t, \quad A(L) = ()1 - L)^{1-d} B(L), \quad B(L) = \Phi - p^{-1}(L)\Theta_q(L). \qquad (3.3)$$

$(1 - L)^d$ can be written as follows by using a binomial expansion:

$$(1 - L)^d = 1 - dL + \frac{d(d-1)}{2!}L^2 + \frac{d(d-1)(d-2)}{3!}L^3 + \cdots$$

$$= \sum_{j=0}^{\infty} \frac{\Gamma(j-d)L^j}{\Gamma(-d)\Gamma(j+1)}. \tag{3.4}$$

where $\Gamma(.)$ is the gamma function (generalized factorial). $(1 - L)^d)$ is therefore an infinite-order lag operator polynomial with slowly decaying weights.

Considering the h-order autocorrelation function $\rho_X(h)$ for large h, this function is bounded by the following power-law function:

$$\rho_X(h) \approx C(d)h^{2d-1}, \ C(d) \neq 0. \tag{3.5}$$

ARFIMA models have a slower hyperbolic autocorrelation decay than ARMA models, which have geometrically decaying autocorrelation:

$$\rho_X(h) \approx Ck^h, \ |k| < 1. \tag{3.6}$$

An aggregate output following an ARFIMA process is obtained by aggregating individual sectors' or firms' production, each following AR(1) processes and Beta-distributed (or mild semi-parametric distributed) across cross-sections (see Granger 1980; Haubrick and Lo 1989; Zaffaroni 2004). These processes have other interesting properties which are not presented here (see the references in Guégan 2005). They are used to detect underlying processes with regime-switching dynamics, stochastic permanent breaks, dynamics with abrupt or smooth transition regimes).

3.1.2   Examples of Losses of Potential GDP

We start with the charts in Figs. 3.1 and 3.2 which show how potential GDP losses can be recognized. For the three example countries, we proceed as follows. We estimate a linear trend over the periods preceding a significant drop in GDP and extend this trend over the following quarters. We re-estimate a linear trend, taking as a starting point the quarters following the end of the fall in GDP. The figures show that shocks cause

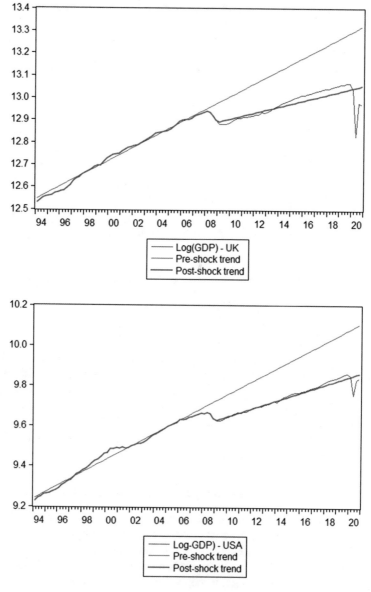

Fig. 3.1 Losses of potential GDP. Examples: UK and USA

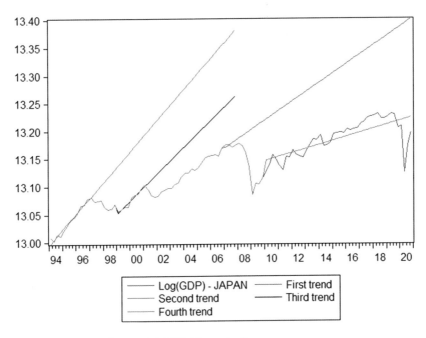

Fig. 3.2 Losses of potential GDP. Example: Japan

regime shifts. We consider the trend dynamics of GDP to be those of potential GDP. A shock such as the 2008 crisis caused the GDP trajectory to fall in all three countries. We see that the trajectories are no longer in line with those observed before the shock. Beyond that, the slopes of the lines have decreased. The combination of these two phenomena has the effect of delaying the return of GDP to the level observed before the shock. These breaks in the long-term trajectories illustrate a situation of "de-capping" of potential GDP, that is, losses of potential GDP. The changes in slope suggest that this may also affect potential growth (the growth rate of potential GDP given by the coefficient of the slope). The case of Japan is the most impressive. Looking at the different shocks, before 2008, as well as the GFC shock, one can observe that the trends are at increasingly lower levels.

To characterize the dynamics associated with this phenomenon, note that a shock can cause several scenarios.

Scenario 1 is similar to an "air-pocket" as in atmospheric turbulence. A shock causes a temporary stall in the initial trajectory of the GDP. The gap with potential GDP is closed more or less quickly.

In scenario 2, the shock causes a new potential GDP path to emerge and become the new GDP attractor. The output gap then measures the deviation from the new potential GDP trend and closes more or less quickly.

In scenario 3, in addition to the effects observed in scenario 2, the new potential GDP is described by a lower slope than the initial one. There is not only a loss of potential GDP level, but also a loss of potential growth.

To model these scenarios, here is a simple approach.

Formally, the losses in potential GDP (the existence of different potential GDP regimes) are captured by the existence of a long memory. In this case, beyond the known property of unit roots in GDP, one can additionally detect the presence of a long memory in the series. GDP series with a stochastic trend subject to "breaks" or regime changes therefore have an integration order between 1 and 2:

$$(1 - L)^{1+d} y^*_{t+1} = \epsilon_{t+1}, \quad \epsilon_{t+1} \approx ARMA(p, q). \tag{3.7}$$

y^*_t is pential GDP, ϵ_{t+1} is assumed to follow a stationary ARMA process. Theoretically, we assume $|d| < 0.5$, but estimates n data can reveals non-stationarity in the long memory itself. To take a simple case, the output gap follows an AR(1) process:

$$y_t = y^*_t + \beta(y_{t-1} - y^*_{t-1}) + v_t, \quad v_t \approx iid(0, \sigma_v^2). \tag{3.8}$$

Using the estimates of the coefficients, we can characterize several scenarios:

1. $d = 0$ and $|\beta| < 1$. Air-pocket scenario. Any deviation of GDP from its initial trend is quickly recovered after a few quarters. GDP has a stochastic trend with no breaks and the output gap is mean-reverting and close quickly after a shock.

2. $d = 0$ and $|\beta| = 1$. There is no regime switches in GDP, but the output gap shows a high persistence. It may take a long time after a shock before the economies retrieves its potential GDP.

3. $d > 0$ and $|\beta| < 1$. GDP stochastic trend is characterized by regime changes (loss of potential GDP after a negative shock, or gains of GDP following a positive shock). The output gap close quickly.

4. $d > 0$ and $|\beta| = 1$. Not only does the stochastic GDP trend undergo regime changes, but the output gap also shows persistent dynamics. One possible explanation may be that the path of potential GDP itself is changing.

To differentiate between the different scenarios, we proceed as follows. First, we estimate an ARFIMA(1,d,1) model on the logarithm of GDP (for Japan we additionally estimate an ARFIMA(0,d,0) model to highlight the presence of long-memory dynamics). Then, we apply a Christiano-Fitzgerald filter to this series and estimate an ARMA(1,1) model. The results of the estimations are shown in Table 3.1. The estimates are obtained by the maximum likelihood method. The table shows the coefficients, the p-values of the null hypothesis tests of the coefficients and the lower and upper bounds of the 95% confidence interval.

We see that GDP has both a unit root and a long-memory component (parameter d significantly positive and coefficient AR(1) close to 1). The case of Japan is specific. Indeed, when estimating an ARFIMA model, the unit root of the AR component captures all the persistent components of

Table 3.1 Estimation of ARFIMA model on log(GDP)

		Coeff.	P-value	Lower bound	Upper bound
USA	AR(1)	0.99	0.0	0.98	1.01
	MA(1)	−0.56	0.05	−1.13	−0.002
	d	0.41	0.0	0.32	0.501
UK	AR(1)	0.98	0.0	0.97	1.03
	MA(1)	−0.38	0.0	−0.50	−0.26
	d	0.22	0.015	0.04	0.39
Japan	$d(p = q = 0)$	0.49	0.0	0.41	0.502
	AR(1)	0.99	0.0	0.96	1.02
	MA(1)	−0.06	0.74	−0.45	0.32
	d	−0.004	0.34	−0.014	0.005

Note Numbers in the column showing the p-values of the test of significance of the parameters must be compared to 10%, 5%, or 1%. The coefficients are statistically significant when the p-values are below these numbers

Table 3.2 Estimation of AR(1) coefficients on the cyclical component of log(GDP)

	Positive output gap		Negative output gap	
	Coeff.	*P*-value	*Coeff.*	*P*-value
USA				
Intercept	0.0006	0.046	−0.002	0.134
AR(1)	0.98	0.0	0.83	0.0
UK				
Intercept	0.003	0.41	−0.003	0.41
AR(1)	0.82	0.0	0.90	0.0
Japan				
Intercept	0.002	0.0003	−0.009	0.0
AR(1)	0.87	0.0	1.14	0.0

Note Numbers in the column showing the *p*-values of the test of significance of the parameters must be compared to 0.1, 0.05, or 0.01. The coefficients are statistically significant when the *p*-values are below these numbers

the level of GDP. The unit root appears as such only when we assume $p = q = 0$.

In Table 3.2, we estimate an AR(1) model using the cyclical component of log(GDP) by distinguishing the observations according to whether the output gap is positive or negative. The identification of the regimes is obtained by estimating a TVTPMS model, as in the previous chapter, to the filtered variable and taking as transition variable its lagged values (maximum 3 lags). In the three countries, we note that in both cases, the dynamics have quasi-unit roots, which means that the output gap is persistent over time and may have difficulty closing quickly after a shock. In the case of Japan, we have an interesting result. Recessionary phases (negative output gaps) can last a very long time. Indeed, the coefficient significantly higher than 1 indicates the presence of non-stationary dynamics.

Equation (3.7) suggests that it is not appropriate to separate the level of GDP from its growth rate to study the effects of persistent shocks. It can be seen that the equation is also interpreted as a long-run model of the growth rate of potential GDP (the first difference of the log of potential GDP). If d is significantly positive, shocks that induce a very high persistence on the level can also induce a persistence on the growth rate (in the form of a long-memory process). This illustrates the phenomenon of super-hysteresis which is not seen if we separate the study of level dynamics from growth rates. A common practice is to differentiate the GDP series, once the presence of a unit root has been identified. Then the first difference is treated as an $I(0)$ process characterized by fast mean-reverting dynamics. This approach masks the presence of forms of persistence in the first differences other than unit roots.

The identification of super-hysteresis paves the way for future new approaches to economic policy. If the level of GDP contains persistence mixed with regime shifts, it is difficult to consider the set of long-term variables on which it depends (all natural variables: unemployment rate, inflation rate, debt ratio, etc.) as fixed points. On the contrary, long-term stationary equilibria can change over time. It would then be better for economic policy to focus on natural states described by stationary distributions. Another important element concerns the persistence of output gaps. If this is ignored, then there is a great risk of overestimating or underestimating the extent of goods market imbalances and may distort the search for optimal equilibria. For example, following a negative shock, the central bank could underestimate the extent of recessions, or even prolong them, by adopting too early a monetary policy aimed at controlling inflationary pressures in recovery phases. This adds to the policymaker's decision a dimension where it is necessary to identify in the changes in the output gap, what is caused by changes in actual output, and what is caused by changes in potential GDP.

3.2   ARE EXPANSIONS GOOD AND RECESSIONS BAD FOR JOBS?

We now turn to an important relationship in macroeconomics that is commonly described as Okun's law. We want to know if economic expansions create jobs and if recessions lead to higher unemployment. Behind this question, we want to know if the variations of unemployment are cyclical or not. Okun's law is valid during a recession if firms accept that employee productivity falls and adopt a labor hoarding strategy, allowing unemployment to rise only slightly. On the contrary, if they reduce employment and hours worked disproportionately to the fall in output, unemployment increases significantly. Gordon (2010) shows that in the United States, since 1990, economic recoveries have been jobless recoveries, because firms have responded by sharply increasing labor productivity and slowly increasing the number of hours worked (productivity changes are procyclical). On the contrary, during recessions, they have laid off heavily to reduce labor costs.

The question of the effects of expansions on unemployment reduction and job creation has become a crucial issue in economic policy, in a context where the institutions governing the relationship between employees and employers have evolved, the nature of jobs has changed, advanced countries are increasingly innovative and labor markets have become globalized.

3.2.1   Some Analytical Relationships for the Okun Law

A simple way to introduce Okun's Law is to decompose GDP into several components. We define the following variables:

- Y: real output,
- E: number of persons employed,
- H: number of hours worked,
- N: working-age population,
- L: labor force.

The output can be broken down into several parts:

$$Y_t = \frac{Y_t}{H_t} \times \frac{H_t}{E_t} \times \frac{E_t}{L_t} \times \frac{L_t}{N_t} \times N_t. \tag{3.9}$$

Total output can be defined as the product of the following quantities:

- $y_t = \frac{Y_t}{H_t}$: output per hour (labor productivity),
- $h_t = \frac{H_t}{E_t}$: hours per employee,
- $e_t = \frac{E_t}{L_t}$: employment rate,
- $l_t = \frac{L_t}{N_t}$: labor force participation rate,
- N_t: working-age population.

Equation (3.9) implies

$$e_t = \frac{Y_t}{y_t \times h_t \times l_t \times N_t}. \tag{3.10}$$

To this identity, we add behavioral equations for the variables in the denominator. To do this, we make the following assumptions.

(H1)   The working-age population grows at a constant exogenous rate n:

$$N_t = N_0(1 + \alpha)^t. \tag{3.11}$$

(H2)   The number of hours worked and productivity vary according to the output. There is a debate in the literature about the degree of flexibility in labor management. In particular, it is interesting to know whether hourly productivity and hours worked respond in the same direction to changes in output. This is an empirical question. We assume that

$$h_t = h_0(1 + n)^t Y_t^{\beta}, \ \alpha > 0, \ \beta \geq 0 \text{ or } \beta \leq 0. \tag{3.12}$$

$$y_t = y_0(1 + \omega)^t Y_t^{\nu}, \ \omega > 0, \ \nu \geq 0 \text{ or } \nu \leq 0. \tag{3.13}$$

β and ν are the elasticities of hours per employee and output per hour with respect to output.

(H3)   Changes in labor participation rate are caused by changes in employment rate:

$$l_t = h_0(1 + d)^t e_t^k, \ d > 0, \ k \geq 0. \tag{3.14}$$

k is the elasticity of l_t with respect to e_t.

Putting Eqs. (3.11)–(3.14) into (3.10) and taking the log, we get:

$$\log(e_t) = \eta_1 + \eta_2 \, t + \kappa \, \log(Y_t), \tag{3.15}$$

$$\eta_1 = - \left(\frac{1}{k + 1} \right) \log(y_0 k_0 N_0), \tag{3.16}$$

$$\eta_2 = - \left(\frac{1}{k + 1} \right) \log[(1 + \omega)(1 + \alpha)(1 + d)(1 + n)]. \tag{3.17}$$

The potential level of employment rate is defined as e_t^* and potential GDP by Y_t^*. From Eq. (3.15), we have

$$\log(e_t^*) = \eta_1 + \eta_2 \, t + \kappa \, \log(Y_t^*). \tag{3.18}$$

Subtracting (3.18) from (3.15), we obtain:

$$\log\left(\frac{e_t}{e_t^*}\right) = \kappa \, \log\left(\frac{Y_t}{Y_t^*}\right). \tag{3.19}$$

The left-hand side is the employment rate and in the right-hand side we have the output gap. Instead of employment, we can also consider the unemployment rate (since $u_t + e_t = 1$, where u_t is the unemployment rate). In logarithmic term, we write:

$$u_t - u_t^* = -\kappa \, \text{output gap}_t. \tag{3.20}$$

3.2.2   Econometric Evidence

From the relations of the previous section, we estimate several long-term relations from ARDL (autoregressive distributed lags) models. From several databases we select the following variables over the period 1990q1 to 2020q4 (q means quarter):

1. Labor force: Total, Thousand persons, OECD, quarterly;
2. Working-age population: aged 15–64, FRED Fed St. Louis, quarterly;
3. Employment rate: Total, % of working-age population, OECD, quarterly;
4. Hours worked per worker: Annual, OECD;
5. GDP per hour worked, Annual, OECD;
6. Unemployment rate: Total, % of labor force, OECD, quarter.

Annual data are converted to quarterly. The series 1, 2, 4, 5 are log-transformed. For each series, we calculate the gaps from a Christiano-Fitzgerald filter with cycle lengths between 6 and 32 quarters. Then, we run ARDL regressions with output as the explanatory variable and the variables on the right-hand side of the equation as independent variables. The long-run relationship is obtained by writing the ARDL equation in the form of an error correction model (ECM) and then deriving the level relationship. For each ARDL model, we choose four lags on all variables (explanatory and endogenous).

One of the motivations for starting with a dynamic autoregressive specification is the need to take into account the adjustment behavior of the different variables to their long-run level. For example, to bring employment to the desired level, firms gradually adjust productivity and hours worked.

Table 3.3 shows the long-term responses of the variables to changes in the output gap. In all three countries, changes in the output gap lead to significant changes in the employment rate and the other two components of aggregate hours. The employment content of growth increases after the GFC (the coefficient of the employment rate is positive and higher over the period 2008–2020). The response of the hour per employee remains identical between the two sub-periods. Everywhere, changes in the output gap have led to a stronger response in hours than in productivity. In the United States, the two variables adjust in opposite directions. In Japan, they changed in the same direction. In the United Kingdom the relationship between the two changes between the two sub-periods. The proportions of 2/3 for aggregate hours and 1/3 for output per hour are not found in this table, which in itself is not a problem. In fact, since the 1960s, the US economy and those of other countries have undergone major changes. The interesting point is this. Although significant, the coefficients on the productivity variable (output per hour) are small. This goes against a common assumption in RBC models that productivity shocks are highly procyclical. On the other hand, the response of the number of hours worked is procyclical (positive coefficients mean that this variable varies in the same direction as the output gap). But the magnitude of the variation varies from one country to another. It is stronger in the United States than in Japan and the United Kingdom. In all three countries, the coefficients are higher in the post-GFC period.

In Table 3.4, we report the results of the regressions where unemployment gap is regressed on the output gap taking into account the variables of the previous table as control variables. As before, the relationships are the long-run equations obtained from an ARDL model.

In all countries, and in both sub-periods, we find an expected negative sign for the output-gap coefficient. Consequently, employment has been, since 1990, one of the adjustment variables of firms to cyclical variations. This finding is in line with some previous papers in the literature that find a strong Okun effect in advanced economies (see, among others, Ball et al. 2017 and Ball et al. 2019).

The need to include the variables y_t, h_t and l_t as control variables in the regressions is motivated by identification issues. An implicit assumption here is that potential GDP and the natural unemployment rate follow a trend governed by productivity, the labor force participation rate, demo-

Table 3.3 Long-run changes in the responses to the output gap

Dependent variable	United Kingdom		United States		Japan	
	1990–2007	2008–2020	1990–2007	2008–2020	1990–2007	2008–2020
Output per hour	0.06***	−0.03**	−0.01	−0.06***	0.06***	0.06***
	(3.90)	(−2.35)	(−1.17)	(−3.49)	(3.01)	(3.87)
Aggregate hours, among which	0.1	0.41	0.51	0.81	0.25	0.35
Hours per employee	0.001*	0.009***	0.003**	0.002***	0.0009	0.001
	(2.33)	(13.57)	(6.57)	(4.26)	(1.17)	(0.15)
Employment rate	0.10*	0.21***	0.42***	0.59***	0.16***	0.35***
	(1.71)	(3.92)	(5.52)	(6.69)	(3.36)	(2.88)
Labor force participation rate	0.01	0.19***	0.09***	0.22***	0.09*	0.07
	(0.54)	(5.24)	(3.68)	(6.01)	(1.90)	(1.00)

Note Numbers between brackets are the Student-*t*. *, **, ***: statistically significant at 10%, 5%, and 1% level of confidence

Table 3.4 Augmented Okun equations

	United Kingdom		United States		Japan	
	1990–2007	*2008–2020*	*1990–2007*	*2008–2020*	*1990–2007*	*2008–2020*
Without control variables	−0.12	−0.08***	−0.42***	−0.56***	−0.20***	−0.09
Output gap	(0.34)	(0.1)	(0.0)	(0.0)	(0.0)	(0.25)
With control variables						
Output gap	−0.34***	−0.74***	−0.54***	−0.48***	−0.57**	−0.45***
	(0.0)	(0.0)	(0.0)	(0.0)	(0.0)	(0.0)
Output per hour (gap)	2.53***	4.2***	5.48***	1.45***	2.12*	−0.44***
	(0.0)	(0.0)	(0.0)	(0.0)	(0.07)	(0.0)
Hours/worker (gap)	39.36***	104.22***	−1.44**	17.08***	60.39***	29.10***
	(0.0)	(0.0)	(0.02)	(0.0)	(0.01)	(0.0)
Labor force participation rate	−1.17***	5.83***	1.18***	0.03***	−0.39***	0.64***
	(0.0)	(0.0)	(0.0)	(0.0)	(0.0)	(0.0)

Note Numbers between brackets are the *p*-values. *, **, ***: statistically significant at 10%, 5%, and 1% level of confidence graphic variables such as the working age population, and so on. Including them in the regression allows to neutralize the effects of changes in potential GDP on the unemployment gap, so that the coefficient measures the response to cyclical variations in activity.

Outside Japan, in the second sub-period, the employment rate and productivity were adjusted in the opposite direction following cyclical changes in GDP. Indeed, we see that in most of the regressions, the output per hour coefficient is positive. This seems to contradict Okun's law, in the sense that firms seem to make a trade-off between adjusting productivity and adjusting employment.

Can we conclude from these regressions that periods of economic expansion have created jobs, while recessions have led to higher unemployment rates? In the above table, are we right to assume that the effects are symmetrical? To answer this, we re-estimate the equations by differentiating the effect of positive and negative values of the output gap. Table 3.5 shows the new results.

As we see, the coefficients are not identical. This result is in line with previous findings in the literature. Some authors, using other econometric approaches, find that the sign of the output gap has been reversed since the early 1980s (see, e.g., Compagnucci et al. 2021). Growth in the advanced countries has become jobless due to the decoupling of productivity from wages and capacity utilization. When we take into account the asymmetry of the cycle, we find a result common in some papers (at least here for the United States and Japan); that is, that Okun's law negative correlation between unemployment gap and output gap seems to be validated in OECD countries during recessions periods and invalidated during expansion periods (the sign turns to positive in the United States and Japan. In these countries recessions are accompanied by an increase in unemployment, but expansions are not necessarily job-creating (Bod'a and Povazanová 2021 find a similar result).

The non-reaction of the unemployment rate to the output gap, or the existence of a positive sign, is sometimes interpreted as a consequence of the existence of wage rigidities (or classical unemployment), especially in the expansion phases of the cycle. In the United Kingdom, we find the opposite result; that is, that periods of expansion create jobs, but during recessions unemployment does not increase (which could be explained, e.g., by the multiplication of precarious forms of work allowing companies to lower labor costs when activity is low).

Table 3.5 Impact of positive and negative output gaps on unemployment gap

	United Kingdom		United States		Japan	
	Pos	Neg	Pos	Neg	Pos	Neg
Without control variables						
Output gap	0.006	0.02*	−0.09	−0.16**	0.02	−0.03*
	(−0.39)	(1.64)	(−0.92)	(−1.99)	(0.54)	(0.10)
With control variables						
Output gap	−0.09*	0.03***	0.29***	−0.30***	0.01**	−0.01***
	(−1.68)	(6.89)	(10.59)	(−15.08)	(13.94)	(−13.98)
Output per hour (gap)	−0.46	0.38***	2.80***	3.38***	−1.38***	−1.41***
	(−0.71)	(6.89)	(11.28)	(26.02)	(−489.45)	(−362.75)
Hours/worker (gap)	−13.31*	−0.25	−63.41***	−27.22***	−18.80***	−19.89**
	('−1.83)	(−0.11)	(−22.84)	(−26.63)	(−42.27)	(−47.50)
Labor force participation rate	−2.71***	−1.02***	−3.03***	−2.05***	−0.03	−0.12***
	('−3.80)	(−12.15)	(−13.30)	(−20.31)	(−17.61)	(−24.43)

Note Numbers between brackets are Student-t. *, **, ***: statistically significant at 10%, 5%, and 1% level of confidence

There are other aspects in the literature that are not discussed here, but are important. The coefficients of the Okun relationship are heterogeneous from one country to another, but above all vary according to the categories of worker populations. The unemployment rate of young workers is twice as responsive to the business cycle as that of adults. The coefficient is lower for the unemployment rate of women than for men (see, among many works, Dixon et al. 2017; Na 2019). Another point of debate is the time-varying aspects of the Okun coefficients (see Lim et al. 2021).

3.3   Is the Phillips Curve Obsolete?

As explained in the introduction, the Phillips curve has been the subject of much debate among economists over the past decade. In its simple version, it is based on two relationships. The first relates wage changes to several variables: the unemployment gap, the level of past wages and past inflation (to capture the degree of nominal wage rigidity). The second relationship is a consumer price equation that incorporates input costs, including wage costs, and price expectations. Combining these two relationships, we obtain an equation in which the rate of inflation (or its acceleration) depends on the unemployment gap (an indicator of labor market pressure). Below we provide an illustration of a formal model. One difficulty with the Phillips curve comes from the fact that the inflation/unemployment relationship is not stable over time. Figure 3.3 shows an example, even over a short historical period since 1990, for Japan and the United States. We explore here some of the elements described in the introduction to explain this phenomenon.

In a detailed investigation of 20 industrialized countries since 1960, Blanchard et al. (2015) and Blanchard (2016) highlight a change in the slope of the curve over time. The authors regress headline CPI inflation on unemployment gap, long-run inflation expectations and past inflation. They estimate a model with variable coefficients and show that the slope coefficient of the Phillips curve first declined sharply between the mid-1970s and the early 1990s. After that, the curve tended to flatten. Ball et al. (2019) analyze the US core inflation and find that inflation expectations were backward looking until 1990, and then they became strongly anchored at the Fed's inflation target. Obviously, this raises a problem. If there is no longer a trade-off between inflation and unemployment, central bankers lose one of their important analytical tools for targeting

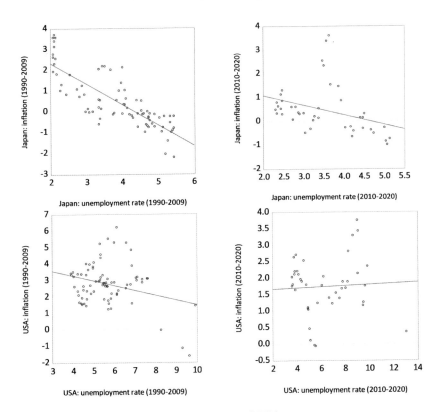

Fig. 3.3   Phillips curves. Examples: Japan and USA

inflation. This type of result usually elicits three types of reactions. The first is skepticism, which is motivated by the fact that the econometric methods used are biased, or that the econometrician finds this result because he omits determinants of inflation as explanatory variables. Macroeconomists, and policymakers, find it very difficult to get rid of a result that has been ingrained in people's minds since the 1960s. The second reaction is to look to microeconomic models for the causes of price and labor market rigidities that would explain the reduction in the slope. A third attitude is to point out that it is possible that inflation is less sensitive to tensions in domestic labor markets, because it is more sensitive to other factors whose influence has grown over the last three decades. As we pointed out in the introduction, we can mention the phenomenon of globalization and the role of financial cycles.

3.3.1   How Does Unemployment Affect Inflation? A Very Simple Model

The Phillips curve is a reduced form derived from various structural models, depending on what we wish to highlight. We propose here a simple model under the following assumptions:

1. Unemployment is involuntary and wage earners negotiate the nominal wage according to expected prices and their reservation wage;
2. Firms set the real wage (they choose their selling price). Employment is determined by labor demand (firms) according to expected market opportunities. The unemployment rate therefore depends on economic activity.
3. Price expectations depend on the inflationary environment of the country.

Nominal Wages and Consumer Prices

Wage earners pay a payroll tax t^d that is applied to wage W_t^s. We define P_{ct}^e the expected level of consumer prices. On these net prices, the government applies a VAT t^v. P_t denotes domestic output prices and P_t^* denotes foreign output prices. Z is the reservation wage. We define the following two equations for the nominal wage and consumer prices:

$$(1 + t^d)W_t^s = (1 + t^v)P_{ct}^e Z. \tag{3.21}$$

$$P_{ct} = P_t^{(1-\phi)}(P_t^* E_t)^\phi, \ 0 \le \phi \le 1. \tag{3.22}$$

E_t is the nominal exchange rate. ϕ is the weight of foreign prices in domestic consumer prices.

By log-linearizing and denoting the logarithms by lower case letters, we rewrite these two equations as follows (Z is normalized to 1):

$$w_t^s = (t^d - t^v) + p_{ct}^e, \ p_{ct} = p_t + \phi\theta_t. \tag{3.23}$$

θ_t is the log-linearized real exchange rate.

Producer Price

Firms produce Y_t with N_t units of labor (N_t is the level of employment). The production function is written as $Y_t = N_t^\gamma$, where γ is the elasticity of output to employment. For simplicity, the capital stock is fixed and normalized to 1. The first-order condition of the profit-maximizing program gives the firm's desired employment level. This leads to a relationship between the relative price and output:

$$p_t - p_{ct}^e = -\ln(\gamma) + \frac{1-\gamma}{\gamma} n_t + (t^v - t^d). \tag{3.24}$$

Price Expectations

The anchoring of inflation expectations depends on the level of inflation. It is conceivable that in a highly inflationary environment, wage earners will negotiate a nominal wage indexed to past prices. The lower the inflation, the more they anchor their expectations to the central bank's forecasts or price target:

$$p_{ct}^e = (1 - \rho_t)\bar{p}_{ct} + \rho_t p_{ct-1},$$

$$\rho_t = F(\pi_{t-d}) = \frac{1}{1 + exp-\delta(\pi_{t-d} - c)}, \quad \delta > 0, \quad \pi_t = \Delta p_t. \tag{3.25}$$

$\bar{p}_{ct}$ is the anchor price (central bank forecast). ρ_t is the weight assigned to past inflation. In this example, we use a formulation where the weight can vary over time depending on the inflation regime. The logistic function allows us to define two extreme regimes, low inflation and high inflation. The two regimes are delimited by a threshold c and the transition from one to the other is either abrupt (if γ is very large) or gradual if $0 < \gamma < \infty$. $d >$ is the lag in inflation. The choice of the logistics function implies that $0 \leq \rho_t \leq \infty$.

Figure 3.4 shows two illustrations for Japan and the United Kingdom. We represent a scatter plot with on the x-axis core inflation calculated by an HP filter of observed inflation, and inflation expectations at 10 years (for the United Kingdom) and 6–10 years (for Japan). On this graph we represent the relationship obtained using a non-parametric LOESS regression. We can see that the link between the two variables is weaker for values of the inflation rate below a certain threshold.

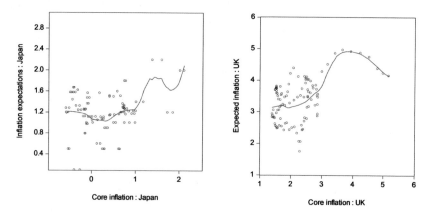

Fig. 3.4   Core inflation and expectated inflation. Examples: Japan and UK

Okun Law

The Okun relationship is deduced from the production function. Denoting n_t^* and y_t^* the natural rate of unemployment and the medium-/long-run output (in log), we have

$$n_t - n_t^* = \left(\frac{1}{\gamma}\right)(y_t - y_t^*). \tag{3.26}$$

Phillips Curve

We define, for any variable x, $\Delta x_t = x_t - x_{t-1}$. Let us note CPI inflation by $\pi_{ct} = \Delta p_{ct}$, expected inflation by $\pi_{ct}^e = \Delta p_{ct}^e$ and producer inflation by $\pi_t = \Delta p_t$. From Eq. (3.23) we obtain

$$\pi_{ct} = \pi_t + \phi \, \Delta \theta_t. \tag{3.27}$$

From Eq. (3.24), we get

$$\pi_t = \pi_{ct}^e + \left(\frac{1-\gamma}{\gamma}\right)\Delta n_t. \tag{3.28}$$

From Eq. (3.25), we have

$$\pi_{ct}^e = (1 - \rho_t)\,\bar{\pi}_t + \rho_t\pi_{ct-1} - \Delta\rho_t\,[\bar{p}_{ct} - p_{ct-1}]. \tag{3.29}$$

$[\bar{p}_{ct} - p_{ct-1}]$ measures the difference between the central bank's forecast of the consumer price level for date t and that of private agents for the same date if expectations are extrapolative (i.e., if $p_{ct}^e = p_{ct-1}$).

Let $u_t = 1 - n_t$ be the unemployment rate and u_t^* the natural unemployment rate. Equation (3.26) implies

$$\delta u_t = -(1/\gamma)\,\Delta(y_t - y_t^*) + \Delta u_t^*, \tag{3.30}$$

and from Eq. (3.28), we obtain

$$\pi_t = \pi_{ct}^e - \left(\frac{1-\gamma}{\gamma}\right)\Delta u_t. \tag{3.31}$$

The Phillips curve is described by the system of Eqs. (3.27), (3.29), (3.30), and (3.31). The reduced form is the following system of two equations

$$\pi_t = (1 - \rho_t)\bar{\pi}_{ct} + +\phi\pi_{t-1}^* + (\rho_t - \phi)\,\pi_{t-1}$$

$$- \Delta\rho_t\,(\bar{p}_{ct} - p_{ct-1}) - \left(\frac{1-\gamma}{\gamma}\right)\Delta u_t, \tag{3.32}$$

$$\Delta u_t = -(1/\gamma)\,\Delta(y_t - y_t^*) + \Delta u_t^*. \tag{3.33}$$

In our simple model, the inflation rate depends on the output gap and on changes in the medium-/long-term unemployment rate. The slope of the Phillips curve depends on the responsiveness of employment to economic growth. In situations of low job recoveries, the Phillips curve becomes flatter (γ is lower).

While there has been much recent discussion of the flattening of Phillips curves, there has been less discussion of their shift. Here, several factors are worth mentioning.

World inflation impacts domestic inflation. Its influence is captured here by foreign price inflation. The coefficient is an indicator of the degree of pass-through of foreign prices into domestic prices. Given the importance of value chains in international trade and of intermediate goods and services, it is important to look at cost-pass-through, that is, the way in which domestic producers pass on the prices of the international intermediate goods they buy in the selling price. The price of imports thus measures not only the effects of competition on final consumer goods and services. If domestic firms maintain their margins, without passing on the declines in world prices of inputs produced cheaper by foreign competitors, the sign of ϕ can be negative.

As is seen, the influence of past inflation depends on two offsetting factors. First, the degree of anchoring of expectations, measured here by ρ_t. Second, the degree of pass-through of foreign prices captured by ϕ.

The equation also shows the importance of expectations of the general price level. If the expected level is higher/lower than that forecast by the central bank, this fuels/mitigates inflationary pressures, when agents revise their expectations (i.e., when $\rho_t \neq 0$).

This simple model could be enriched in several ways. One could introduce monetary illusion or an overreaction of wage earners to past inflation when they negotiate the nominal wage. Instead of a unit coefficient, we could, for example, put a coefficient less than 1 in front of p^e_{ct} in Eq. (3.23). We could also introduce a pass-through from wages to prices.

3.3.2   Some Empirical Evidence

We consider several specifications of the Phillips curve, where CPI inflation is regressed on the explanatory variables in Table 3.6. A cross means that the variable is included in the equation. Dynamic effects are taken into account in an ARDL model and we report the coefficients of the relationship in level (cointegration relationship). It tells us about the links between the inflation rate and the structural components of its determinants.

We also consider the following variables:

1. Food price index, quarterly, World Bank;
2. Energy price index, quarterly, World Bank;
3. Emerging market and developing economies producer price index (PPI) inflation, annual average, World Bank;
4. UK: 10-year inflation implied forward, monthly average of yield from British Government securities;
5. USA: 10-year expected inflation, monthly, Fed of St. Louis (FRED);
6. Japan: 6- to 10-year inflation forecasts, monthly, Bank of Japan;
7. Financial cycles as described in the previous chapter.

Table 3.6
Specifications of the
Phillips curve

Explanatory variables	(1)	(2)	(3)	(4)
Unemployment rate	×	×	×	−
Food prices	×	×	×	×
Energy prices	×	×	×	×
Emerging market inflation	×	×	×	×
Inflation expectations	×	×	×	×
Labor force	−	×	−	×
Intercept	×	×	×	×
Financial cycle	−	−	×	−
Employment rate	−	−	−	×
Labor productivity	−	−	−	×

Note A cross means that the variable is included in the regression

All variables are transformed into quarterly frequencies. The estimates are made by distinguishing two sub-periods, before and after the GFC.

In Regressions (1), (2), and (3), the inflation rate is equal to the unemployment rate. The basic Regression (1) also includes sources of inflation volatility (energy and food prices), the influence of globalization and competition from emerging and developing countries (production prices of firms in these countries), and long-term inflation expectations. In Regression (2), we add the labor force. In Regression (3), we add to the variables of Regression (1), the influence of the financial cycle. Regression (4) differs from Regression (2) in that instead of the unemployment rate, the inflation rate reacts to the employment rate and hourly labor productivity.

We select results for the United States, the United Kingdom, and Japan. The regression results are shown in Tables 3.7, 3.8, 3.9, 3.10, 3.11, and 3.12. Bold numbers denote coefficients significant at least at the 10% level.

In the basic Regression (1), in the United States and Japan, the slope of the Phillips curve decreases significantly, from −0.33 to −0.06 in the first country and from −0.55 to −0.10. In the English case, the coefficient of the unemployment rate has a negative sign only when the financial cycle is introduced among the explanatory variables. This suggests that for this

Table 3.7 Phillips curve estimates: United States, 1990–2007

Variable	(1) Coeff.	(1) t-Stat.	(2) Coeff.	(2) t-Stat.	(3) Coeff.	(3) t-Stat.	(4) Coeff.	(4) t-Stat.
Unemployment rate	**-0.33**	-3.86	**-0.35**	-4.39	**-0.22**	-4.08	–	–
Food prices	**0.78**	3.10	**1.08**	3.67	**0.75**	4.59	0.12	0.45
Energy prices	**0.38**	12.64	**0.39**	13.67	**0.27**	8.86	**0.48**	9.99
Emerging market inflation	**-0.15**	-2.13	**-0.20**	-2.91	**-0.09**	-1.84	**-0.17**	-2.19
Inflation expectations	**1.51**	8.17	**1.52**	8.59	**1.42**	11.02	**1.15**	8.54
Labor force	–	–	0.12	0.49	–	–	**-1.49**	-2.68
Intercept	-0.37	-1.21	-0.37	-1.26	**-1.17**	-4.66	**-8.97**	-2.26
Financial cycle	–	–	–	–	**1.20**	4.77	–	–
Employment rate	–	–	–	–	–	–	**0.11**	2.15
Labor productivity	–	–	–	–	–	–	**-3.47**	-4.58

Note The coefficients in bold are statistically significant at least at 10% level of confidence

Table 3.8 Phillips curve estimates: United States, 2008–2020

Variable	(1) Coeff.	(1) t-Stat.	(2) Coeff.	(2) t-Stat.	(3) Coeff.	(3) t-Stat.	(4) Coeff.	(4) t-Stat.
Unemployment rate	−0.06	−2.16	−0.01	−0.43	−0.25	−10.84	—	—
Food prices	1.23	6.85	1.46	8.74	1.60	13.29	1.15	11.53
Energy prices	0.48	8.94	0.44	10.68	0.65	13.37	0.25	6.85
Emerging market inflation	−0.29	−2.35	−0.60	−4.26	−0.86	−6.28	−0.08	−0.63
Inflation expectations	−0.94	−1.01	−0.48	−0.61	0.06	0.15	−2.24	−2.99
Labor force	—	—	−0.01	−0.03	—	—	−1.50	−3.00
Intercept	4.09	2.12	3.00	1.90	4.66	4.92	5.86	4.11
Financial cycle	—	—	—	—	−3.70	−6.77	—	—
Employment rate	—	—	—	—	—	—	0.08	2.59
Labor productivity	—	—	—	—	—	—	−4.90	−3.74

Note the coefficients in bold are statistically significant at least at 10% level of confidence

Table 3.9 Phillips curve estimates: United Kingdom, 1990–2007

Variable	(1) Coeff.	(1) t-Stat.	(2) Coeff.	(2) t-Stat.	(3) Coeff.	(3) t-Stat.	(4) Coeff.	(4) t-Stat.
Unemployment rate	−0.06	−0.35	4.91	0.88	−0.14	−0.61	–	–
Food prices	**0.93**	2.08	−2.88	−0.63	**1.80**	3.04	**1.90**	5.10
Energy prices	**0.32**	2.37	−0.48	−0.54	**0.81**	3.15	**0.76**	4.81
Emerging market inflation	**0.30**	1.76	−4.80	−0.83	0.03	0.15	−0.65	−2.43
Inflation expectations	0.43	1.27	−3.43	−0.76	0.00	0.00	−0.58	−1.52
Labor force	–	–	60.45	0.91	–	–	**4.92**	3.13
Intercept	−0.41	−0.80	−2.92	−0.89	**3.65**	1.97	**42.63**	2.39
Financial cycle	–	–	–	–	**−5.92**	−2.38	–	–
Employment rate	–	–	–	–	–	–	**−0.54**	−2.34
Labor productivity	–	–	–	–	–	–	**−6.70**	−4.52

Note The coefficients in bold are statistically significant at least at 10% level of confidence

Table 3.10 Phillips curve estimates: United Kingdom, 2008–2020

Variable	(1) Coeff.	t-Stat.	(2) Coeff.	t-Stat.	(3) Coeff.	t-Stat.	(4) Coeff.	t-Stat.
Unemployment rate	**0.10**	2.17	0.06	1.40	**−0.06**	−2.13	—	—
Food prices	**0.21**	1.76	0.32	1.43	**0.69**	8.37	**1.40**	2.71
Energy prices	**0.51**	4.79	**0.37**	3.71	**0.19**	2.30	**0.71**	2.59
Emerging market inflation	−0.03	−0.14	0.18	1.44	**0.47**	2.17	−1.19	−1.28
Inflation expectations	0.00	0.00	0.04	0.12	0.07	0.47	1.34	0.87
Labor force	—	—	**−0.55**	−1.71	—	—	−4.89	−1.51
Intercept	0.99	0.74	0.83	0.60	**3.10**	5.10	−8.92	−0.98
Financial cycle	—	—	—	—	**−5.61**	−5.46	—	—
Employment rate	—	—	—	—	—	—	0.09	1.44
Labor productivity	—	—	—	—	—	—	10.39	1.20

Note The coefficients in bold are statistically significant at least at 10% level of confidence

Table 3.11 Phillips curve estimates: Japan, 1990–2007

Variable	(1) Coeff.	t-Stat.	(2) Coeff.	t-Stat.	(3) Coeff.	t-Stat.	(4) Coeff.	t-Stat.
Unemployment rate	**-0.55**	-4.57	**-0.61**	-2.98	**-0.43**	-5.01	–	–
Food prices	**2.02**	9.19	**1.87**	6.93	**1.44**	9.76	**1.95**	4.75
Energy prices	**0.36**	2.88	**0.32**	2.26	**0.37**	4.31	**0.68**	2.80
Emerging market inflation	0.16	1.53	**0.26**	2.34	-0.06	-0.84	**0.67**	3.57
Inflation expectations	**-0.44**	-1.73	-0.62	-1.33	0.14	0.75	0.06	0.16
Labor force	–	–	**1.36**	2.30	–	–	**2.76**	4.25
Intercept	**2.46**	3.14	**2.72**	1.95	**0.99**	1.68	-9.60	-1.04
Financial cycle	–	–	–	–	**2.28**	5.73	–	–
Employment rate	–	–	–	–	–	–	0.11	0.84
Labor productivity	–	–	–	–	–	–	**-4.91**	-2.62

Note The coefficients in bold are statistically significant at least at 10% level of confidence

Table 3.12 Phillips curve estimates: Japan, 2008–2020

Variable	(1) Coeff.	t-Stat.	(2) Coeff.	t-Stat.	(3) Coeff.	t-Stat.	(4) Coeff.	t-Stat.
Unempl. rate	**-0.10**	-2.00	0.00	-0.06	**0.47**	2.93	–	–
Food prices	**2.19**	13.05	**2.68**	8.39	**1.43**	3.97	**1.72**	11.94
Energy prices	**0.42**	9.65	**0.48**	8.02	**0.60**	5.73	**0.33**	11.34
Emerg. mark. infl.	**-0.22**	-3.05	**-0.43**	-4.63	**-0.99**	-4.44	-0.03	-0.59
Inflation expectations	0.17	0.56	-1.05	-1.84	0.25	0.32	**0.57**	2.98
Labor force	–	–	-0.93	-1.40	–	–	**0.68**	3.30
Intercept	0.11	0.27	1.39	2.29	-0.19	-0.22	**-4.12**	-4.16
Financial cycle	–	–	–	–	**-2.27**	-2.74	–	–
Employ. rate	–	–	–	–	–	–	**0.04**	3.75
Labor product.	–	–	–	–	–	–	**2.66**	3.78

Note The coefficients in bold are statistically significant at least at 10% level of confidence

Table 3.13 Inflation and slack variables: Japan: 1990–2020

	Coeff.	St. Err.	z-Stat.	Coeff.	St. Err.	z-Stat.
Variance	**−1.97**	**0.38**	**−5.19**	**−2.18**	**0.69**	**−3.14**
Intercept	0.01	0.10	0.08	**0.73**	**0.13**	**5.73**
Infl. expect.	**0.45**	**0.07**	**6.57**	**0.28**	**0.05**	**6.15**
Output gap	**0.14**	**0.03**	**5.17**	–	–	–
Unemployment rate	–	–	–	**−0.03**	**0.02**	**−1.71**
Lagged inflation	**0.72**	**0.04**	**20.52**	**0.79**	**0.02**	**35.77**
	Variance Equation			Variance Equation		
Intercept	**0.32**	**0.05**	**6.18**	**0.43**	**0.11**	**3.80**
ϵ^2_{t-1}	**−0.08**	**0.02**	**−3.41**	**−0.03**	**0.01**	**−2.56**
ϵ^2_{t-2}	**−0.05**	**0.02**	**−2.64**	**−0.06**	**0.02**	**−2.39**
ϵ^2_{t-3}	**−0.06**	**0.02**	**−3.33**	–	–	–
Food prices	**−0.06**	**0.02**	**−3.16**	**−0.09**	**0.03**	**−3.10**
Energy prices	**−0.01**	**0.01**	**−1.91**	**−0.03**	**0.01**	**−3.06**
Import prices	0.00	0.01	−0.47	−0.01	0.00	−1.61
Shape parameter	**0.79**	**0.12**	**6.64**	**0.59**	**0.10**	**6.09**
Adjusted R-squared	0.85			0.87		
S.E. of regression	0.44			0.87		
Durbin–Watson stat	1.94			1.87		
Mean dependent var	0.41			0.41		
S.D. dependent var	1.16			1.16		
Akaike info criterion	1.31			1.21		

Note The coefficients in bold are statistically significant at least at 10% level of confidence

Table 3.14 Inflation and slack variables: United Kingdom: 1990–2020

Variable	Coeff.	Std. Err.	z-Stat	Coeff.	Std. Err.	z-Stat.
Variance	**4.34**	1.66	2.62	**4.65**	1.18	3.95
Intercept	**-0.27**	0.13	-2.03	**-0.48**	0.15	-3.20
Infl. Exp.	0.00	0.03	0.16	**0.11**	0.04	2.82
Output gap	**0.05**	0.02	2.54	–	–	–
Unempl. rate	–	–	–	-0.01	0.02	-0.76
Lagged infl.	**0.81**	0.02	33.22	**0.78**	0.03	23.81
Variance Equation						
Intercept	**0.08**	0.02	3.40	**0.05**	0.01	3.84
ϵ^2_{t-1}	-0.02	0.02	-0.70	-0.05	0.03	-1.52
ϵ^2_{t-2}	**0.09**	0.04	2.17	**0.07**	0.04	1.98
ϵ^2_{t-3}	**0.11**	0.05	2.39	**0.45**	0.11	4.10
Food prices	**0.01**	0.01	1.77	**0.01**	0.01	1.74
Energy prices	**0.01**	0.00	2.69	**0.01**	0.00	2.95
Import prices	0.01	0.01	1.21	0.01	0.00	1.42
Shape parameter	1.37	0.40	3.46	0.98	0.19	5.05
Adjusted R-squared	0.95			0.94		
S.E. of regression	0.36			0.39		
Durbin-Watson stat	1.41			1.88		
Mean dependent var	2.50			2.50		
S.D. dependent var	1.68			1.68		
AIC	0.68			0.78		

Note The coefficients in bold are statistically significant at least at 10% level of confidence

Table 3.15 Inflation and slack variables: United States: 1990–2020

Variable	Coeff.	Std. Err.	z-Stat.	Coeff.	Std. Err.	z-Stat.
Variance	**-0.58**	**0.29**	**-2.02**	**-0.94**	**0.20**	**-4.62**
Intercept	**0.31**	**0.13**	**2.36**	**0.42**	**0.15**	**2.83**
Infl. Expect.	**0.19**	**0.05**	**4.25**	**0.20**	**0.05**	**4.28**
Output gap	**0.08**	**0.03**	**2.98**	–	–	–
Unempl. Rate	–	–	–	**-0.01**	**0.00**	**-2.10**
Lagged infl.	**0.74**	**0.02**	**33.04**	**0.81**	**0.03**	**31.04**
Variance Equation						
C	**0.35**	**0.14**	**2.48**	**0.53**	**0.10**	**5.13**
ϵ_{t-1}^2	0.18	0.15	1.21	**0.15**	**0.08**	**1.83**
ϵ_{t-2}^2	0.01	0.03	0.49	–	–	–
$\epsilon_t - 3^2$	**0.14**	**0.06**	**2.30**	–	–	–
Food prices	0.03	0.08	0.31	-0.03	0.02	-1.17
Energy prices	**-0.02**	**0.01**	**-2.10**	**-0.03**	**0.01**	**-4.57**
Import prices	-0.05	0.04	-1.25	-0.03	0.03	-1.09
Shape parameter	**0.79**	**0.15**	**5.12**	**0.68**	**0.10**	**6.51**
Adjusted R-squared	0.72			0.75		
S.E. of regression	0.62			0.59		
Durbin-Watson stat	1.52			1.56		
Mean dependent var	2.35			2.35		
S.D. dependent var	1.18			1.18		
AIC	1.63			1.61		

Note The coefficients in bold are statistically significant at least at 10% level of confidence

country, not taking into account the effects of financial globalization may lead to omission biases.

However, as seen in some regressions, it can happen that the sign of the coefficient on the unemployment rate comes out positive and significant (as in the case of the United Kingdom in Regression 1 for the period 2008–2020 and Japan in Regression 3 for the period 2008–2020). This occurs in two contexts. The first has been observed historically since the late 1970s after the oil shocks. In this case, we had both high inflation rates and high unemployment rates. In another context, it is possible to observe both a fall in the unemployment rate and disinflationary or deflationary pressures. This typically occurs in secular stagnation regimes (a topic that has been much debated in recent years).

An interesting result in the regressions is that, since 2008, the boom phases of the financial cycle (a rise in the corresponding variable) have exerted deflationary pressures in the real sector. Indeed, we see that in all countries, the coefficient on this variable is systematically significantly negative over the period 2008–2020.

Regression 4 leads to different conclusions depending on the country. In the United States, the coefficient on the employment rate is positive and not significantly different between the two sub-periods. In the United Kingdom, it is negative in the first sub-period, then insignificant after 2008. In Japan, it is insignificant or weakly positive. This shows that the response of inflation to employment is not homogeneous from one country to another, especially since the impact of labor force varies from one country and one sub-period to another.

3.3.3   Inflation and Economic Slack

The reduced responsiveness of inflation to the unemployment rate in the usual formulations of the Phillips curve does not necessarily imply that the latter is no longer valid. It also indicates that the variable that influences prices may not be the unemployment rate, or the employment rate, but rather the rate of capacity utilization or the output gap. Indeed, the theoretical link between the employment situation and wages has become more tenuous in industrialized countries. The same is true for the price-wage loop, which is much less important than it was during the 30 glorious years. Wage moderation has been part of the structural changes that have affected labor markets. One of the major changes in labor markets over the last 20 years or so has been the emergence and multiplication of new forms of employment, different from the wage labor that had been the norm in the economies that industrialized in the wake of the two industrial revolutions of the nineteenth century. These new forms of employment have had the effect of modifying the bargaining relationship between employers and employees, and have accentuated competition between workers by atomizing jobs.

The growth model of the 30 glorious years was that of a society of mass consumption, driven by a strong demand made up of people who had to be paid in return for their participation in a productive system whose pillars of operation were Taylorization and mass production. From the mid-1990s onward, a break occurred with the rise of supply-side policies when it was a question of introducing more flexibility into labor markets in order to gain competitiveness (which sometimes led to a de-indexation of wages to factor productivity). Collective wage bargaining has weakened and the wage contract has become more individualized. In this context, several variables have weakened the links between unemployment and wage and price changes.

The first key variable has been the rate of participation in the labor market (i.e., flows into and out of labor markets). There is a correlation between the business cycle and the phenomena of discouraged workers or involuntary part-time workers. In periods of economic slowdown or recession, "atypical" forms of work, leading to working less time than in normal periods, multiply: fixed-term contracts, temporary work, part-time work. These phenomena have been accentuated by (a) the entry into the global market of millions of low-skilled workers from emerging and developing countries, (b) the rise of subcontracting activities at the global level, and (c) the increase in the share of services in GDP and the decrease in the share of industry, especially manufacturing. Similarly, during periods of economic recovery, the labor force participation rate is a key variable whose variations are difficult to interpret. The participation rate may increase, not because new people are employed, but simply because exits from the labor market slow down. Thus, one can observe recoveries without jobs, or recoveries accompanied by an increase in precarious jobs (e.g., jobs with no fixed duration). Typical examples are payrolling or contracting, where workers are hired temporarily to do odd jobs.

The second key variable is, as we have seen, productivity. With the rise of highly flexible employment contracts, the aim has been to increase

Table 3.16 Wage levels, low paid %

	Germany	Japan	United Kingdom	United States	OECD
1992	20.80	16.07	20.90	23.15	16.38
2000	15.80	14.56	20.84	24.70	16.45
2015	19.35	13.46	19.98	25.02	14.69
2019	17.63	11.78	18.09	23.37	13.88

Source OECD

productivity by reducing wage costs, especially for the least qualified workers. This is the so-called flexibility of labor markets approach.

Table 3.16 shows examples of some countries where the proportion of low-paid workers is above the average for all OECD countries. In the Euro area, Germany and Great Britain are the countries where this phenomenon has developed the most with the rise of non-standard work and the decentralization of wage bargaining to the firm level. In the OECD countries, the United States is among the countries where this phenomenon has spread because of the fragmentation of the labor market: workers under the control of companies alongside those whose labor force is rented. In the statistics, the cost of labor is always an average cost. If it were weighted by the proportion of workers with typical and atypical jobs, the observed developments would probably be different.

In any case, these developments take us away from the view of the functioning of labor markets in the 1950s and 1960s, when the first work on the Phillips curve began. The strategy adopted by many industrialized countries was to consider that employment was linked above all to the relative cost of labor and to favor legislative frameworks that led to its moderation by increasing competition between labor suppliers. One of the difficulties is that this reasoning only works when all else is equal. In particular, this strategy is only good if the prospects for firms are high. As we shall see in the next section, the potential growth trajectories of industrialized countries have been on a downward trend for three decades. We are no longer in the period of the 30 glorious years. Wage moderation has caused consumer spending to fall and the slowdown in potential growth has caused investment to fall sharply. It is therefore not certain that this approach is sustainable. It explains, in particular, why trend inflation has also been falling for several decades. But above all, it has disastrous social consequences, increasing inequality and poverty (see the next chapter).

For all the reasons discussed above, the response of inflation to employment or the unemployment rate may be more lax. If the rise between employment and wages is distended, then a more reliable indicator for measuring the effects of macroeconomic imbalances on inflation is the output gap. To investigate this empirically, we propose the following simple regressions.

We assume that headline inflation is determined by the following GARCH-M process:

$$\pi_t = c + \alpha \pi_t^e + \beta \, \overline{gap}_{t-1} + \lambda \sigma_t^2 + \epsilon_t, \; \epsilon_t \approx GED(0, h_t)$$

$$h_t = \sigma_t^2 = \omega + A_p(L)\epsilon_t + B_q(L)\sigma_t^2 + \gamma X_{t-1}. \tag{3.34}$$

π_t is the inflation rate, π_t^e is inflation expectations, $\overline{gap}_t$ is the average of the output gap over the quarters $t - 3$ to t. σ_t^2 is the volatility of inflation which we assume is linked to factors in the vector X_t: food and energy prices, as well as international emerging economies' inflation (a proxy for imported inflation). The volatile component of inflation is modeled through a $GARCH$ process. $A_p(L)$ and $B_q(L)$ are lag polynomials of respective orders p and q. The residual term is not distributed as a Normal law, but has a Generalized Exponential Distribution (GED). c and ω are intercepts. We shall compare this equation, with another one where the average unemployment rate is substituted for the average output gap. This formulation avoids ad-hoc calculations of core inflation, which is the variable sometimes considered in the literature. We directly explain headline inflation and capture the volatile components through the GARCH effects. We test several specifications and select the regressions leading the lowest root mean square error. When the output gap and unemployment rate averages are not statistically significant, we consider the output gap and unemployment of the current or lagged quarter.

Using the example of our three countries, we can see in Tables 3.13, 3.14, and 3.15 that the coefficient of the output-gap variable is higher than that of the unemployment rate (5 times higher in Japan and the United Kingdom, eight times higher in the United States). In all models, the ARCH components are sufficient to capture the volatility. In Japan and the United States, food prices, energy prices and output prices in emerging countries were factors that mitigated price volatility. In all three countries, inflation has a persistent component captured here by the autoregressive coefficient (Table 3.16).

3.3.4 Directions of the Current Literature on Phillips Curves

Phillips curve analysis at the macroeconomic level is a hot topic in the current literature. We gather here some key ideas and provide some references to the reader who would be interested to work on this topic.

The most debated topic in recent years has been the weakening of the link between inflation and unemployment. The most widely discussed hypothesis is that of econometric measurement error. For example, our measures of the output gap are flawed, because we do not take into account the influence of the financial cycle, of changes in demographic structure. Another much-debated hypothesis concerns the role of expectations. Today's Phillips curve would look like the original one (and not the accelerationist version of the monetarists). The reason is that industrialized countries have been in a low-inflation regime for several decades. When inflation evolves below a certain threshold, the expectations of the private sector do not change (the new inflation rates observed do not modify their expectations). Consequently, in a regime of low inflation, there is a link between the inflation rate and the output gap, whereas this link is tenuous when inflation expectations are a determinant of the Phillips curve (see, e.g., in the case of the United States, Jorgensen and Lansing (2021), and for a complete study of a large number of countries, Blanchard 2016). Some authors believe that the flattening of the Phillips curve can be explained above all by the phenomenon of job polarization, which has been one of the major structural changes in the labor markets of advanced countries over the last 20 years. This phenomenon is particularly accentuated during economic recessions. Regressions must therefore take into account the composition of employment: fixed-term contracts, temporary work, self-employment, piece-rate jobs, and so on. For an illustration in the European case, see, for example, Siena and Zago (2021).

Work has been done on non-linear models of the Phillips curve. This assumption of non-linearity has several interpretations. Some authors see it as a consequence of structural changes involving a temporal variation of the coefficients. However, these changes go unnoticed when the econometricians run their regressions assuming that the slopes are constant. For example, Albuquerque and Baumann (2017) show in the US case that a Phillips curve with variable coefficients reveals strong links between inflation and unemployment, in a regression that includes lagged inflation, inflation expectations and supply shocks as other explanatory variables. Another explanation is that the elasticity of inflation to unemployment depends on the level of the unemployment rate. It is high when unemployment is high, and low when it is low. Other authors think that this elasticity varies with the level of inflation (this is the anchored expectations thesis). There are many papers on non-linear Phillips curves. For some works, see Albuquerque and Baumann (2017), Nailewaik (2016), Doser et al. (2017), Forbes et al. (2021), Speiner (2014), and the many references in these papers.

The question of the endogeneity of the variables describing the slack in the labor market or activity is also the subject of recent work. Bad instrumental variables for the unemployment rate and the output gap can produce an inversion of the sign of the slope of the Phillips curve. The question of the right instruments is still the subject of much debate. A first approach is usually to add variables capturing supply shocks (commodity inflation, exchange rates, or monetary policy variables) to the equations. Another approach is to use the instrumental variables method. But the choice of instruments is based on the modelers' a priori. An alternative is to use semi-structural or structural models instead. For an overview of the discussion, Dovi et al. (2021).

A burgeoning literature is devoted to pandemic inflation. Questions are being raised about the resumption of inflation in industrialized countries after several decades of low inflation. The lockdown measures had two effects. They were a supply shock following the supply disruptions, and a demand shock due to the global recession. In the rich countries, the combination of weak demand and falling output kept inflation low. But as the crisis ended, the recovery in aggregate demand combined with bottleneck effects led to a resumption of inflationary pressures. The price movements observed during and after the pandemic therefore have a significant headline inflation component, although it is not clear whether the increases are temporary or permanent (see Ha et al. 2021). Forbes et al. (2021) explain the global inflation of the pandemic period by a combination of global factors (exchange rate changes, global economic recovery, commodity price pressures) and non-linearities effects reflected by the fact that inflation at the end of a health crisis reacts much more strongly than it decreases when output falls below potential.

The literature has also turned to the study of country-specific Phillips curves. We thus find the names "Euro area Phillips curve," "Japanese Phillips curve," and so on. The aim is to take into account idiosyncratic factors (the "slack" variables—output gap, unemployment rate) which do not have the same effects on inflation from one country to another. But it is also a question of differentiating the effects of global factors from one zone to another. For the Eurozone, the papers try to explain the phenomena of missing disinflation and missing inflation (understanding why inflation is less reactive to recessions and economic expansions), as well as the higher volatility of headline inflation over the last decade—even if core inflation has remained below the ECB's target.) According to the conclusions of this work, the fall in inflation after 2008 was offset by factors outside the euro zone, while the period of missing inflation was mainly explained by domestic slacks, the pass-through from wages to prices, and the anchoring of short- to medium-term inflation expectations. See, among others, Ball and Mazumder (2021), Bordes and Clerc (2007), Eser et al. (2019), Moretti et al. (2019), Jarocinski and Lenza (2018), Bobeica and Sokal (2019). Smith (2008) and Nishizaki et al. (2014) show that the Phillips curve perfectly explains the high unemployment rates and the very low inflation rates in Japan since the mid-1990s. In particular, Japan's chronic deflation episodes can be explained when the following variables are introduced into the Phillips curve: lower inflationary and growth expectations, output gaps that remain negative for a long time, lower import prices, a higher exchange rate, a continuous deterioration of potential output, and a lower natural rate of interest of the economies (i.e., the low rate of return on capital).

3.4   THE SECULAR STAGNATION HYPOTHESIS

3.4.1   How to Characterize Secular Stagnation?

For the past three decades or so, industrialized countries have been experiencing a combination of three phenomena: (a) low potential growth or trend GDP, (b) low nominal and real interest rates and (c) low core inflation levels. Over the last 30 years, potential growth has fallen from the high levels observed during the 30 glorious years, or when capitalism was booming at the end of the nineteenth century and the beginning of the twentieth century until 1914, and then during the inter-war period.

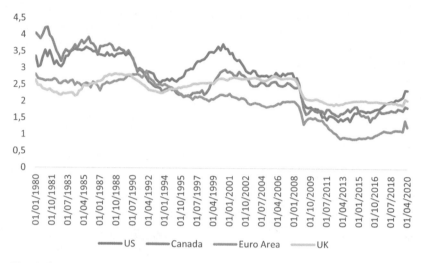

Fig. 3.5   Potential growth: US, Canada, Euro area, UK

Figures 3.5 and 3.6 were produced from data constructed by Holston et al. (2017) and regularly updated. These are potential growth and output gaps since 1980, for the United States, Canada, the Eurozone and the United Kingdom.[2] Figure 3.5 shows that potential growth evolves along a downward trend. And we also see declines in levels with two turning points: the early 1990s and 2008/2009, that is, years where major shocks had an impact on growth and GDP. In the 1990s, the world experienced a recession triggered by the Gulf crisis and soaring oil prices, not to mention the ERM currency crisis in Europe. 2008 is the year of the Great financial crisis. It is as if each major crisis slows down the medium-/long-term growth trajectory. Figure 3.6 shows that, with the exception of the United Kingdom, output gaps take time to close when they are either negative or positive, as was the case throughout the decade from the 2000s until the financial crisis.

---

[2] There are multiple ways to calculate GDP and potential growth, as well as output gaps. One can use statistical filters, like the HP filter. One can also use structural models. The series used here are derived from a semi-structural Holsten-Laubach-William model of secular stagnation.

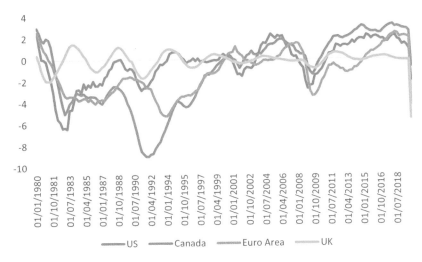

Fig. 3.6 Output gap: US, Canada, Euro area, UK

We have previously documented the long decline in interest rates. In the previous chapter, we said that a number of economists believe that interest rates are driven by the natural rate of interest of the economies, which has not stopped falling. We will see later that econometric estimates of this rate are negative. We have also seen that underlying inflation has experienced a long downward trend and that advanced capitalist economies are now evolving in a regime with low growth rates.

The combination of these two phenomena gives the following result. The economies' natural interest rate is the real interest rate that would be observed if they were operating at full production capacity, that is, if they were close to full employment. When potential growth is low, this rate becomes negative. This means that in order to get out of situations of lasting stagnation, it would be necessary to bring the real interest rate down to the level of the natural rate. But one can understand why this is difficult. Indeed, if nominal rates are already at very low levels, it is difficult to bring them down further. And if, in addition, disinflationary pressures are strong, then real interest rates cannot fall either. This is one reason for the change in approach to monetary policy. Instead of retaining an instrument that no longer works—the nominal interest rate—it is more interesting to use quantitative policies that target the monetary base directly, with a hope to activate the money multiplier.

We have previously documented the long decline in interest rates. In the previous chapter, we said that some economists believe that interest rates are driven by the natural rate of interest, which has not stopped falling since several decades. We have also seen that underlying inflation has experienced a long downward trend and that advanced capitalist economies are now evolving in a regime with low growth rates.

The interpretation of the phenomenon of secular stagnation leads to several interpretations. Some economists believe that it is a proven structural phenomenon that is part of the long term and reflects changes in the mode of regulation of industrialized economies: secular stagnation due to supply, that is, linked to the productive capacity of economies and aging population, secular stagnation due to the weakness of aggregate demand. On the other hand, some economists interpret what is happening as something transitory. The "optimists" put forward Schumpeter-like interpretations, based on the concept of creative destruction. The "pessimists" believe that secular stagnation heralds the entry into a new growth regime for several centuries to come.

As for supply-side explanations, we saw in the previous chapter what a demographic slowdown, a slowdown in productivity gains, and a deterioration in human capital can produce on economic growth. The paper by Gordon (2015) summarizes the main ideas. The author links secular stagnation to a global phenomenon that he describes as "socioeconomic decay." See also the references in Chap. 2. If productivity gains slow down for a long time, then the so-called Baumol's disease occurs, that is, excess costs in sectors where productivity is growing slowly. Firms must therefore lay off workers, which degrades human capital and opens a vicious circle of continuous productivity decline.

Economists who emphasize demand factors have a more Keynesian interpretation. Indeed, they analyze secular stagnation as a situation of durable underemployment of production factors. We find ideas that are already familiar. One is that lasting involuntary unemployment can occur because of an excess of supply in the goods market (or, equivalently, excessive aggregate net savings, or low capacity utilization rates), even if prices and wages are perfectly flexible. The other idea is that supply does not create its own demand, so there is no reason why, ex ante, savings should equal investment. Secular stagnation occurs when economies are

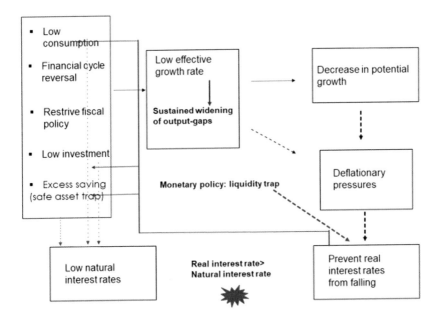

Fig. 3.7 Demand factors of secular stagnation

drawn into a vicious circle of weak aggregate demand. Figure 3.7 provides a summary of how this can happen.

On the side of those who interpret secular stagnation as a temporary phenomenon we find the Schumpeterian. See the previous chapter for references on the analysis of the effects of innovation and technological progress on long-term growth. Their analysis is interesting. Historically, we observe that it usually takes at least two decades between the birth of new innovations and their positive effect on medium-term growth. Between two technological revolutions, there is a transition phase characterized by a productivity crisis (changes in the production system and reorganization in companies). This is a normal phase for benefiting from new productivity gains. For example, the fall in the Solow residual observed during the 1970s and 1980s corresponded to the entry into a new economy, the reality of which was not seen until the end of the 1990s (which corresponds to the rise of the user and producer sectors of the ICTs: Internet, microprocessors, lasers, optical fiber, satellite technologies). If we go back further in time,

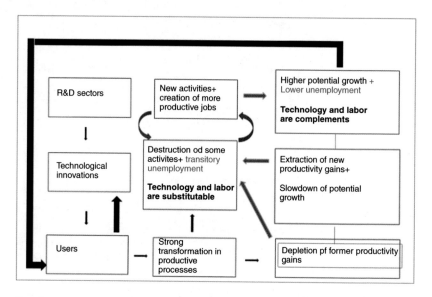

Fig. 3.8 Secular stagnation and the process of creative destruction

between the innovations of the eighteenth and nineteenth centuries, between 1870 and 1900, and the exploitation and the industrial boom, there were about 30 years. Today we are living a new transition with major innovations: digital, robotics, nanotechnologies, automation, and so on. If we place their start at the beginning of the 2000s, their diffusion on a large scale among users could be realized around 2030. There is therefore no secular stagnation, but rather a phase of creative destruction with changes in production processes, consumption patterns and the use of technology.

Figure 3.8 shows how the phenomenon of secular stagnation can be analyzed as a phenomenon of creative destruction. For the Schumpeterian, it is the motor of capitalism. This vision is part of a long-wave view in which what is interpreted—wrongly—as stagnation corresponds to a period of maturation of a new long technological cycle.

Finally, some economists interpret secular stagnation as reflecting the end of the current growth regime. Capitalism generates forces that wear it down and destroy it. The solution is then that of "degrowth," imperative to start a rapid reversal and change of direction of our modes of production and consumption. We can achieve a new growth rates under several conditions: (i) move toward new productive systems (ecological transition), (ii) modify corporate governance to recover the link between financial cycles and productive investments, and (iii) implement economic policies that support long-term growth (innovation). In the second part of the book, we address the issue of sustainable growth.

Beyond theoretical interpretations, there is an extensive empirical literature on natural rates and potential growth rates. The reader can consult the references in Brand et al. (2021) for an overview. The literature continues to grow. In a recent paper Dufrénot et al. (2022) have proposed to extend the concept of natural rate to the whole yield curve and construct a measure of the neutral yield curve gap for Japan. The idea is to take into account not only short rates, but all yields. The authors show that monetary and fiscal policies have been ineffective in bringing real rates below the natural rate at all maturities. Rungcharoenkitkul and Winkler (2021) proposes a measure based on the beliefs of central bankers and the private sector. Private sector agents interpret any expansive monetary policy as a signal that the unobservable natural rate has fallen or is falling, which they associate with poor economic conditions. They therefore have bearish expectations about the future growth rate and reduce their spending accordingly. For its part, the central bank, which observes the fall in aggregate demand, interprets it as confirmation that the interest rate has fallen. It then cuts its interest rate. So there is a learning feedback mechanism that works in the wrong direction.

The interested reader will find regularly updated measures of the natural interest rate for various industrialized countries online. Holston et al. (2017) propose such estimates based on a semi-structural model that includes, in addition to an aggregate demand and supply function, state variables—those that are unobservable such as the level of potential output and potential growth. In their model, one obtains a joint estimate of the natural rate, the output gap and potential growth (on the website of the New York Federal Reserve). Lubik and Matthes (2015) also offers online estimates on the website of the Richmond Federal Reserve. Their methodology is different from the previous authors. They rely on a time-varying parameter VAR model with stochastic volatility. Their approach is purely empirical and has no theoretical foundation.

3.4.2   Some Theoretical Models of Secular Stagnation

The Farmer and Platonov Model: The Role of Pessimistic Beliefs (See Farmer and Platonov 2016)

The authors want to highlight the role of financial markets as the engine of secular stagnation. However, their approach is different from Minsky-style models, where irrational animal spirits generate a strong instability of the financial cycle and negatively impact economic growth. Their model challenges one of the assumptions of New-Keynesian models, which explain the occurrence of long-term unemployment by price rigidity phenomena. The authors substitute a belief function and a no-labor condition for the New-Keynesian Phillips curve. It is not downward price rigidities that cause lasting unemployment. Rather, they argue, it is the beliefs— or expectations—that actors make about the probability that financial markets will move in the future in a bullish or bearish phase (because these expectations have an implication on the expectations they make about the evolution of their wealth). These expectations are therefore completely rational. They have no reason to be irrational as long as agents use their current observations to project themselves into the future. Indeed, in a sluggish economy, or if growth is low, it is rational to think that stock market assets will follow a downward trend in the future.

Their theoretical models rely on the following framework. Generations of households follow one another, each living through two periods. Young people work, consume and invest in three assets: money, a physical asset, capital, whose services they rent to a firm and pocket an annuity and an underground bond that yields a certain interest rate. When they become old, they sell the capital and the money to the next generation. The utility function is logarithmic (with labor no causing disutility) and they use a Cobb-Douglas production function with capital and labor as inputs.

At steady state equilibrium, their model is summarized by the following three equations:

$$IS: \frac{1-\alpha}{1+\beta+\delta}\left(\beta - \frac{\delta}{i_t}\right)Y_t = \Theta_t, \quad \Theta_t = E_t\left[\frac{P_{K,t+1}}{P_{t+1}}\right], \tag{3.35}$$

$$LM: \frac{M_t}{P_t} = \frac{(1-\alpha)\delta}{1+\beta+\delta}\frac{(1+i_t)}{i_t}Y_t, \tag{3.36}$$

$$NAC: i_t = \frac{\alpha Y_t}{\Theta_t}. \tag{3.37}$$

with the following definitions of the variables:

- $(1-\alpha)$: elasticity of output to employment in the production function,
- β: discount factor in the household's utility function,
- δ: coefficient of real money balance in the household's utility function,
- Y, i Output and return to sovereign bond,
- M/P: real money balance
- Θ: belief function,
- P_K: price of capital,
- P: general level of prices.

Equation (3.35) is obtained from the saving function. It can be seen that i and Y vary in the same direction (the IS curve is upward sloping in the (Y, i) space). It also depends on Θ A decrease in Θ (more pessimistic expectations) moves the IS curve upward or to the left. Equation (3.36) is the equation of the demand for real money. It is also upward sloping in the (Y, i) space. Equation (3.37) is obtained from a no-arbitrate equation saying that the young are indifferent between investing in capital and bonds. This curve has also a positive slope.

The authors show that, with a Cobb-Douglas production function and a logarithmic utility function, the steady state is uniquely determined. A negative shock on Θ reflects a situation where households anticipates a future decrease of their financial wealth, because they anticipate lower relative financial prices. This leads them to reduce their consumption, which reduces output and shifts the IS curve to the left. At the same time, they sell assets, which lower prices—their expectations are therefore self-fulfilling) and this rises the interest rate. This in turn increases saving. The NAC curve also shits upward. Since output decreases, the demand for real money balance decreases and the price level must be higher in the new steady state. In addition to the study of comparative static, the author show that their model displays dynamic indeterminacy. In all cases, secular stagnation is caused by pessimistic expectations about the future evolution of financial asset prices.

Farmer and Platonov's arguments have not received the attention they deserve. Indeed, one consequence of what they say is that the way out of a situation of secular stagnation does not necessarily lie in vigorous fiscal policies (even if this idea is very popular today in economic policy circles), but in policies that reduce the runaway nature of the financial cycle in order to prevent economic agents from losing a lot of their financial wealth when prices fall sharply.

Chronically Low Natural Interest Rates in Overlapping Generations Models

Secular stagnation has been investigated through one of its consequences, that is, the chronically low level of the natural interest rate, that is, the real interest rate observed when the economy is at full employment and the output gap is 0. In the previous chapter, we presented the overlapping generations models of Eggertsson (2014). Others models in a similar framework have been proposed by Eggertsson (2010), Eggertsson et al. (2019).

The key results obtained from these models are the following.

In such models, secular stagnation is a situation illustrating a long-lasting underemployment equilibrium with a negative natural interest rate. This equilibrium occurs because of excessive net savings. Low potential growth prevents investment from recovering, and central banks find it difficult to stimulate aggregate demand by lowering the real interest rate to the level of the natural interest rate, due to a strong disinflationary (or even deflationary) regime. What causes the most disagreement among economists today is the fact that the equilibrium interest rate is negative. Those who contest this hypothesis criticize both the empirical assumptions—such as the fact that the output gap is measured incorrectly—and logical inconsistency of the New-Keynesian models of secular stagnation.

Some examples of such models are OLG models linking secular stagnation to a theory of negative natural interest rates. The authors' vision is influenced by a Wicksellian reading of monetary policy. They assume the existence of real interest rate corresponding to a situation of full employment. And, a key role is played by central banks's policy nominal rates, which are modified in such a way that the real rate reaches the natural rate.

If the natural rate of interest is too low or negative, it may be difficult for a central bank to cut its nominal rate so that the observed real rate reaches the natural rate. This happens both because of the zero lower bound (the nominal policy is constrained to be negative) and because economies evolves in a low inflation regime. The other important point concerns the path followed by the natural rate. It is possible that despite a prolonged decline in the natural rate, unemployment will not fall. The reason is as follows.

Consider the simple case of a demand shock caused by a financial crisis, such as bursting bubbles. The collapse of financial asset prices causes wealth and balance sheet effects that lead households and firms to deleverage. It is the prolonged deleveraging that follows the crisis that leads the economy into a deep recession (as the private sector sharply reduces its spending in order to deleverage). But deleveraging causes a vicious circle. Indeed, it implies an increase in future savings and thus an excessive supply of savings which continues to depress demand and keeps the real interest rate low.

This dynamic is aggravated when aggregate demand is weakened by strong inequalities, overly restrictive fiscal policies, slowing population growth, and falling investment prices.

In a flexible price regime, if the natural interest rate is too negative, it cannot be "caught up" by the real interest rates observed. Even if a large inflationary shock were to occur, the negative repercussions on demand would push the economy into a lasting recession. Wage flexibility worsens the fall in output.

If wages are downward rigid, we get several paradoxes. The first is the thrift paradox. In a crisis, private savings increase, which reduces spending and aggregate output. Eventually, aggregate savings fall. The second paradox is the paradox of toil: a positive demand shock reduces current output. The exit from a regime of secular stagnation is facilitated by very expansionary fiscal policies, or by monetary policies where central banks raise their inflation target.

We now present some examples of secular stagnation models from which these results are obtained.

The Eggertsson-Mehrotra-Summers Model (see Eggertsson et al. 2016)

In the previous chapter, we saw that models à la Eggertsson-Summers allow to define an equilibrium interest rate by taking into account households' life cycle, demographic factors and the wealth structure of young and old generations. Here, we analyze secular stagnation equilibria using the reduced forms of such models.

The economic equilibrium is described by three equations: IS curve, Taylor rule and aggregate supply equations.

The IS equation is represented by the equality between the supply of financial capital and the demand for financial capital.

The demand for financial capital is equal to the sum of the budget deficit and private investment. For simplicity, we assume that revenues are zero and that investment varies negatively with the interest rate. The demand for financial capital is written:

$$DFC = -\alpha(i - \pi) + \delta G, \quad \alpha > 0, \quad \delta > 0,$$

where DFC means demand for financial capital, i is the nominal interest rate, G is public spending, π is inflation rate.

The supply of financial capital is the sum of domestic savings, global external balance (trade balance plus capital and financial account balance), the loans received from abroad by foreign investors holding a fraction of the domestic country's sovereign bonds and the loans received by the governments from domestic agents who also hold a share of domestic sovereign bonds. For simplicity, we assume that private consumption equals imports and that the financial inflows in the BOP financial accounts are portfolio investment and FDI. We define the supply of financial capital as follows:

$$SFC = Y + Xq + \omega K^* - \theta(B^g - IR),$$

where SFC denotes the supply of financial capital, X denotes exports and q is the real exchange rate (an increase means an appreciation of the domestic currency, K^* is capital inflows (portfolio investment and FDI), IR denotes international reserves (foreign investors lend in foreign currency which increases the country's liabilities to foreigners), B^g is the value of sovereign bonds.

Equalizing DFC and SFC, we get the IS curve:

$$Y = -\alpha(i - \pi) + \delta G - Xq - \omega K^* + \theta(B^g - IR) + \epsilon,$$
$$K = \bar{K}^* + \eta(R - R^*). \tag{3.38}$$

ϵ is added for demand shock variables. A central assumption of the model is that the real interest rate is higher than the natural interest rate of the economy: $R = i - \pi > R^n$. Capital inflows depends on an exogenous components and interest rate differentials (a $*$ in Eq. 3.38 represent the foreign country).

Monetary policy is described by an interest rate rule subject to the ZLB constraint. The central bank targets an inflation rate $\bar{\pi}$:

$$i = \max\left\{0, R^n + \bar{\pi} + \phi_\pi(\pi - \bar{\pi})\right\}, \quad \pi > 1. \tag{3.39}$$

R^n is the natural interest rate observed when $\pi = \bar{\pi}$ and $Y = Y^f$, where Y^f corresponds to full-employment output gap.

The aggregate demand function AD is obtained by combining Eqs. (3.38) and (3.39). This curve is non-linear and has a kink, due to the ZLB constraint. Indeed, we have:

$$Y = \begin{cases} \alpha(1 - \phi_\pi)\pi + A + B, & \text{if } i \geq 0, \ \text{Regime AD1}, \\ \alpha\pi + B, & \text{if } i < 0, \ \text{Regime AD2}. \end{cases} \qquad (3.40)$$

where

$$A = -\alpha(R^n + \bar{\pi} + \phi_\pi\bar{\pi}), \quad B = \delta G - Xq - \omega K^* + \theta(B^g - IR) + \epsilon.$$

If $\phi > 1$ and $\alpha > 0$ AD has a positive slope for negative values of i. This non-linearity is the source of secular stagnation equilibria. The positive slope is explained by the fact that the central bank can no longer use to adjust its nominal interest rate below zero. A drop in inflation raises real interest rates and lowers output.

The aggregate supply function is defined as follows. When output reaches its potential level, it does not depend on the inflation rate and is vertical. On the other hand, below the potential, there is a positive correlation between inflation and unemployment. The authors consider the illustration of an economy where lower production costs allow firms to improve their output. There is a deflationary regime—a fall in the price level—where they can increase their production capacity and productive efficiency. However, when they can no longer do so, they are already producing at full capacity and prices are rise (inflation is positive):

$$Y = \begin{cases} Y^f, & \text{if } \pi \geq 0, \qquad \text{Regime AS1}, \\ \kappa\pi, & \text{if } \pi < 0, \ \kappa > 0, \ \text{Regime AS2}. \end{cases} \qquad (3.41)$$

The supply curve therefore also has a kink at the point where inflation is zero.

A secular stagnation equilibrium occurs when the real interest rate corresponding to full employment is sufficiently negative so that the nominal interest rate hit the ZLB ($R^n + \bar{\pi} < 0$), and production is below potential ($Y < Y^f$). Combining Regime AS2 in Eq. (3.41) and Regime

AD2 in Eq. (3.40) at $\pi = \bar{\pi}$, we obtain

$$\hat{\pi} = \frac{B}{\kappa - \alpha}, \quad \hat{Y} = \alpha\hat{\pi}, \quad R^n < \bar{\pi}. \tag{3.42}$$

$\hat{Y}$ and $\hat{\pi}$ are respectively production and inflation at equilibrium. A decrease in government spending G decreases B, hence reduces $\hat{\pi}$ and $\hat{Y}$. An increase in exports, capital inflows, or foreign purchases of sovereign securities has the opposite effect on output and the equilibrium inflation rate. This basic model can be extended to study other effects. For example, deflationary shocks (e.g., an increase in labor productivity or a decrease in wages) prevent the exit from a secular stagnation because they increase the real interest rate. It is output that adjusts downward. To get out of it, you need an aggressive fiscal policy. When you take into account the dynamics of public debt, the public debt needed to finance public spending is sustainable because the interest rate is negative.

Secular Stagnation and Balance Sheet Effects

A prolonged recession can occur when, following financial crises, bubbles burst and force companies and households to deleverage. A cut in the central bank's policy rate has little effect on spending, as the private sector is forced to deleverage to regain liquidity on their balance sheets. In the event of widespread deleveraging, an economy can become trapped in a vicious cycle of debt-deflation. This was highlighted by Koo (2011) and formalized by Eggertsson and Krugman (2012).

These authors describe an economy composed of impatient and patient agents. They have different rates of preference for the present. The former borrow from the latter and face a debt ceiling that changes over time according to the evolution of financial asset prices. They are subject to "Minsky moments," reflected in waves of optimism and pessimism and self-fulfilling prophecies. During reversals in financial cycles, the debt ceiling falls. To restore balance sheet liquidity, borrowers reduce their consumption. But the fall in prices increases the real value of their debts. This forces them to accelerate their deleveraging. A vicious circle of debt-deflation is set in motion, leading to prolonged recessions and deep depressions.

A simple formalization of these mechanisms is as follows.

The output gap depends on aggregate consumption obtained by combining the consumption of two types of agents: borrowers (C_t^b) and savers (C_t^s):

$$Y_t - \bar{Y} = \Xi_s \hat{C}_t^s + (1 - \Xi_s)\hat{C}_t^b, \tag{3.43}$$

where Ξ is the proportion of savers. Consumption is expressed as per capita and as a deviation from potential output $\bar{Y}$. A variable topped by a hat symbolizes this gap. $Y_t - \bar{Y}$ is the output gap.

The model also includes a New-Keynesian Phillips curve and an interest rate rule with a ZLB constraint:

$$\pi_t = \kappa(Y_t - \bar{Y}) + E_{t-1}\pi_t, \tag{3.44}$$

where π_t is inflation rate at time t, and $E_{t-1}\pi_t$ is inflation expectation made at time $t-1$ for time t. The coefficient κ depends on the fraction of monopolistic competitive firms that leave their prices unchanged for a certain time.

The interest rate rule is written

$$i_t = max\left\{0, R_t^n + \phi_\pi \pi_t\right\}, \ \phi_\pi > 1. \tag{3.45}$$

R_t^n is the natural interest rate.

Borrowers and savers set their consumption by maximizing an intertemporal utility function subject to resource constraints (for details, see Eggertsson and Krugman 2012). The linearized Euler equation of the savers, at steady state equilibrium, is written:

$$\hat{C}_S^s = \hat{C}_L^s - \sigma(i_S - \pi_L - \bar{R}), \tag{3.46}$$

and that of the borrowers is:

$$\hat{C}_S^b = \hat{Y}_s - \hat{D} + \gamma_D \pi_S - \gamma_D \beta(i_S - \pi_L - \bar{R}) \tag{3.47}$$

Lower subscripts S and L mean "short-term" and "long-term" equilibrium. The hat means that the variables are measured as deviation to potential output. σ is a parameter. γ_D is the debt ratio when output is at potential. $\bar{R}$ is the natural interest rate, observed when $Y = \bar{Y}$.

The short-term steady state equilibrium leads the following equations:

$$\hat{Y}_S = -\frac{\Xi_s \sigma + (1 - \Xi_s)\gamma_D \beta}{\Xi_s}\left(i_S - R_S^n\right),$$ (3.48)

$$R_S^n = \bar{R} - \frac{1 - \Xi_s}{\Xi_s \sigma(1 - \Xi_s)\gamma_D \beta}\hat{D} + \frac{\gamma_D}{\Xi_s \sigma(1 - \Xi_s)\gamma_D}\pi_S.$$ (3.49)

Equation (3.49) says that the natural interest is endogenous and varies according to the debt ratio $\hat{D}$ defined by $\hat{D} = (B^{\text{high}} - \bar{D})/\bar{Y}$. It can be interpreted as the level of debt overhang. A decrease in π_S reduces R_S^n.

Equation (3.48) is an IS curve. The AD curve is obtained by combining Eqs. (3.48), (3.49) and the interest rate rule at the steady state. It has a positive slope in case of a debt-deflation phenomenon. Low prices force borrowers to reduce consumption since the real value of debt increases. Savers do not change their consumption. When the economy is not in secular stagnation equilibrium, cutting the short-term interest rate boost savers' consumption (since they reduce their savings) and total production increases. since the latter implies higher income, borrowers' consumption in turn increases. This raises production and so forth. Assuming that deflationary shocks are unexpected ($E\bar{\pi} = 0$), the aggregate supply function at steady state is written: $\pi_S = \kappa \hat{Y}_S$. Combining Eqs. (3.48) and (3.49) we obtain the output and inflation rate of the short-term stationary equilibrium, in the case where a deleveraging shock causes the interest rate to fall to zero and the natural interest rate becomes negative. The economy then falls into a trap of chronic deflation and long lasting recession:

$$\hat{Y}_S = \Gamma - \frac{1 - \Xi_s}{\Xi_s \sigma(1 - \Xi_s)\gamma_D \kappa}\hat{D} < 0,$$ (3.50)

$$\pi_S = \kappa \Gamma - \frac{1 - \Xi_s}{\Xi_s \sigma(1 - \Xi_s)\gamma_D \kappa}\hat{D} < 0.$$ (3.51)

where Γ is a function of the coefficients $\Xi_S, \sigma, \gamma_D, \bar{R}$.

Other Theoretical Models of Secular Stagnation

Other models of secular stagnation have been proposed in the literature. The concept of stagnation traps is introduced by Benigno and Fornaro

(2018). The authors explain secular stagnation by the coexistence of a liquidity trap, very weak growth due to low aggregate demand and a low investment rate, but also pessimistic expectations of future growth by economic agents.

Secular stagnation has also been studied as a cause of growing inequalities. Jackson (2019) proposes a model in which a limit to exponential growth comes from the combination of creeping inequality and the gap between the evolution of productivity and wages. The novelty of his analysis is that these inequalities come from the strategy of growth at all costs, whereas the evolution of incomes should be adapted to a regime of low growth considered as the "new normal," if only because there are natural limits to economic growth. An important argument in the literature is that inequalities create negative externalities that are harmful to growth: social conflict, rent-seeking behavior, poverty, capital concentration, and under-investment in human capital (see Pichelman 2015 for a review of the arguments). There are thus effects on supply and productive capacity that can explain weak growth regimes.

The interested reader can refer to Lo and Rogoff (2015)'s survey, where the authors review all the arguments put forward in theoretical models to explain secular stagnation: weak demand, debt overhang, demographic factors, political fragmentation, and so on.

3.5 IMPLICATIONS ON HOW TO TEACH MACROECONOMICS

What we have studied here has implications for how we teach and study the aggregate supply function. How can we realistically describe the relationship between inflation and activity? And for what purpose? The objectives are usually the following: (a) to motivate the non-neutrality of monetary policy by an assumption of price rigidity; (b) to highlight the persistence of inflation, so as to understand that monetary shocks have progressive inflationary/disinflationary effects; and (c) to show that there is indeed a trade-off between inflation and unemployment, in the sense that disinflation policies are not costless—they generally produce recessions. On the first aspect, the standard New-Keynesian Phillips curve approach is based on the Calvo explanation of rigidities. In this type of model, inflation is persistent only if output is governed by a persistent process. There are several ways of introducing the influence of past prices. The first is to consider that workers negotiate on real—and not nominal—wages, which leads to assumptions about price expectations. The second is to assume that firms use backward-looking pricing rules with adaptive expectations to set their real marginal cost. A third way is to assume that firms revise their prices in a context of imperfect information.

One way to present the aggregate supply curve to students without excessive and unnecessary complication is as follows.

The first important point is the determination of output levels and/or the long-run unemployment rate. These ("natural") levels are not fixed, nor even unique, but vary over time. It is therefore important to present some theoretical models whose reduced forms show the existence of hysteresis effects. As we have seen, such models have existed since the 1980s and are based on the presentation of price and wage determination strategies. We can also present recent theoretical models where the natural interest rate is co-determined with potential growth and potential unemployment rate. The determination of long-term output and unemployment is the first step in the reasoning, because output gaps/unemployment gaps trigger inflationary or deflationary pressures.

The second important point is: what is the right formulation of the supply curve, accelerationist or level? The answer depends on the nature of expectations. If they are adaptive, then the pressures are in the form of an acceleration or deceleration of prices. If expectations are anchored, then output gaps lead to higher or lower levels of inflation.

In macroeconomics courses, we cannot ignore the presentation of specific growth regimes, such as secular stagnation equilibria. It is now easier to understand the context in which the accumulation of capital (physical and financial) can impact investment and savings, the effects of which, although positive in principle, can be counteracted: the existence of a ZLB constraint in a low-inflation regime, a domestic or international saving glut, a very low marginal net rate of return on capital, forced deleveraging by private agents, and rising inequalities. The literature, both theoretical and empirical, devoted to these subjects has become voluminous.

Finally, we need to incorporate modern developments on the Phillips curve into our macroeconomic courses. This implies in particular to take into account three facts.

First, students need to be aware that there are two types of inflation. One is for non-financial, non-monetary assets. This is the one that macroeconomists were primarily interested in until recently. The second concerns the evolution of financial asset prices. This inflation and the first one are mutually dependent. We can say that inflation has become a financial phenomenon.

Second, even if the level of analysis of macroeconomics is aggregate, there is not one but many wages defined according to the type of job that workers find. The last quarter of the twentieth century and the beginning of the twenty-first century have been characterized by a fragmentation of labor markets that has affected the way wages are set. The strategies of negotiation of labor contracts by employees that are emphasized in the models represent only part of the reality.

Thirdly, many of the causes of domestic inflation rates are international. This is why financial globalization variables—real or financial—must be incorporated into the Phillips curves. The financial cycle should be presented as a determinant of real household wealth, which is an element, in addition to wages, that enters into the bargaining process.

Interested readers will find examples of what stylized models of macroeconomics might look like for students taking into account all that has been discussed here in several books. Romer (2000) is an excellent reference. The LM curve is replaced by a monetary policy rule that better reflects reality. Instead of prices, inflation becomes a key variable and changes are observed according to the gap between output and its potential level. Thus, demand shocks first cause changes in GDP, and only then do inflationary or deflationary pressures appear. This eliminates the simultaneity that exists between the price level and output in the usual IS/LM model. Readers can also consult the 8th edition of Olivier Blanchard's book (see Blanchard 2021). Of particular interest is the link between financial markets and aggregate supply and demand.

3.6   CONCLUSION

The renewal of the concepts of macroeconomics concerning hysteresis effects, the business cycle and inflation are the subject of intense debate among economists.

If we consider the debate on hysteresis, in addition to the concepts of super-hysteresis presented in this chapter, we can mention a recent new concept which is reverse hysteresis, that is, a situation in which a positive demand shock has persistent effects in the medium/long term. Giradi et al. (2020) study the effects of a hundred or so demand expansions in OECD countries since 1960 and showed that these were the source of positive hysteresis effects on the participation rate, the capital stock and GDP. One of the explanations for this phenomenon is a change of vision of what impulse-propagation mechanisms are for economies. Macroeconomists are used to Frisch-Slutsky type dynamics, where shocks propagate in a system whose job is to diffuse them, absorb them and gradually make them disappear (we are used to reasoning about stationary systems). However, the mechanisms of propagation of shocks can cause regime changes; that is, the shocks move the equilibrium states (they are not mean-reverting). In this context, our job is to explain what explains these multiple equilibria: the state of technology, demographic cycles, inequality, the financial cycle, structural transformations of labor markets, and so on. What this shows is that macroeconomists are increasingly interested in structural phenomena and not only in short-term macroeconomic stabilization.

An illustration is the debates that arise from the use of the Phillips curve to understand the trade-off between inflation and unemployment. One of the major facts is the lower sensitivity of the rate of change of prices to the indicator of tension in the labor market. The Phillips curve is less steep. This probably reflects deep structural changes, including the strong dependence of domestic inflation on non-domestic factors, the atomization of labor markets, the change in corporate governance that has made real sector inflation dependent on financial asset price inflation, the change in the orientation of inflation expectations, and the disappearance of the price-wage loop.

The issue of secular stagnation continues raising questions. A distinction must be made between criticisms of the internal consistency of the models and criticisms of the assumptions of mainstream models. The first type of criticism consists in questioning the "fidelity" of the frameworks to the theoretical schools of thought to which they refer. The Eggerts-son/Summers models are criticized for not being in line with Keynes's thinking by representing the economy as a market of loanable funds and by forgetting that savings depend on income and investment on the rate of profit. See, for example, Di Bucchianico (2020), Levrero (2021). The second type of criticism concerns, as we have seen, the causes of secular stagnation. Those who make these criticisms describe mainstream models as orthodox. By orthodox, they mean "neoclassical." In fact, the ideas developed in the New-Keynesian models are rather close to the ideas of the classical economists of the 1950s: Pigou, Haberler, Mills, and Scitovsky in the 1950s. After having been opposed by Keynes during the Great Depression, these ideas had made a strong comeback during the period of the 30 glorious years. But the context was not one of stagnation, but on the contrary of a strong expansion of economies in the midst of post-war reconstruction. The discussions focused on the question of the determinants of savings. The authors mentioned earlier took up the notion of the interest rate as a variable for adjusting savings and investment from the classical economists. But they considered that the interest rate had monetary and financial—not just real—determinants. Moreover, they highlighted the multiplicity of possible equilibria and the central role played by monetary policy in their selection. For an overview of these discussions, the interested reader can read Metzler (1951)'s paper.

The so-called mainstream models differ from the neoclassical models in that equilibrium interest rates can be negative. They should rather be called "Classical-Keynesian." The important point is to know why an economy can remain trapped in this type of equilibrium. One answer is that the natural interest rate is obtained at the intersection of two curves in the (i, Y) plane: a short-term IS curve, and a long-term supply curve when output is equal to its potential level. Therefore, every time the IS curve moves, the natural interest rate moves. In the case of a continuous fall in investment or consumption, it therefore moves continuously downward. And if prolonged recessionary regimes have an impact on potential GDP (i.e., if they cause it to fall), this further increases the fall in the natural rate of interest. The latter therefore depends on both the shifts in the IS curve and the growth rate of potential GDP.

There are therefore two questions to be answered. The first is whether the decline in the natural rate is explained by changes in the IS curve (demand factors), or by significant changes in potential output (supply factors). The second question is: Why do economies remain trapped in this type of equilibrium? The New-Keynesian models point to the ZLB and the fact that economic agents have anchored their inflation expectations at low levels. We have seen that other authors emphasize the need to correct imbalances that lead to excess net savings.

PIONEERS IN THE FIELD

Olivier Blanchard

Olivier Blanchard is a macroeconomist who has made major contributions to macroeconomic issues over the last 30 years. He contributes to current economic policy debates by proposing new ideas to adapt to recent changes in economies. For example, the attention to be paid to fiscal multipliers during periods of fiscal retrenchment; the important role of counter-cyclical policies; the opportunity for governments to take on debt to boost economic growth without fearing that public debt will become unsustainable when interest rates are far below growth rates; the possibility of taxing inheritance to reduce inequalities of opportunity between individuals, the central role of liquidity outside periods of crisis, the use of taxation to activate automatic multipliers during periods of crisis. He is an academic, but also an economic practitioner—he was Chief Economist of the IMF and has advised several governments on macroeconomic issues. He is one of the economists who have pointed out the need for the Eurozone to favour an approach to economic policies (especially fiscal policies) based on cooperation and coordination of decisions, rather than exclusively on rules. Reading his recent work on the Phillips curve, one might think that there is a low probability of a return to high structural inflation in the next few years. Unless commodity and energy prices continue to soar. And unless aggregate demand surges unexpectedly, which is unlikely.

Lawrence Summers

In 2013, he "resurrected" the concept of secular stagnation proposed by Hansen during the 1930s, suggesting that it can be used to characterize the evolution of industrialized economies since at least the last 20 years. His works aim to show that the slacks experienced by economies can last for a long time, or take time to improve. The consequence is that potential growth trajectories can slump durably and force real rates of return on capital (natural interest rates) to follow a downward path, and inflation to remain durably low. To get out of this situation, he proposes a return to a new old Keynesian

(continued)

economy, to get out of a regime of excess savings and insufficient aggregate demand.

Summers' contribution is mainly theoretical, and the overlapping generations models he and his co-authors proposed are a reference for understanding a phenomenon that neoclassical models generally exclude, that is, the possibility of having a negative equilibrium interest rate. The frameworks proposed by this author make this possible thanks to demand functions that are non-linear and positively sloped over a part of their portion. The novelty is that demand does not react in the "right" direction to changes in the interest rate.

Michel Aglietta

He is one of the French economists who have made major contributions in several recent fields of macroeconomics. He is interested in the transformations of capitalism over the long term, by studying the mutations of the monetary and financial systems. According to Aglietta, it is the developments in finance that make the breaking points in capitalism. He highlights the role of self-referential mechanisms at the origin of Minsky moments. It is the regular reversals of the private credit cycle and of asset prices that explain the phases of long recession. According to him, the preferred interpretation is that of a change in the modes of regulation since the beginning of the 1980s. These changes are both microeconomic and global. The shareholder governance of companies has had consequences on the evolution of investment, but also on the nature of inflation, which is no longer only real, but also financial. At the macroeconomic level, the decline in state intervention has modified social relations, leading to a number of phenomena: the detachment of wage and productivity trends, and the transformation of labor markets. Today, he participates as a key actor in the debate on secular stagnation in Europe.

REFERENCES

Albuquerque B, Baumann U (2017) Will US inflation awake from the dead? The role of slack and non-linearities in the Phillis curve. ECB Working Paper 2011

Backhouse RE, Boianovsky M (2016) Secular stagnation: the history of a macroeconomic heresy. Eur J Hist Econ Thought 23(6):946–970

Ball L, Mazumder S (2019) A Phillips curve with anchored expectations and short-term unemployment. J Mon Cred Bank 51(1):111–137

Ball L, Mazumder S (2021) A Phillips curve for the Euro area. Int Fin 24:2–17

Ball LM, Onken L (2021) Hysteresis in unemployment evidence from OECD estimates of the natural rate. NBER Working Paper 29343

Ball L, Leigh D, Loungani P (2017) Okun's law: fit at 50's? J Mon Cred Bank 49(7):1413–1441

Ball L, Furceri D, Leigh D, Loungani P (2019) Does one law fit all? Cross-country evidence on Okun law. Open Econ Rev 30(5):841–874

Benigno G, Fornaro L (2018) Stagnation traps. Rev Econ Stud 85(3):1425–1470

Blanchard K (2016) The changing curve: back to the 60's? Am Econ Rev Pap Proc 106(5):31–34

Blanchard O (2021) Macroeconomics, 8th edn. Pearson.

Blanchard OJ, Summers LH (1986) Hysteresis and the European unemployment problem. NBER Working Paper 1950

Blanchard O, Cerutti E, Summers L (2015) Inflation and activity. Two explorations and their monetary policy implications. IMF Working Paper 15/230

Bobeica E, Sokal A (2019) Drivers of underlying inflation in the euro area over time: a Phillips curveperspective. ECB Econ Bull 4:87–105

Bod'a M, Povazanová M (2021) Output-unemployment asymmetries in Okun coefficient for OECD countries. Econ Anal Pol 69:307–323

Bordes C, Clerc L (2007) Price stability and the ECB's monetary policy strategy. J Econ Surv 21(2):268–326

Brand T, Dufrénot G, Mayerowitz A (2021) A state-space model to estimate potential growth in the industrialized countries. In: Dufrénot G, Matsuki T (eds) Recent econometric techniques for macroeconomic and financial data. Springer, Berlin

Cerra V, Fatás A, Saxena SC (2020) Hysteresis and business cycle. IMF Working Paper 20/73

Clark P (1989) Trend reversion in real output and in employment. J Econ May:15–32

Compagnucci F, Gentili A, Valentini E, Gallegati M (2021) Have jobs and wages stopped rising? Productivity and structural change in advanced economies. Struct Change Econ Dyn 56:412–430

Di Bucchianico S (2020) Discussing secular stagnation: a case of freeing good ideas from the theoretical constraints? Struct Change Econ Dyn 55:288–297

Diebold F, Inoue A (2001) Long-memory and regime-switching. J Econ 105(1):131–159

Diebold F, Rudebusch G (1989) Long-memory and persistence in aggregate output. J Mon Econ 24:189–209

Dixon R, Lim GC, van Ours JC (2017) Revisitng the Okun relationship. Appl Econ 49(28):2748–2765

Doser A, Nunes RC, Rao N, Shcremirov V (2017) Inflation expectations and nonlinearities in the Phillips curve. Fed Res B Boston Working Paper 1711

Dovi M-S, Koester G, Nickel C (2021) Adressing the endogeneity of slack in Phillips curves. ECB Working Paper 2613

Dufrénot G, Rhouzlane M, Vaccaro-Grange E (2022) Potential growth and natural yield curve in Japan. J Int Mon Fin forthcoming

Eggertsson GB (2010) The paradox of tail. Fed. Res. B. NY, Staff Report, n°433

Eggertsson GB (2014) A model of secular stagnation. NBER Working Paper n°20574

Eggertsson GB, Krugman P (2012) Debt, delevaring and the liquidity trap: a Fisher-Minsky-Koo approach. Q J Econ 127(3):1469–1513

Eggertsson GB, Mehrotra NR, Summers LH (2016) Secular stagnation in the global economy. Am Econ Rev 106(5):503–507

Eggertsson GB, Mehrotra NR, Robbins JA (2019) A model of secular stagnation. Theory and quantitative evaluation. Am Econ J Macroecon 11(1):1–48

Eser F, Karadi P, Lane PR, Moretti L, Osbat C (2019) The Phillips curve at the ECB. Manchester Sch 2020 88(51):50–85

Fátas, A (2000) Endogenous growth and stochastic trends. J Mon Econ 45(1):107–128

Farmer RE, Platonov K (2016) Animal spirits in a monetary economy. CEPR discussion paper 11197

Forbes K, Gagnon JE, Collins CG (2021) Low inflation bends the Phillips curve around the world: extended results. PIIE Working Paper 21–15

Galí J (2015) Hysteresis and the European unemployment problem revisited. NBER Working Paper 21430

Giradi D, Paterni Meloni W, Stirati A (2020) Reverse hysteresis? Persistent effects of autonomous demand expansions. Can J Econ 44(4):835–869

Gordon RJ (2010) Okun's law and productivity innovations. Am Econ Rev Papers Proc 100:11–15

Gordon R (2015) Secular stagnation: a supply-side view. Am Econ Rev 105(5):54–59

Granger CWJ (1980) Long-memory relationships and the aggregation of dynamic models. J Econ 14:227–238

Guégan D (2005) How can we define the concept of long-memory? An econometric survey. Econ Rev 24(2):113–149

Ha J, Kose MA, Ohnsorge F (2021) Inflation during the pandemic: what happened? What is next? CEPR Disc. Pap. 16328

Haubrick JG, Lo AW (1989) The sources and nature of long-term memory in the business cycle. NBER Working Paper 2951

Holston K, Laubach T, Williams JC (2017) Measuring the natural rate of interest: international trends and determinants. J Int Econ 108(1):559–575

Jackson T (2019) The Post-growth challenge secular stagnation, inequality and the limits to growth. Ecol Econ 156:236–246

Jarocinski M, Lenza M (2018) An inflation predicting measure of the output gap in the euro area. J Mon Cred Bank 50:1189–1224

Jordá O, Schularick MMP, Taylor AM (2011) When credits bites back: leverage, business cycles and crises. NBER Working Paper 17621

Jorgensen PL, Lansing KL (2021) Anchored inflation expectations and the slope of the Phillips curve. FFRB S. Franc. Working Paper 2019-27

Koo R (2011) The world in balance sheet recession: causes, cure, and politics. R W Econ Rev 58(12):19–37

Levrero ES (2021) Estimates of the natural rate of interest and the stance of monetary policies: a critical assessment. Int J Pol Econ 50(1):5–27

Lim GC, Dixon R, van Ours JC (2021) Beyond Okun's law: output growth and labor market flows. Emp Econ 60(3):1387–1409

Lindbeck A, Snower JD (1988) The insider-outsider theory of employment and unemployment. MIT PRess, Cambridge

Lo S, Rogoff K (2015) Secular stagnation, debt overhang and other rationales for sluggish growth, six years on. BIS Working Papers n°482

Lubik TA, Matthes C(2015) Time-varying parameter vector autoregressions: specification, estimation, and an application. Fed Res Richm Econ Qua 101(4):323–352

Metzler LA (1951) Welath, saving and the interest rate. J Pol Econ 59(2):93–116

Moretti L, Onorante L, Saber S (2019) Phillips curves in the Euro area. ECB Working Paper 2295

Na M (2019) Examining the stability of Okun's coefficient. Bull Econ Res 71(3):240–256

Nailewaik J (2016) Non-linear Phillips curves with inflation regime-switching. Fin and Econ. Discussion Series 2016-078. B. of Gov. of the Fed. Res. Sys.

Nishizaki K, Sekine T, Ueno Y (2014) Chronic deflation in Japan. Asian Econ. Policy Rev 9(1):20–39

Palley TI (2018) The atural interest rate fallacy: why negative interest rate policy may worsen Keynesian unemployment? Inv Econ 77(304):7–39

Palley TI (2019) The fallacy of the natural interest rate and zero lower bound economics: why negative interest rate may not remedy Keynesian unemployment. Rec Keyn Econ 7(2):151–170

Pichelman K (2015) When "secular stagnation" meets Piketty's capitalism in the 21st century. Growth and inequality trends in Europe reconsidered. Eur. Comm. Econ. Pap. n°551

Reinhart CM, Rogoff KS (2014) Recovery from financial crisis: evidence from 100 episodes. Am Econ Rev 104(5):50–55

Romer P (2000) Keynesian macroeconomics without the LM curve. J Econ Lit 14(2):149–169

Rungcharoenkitkul P, Winkler F (2021) The natural rate of interest through a hall of mirror. BIS Working Papers n°974

Siena D, Zago R (2021) Job polarization and the flattening of the Phillips curve. B. de France Working Paper 819

Smith F (2008) Japan's Phillips curve looks like Japan. J Mon Cred Bank 40(6):1325–1326

Speiner B (2014) Long-term unemployment and convexity in the Phillips curve. B. of England Working Paper 519

Zaffaroni P (2004) Contemporaneous aggregation of linear dynamic models in large economies. J Econ 120(1):75–102

Zidong A, Bluedorn J, Ciminelli G (2021) Okun's law, development and demographics: differences in the cyclical sensitivities of unemployment across economy and worker groups. IMF Working Paper 21/270

CHAPTER 4

New Thinking on Sustainable Development and Growth

There is abundant work by economists on sustainable growth and development. However, this chapter does not review what has been written so far in this voluminous literature. Rather, we discuss new, and as yet little explored, avenues. This chapter is deliberately not technical and is shorter than the others in the volume. Indeed, our aim is simply to review some new ideas and approaches that are emerging at the beginning of the twenty-first century on the question of the sustainability of growth. The concept of sustainable growth (or development) is usually used to study the interactions between economy and environment. However, it maps several dimensions, including sociopolitical stability, pathogenesis in societies, conservation of resources for future generations, and preservation of planetary balances.

A standard approach to growth for an economist is to ask what conditions allow capitalist economies to generate a flow of income (GDP) in the most efficient way, taking into account structural changes in the productive capacity of economies. This explains why their attention is focused on some specific aspects, such as technological innovations, the digital economy, the slowdown in productivity gains, the rate of accumulation of physical capital, the role of demographic factors, and the contribution of finance. But all productive activities take place in an environment of increasing uncertainty: the increase in natural disasters, global warming, the resurgence of viral epidemics, the spread of metabolic diseases across the planet (hypercholesterolemia, diabetes, overweight), and so on.

G. Dufrénot, *New Challenges for Macroeconomic Policies*, https://doi.org/10.1007/978-3-031-15754-7_4

To approach the notion of sustainability of growth and economic development, we must therefore not only reason in terms of efficiency in the transformation of capital, but also in terms of opportunities in the perpetuation of the productive capacity of economies. An important issue is understanding under what conditions future generations will have the same opportunities as present generations to be able to produce, to have a good quality of life, to have sufficient natural resources, and to choose new technological paradigms. These opportunities are measured by net wealth: the difference between the value of the assets that we accumulate and that can be mobilized in productive activity, and their devaluation caused by today's activities. The concept of sustainability states that the rate of transformation of existing assets into income flows (i.e., the rate of growth of GDP) can only be maintained if net assets grow at a sufficient rate (which implies that their depletion over the decades and centuries should not be too rapid).

The notion of assets (the term "capital" is also used) must be understood in a generic sense. There are different forms of assets: natural capital, produced equipment, buildings, human capital, social capital, monetary capital, freshwater resources, food, ecosystem balances, and so on. The question of sustainable development (this term is more neutral than "human progress") has become central for macroeconomists today. Indeed, for good reason, we have spent the nineteenth and twentieth centuries asking ourselves what is the best way to improve our productive efficiency thanks to technical progress. There is a new question on the table for the twenty-first century: How can we do this while preserving as much as possible of the resources that will have to be equally available for all future generations? There are several possible answers.

A first angle is to consider that there is no issue at all because there are natural mechanisms for regulating these resources: cycles of oxygen, water, geochemical elements, and so on. Our concern could therefore be to continue to deal with efficiency (because to live we must continue to generate income flows) by considering assets as constraints whose reproduction cycles and risks of depletion we must internalize. This philosophy is one of the foundations of the idea that other ecosystems could represent "constraints" and limits to growth. Classical economists (e.g., Ricardo, Smith, Malthus) were very much afraid of such a perspective. As a result, this philosophy also helped to shape the debate among economists, with attention focused on technical means to circumvent its limits and prevent growth from running out of steam. The foundation of the neoclassical endogenous growth models of the 1990s was to understand how the productive apparatus could generate non-decreasing returns to scale. Schumpeterian economists believe that technical progress can help push the limits of growth, for example by finding innovations to trap greenhouse gases, or to have technologies that are more carbon efficient.

But this reasoning has a flaw. It does not take into account conflicts of temporalities. This means that the short period of human production activities is the opposite of the longer period of the regulation of ecosystems and social organizations. The intensification of production methods and consumption thanks to technology can cause breaks in equilibrium. This is the thesis of scientists who defend the idea of the Anthropocene (economic activity, since it "oppresses" the various ecosystems, modifies the duration of natural cycles, and increases the chances of tipping points occurring). For this reason, it is not enough to internalize the dynamics of non-economic ecosystems. It is also necessary that the growth process be "co-determined" with the realization of other natural, sociopolitical equilibria.

Our attention must therefore focus on the following points. First, sustainability implies focusing on a global approach to investigate the interdependencies between economic activities and other ecosystems. In this perspective, a statistically interesting method to measure the wealth of nations in a context of sustainable development is the United Nations' Inclusive Wealth Index (IWI) (see below). Secondly, since the economy is necessarily embedded in social organization, we cannot ignore the phenomena of poverty and discrimination inherent to capitalism. A dazzling growth of GDP is not necessarily socially sustainable if it generates and accentuates social disparities and situations of precariousness. Indeed, such situations cause wars and conflicts and degrade the social climate, and thus the stability of social organizations. Finally, sustainability implies a better understanding of the relationships between macroeconomic and epidemiological equilibria. A country can have dazzling growth rates with a deteriorating human capital (because access to quality health care becomes difficult, since part of the population suffers from human metabolic diseases, because access to education is expensive, or because the population is aging).

4.1   A Global Approach to Sustainable Growth and Development

4.1.1   Economic Ecosystems Interact with Other Ecosystems

Sustainable development has two dimensions that require a global approach to growth. The first refers to the viability of interdependencies between human activities and other ecosystems. The second dimension refers to the polarities generated by the growth processes of capitalist economies.

One of the greatest challenges for researchers investigating sustainable development and growth in the twenty-first century will be that of a global approach to economic growth. Indeed, economic activities interact with the equilibrium of other ecosystems, whether geophysical, environmental, or animal. The economic activities can disrupt these equilibria, but such disruptions can also generate "feedback loops" that can threaten the viability of the fundamental functions that a strong economic growth should fulfill: producing to give people food; curbing demographic growth; managing the natural resources that are essential to human life; enhancing soils to facilitate agricultural productivity; preserving the workforce's health; and improving people's living conditions by facilitating access to clean water, decent housing, breathable air, and so on. Figures 4.1 and 4.2 help to visualize a global approach to sustainable growth.

To understand why economic growth and the activities it generates have several dimensions (environmental, material, epidemiological, etc.) we must bear in mind that humans coexist with other worlds (see Fig. 4.1), each of which forms an ecosystem. These ecosystems interfere with each other, and this is how local and global balances are defined. In these ecosystems, geography is important: Humans have taken over much forest space for agriculture and housing. Humans and animals serve as a vehicle for millions of micro-organisms, bacteria, and viruses to move around the world. The epidemiological equilibrium of a country and the world reflects these balances. Sometimes, this coexistence is difficult: Some viruses and bacteria kill people and animals (see Fig. 4.2).

Therefore, there can be a struggle between humans and these micro-organisms for their survival. Sometimes, things function very well: The immune system of wild fauna (e.g., bats) is highly acclimatized to viruses that are dangerous for humans. Soils provide services to human beings. They allow the supply of drinking water (purification of rainwater during

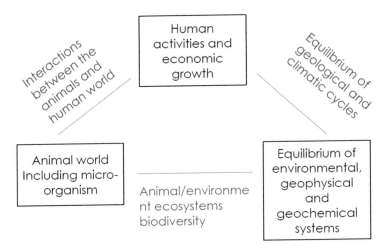

Fig. 4.1 The interference of the worlds: everything is linked

its infiltration to the water table), facilitate agricultural production, and provide medicinal remedies (plants). Geochemical, geophysical, and ecological cycles also illustrate the services provided to human beings by other ecosystems. The oceans and forests absorb carbon dioxide and bacteria. The Earth decomposes organic matter, providing a home for millions of micro-organisms, allowing fauna and flora to find living spaces.

Economic growth since the beginning of the nineteenth century has had the following characteristics: (1) It has taken place in a context of massification (mass production and consumption), (2) it happened within a thermo-industrial civilization (through the intensive use of carbon-based energies), and (3) it has been based on a strong geographical expansion (first by states, then by multinational companies with the multiplication of value chains). It has therefore entailed several costs:

- Deforestation to favor cash crops and livestock (oil palms in Asia, timber in Africa, soybeans in Brazil,…).
- Increase in maritime, air, rail, and road transport that accompanied the multiplication of value chains (crushing costs) has contributed to global warming.
- Intensive livestock farming and agriculture to meet demographic growth and the strong increase in demand for animal protein. Inten-

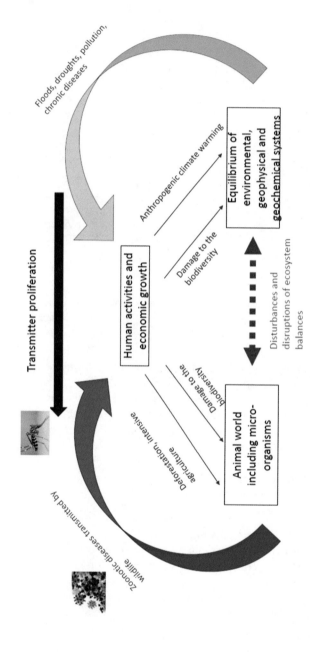

Fig. 4.2 Disturbances in the global equilibrium

sive agriculture has increased yields, but it has also caused environmental pollution.

- Damage to biodiversity.

There are tolerable thresholds for other ecosystems (environment, animal, wildlife, Earth system) beyond which they can no longer provide the services necessary for the security of human life and production activities:

- Biodiversity becomes insufficient to protect against zoonotic diseases.
- Intensive breeding allows us to feed more people with animal proteins, but breeding sites are incubation sites for new viruses and create externalities (groundwater pollution).
- Global warming favors the proliferation of virus and disease vectors, for example mosquitoes, rats, and insects.
- Toxic substances and air pollution contaminate the water table and the air, causing health problems for individuals and the public.
- Deforestation increases the production and living space of human beings, but destroys the natural habitats of wild fauna and causes new diseases for domestic animals, livestock, and humans in the case of zoonoses.

4.1.2   Why Has the Global Approach Had Little Success with Economists?

Such a global approach to growth has long been neglected by macroeconomists working on growth, for several reasons.

The First Reason is Historical

We should remember that until the technological innovations of the industrial revolutions of the nineteenth century, a large part of the world lived in great misery and material poverty. The relationship with climate, micro-organisms, the Earth system, and the environment was conceived in a conflictual approach: The seasons gave rhythm to the periods of famine and abundance, while the epidemic and disease cycles regulated those of demography. The exclusively economic approach to growth during a good part of the nineteenth and twentieth centuries was justified, because the countries that are now industrialized-but that were underdeveloped until then-were emerging from several millennia of very low living standards. Production was the result of the interweaving of three cycles: that of agriculture according to climatic variations, that of wars according to the moods of political powers, and that of diseases according to recurrent epidemics.

Figure 4.3 shows the share of GDP in the global GDP of select countries and regions from year 1 until 2008, based on statistics collected by the Angus Maddison Project. Until the nineteenth century, only two countries in the world had standards of living far above those of the others, that is, India and China. The changeover for Western Europe and the United States occurred "only" from 1870 onward. The downgrading of India and China took place with the rise of the technological and industrial revolutions, first in Europe, then in the United States. When countries emerge from very long periods during which means of subsistence have been lacking, it is not surprising that attention is mobilized on the question of how to ensure their sustainability, without the means of subsistence being subject to the vagaries of the natural elements. Long before the industrial revolutions of the eighteenth and nineteenth centuries, growth economists were already primarily concerned with the conditions that would guarantee sufficient yields from agriculture in the long term. Many economists, first and foremost the classics, were haunted by the idea that economies could in the long run converge to steady states because of non-

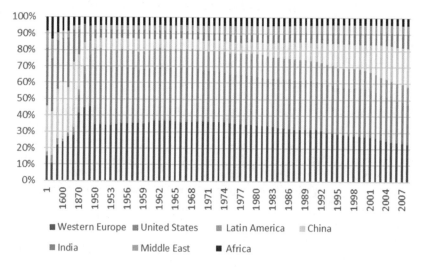

Fig. 4.3 Share of GDP in World GDP (%). Source: Historical Statistics of the World Economy 1-2008

economic factors: demographic behavior, land yields, diseases, or depletion of natural resources. With the industrial revolutions, the debates continued with the question of the best technology to achieve the highest yields while preserving scarce resources. During the periods following the two world wars, the urgency was to rebuild completely destroyed economies. The industrial boom was more important than the problems of externalities caused to the environment and other ecosystems.

The Second Reason Is due to Certain Misconceptions about Reality

The risks raised by the environmental externalities of rapid industrial growth were highlighted very early on. As early as the 1950s, there were heated debates on the ecological effects of growth within the civil societies of industrialized countries. In 1972, the Meadows report underlined the limits to this type of growth: depletion of resources and, above all, damage to the environment leading to additional human, physical, and financial costs.[1] An International Union for Conservation of Nature (IUCN) document from 1980 discussed the links between the global growth strategy and the issue and preservation of living species. The Bruntland Commission in 1987 wrote a highly publicized report on a reversal of hierarchies: Sustainable development and meeting the needs of the poorest is more important than the search for maximization of economic activities.

But these ideas, which today seem to be widely accepted by societies, were not in vogue for a long time. This is due to several misconceptions.

Economists have long believed that as countries succeed in raising their standard of living, the pollution generated by growth would decrease thanks to two effects: (1) a compositional effect due to the fact that countries specialize in the production of less polluting goods and services (richer consumers become more attentive to quality of life and therefore more demanding in terms of clean energy) and (2) a technical effect. Rising living standards lead to production changes (companies innovate in less polluting technologies because of regulatory constraints). These phenomena have never been observed.

---

[1] The first version of the Meadows report on the limits to economic growth dates from 1972 and evokes the possibility of a stationary state of the economies characterized by a growth rate that would become equal to 0, because of two factors, that is, demography in certain countries and the depletion of underground resources. The authors developed a planetary model, called World3, which includes several other dimensions in addition to growth: demographics, available reserves in the subsoil, pollution.

Another misconception is the result of ignorance. With the disruption represented by the industrial revolutions, the structuring of production and consumption patterns has progressively created conditions conducive to the acceleration of viral transfers: deforestation, the destruction of natural wildlife habitats during the conversion of land for intensive export agriculture, industrial livestock parks that are incubators for the spread of epidemics, excessive urbanization that favors animal migration zones, and excessive mining. Recent works show the existence of a correlation between the destruction of animal biodiversity and the appearance of emerging viruses from the animal world. This affects human capital, annihilates the demographic dividend, and can lead to a drop in activity in the event of major pandemics, as was the case historically before the micro-biological revolution of the nineteenth century and the progress made in medicine. We have not paid attention to the fact that global warming is likely to favor the adaptation of disease vectors and of a number of hosts constituting reservoirs for viruses at higher latitudes: insects, mosquitoes, birds, and ticks (in temperate as well as subtropical geographical areas).

4.1.3 Sustainable Development and Polarities

Industrial development has provided the means of subsistence and of living decently to millions of people. But this progress has a cost that is increasingly difficult to bear for societies and has produced polarities (see Fig. 4.4). On the one hand, we have overabundance (financial hypertrophy,

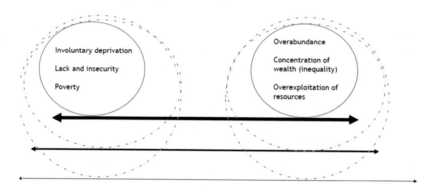

Fig. 4.4 Growth can generate excesses and shortages

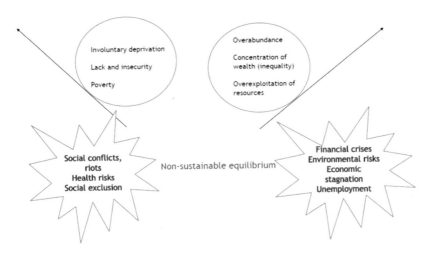

Fig. 4.5 Non-sustainable socioeconomic equilibrium

overproduction generating a proliferation of waste, over-exploitation of natural resources and the living environment, a high concentration of wealth creating inequalities). On the other hand, the productive systems have generated a proliferation of phenomena of "lack": Poverty still affects entire subgroups of populations, and there are involuntary deprivations reflected by the phenomena of precariousness. The social, political, social, and environmental equilibrium of a society cannot be achieved when the distance between these poles grows. It is as if two weights are placed at the ends of a wire and their mass increases more and more. At a certain point the thread breaks (see Fig. 4.5), and this break is materialized by various types of crisis (epidemic, social, environmental) that can call into question the viability of productive systems to maintain decent living standards for populations and future generations.

One of the reasons why this phenomenon has gone unnoticed is that economists are very optimistic about the role of technology in economic development, based on the historical experience of European countries. There is a strong belief among some economists that innovations contribute to reducing inequality and poverty when they become accessible to the greatest number of people. Economists such as Baumol, Okun, and Schumpeter have defended this idea (productivity gains leading to higher real wages). However, this is not what we have observed: Since the 1980s, the evolution of wages and productivity gains has been uncorrelated, and poverty and inequality have increased in countries located on the global technological frontier (e.g., the United States and Japan).

Moreover, the technological discoveries of the end of the twentieth and beginning of the twenty-first century have been obtained through the creation of oligopolistic rents and through an increase in the concentration of capital (digital and communication sectors, pharmaceutical sector, etc.).

What Are the Implications for the Study of Growth and Sustainable Development?

There are several ways to model sustainable development taking account of the elements outlined above.

The first approach is the most difficult. It can be described as a "general equilibrium" analysis in the sense that it requires a global model that summarizes the mechanisms of each ecosystem (human, land, marine, animal, environmental) that captures the interdependencies and is interested in the co-determination of equilibria. This implies interdisciplinarity and transversality. This scientific approach is recent, dating back barely 20 years. It appeared in health disciplines (One Health approach) and in the Earth sciences. In economics, the so-called integrated approach (meaning "with other disciplines") is embryonic in some fields (e.g., regarding the role of economic behaviors in the spread of epidemics and the effects of these on macroeconomic indicators, models have recently been developed in a literature devoted to the macroeconomics of Covid-19; see Eichenbaum et al. 2020). In other fields, advances have been made for a longer period of time, for example on the links between economic behaviors and climate change. The aim is to define, within a consistent framework, the causal interactions and feedback loops between greenhouse gas emissions, the effects of climate change, and the repercussions of these. Such models require skills in environmental sciences (climatology, oceanography, ecology), in economics, and in the sciences. William Nordhaus has played an important role in proposing integrated models to assess the impacts of climate change on the economy.

The second approach, the most widespread, consists of internalizing the equilibria of environmental, animal, land-system, and epidemiological ecosystems in macroeconomic models, without necessarily exploring in detail their dynamics, whose complexity is summarized by simple relationships. Symmetrically, partial equilibrium models from other disciplines may favor a geophysical, medical, biophysical, or environmental approach, reducing the complexity of macroeconomic and social relationships to simple mechanisms.

Thirdly, as we pointed out earlier, one of the causes of a growing interest of civil societies in sustainable development is that crises, whatever their nature, are caused by breaks. Approaches that can be described as "indirect" therefore aim to agree on and construct indicators in each discipline, to identify thresholds beyond which the equilibrium of each subsystem is called into question, and finally to look at the links that exist between the indicators of the various disciplines and the thresholds crossed. Economists have their indicators of sustainable development but they are also interested in indicators developed by other disciplines. Each time thresholds are crossed, we identify "limits" to growth, to development, or to the planet, in the sense that we enter zones of uncertainty concerning the viability of ecosystems due to a deterioration in their functioning.

Since 2009, sciences outside of economics have defined the concept of "planetary boundaries", that is, thresholds that must not be exceeded to maintain the environmental, epidemiological, ecological, and social conditions of the Earth system in which human life can develop. The crossing of thresholds increases the risks of chain reactions that we want to avoid imperatively. Today, there are nine indicators that are particularly scrutinized and that define the equilibrium of the biosphere: (1) the water cycle, (2) chemical pollution (including plastics), (3) greenhouse gas emissions and their effects on the ozone layer, (4) biogeochemical cycles (phosphorus and nitrogen), (5) the degree of ocean acidification, 6) the erosion of biodiversity, (7) climate change, (8) changes in land use, and (9) the increase of aerosols in the atmosphere. It is difficult to deny that human activities have some influence on the evolution of these indicators, and that in turn the latter affect the economic variables (see Rockström et al. 2009).

The challenge for macroeconomists is to define a growth rate that avoids approaching the planet's frontier and to define a sustainability space for growth, that is, a minimum distance from ecological thresholds. The complexity of the topics lies in the fact that we cannot be satisfied with aggregate production functions, because they do not allow us to account for the interactions with other ecosystems. Any model must integrate production processes built on green innovations, and behavioral mechanisms that promote pro-environmental and "pro-Earth" behaviors, and that take into account the services provided by other ecosystems. The notion of well-being then consists in retaining growth and economic development trajectories that reduce the risks of bifurcations, of disruptions in the planetary physical equilibrium, because these are the bearers of extreme events harmful to human life: Climate disruption accentuates periods of drought, floods, and extreme cold; severe pollution has high costs for human health; melting ice favors the emission of methane, and so on.

In addition to environmental factors, we should also consider some additional indicators to monitor and ensure a sociopolitical dimension of sustainable development. We can take up some indicators retained in the objectives of sustainable development such as access to drinking water and energy, decent housing conditions, free education, food, gender equality, and the reduction of poverty and sociopolitical indicators such as social peace and security. We can also add indicators of reduction of inequalities, poverty, and social discrimination.

With the global approach, the interesting point is that the different regimes of capitalism in relation to the states of equilibrium of the various ecosystems can be defined from the economic decline of the Anthropocene. This concept is debated among scientists. But if we retain it, the Anthropocene designates recent periods in the history of the Earth during which human activities have begun to have an influence on biogeochemical cycles, climate change, ocean acidity, and so on. This definition can be generalized to all ecosystems. This means that the regulations of non-human ecosystems are no longer on a long time scale, but on an increasingly shorter one. Furthermore, it is assumed that this change is related to human activities. In this perspective, the Capitalocene designates historical periods during which different modes of production and exploitation of natural resources have begun to play a role in modifying the temporal scales on which the equilibrium of the biosphere, geophysical, geochemical, lithosphere, and other living ecosystems is defined.

If we go back to the industrial revolutions of the nineteenth century in Europe, we can distinguish two eras that followed one another rapidly, both marked by an intensive use of carbon-based energies. These periods are always part of a context of hegemonic stability-to use Kindleberger's term-where one or more countries impose their vision of the world and modes of production on the hierarchy of nations. This power is based on a combination of technical innovations and the discovery and large-scale exploitation of new energy sources. The first corresponds to the domination of the United Kingdom over the world, whose industrial superiority was based on the large-scale exploitation of coal from the middle of the eighteenth century, at a time when transport costs were high. The development of the iron and steel industry, the textile industry, and transportation was based on the exploitation of coal mines. The second era is the one that established the hegemony of the United States from the end of the Second World War, because the country was able to access cheap carbon resources: oil, gas, and coal. The central role of these resources would be confirmed in the early 2000s, when the United States embarked on a program of energy independence because its dependence on oil imports from foreign countries was analyzed as a problem of national security (in 2007 the Energy Independence and Security Act was passed). Behind these dominant nations, the other powers emerging in their wake have also used the same modes of production based on carbon energies (Germany, France, Italy, Australia, Japan, the United Kingdom, etc). More recently, the rise of China and its global role, and its dazzling economic growth rates, have also relied on the combination of technological innovations and an intensive use of carbon-based energies (coal, in particular).

One of the difficulties in studying the consequences of the exploitation of carbon resources corresponding to different eras of the Capitalocene is that we do not yet have complete theoretical models that take into account all the interdependencies between economic and ecological variables in order to establish causalities and identify the underlying mechanisms. The current models (e.g., those of the IPCC) are simulation models and are based on hypotheses (these models have a predictive purpose by giving ranges on the probability of evolution of key variables). Those who contest their conclusions and refute the idea of anthropogenic climate warming rely on the fact that we cannot theoretically differentiate the effects due to human activities and those due to the functioning of the Earth system. At best, the empirical data we observe are correlations.

What do the scientific data on anthropogenic warming during the twentieth century show us? First, the concentration of CO_2 in the atmosphere has increased by 49.6% compared to the pre-industrial period between 1850 and 2020, from 278 ppm (parts per million) to 416 ppm (according to data from the US Earth Systems Research Laboratories). This is the stock resulting from the part of the emissions not absorbed by the natural carbon sinks (lithosphere, biosphere, and hydrosphere). Second, the evolution of the global annual mean temperature between 1850 and 2019 is described by a convex increasing curve with a flat part. Indeed, between 1850 and 1940 the increase was modest, but then accelerated from this date. Taking the decade sliding average, between 1850 and 1950, the temperature anomalies remained around zero and were even negative between 1900 and 1920. Between 1940 and 1960, these figures became positive between +0.20 °C and +0.40 °C. In 2020, the anomalies were around +1.20 °C. Third, the average sea level has risen since 1900 (until 2010) by 1.7+/−0.3 mm, and the increase has accelerated to reach between 1993 and 2019 3.3+/−0.4 mm/year.

It is difficult to establish the existence of a correlation between pollution and global warming using econometric models that are necessarily simplified and that do not take into account the complex feedback loops specific to the Earth system and between different ecosystems. By relying only on data, we risk encountering a problem of selection bias. To see this, one only has to look at the evolution of temperatures before the industrial boom in Europe, that is, during periods when anthropogenic CO_2 emissions were lower. An important fact is that, historically, large temperature cycles have existed and have been characterized by periods of warming and periods of cooling. For example, between 900 and 1250, average temperatures were higher than in 2000. This period is known as the Medieval Warm Period (or in scientific language, the Medieval Optimum Period, the term "optimum" referring to periods of warming that are considered more favorable to human life than periods of cooling). Apart from temperature, other climate-related disturbances were also observed during the same period (see, e.g., Bradley et al. 2003; Follc et al. 2001; Jones and Mann 2004; Le Roy Ladurie 1988).

Will another capitalocene emerge in the coming years and decades, following the one based on the use of carbon resources? This is an important question. Indeed, the economically hegemonic nations are faced with the risk of downgrading in a context where the objectives of reducing greenhouse gases and mitigating the effects of global warming require a drastic reduction in the use of carbon-based energy.

The decision of the United Kingdom from the middle of the nineteenth century to base its economic, commercial, monetary, and geopolitical hegemony in the world on the carbonaceous resources of the subsoil took place at a time when the country had high growth rates but was in danger of being stopped by the depletion of organic resources, in particular precious metals, forestry resources, and wood. The potential costs of a halt in growth were all the more important as the country was also experiencing high demographic growth, an increase in agricultural productivity, and an advanced division of labor. The standard of living of the population was higher than in the rest of Europe (the other country in the world that was in the same situation of prosperity at that time was China). It is by imagining the potentially high costs of stopping growth that the English decided to base an economy on a new resource to which they had unlimited access: coal (and later oil thanks to territorial wars). They also had the formidable steam engine and a vast colonial empire that helped them establish an industrial model based on coal (see Malm 2016; Wrigley 2010).

Energy transitions occur whenever hegemonic nations face constraints. During the 1980s, fossil fuels were referred to as non-renewable energy sources. A popular theory was Hubbert's peak, and each country estimated an end date for its assumed carbon energy reserves. But, in addition to the fact that more and more new deposits of high-quality oil and gas have been discovered in the rocks of the oceans, shale oil and gas have allowed the United States- a hegemonic nation-to pursue its growth model by ridding itself of its dependence on other countries, particularly those in the Middle East. The constraint today does not come from the unavailability of underground resources, but from the environmental disturbances linked to the intensive exploitation of these energies and the negative effects caused to the different ecosystems. A new technological paradigm must therefore be found, and this requires a transition toward the exploitation of new energy sources.

A new hegemonic race based on the capture of new resources has been under way for at least 15 years. It has prefigured an orientation of productive systems toward a new model of digital economy. Countries are gradually entering a new capitalocene, that of metals and minerals, whose strategic nature has become obvious. These are both abundant and rare metals: iron, silver, copper, nickel, cobalt, berylim, tungsten, bauxite, niobium, etc. There are at least 100 of these. These minerals and metals, which are supposed to have a low carbon footprint, are used in the technologies of the future: batteries, solar panels, televisions, computers, electronic circuits, lasers, robots, nanotechnologies, traction motors, drones, and so on. The strategies for capturing these resources reveal a dominant nation, sub-dominant nations, and "secondary" nations. The dominant nation is China. In addition to the strategies of monopolizing these resources from all the countries of the world (thanks in particular to extensive foreign direct investment policies), China has many of these minerals in its subsoil. But above all, this country has taken control and a dominant position in the mineral refining sector. The "sub-dominant" nations are the United States and the European countries (if we include polymetallic nodules). The "secondary" nations are made up of countries which, although they have certain strategic resources, are not hegemonic powers on the geopolitical, economic, or financial level. On the contrary, the fact that they have these resources has made them dependent on China and the industrialized countries: Brazil, Chile, South Africa, the Democratic Republic of the Congo, and Australia. This is a new capitalocene because the extraction and refining of these metals and ores are highly polluting for the environment. Indeed, in addition to the release of radioactive elements during the separation stage for rare metals, their exploitation implies the use of vast quantities of water, and can lead to the pollution of water tables and soils and to the degradation of biodiversity. Moreover, the transition to the digital economy is not necessarily a low-carbon strategy. The raw material is the trillions of data and the necessary equipment (computers, servers) are sources of greenhouse gas production.

4.1.4   What Are the Directions for Future Research?

Attempts to propose a global approach to the links between economies and the equilibria of other ecosystems date back several decades, although this path has been little followed. However, several important contributions, both old and more recent, should be mentioned.

During the 1970s, an interdisciplinary team of 70 researchers from a wide range of disciplines (meteorology, economics, oceanography, law, ecology, atmospheric chemistry, biology, physics, etc.) was interested in global climate change and the environmental effects of human activities. The study was sponsored by MIT. Their work resulted in a report entitled *Study of Critical Environmental Problems*. The authors were already highlighting the effects of transportation- which was booming at the time, especially in the airline industry-on the rates of carbon dioxide accumulation in the atmosphere (especially the part not absorbed by the oceans and forests). They relied on a mathematical model showing the interactions between economic activities and the atmosphere–land balance. In the conclusion of their report, the authors called for a precautionary principle and for corrective measures in the pace of economic growth.

However, the report was subject to two major criticisms. The first was that it was too abstract (because it was complex), that is, not sufficiently accessible to non-specialists to attract attention from policymakers. The second criticism was that the predictions made for the long term seemed exaggerated, even though their simulations showed that in the 100 years from 1970, the probability of climate change directly linked to the concentration of CO_2 in the atmosphere was low.

William Nordhaus has made a significant contribution to the development of multidisciplinary models to study the interactions between economic growth, geochemical cycles, greenhouse gas emissions, and climate change. Some seminal contributions are Nordhaus (1991), Nordhaus (1992), Nordhaus (1994), and Nordhaus and Yang (1996). The models proposed by this author (DICE and RICE models: Dynamic Integrated model of Climate and the Economy, and Regional, Integrated model of Climate and the Economy) have given rise to numerous extensions in the literature (see, e.g., Nordhaus and Boyer 2000 and Traeger 2014). But one of the criticisms of this type of modeling is that it remains very economy-centric. The models are not global in the sense that we have defined above, but they integrate climatic and ecological modules into the functioning of the economy by looking, for example, at the costs generated by damage to the environment. Their principle is to have a module tracing the dynamics of the economy by integrating a damage function (harmful to growth) and a climate module that models the cycles of geochemical elements (notably carbon) as well as the dynamics of the climate (with a link based on the fact that atmospheric carbon concentration rates have an impact on the climate). An important limitation of these models is that the welfare function of different regions of the world or globe is defined according to different trajectories of future per capita consumption with economic and geophysical constraints. Given the issues related to the balances of all physical, natural, and other living ecosystems, summarizing well-being as what people want to consume or invest optimally in the future is very limited. It does not take into account the concept of the planetary boundary mentioned earlier.

Recent work based on a truly global approach allows for modeling the services provided by other ecosystems (see Boehnert 2021; Daw et al. 2011). The interested reader will also find abundant references on socio-ecological Earth system models to study the dynamics of the Anthropocene in Bates and Saint-Pierre (2018) and Verburg et al. (2016). The branch of economics that currently seems most open to the global approach is ecological economics. It was born in the 1980s and includes various currents of thought. But all of them have in common that in their models the economy is inserted into the other ecosystems of which it is a component and not the final goal (for a synthesis, see Costanza 1989,

2020; Harris et al. 2006; Lagrue et al. 2012; Melgar-Melgar and Hall 2020; Pushpam 2010, and Washington and Maloney 2020).

4.2   ECONOMIC WELL-BEING AND SUSTAINABLE GROWTH

We must remember that the objective sought by one of the founders of GDP, Simon Kuznets, was to find an indicator measuring social well-being. This is the purpose, beyond understanding the determinants of GDP growth over time. The goal is to find indicators that allow us to live decently for present and future generations. In the literature, there are two approaches to measuring wealth (and the theoretical models that follow from them).

On the one hand, one can reason in terms of flows and ask what use human beings get out of the income flows they generate (the GDP that is produced with capital): They consume, but must keep some of their income (savings) in order to continue to produce an income flow continuously over time. Growth models are interested in this: How to create wealth by satisfying various criteria (maximizing the well-being derived today from consumption, allocating consumption and savings in an optimal way over time, arranging for the flow of income that is generated to grow at the same rate as the resources that allow it to be generated-this is balanced growth). This flow approach can take into account demographic constraints and constraints related to the availability of natural resources. Theoretical models can also take into account the environmental externalities caused by productive activities, as well as the optimal rate of exploitation of natural resources (fish, minerals, etc.). There is an abundant literature, for example, on the economics of natural resources and ecological economics. However, this is not what interests us here.

An alternative approach is based on stocks. Welfare is measured by the-intertemporal-utility that one derives from the fact that a country has a capital that is multiple. What matters here are assets and liabilities. Capital cannot be understood only in the sense of growth theories (equipment, infrastructure, intangible capital, total factor productivity, human capital), but also consists of natural capital (forests, arable land, non-renewable and renewable resources, subsoil water resources) and the biosphere (ocean and atmospheric resources). In order to give them a value, one is obliged to take into account the services rendered by the different forms of capital, but also the costs incurred by their use. Sustainability refers to the fact that the damage caused to ecosystems, and the losses of natural capital induced by economic growth, must not be greater than the gains from the use of resources for production. Otherwise this means that present generations cannot pass on to future generations a productive base that ensures a decent standard of living. Capital must also include certain common goods such as peace, stability, and social justice, and the reduction of poverty and inequality. Strong growth that is accompanied by rising inequality or increasing poverty is not sustainable if it increases the risk of future social conflicts and degrades the social capital necessary for productive activities.

The investigation of sustainable growth thus responds to two different objectives. In the first case, the focus is on the capacity of economies to transform capital into income flows. We study the efficiency of this transformation and the conditions that allow it. In the second case, we are more interested in the capacity of today's generations to pass on to future generations a productive capacity that is not degraded and that gives them the same opportunities as previous generations to continue to generate income flows to live, but also to have a decent quality of life.

To illustrate this, Fig. 4.6 compares the average annual growth rate of wealth in certain countries, measured using three indicators. Data are

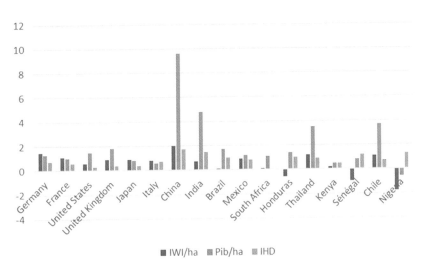

Fig. 4.6 Comparing growth per capita rates using three approaches

taken from the UNEP report on inclusive growth from 2014. The first indicator is standard GDP per capita growth. The second is the growth rate of the Human Development Index (HDI), which combines GDP per capita with a variable of life expectancy of the population and the level of education of those aged 15 and over. The third indicator is based on the IWI mentioned above. It is composed of three forms of capital: goods and services produced, but also human and natural capital. It has been proposed by the UNEP (UN Environment Programme as of 2012). The statistics concern a long period of 20 years between 1990 and 2010. The reader can refer to the 2014 Inclusive Wealth Report, measuring progress toward sustainability, UNU-IHPP, UNEP, Cambridge. The report presents data from 140 countries.

A country that experiences sustained per capita growth rates but at the same time "drains" its natural capital runs the risk of eventually running up against a natural constraint because the soil and subsoil resources will not have had time to renew themselves. The sustainability of growth depends on the management of natural resources and their availability for future generations. The figure shows that, according to the standard criterion of growth measured by GDP per-capita, the important performances are observed for emerging countries (notably, China, India, Thailand, and Chile). Countries such as Brazil, South Africa, and Honduras have per-capita growth rates very close to those of the industrialized countries (France, Germany, Japan, the United States, and the United Kingdom). However, per capita GDP growth does not always improve welfare growth, which, in addition to GDP, also takes into account the effects on human capital (health and education). We observe the large difference between GDP growth measured by GDP per capita and that obtained from the HDI. The changes in lifestyle and production implied by sustained growth rates cause damage to the environment and degrade the health of populations. Poor nutrition (overeating or nutritional deficiencies) has also shortened life expectancy through increased premature death. The differential is particularly striking in emerging and developing countries, and less so in industrialized countries (except in the United Kingdom and the United States). The same observation applies to the comparison of the growth rate of the HDI per capita and that of the IWI indicator. The difference is very marked in the emerging economies. In some developing countries such as Brazil, South Africa, Honduras, Senegal, and Nigeria, growth causes destruction of natural capital (negative growth rate of the IWI). In these countries, growth rates do not seem compatible with the sustainability criterion based on the preservation of resources for future generations.

Factors change radically when we take into account the valuation (and destruction) effects of different forms of capital. For example, if companies build technologies to improve the energy efficiency of carbon-based energies (increasing the quantities produced with less coal, oil, or gas used), this increases production while decreasing the negative effects on the environment linked to the release into the atmosphere of fine particles and toxic fumes. In this case, the IWI is likely to increase. Another example is that the increase (decrease) in the price of oil on the world markets increases (decreases) the value of crude oil in the subsoil of a country.

Figure 4.7 takes into account several factors that may affect the measurement of IWI: environmental damage caused by carbon-based energy sources (Carbon), valuation effects related to oil price variations (Oil), and factor productivity (R&D). These figures show a world divided in two. In industrialized countries, the per capita growth rate is positive, while it is frequently negative in emerging and developing countries. The cases of China and Nigeria are an illustration. In most of these countries, the slowdown in factor productivity (the insufficiency of technologies

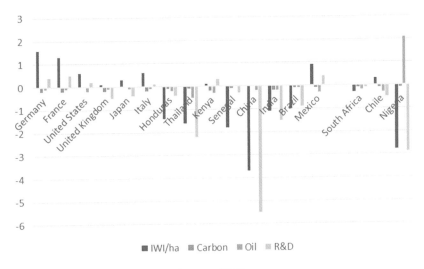

Fig. 4.7 Comparing the determinants of IWI

to safeguard human and natural capital) lowers the level of sustainable growth. In all these countries, the valuation effects of oil or the negative environmental externalities of the use of carbon resources have led to negative growth everywhere. In the industrialized countries, growth rates, even positive ones, are relatively low. There is heterogeneity between countries. For example, France and Germany have growth rates that are twice, and in the case of Germany three times, that of the United States, more than 10 times that of the United Kingdom, and four to five times that of Japan. The difference comes from technical progress, which is higher in these two countries than in other nations.

4.3   SUSTAINABLE GROWTH AND SOCIAL INCLUSION: A TRADE-OFF BETWEEN INEQUALITY AND POVERTY?

4.3.1   Fighting Poverty: The First Objective of Inclusive Growth

The notion of sustainable growth goes beyond preserving the balance of the various ecosystems. In social and political terms, it also implies that everyone benefits from economic growth. In recent years, there has been a voluminous economic literature on poverty and inequality, both theoretical and empirical. However, few works and models explicitly link these notions to the sustainability of growth (in the sense of "inclusive growth"). At best, papers focus on pro-poor growth. But theoretical and empirical progress still needs to be made on several points, which justifies the need to privilege a global approach, this time with the disciplines of the human sciences: sociology, psychology, and anthropology.

From a statistical point of view, a new multidimensional measure of poverty is now being proposed, based on the experiences of poor people (let us say that it is a behavioral approach). The method has nothing to do with experimental economics or randomized experiments. It is similar to what anthropologists do. Based on fieldwork conducted since 2016 by the OECD, ATD Fourth World, and Oxford University in six countries (Bangladesh, Bolivia, the United States, France, the United Kingdom, and Tanzania), a new indicator of non-inclusiveness of growth has been proposed by these institutions based on the feelings of people who are not beneficiaries of growth. This indicator has four dimensions.

The first dimension includes variables describing the core of the poverty experience and is related to disempowerment (in other words, the way in which the poor feel disempowered to act to improve their living conditions: psychological disincentives related to social suffering). The second dimension includes variables related to relational dynamics (social and institutional abuses, as well as unacknowledged contributions).

The third dimension deals with deprivation (lack of decent work, material deprivation, precarious income).

The fourth dimension includes "modifiers" (including cultural beliefs and the political environment).

This approach has several implications for theoretical modeling.

First, the experiences of people living in poverty suggest that work is not a service like any other. In economic analyses, it is a service from which both employers and those they employ derive income (a factor of production): On the side of firms, workers are hired for profit, and on the side of employees, a wage is received as compensation. However, when a significant number of people are unemployed, do not receive decent wages, and have precarious jobs due to the fragmentation of labor markets, the deprivation of these goods puts the social survival of individuals at risk. The work deprivation that accompanies poverty is, very often, correlated with situations of material deprivation, illiteracy, and social isolation, as well as with situations of opportunity inequality.

Second, there are implications for the way in which anti-poverty policies are designed. Field research (which extends beyond randomized experiments) shows a correlation between social inequality and poverty, in rich and poor countries. But poverty will not be eradicated through exclusively distributive policies, by heavily taxing the richest or capital. The solution is not only ex-post (through redistribution once the production of wealth has been achieved), but also ex-ante through the establishment of principles for the evaluation of social well-being that take into account the position of individuals in terms of access to primary goods and services: decent wages and employment, decent living conditions (access to good-quality health and education services, decent housing, equity in access to justice services), and today, the struggles against digital illiteracy and gender discrimination, as well as the search for more inclusive collective choice procedures. These are not ideological principles, but ethical ones in the sense of theories of social justice, notably those of Rawls and Sen. However, the reality on the ground suggests that one of the primary causes of poverty is inequalities in access to these primary goods and services. Indeed, in recent decades, the trend has been toward greater fragmentation of labor markets at the global level, a nuclearization of work and a return to "task-based" remuneration favored by the uberization of economies, an accentuation of spatial segregation of housing due to land speculation (this phenomenon being observed throughout the world), and the deterioration of educational services in some of the world's poorest countries.

While field experiments have been gaining popularity among development economists and those working on inequality and poverty in recent years, there are several pitfalls to be avoided with this approach. The first is to think that a more accurate view of poverty can be obtained from subjective criteria derived from declarative data on the quality of life. We find here an old dilemma in social justice theories, between the welfarist approaches and the primary goods approaches of Rawls and the "capabilities" of Amartya Sen. Our societies will not be able to avoid a debate on what we choose, collectively and "objectively" (i.e., according to ethical principles), to consider as primary goods and services, beyond individual experiences. The second difficulty to overcome concerns randomized experiments. They do not allow the construction of general theories. Economists who use randomized experiments to test anti-poverty strategies have to fight against a strong temptation to seek consensus. This would be to forget that reactions to incentives vary from one group of individuals to another. The results of randomized experiments do not allow the formulation of microeconomic hypotheses that would serve as a basis for poverty reduction policies designed at the macroeconomic level.

How do we know whether a country's growth is socially inclusive? A common idea is that it should raise the average or median standard of living of the population. But we know that this criterion has its limitations, because it does not provide information about how what is produced is distributed. Nor does it provide information on the quality of life, let alone the thresholds at which income can be considered sufficient to live on. Inclusive growth improves people's quality of life.

The European Union, for example, uses a multidimensional indicator of material deprivation. Inclusive growth or development reduces people's deprivation. In Europe, poverty is defined as the inability of a household or individual to afford at least four of the following:

- Pay rent or utility bills,
- Keep the home adequately heated,
- Meet unexpected expenses,

- Eat fish, meat, or one protein equivalent every two days,
- Go on vacation away from home one week per year,
- Buy a washing machine,
- Buy a color television,
- Pay for one telephone connection.

Based on this criterion, it is estimated that 5.6% of the EU population is in this situation (24 million people). The populations at risk are young people, the least educated, and single-parent families. The countries with high rates of multidimensional poverty are Bulgaria (19.9%), Romania (12.6%), and Greece (15.9%).

Improvement in quality of life can also be seen in the fact that people's living standards are less subject to uncertainty. The European Union proposes an economic stress indicator that captures the vulnerability to shocks that can push people from a situation of precariousness to a situation of poverty. The dimensions of this indicator as follows:

- Difficulty in balancing the household budget given its income,
- Inability to meet unexpected expenses,
- Accumulation of payment arrears: rent, housing loans, credit purchases, water, electricity and gas bills,
- High burden of the total cost of housing.

Finally, it is necessary to have indicators of poverty. The at-risk-of-poverty rate is the proportion of people with an equivalent disposable income (after social transfers) below the at-risk-of-poverty threshold, which is set in the European Union at 60% of disposable income after social transfers. Based on these criteria, in 2019, the proportion of the population at risk of poverty and social exclusion was 21.1% in Europe (i.e., one fifth of the population). In 10 years (between 2008 and 2018) the risk of poverty has increased by almost 5pp in Luxembourg, 2.8 pp in both Sweden and the Netherlands.

4.3.2 The Question of the Trade-Off between Poverty and Inequality

Rampant inequality is another hot topic linked to the non-inclusive nature of growth in the industrialized countries and the rest of the world. In this chapter we do not address the extensive literature review that exists on this issue. Rather, we focus on a puzzle that has long been discussed by economists: Can economic growth reduce poverty and inequality at the same time? Is this desirable? And is it possible? Kuznets (1955) was the first to suggest an inverted U-curve theory for inequality. In an initially poor country that industrializes, inequality jumps. It increases less and less rapidly as the country increases the standard of living of its population. Then, above a certain level of GDP, inequality falls. This was the case in most industrialized countries at the beginning of the twentieth century, reflecting the emergence of a pauperized working class. Some authors, such as Okun (1975), argue that a more equal distribution of resources can be disastrous for the production of wealth and therefore detrimental to the growth of average income because it reduces the incentives to work and invest.

But there is also a more anthropological reading. The forces that reduce poverty are technological and economic in nature. They are linked to the productive system, to technology, to the market, to trade, to business activity, to good business, and to industrialization. They correspond to the mechanisms that allow for an increase in wealth that could potentially be distributed in an equitable manner among all economic and social actors. The forces that reduce or increase inequality are sociopolitical in nature. Historically, they have emerged from the great societal demands for more equality, from sociopolitical compromises as in the regime of welfare states. According to a Marxist reading, inequalities are linked to private property and to the unequal ex-ante distribution of capital among social actors.

The answer to our question has been considered from several angles. The first idea is to try to find a link between the two phenomena (poverty and inequality) by focusing on a subgroup of the population. For example, statistically, there are indicators that measure both the poverty rate and its depth by taking into account the distribution of income among the poorest. These are the FGT indicators (Foster–Greer–Thorbecke):

$$P_\alpha = \frac{1}{N} \sum_{\substack{j=1(R_j \le S)}}^{K} \left(\frac{S - R_j}{S} \right), \qquad (4.1)$$

where

N: population size,
R_j: income of individual j (earning less than the income corresponding to the poverty line$S$),
S: poverty line income,

K: number of poor individuals with income less than S,
$\alpha = 0, 1, 2, 3, \ldots$: relative weights of the poorest among the poor inequality aversion parameter.

For $\alpha = 0$, we define the headcount poverty, which corresponds to the proportion of the poor in the total population:

$$P_0 = \frac{K}{N} = \frac{1}{N} \sum_{j=1(R_j \leq S)}^{K} 1. \tag{4.2}$$

For $\alpha = 1$, we define the poverty gap measure or depth of poverty, which provides information about the average location of the poor relative to poor people's average income:

$$P_1 = \frac{1}{N} \sum_{j=1(R_j \leq S)}^{K} \left(\frac{S - \bar{R}_L}{S} \right), \tag{4.3}$$

where $\bar{R}_L$ is the poor individual's average income.

For $\alpha = 2$, we define the severity of poverty, which considers the distribution of income among the poor captured by the standard deviation of income (denoted σ_L) in the following equation:

$$P_2 = \frac{1}{N} \sum_{j=1(R_j \leq S)}^{K} \left[\frac{S - R_j}{S} \right]^2 = \frac{K}{N} \left[\left(\frac{S - \bar{R}_L}{S} \right)^2 + \left(\frac{\sigma}{S} \right)^2 \right]. \tag{4.4}$$

Using the FGT indexes, one can also consider the Sen poverty indicator, which combines all three aspects of poverty: headcount, depth, and severity:

$$Sen = P_0 G_L + P_1 (1 - G_l), \tag{4.5}$$

where G_L is the Gini index computed for individuals' income below the poverty line.

A disadvantage of these measures of poverty is that they can produce surprising results, such as a decline in poverty when income falls, because it creates more deaths. On the other hand, in the opposite direction, the demographic effect is interesting. Even when income increases, poverty may increase due to a demographic effect (poor families have more children). This problem is not solved by taking income per capita, because we do not have detailed statistical data on how deaths and births are distributed in the population according to income level. But they are widely used.

A disadvantage of $\P_\alpha lpha$ indicators is that they focus on the poorest. For public policy, the question must be more universal: How to increase the average standard of living while reducing the dispersion of income within a population? To answer this question, we must not approach it in exclusively economic terms, but also in terms of political philosophy or social justice. Let us make the hypothesis that intra- and intergenerational solidarity is a condition for the viability of societies in the long term. A possible reason is that no social contract, no productive system, can last over the long term without the support of the population. But this adherence presupposes that the needs of everyone are taken into account. But how can we objectively construct a social welfare function? Economists have answered this question by highlighting a paradox: It is impossible if preferences are heterogeneous (Arrow's impossibility theorem). The solution can only be based on normative principles. According to Rawls, a fair society is one in which each member has access to primary goods, any deprivation being equivalent to depriving people of freedom. The fight against poverty is therefore a first objective to aim for (providing everyone with the minimum to live decently). But can it be achieved by fighting against inequalities?

In Fig. 4.8, we show poverty on the x-axis, on a scale of 0–1. This is any indicator that measures the average standard of living of the population. As we approach 1, poverty becomes important in the country. Conversely, as we move toward 0, it decreases. On the ordinate, we represent inequality. Inequality is high when we are close to 1 and low when we are close to 0. On this graph, small numbered circles illustrate different country situations. Circle 1 corresponds to an ideal situation where the distribution of income and wealth is not very unequal and poverty is low. This is the medium-/long-term objective toward which a government that puts inclusive, socially sustainable growth at the heart of its priorities seeks to move. Circle 2 represents a situation of egalitarianism in poverty. This was the case in China throughout the Mao period, and also in the USSR until Perestroika. It is still the case today in many poor countries in sub-Saharan Africa, Asia, and Latin America. Circle 3 describes a case where a few rich people rule in the middle of a mass of poor people. This situation

Fig. 4.8 Fighting
inequality and poverty

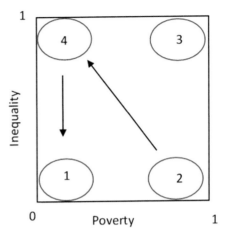

generally characterizes "kleptocracies", that is, economies that function
under the regime (autocratic or liberal) of exploitation of rents. Finally,
circle 4 illustrates the situation of countries with a high average standard
of living in a context of high inequality. This reflects the current situation
in many industrialized countries.

The question we can ask ourselves is: Starting from a given initial
situation, how do we get to circle 1?

Let's start from circle 2, taking two examples. This was the situation
in the Communist People's Republic of China under Mao, between 1949
and 1976. The mass of the population, mainly rural and working class,
was poor, but communism claimed to be different from capitalism in
its ethics in favor of equality among all. The doctrine in vogue was an
adaptation of Soviet communism to the Chinese reality. The policy of
the Great Leap Forward until 1966 marked the collectivization of the
means of production. The Great Cultural Revolution, from 1966 onward,
aimed to give power to the masses (the proletariat and the youth) by
eradicating all symbols of inequality (questioning the bureaucracy, the elites
and all Confucian symbols of meritocracy). Even if daily life was devoid
of comfort, the system drew its strength from an authoritarianism based
on the zeal of the rulers to exalt the sharing of goods in common as
an example of humanity. A similar situation prevailed in a small African
country, Burkina Faso, between 1983 and 1987. Under the leadership of
Thomas Sankara, one of the poorest countries in the world adopted harsh

policies of eradicating corruption, national emancipation, and repression of any opposition to the anti-imperialist struggle. The ideas were close to Russian communism, but were intended to be rooted in the African tradition. Typically, political regimes promote structures for participatory democracy, both politically and economically (e.g., participation in local management structures). In Burkina Faso, as in China, the aim was to give power to the masses. In China, a breakthrough came with Deng Xiaoping's reforms from 1978. The arrival in power of a new generation of leaders led to the following leitmotiv: The people of China want the same standard of living as those in Western countries. From then on, the objective was to create a middle class to which it was hoped to provide a standard of living comparable to that in Europe or the United States. In Burkina Faso, the arrival in power in 1987 of a president more in favor of close relationships with France and industrialized Western countries gradually put an end to the revolutionary experience. Before that, people were living in a country of "men of integrity" (as Burkina Faso means in the Moré language), but the vast majority of them were very poor.

In the figure, arrows are drawn to indicate the case of a country that cannot move directly from circle 2 to circle 1, and that must necessarily join circle 4 first. This seems to be consistent with what the historical and empirical evidence suggests (even if it is only clusters of evidence with no theoretical basis).

Indeed, historical evidence suggests that the two phenomena (declining poverty and declining inequality) have often been decoupled. For example, Perestroika in the early 1990s raised Russian living standards above what they had been before, but it was initially accompanied by a sharp rise in inequality. Developing countries that experience catch-up growth rates of 5–8% for several years experience an increase in GDP per capita, but this is not immediately accompanied by an improvement in inequality indicators (Gini and Theil indices, Palma ratio, etc.). In the case of China, between 1978 and 2012, about 600 million Chinese people were lifted out of extreme poverty. Living standards have risen and a large middle class has emerged. But the meteoric growth has also increased income and wealth inequality. The goal of the Chinese leaders is now to move down to circle 1 by keeping the economy as far to the left as possible in the figure. The quest for a "harmonious society" is the stated goal of the Chinese Communist Party, which means that growth strategies over the next few years will be based more on social justice considerations (even though the country appears to be growing at lower rates than in the past decade).

What makes it difficult to reach both objectives simultaneously (fighting poverty and income inequality) is that the necessary conditions are often difficult to meet. Not only must economic growth be sufficiently fast (to bring about a significant decline in poverty levels), but inequality must not be too pronounced at the beginning and end of the process. This means that countries starting from an initial situation corresponding to point 2 are more likely to achieve these two objectives than countries starting from point 3. This can be easily demonstrated by using two concepts familiar to growth economists, that is, beta and sigma convergence.

Let us consider a population with N individuals $j(j = 1, \ldots, N)$ whose income y is measured between two dates t_0 and t_1. A usual measure of a decrease in income inequality is the σ-convergence, that is, that the variance of income is lower at date t_1 than at date t_0 ($t_0 < t_1$):

$$V(y_{t_0}) > V(y_{t_1}). \tag{4.6}$$

The increase in average income between the two dates can be described by a β-convergence equation:

$$y_{t_1} - y_{t_0} = \alpha - \beta y_{t_0} + \epsilon_{t_1}, \tag{4.7}$$

where ϵ_{t_0} is a residual term. α and β are two coefficients.

If the average per capita income is negatively correlated with the cumulative average income gap between the two periods, this means that the average income has increased between the two periods t_0 and t_1, so beta is positive. There may be several causes. But it is not clear whether this income is increasing because the standard of living of the poorest has increased faster than that of the richest. We could even have an increase in average income if the income of the richest increases greatly and that of the poorest decreases somewhat. Ideally, we would like to see the standard of living of the poor rise faster than that of the rich.

Considering a general form of the convergence equation, we write

$$y_t - y_{t_0} = \beta(y_{t-1} - y_{t_0}) + \epsilon_t, \quad t > t_0. \tag{4.8}$$

Taking the variance of both sides, we obtain

$$\sigma_t^2 = \frac{1}{1 - \beta^2 L}\left[(1 - \beta)^2 \sigma_{t_0}^2 + \beta(1 - \beta)cov(y_{t-1}, y_{t_0}) + \sigma_{\epsilon_t}^2\right], \tag{4.9}$$

where σ_t^2 is the variance of y_t, $\sigma_{t_0}^2$ is the variance of income at time t_0, $\sigma_{\epsilon_t}^2$ is the variance in income due to idiosyncratic factors, L is the lag operator. If $|\beta| < 1$, then we have β-convergence. Under this assumption, the limit behavior of $\sigma_t^2 - \sigma_{t_0}^2$ (when $t \to \infty$, $L = 1$) is given by

$$\sigma_t^2 - \sigma_{t_0}^2 = \frac{1}{1 - \beta^2} \left[\beta(1 - \beta)cov(y_{t-1}, y_{t_0}) + \sigma_{\epsilon_t}^2 \right]. \tag{4.10}$$

Using the fact that, by the OLS (ordinary least squares) estimate of β,

$$cov(y_{t-1}, y_{t_0}) = \frac{1 + \beta}{\sigma_{t_0}^2}, \tag{4.11}$$

We can write

$$\sigma_t^2 - \sigma_{t_0}^2 = \frac{\beta}{\sigma_{t_0}^2} + \frac{\sigma_{\epsilon_t}^2}{1 - \beta^2}. \tag{4.12}$$

Inclusive growth must meet two conditions.

First, it must lead to the production of new wealth (growth), so that the average income initially observed in the population increases. The β-convergence condition must therefore be satisfied. Moreover, the poorest in the initial income distribution move to the right of the distribution, which implies a tightening of the left tail of the distribution. This does not necessarily happen, especially when the convergence is cyclical (when β is less than 1 in absolute value but negative). The β-convergence process is not necessarily monotonic. GDP per capita can increase cyclically around an increasing trend, which means that growth rates vary over time: Sometimes the economy grows rapidly, sometimes its growth slows down. When β is negative, there is σ-convergence (lower income inequality) if the variability of income due to idiosyncratic shocks does not exceed a certain threshold:

$$\sigma_{\epsilon_t}^2 < \left| \frac{\beta(1 - \beta^2)}{\sigma_{t_0}^2} \right|. \tag{4.13}$$

If initially the income distribution is highly unequal (X large), then even a small variability in the growth dynamics can lead to a sigma-divergence in income.

Another way of dealing with the issue of trading off between poverty and inequality is to use the concept of poverty elasticity of growth, which has been extensively studied in the literature.

Let us take the FGT index, discussed above, in continuous time:

$$P_\alpha(S, R)) = \int_0^S \left(\frac{S-R}{S}\right)^\alpha f(R)dR, \qquad (4.14)$$

where $f(R)$ is the density R which measures the distribution of income among the poor. The poverty elasticity of growth is defined by:

$$\eta_\alpha = \frac{\alpha(P_{\alpha-1} - P_\alpha)}{P_\alpha}. \qquad (4.15)$$

To account for the effect of income distribution on the response of poverty indicators to growth, it is necessary to make assumptions about the distribution of the density function $f(R)$. In the literature, we often consider the case where this distribution is log-normal (see, e.g., Bourguignon 2000; Datt and Ravallion 1992; Kakwani 1993). The elasticity of the headcount poverty can be written as:

$$\eta_0 = -\frac{\Delta P_{0t}}{P_{0t}} \frac{1}{\Delta \ln(\bar{R}_L)} = \frac{2}{\sigma_L^2} \lambda \left[\frac{\ln(S/\bar{R}_L)}{\sigma_L^2} + \frac{\sigma_L^2}{2}\right], \qquad (4.16)$$

where $\frac{\Delta P_{0t}}{P_{0t}}$ is the proportional change in headcount poverty, $\bar{R}_L$ and σ_L^2 are respectively the average and standard deviation of log-income among the poor, λ is the hazard function of the standard Normal distribution (i.e., the ratio of the density to the cumulative distribution function). S is the poverty line.

The equation shows the sensitivity of headcount poverty to a 1% increase in the average income, assuming that the inequality of income does not change (σ is given). The elasticity is an increasing function of the economic growth (captured here by $S/\bar{R}_L$). Indeed, a higher growth rate brings the average income closer to the poverty line. Elasticity is a decreasing function of inequality. In the case of a log-normal distribution, there is a relationship between the Gini coefficient and σ:

$$Gini = 2\Phi\left[\frac{\sigma_L}{\sqrt{2}}\right] - 1, \qquad (4.17)$$

where Φ is the cdf of the standard Normal distribution. For a given level of elasticity, we can observe that there is an inverse relationship between poverty and income inequality. The level curves are decreasing and convex. The elasticity of the poverty gap is written as:

$$\eta_1 = \frac{\Phi\left[\ln(S/\bar{R}_L)/\sigma_L - \sigma_L/2\right](\bar{R}_L/2)}{\Phi\left[\ln(S/\bar{R}_L)/\sigma_L + \sigma_L/2\right] - \Phi\left[\ln(S/\bar{R}_L)/\sigma_L - \sigma_L/2\right](\bar{R}_L/2)}$$

(4.18)

As shown earlier, for a given level of η_1, there is a decreasing and convex relationship between poverty and income inequality. To show the effects of changes in income distribution in the indicators, we can use the approach suggested by Datt and Ravallion (1992).

The assumption of a log-normal distribution of income can be criticized, and the literature has highlighted other distributions (see, e.g., Cowell and Flachaire 2007). But the derivation of previous elasticities under these distributions is still an open field of research. In particular, it would be interesting to examine the case of extreme distributions (where, e.g., there are large income disparities within the population of the poor).

Some empirical work argues in favor of the two-step sequence: first fighting poverty, then fighting inequality. Indeed, one of the stylized facts highlighted in the context of globalization over the last 30 years is that the opening up of economies has reduced inequalities between countries, but that these have increased within countries. The convergence of living standards between countries is linked to the phenomenon of economic catch-up and to the fact that the GDP per capita of the poorest countries has grown faster than in the richest countries. The increase in inequalities is linked to various phenomena: the technological shift (skill premium) and its consequences on the widening of wage inequalities, the greater flexibility of labor markets which have increased competition between workers and crushed wages, the decline of welfare states, and disparities in access to land, capital and opportunities, etc.) (see, e.g., on these aspects Autor et al. 2014; Bourguignon 2016; Brandolini and Carta 2016; Dabla-Norris et al. 2015; Milanovic 2016, and Rodrik 2018).

The question of theoretical links (proven or unproven) between inequality and poverty remains open, even though the issue has been debated for a long time. We have, for the moment, essentially empirical and historical answers (see, e.g., in a very extensive literature, Berg and Ostry 2011; Lopez and Serven 2006; Ravallion 2005, and more recently Berg et al. 2018; Lakner et al. 2022, and Seo et al. 2020). It is still not clear whether a better redistribution of wealth is an effective and sustainable policy to fight poverty, because it is also necessary to take into account the factors endogenous to the dynamics of poverty that are at the origin of, for example, poverty traps or recidivism phenomena. All we can say is that more equality of income or wealth is a factor of social stability (and therefore of sustainable growth) because it responds to norms of social justice accepted by the social actors. On the other hand, empirical evidence shows that fighting poverty is not a sufficient criterion for reducing inequality. All these questions are important because they condition the public policies to be adopted. Should policies be universal, or is it better to target subgroups of the population? The economist can approach this question by anchoring his or her reflections in other disciplines, notably sociology, where these questions have long been studied (see, e.g., the seminal paper by Korpi and Palme 1998). Theoretical contributions were first developed with reference to the seminal approaches of Kuznets and Kaldor, but were then abandoned because of the questioning of the empirical stylized facts put forward by these authors. Several authors suggest a new theoretical framework that links inequality to the increase in rents of different types (land, human capital, wealth and intergenerational transfers, distribution of asset ownership). We can add to this the rents accumulated by the GAFAM, whose business is based on the almost free exploitation of massive data collected from the users of their services. The same GAFAM order works to numerous subcontractors or employees in strong competition with each other. There is both an accumulation of rents and a concentration of capital. If there is a link between inequality and poverty, it may be, for example, dynastic inequality, which perpetuates inequality from one generation to the next through the transmission of wealth, but also explains the persistence of situations of poverty (see, e.g., Kanbur and Stiglitz 2015; Stiglitz 2016).

4.4   A HOT TOPIC FOR THE TWENTY-FIRST CENTURY: SHOULD INHERITANCE BE TAXED?

While the debate on inequality has focused on the unequal distribution of wealth and income, the issue of dynastic inequality is at the heart of the debate on what a fair society should look like. The sustainability of growth includes a dimension of social ethics, and this applies to relations between generations.

One of the reasons for the vehemence of the debate today is that recent work seems to show a return of rentier societies. In the United States, 10% of the population holds almost three quarters of the wealth, and the top 10% of the population holds 99% of the financial investments. In Europe, in France, for example, inheritance flows were 15% in 2010 and are projected to be 25% according to Piketty's data. Moreover, sociological data show that in most industrialized countries, the reproduction of elites is a phenomenon due to barriers (cultural, financial) to access to education. This phenomenon is even one of the causes of the slowdown in productivity gains in the United States: Higher education has become expensive and even unaffordable for many people. Does inheritance increase social inequality? The answer is yes, if we consider only movable and immovable capital. Indeed, real estate bubbles increase spatial segregation (by limiting access to city centers to people who do not own property). Moreover, according to Piketty, there is a dynastic reproduction of inequalities linked to the phenomena of rent extraction: monopolies, patents, and financial markets. Finally, real estate and movable capital is today concentrated in the generations born during the baby boom period. There is thus an inequality between generations, since the younger generations who would need capital to invest benefit from it late and often have to go into debt.

If we include public goods and services in the inheritance, the answer is more ambiguous. Societies in industrialized countries benefit from a public heritage, through the social protection systems that are a hallmark of political regimes based on social democracy: pension rights, health expenditures related to old age, and social transfers to senior citizens. This mitigates the effects of wealth inequalities, even if differences between countries may exist depending on the specific regimes (capitalization versus distribution, public versus private health systems). If we include human capital, there is no doubt that inheritance is a cause of dynastic inequality. Emmanuel Todd shows that in the United States, it is a tool for sorting out the elites.

Should inheritance be taxed? If so, should we tax the holding or the transmission? The transfer tax has been abolished in some industrialized countries (e.g., Portugal, Austria, Sweden, Italy, and Australia).

The arguments in favor of taxing inheritances are well known. On the one hand, it generates economic inefficiencies. This argument is put forward by Piketty, for example. If the interest rate is higher than the growth rate, then economic actors have been over-saving by building up financial rents and under-investing by limiting economic risk-taking. On the other hand, inheritance can have a negative effect on the supply of labor (and thus on economic activity). If there are wealth effects due to the revaluation of wealth following increases in asset prices, this affects the intertemporal trade-off between consumption and leisure over the life cycle.

Macroeconomists disagree on the following point. Some believe that wealth ownership should be taxed. Piketty believes that capital should be taxed whatever its origin (whether inheritance or capital gains) in order to fight against the phenomenon of capital concentration-one should tax rent extraction-and to avoid the capture of the state by the richest (lobbying). Other economists, such as Philippe Aghion, posit that we should not tax entrepreneurs (who innovate and take risks), but rather rentiers. Those who believe that it is better to tax inheritance have several motivations. First, there is a redistributive virtue. Inheritances are a source of inequality. Yet democracies favor meritocracy (equality of opportunity must be promoted). It is therefore necessary to correct the inequalities linked to initial endowments. Another argument is that there is an asymmetry of information between those who know how financial markets work and those who do not. Arrondel and Masson suggest that transfers at death should be heavily taxed, so as to encourage in vivo donations. The idea is to reward altruism in order to reduce dynamic inefficiency (accelerating donations during the life cycle alleviates the liquidity constraints of descendants). Readers interested in these topics can consult the following articles (among many others): Adermon et al. (2018), Blancher et al. (2022), Botta et al. (2021), Chancel and Piketty (2021), Corak (2013), Lindahl et al. (2015), Palomino et al. (2021), Piketty and Saez (2013), Piketty (2014), Piketty and Zucman (2015), and Piketty (2020).

4.5   CONCLUSION

The issue of sustainable growth goes beyond the question of limits to growth. We are in an era where scientists from other disciplines are putting forward the hypothesis of potential ruptures in the regulation of environmental ecosystems, micro-organisms, and biodiversity, but also ruptures in sociopolitical stability, the rise of dynastic inequalities, and the phenomena of the recurrence of poverty. Faced with this, the standard models of environmental economics, at the center of which is the economic sphere, have little to tell us. The right approach is that of global models whose purpose is to model what scientists call the Earth's boundaries. Of course, growth or GDP per capita and the allocation of available resources are included in the sustainability objectives, but they are objectives among others (non-economic).

This shows that the question of sustainability is one of the most complex of the many questions that economists face. It challenges our modeling habits. On the statistical side, it is the same. We have given an example here of the IWI indicator proposed by the United Nations to measure the growth of GDP per capita taking into account used and available resources. It is likely that this indicator will be completed in the future to integrate the availability of water resources, as more and more countries are suffering from water stress, as freshwater resources are decreasing, and as the evapo-transpiration cycle seems to be disrupted by human activities as well. We have also addressed the issue of the trade-off between poverty and inequality, to underline the difficulty of strategies trying to fight against these two scourges at the same time. A sequenced strategy seems more appropriate.

In any case, we realize that the question of sustainability of growth and development puts the homo economicus as an element at the heart of different sets: societies, animal, geochemical, and environmental ecosystems. One of the difficulties for economists is that of entering into this perspective by not thinking that growth is the final objective and that ecosystems-or society-are constraints to be taken into account.

PIONEERS IN THE FIELD

Joseph Stiglitz

Stiglitz is known for his theoretical contributions which earned him the Nobel Prize in Economics in 2001. In particular, his papers have contributed to a better understanding of the phenomena of asymmetry of information. In relation to the topic of this chapter, he can be defined as one of the economists with the most innovative theoretical proposals on the issue of the analysis and reduction of inequalities. With Jean-Paul Fitoussi and Amartya Sen, he proposed in 2008 that indicators of well-being should go beyond GDP alone and include ecological and social dimensions. Some of his ideas are summarized in his book *The price of Inequality published* by WW Norton & Co in 2013, where he analyzes the rise of wealth and income inequalities in the United States and the role played by rent-seeking activities and the destabilizing role of the financial cycle for socioeconomic balances. An important aspect of the book is that it shows that the fight against inequality is based on political choices. Stiglitz has contributed to advancing the ideas of redistribution policies through taxes on capital in order to fight inequality and poverty, working with another global specialist on these issues, Anthony Atkinson. Stiglitz can be compared to Joseph Aloy Schumpeter in his approach to economic processes that are embedded in the historical, social, and political dynamics of societies. Readers interested in a comprehensive view of his contributions to the field of social justice can read the book edited by Martin Guzman at Columbia University Press in 2018 entitled *Toward a Just Society: Joseph Stiglitz and Twenty-First Century Economics.*

Thomas Piketty

Like Joseph Stiglitz, this economist has made a major contribution to the analysis of inequality. In addition to Capital in the Twenty-First Century, his other book, Capital and Ideology, which has been translated and published by Harvard University Press, is worth reading. The author has an advantage over other academic authors: He uses statistics but above all his historical knowledge of societies

(continued)

to study past and contemporary inequality regimes, in industrialized and emerging countries. We can retain several key ideas from his work. First, while inequality has become rampant in industrialized economies (the breakthrough being meteoric in the United States), this has not always been so. The period between 1914 and 1980 was one of redistribution through progressive income and inheritance tax systems. This was one of the hallmarks of social democracy in Europe. An important point emphasized by the author is that the decline of this sociopolitical regime is due to the collapse of the USSR in the early 1990s. Among the author's original proposals for reducing inequality are a universal capital endowment equal to 60% of the average adult's wealth, the application of social quotas in access to education, and the restoration of progressive taxes with an increase in the marginal rates on the income of the richest. Piketty considers that in order to allow the least privileged to benefit from the highest standards of living, it is necessary to rethink property relations and the distribution of income and wealth. In his abundant work, the interested reader will find ideas on various subjects: the transformation of capital since the eighteenth century, the division of capital and labor over the long term, the evolution of labor inequalities in industrialized countries, the relationship to inequalities in meritocratic societies, the problem of public debt and its reduction, the constitution and evolution of the social state, and the history of the progressive income tax.

REFERENCES

Adermon A, Lindahl M, Waldenström D (2018) Intergenerational wealth mobility and the role of inheritance: evidence from multiple generations. Econ J 128(612): F482–F513

Autor DH, Dorn D, Hanson GH, Song J (2014) Trade adjustment: worker-Level evidence. Q J Econ 129(4):1799–1860

Bates S, Saint-Pierre P (2018) Adaptive policy framework through the lens of the viability theory: a theoretical contribution to sustainability in the anthropocene era. Ecol. Econ. 145:244–262

Berg A, Ostry JD (2011) Inequality and unsustainable growth: two sides of the same Coin? IMF Staff Discussion Note 11/08

Berg A, Ostry JD, Tsangarides CG, Yakhshilikov Y (2018) Redistribution, inequality, and growth: new evidence. J Econ Growth 23:259–305

Blancher T, Fournier J, Piketty T (2022) Generalized Pareto curves: theory and applications. Rev Income Wealth 68(1):263–288

Boehnert J (2021) Anthropocene economics and design: heterodox economics for design transitions. She Ji: J Design Econ Innov 4(4):355–374

Botta A, Caverzasi E, Gallegati M, Piketty T, Russo A (2021) Inequality and finance in a rent economy. J Econ Behav Org 183:998–1029

Bourguignon F (2000) The pace of economic growth and poverty alleviation. The World Bank and Delta, Unpublished Manuscript

Bourguignon F (2016) The globalization of inequality. Princeton University Press, Princeton

Bradley RS, Hughes MK, Diaz, HF (2003) Climate change: climate in Medieval time. Science 302(5644):404–405

Brandolini A, Carta F (2016) Some reflections on the social welfare bases of the measurement of global income inequality. J Global Dev 7(1):1–15

Chancel L, Piketty T (2021) Global income inequality 1820–2020: the persistence and mutation of extreme inequality. J Eur Econ Assoc 19(6):3025–3062

Corak M (2013) Income inequality, equality of opportunity, and intergenerational mobility. J Econ Perspect 27(3):79–102

Costanza R (1989) What is ecological economics? Ecol Econ 1:1–7

Costanza R (2020) Ecological economics in 2049: getting beyond the argument culture to the world we all want. Ecol Econ 168:106484

Cowell FA, Flachaire E (2007) Income distribution and inequality measurement: the problem of extreme values. J Econ 141(2):1044–1072

Dabla-Norris E, Kochhar K, Nujin S, Ricka F, Tsounta E (2015) Causes and consequences of income inequality: a global perspective. IMF Staff Disc Note No. SDN/15/13

Datt G, Ravallion M (1992) Growth and redistribution components of changes in poverty measures: a decomposition with application to Brazil and India in the 1980s. J Dev Econ 38(2): 275–295

Daw T, Brown K, Rosendo S, Pomeroy R (2011) Applying the ecosystem services concept to poverty alleviation: the need to disaggregate human well-being. Environ Conserv 38(4):370–379

Eichenbaum MS, Rebelo S, Trabandt T (2020) The macroeconomics of epidemics. NBER Working Paper No. 26882

Folland CK, Karl TR, Christy JR et al. (2001) Was there a "Little Ice Age" and a "Medieval Warm Period"? In: Houghton JT, Ding Y, Griggs DJ, Noguer M et al. (eds). Working group I: the scientific basis. Intergovernmental panel on climate change. Cambridge University Press, Cambridge, p 881

Harris J (2006) Environmental and natural resource economics: a contemporary approach. Houghton Mifflin Company

Jones PD, Mann ME (2004) Climate over past millennia. Rev Geophys 42(2): RG2002

Kakwani N (1993) Poverty and economic growth with application to Cote d'Ivoire. Review Income Wealth 39:121–39

Kanbur R, Stiglitz JE (2015) Dynastic inequality, mobility and equality of opportunity. CEPR Disc Pap No. 10542

Korpi W, Palme J (1998) The Paradox of redistribution and strategies of equality: welfare state institutions, inequality, and poverty in the Western countries. Am Soc Rev 63(5):661–687

Kuznets S (1955) Economic growth and income inequality. Am Econ Rev 45 (1):1–28

Lagrue J, Spash CL, Ryan A (2012) Economic schools of thought on the environment: investigating unity and division. Camb J Econ 36(5):1091–1121

Lakner C, Mahler DG, Negre M, Prydz EB (2022) How much does reducing inequality matter for global poverty? J Econ Inequality forthcoming

Le Roy Ladurie E (1988) Times of feast, times of famine: a history of climate since the year 1000, Farrar Straus & Giroux, Reissue edition

Lindahl M M, Palme S, Sandgren M, Sjögren A (2015), "Long-term intergenerational persistence of human capital: an empirical analysis of four generations. J Hum Resour 50 (1):1–33

Lopez JH, Serven L (2006) A normal relationship? Poverty, growth, and inequality, World Bank working paper WPS3814

Malm A (2016) Fossil capital: the rise of steam power and the roots of global warming. Brooklyn, Verso

Melgar-Melgar RE, Hall CA (2020) Why ecological economics needs to return to its roots: the biophysical foundation of socio-economic systems. Ecol Econ 169:106567

Milanovic B (2016) Global inequality: a new approach for the age of globalization. Harvard Univ Press, Cambridge

Nordhaus W (1991) To Slow or not to slow: the economics of the greenhouse effect. Econ J 101(407):920–937

Nordhaus W (1992) An optimal transition path for controlling greenhouse gases. Science 258:1315–1319

Nordhaus W (1994) Managing the global commons: the economics of climate change. MIT Press, Cambridge, MA

Nordhaus W, Boyer J (2000) Warming the world: economic models of global warming. MIT Press, Cambridge, MA

Nordhaus WD, Yang Z (1996) A regional dynamic general-equilibrium model of alternative climate-change strategies. Am Econ Rev 86(4):741–765

Okun A (1975) Equality and efficiency: the big tradeoff. Brookings Institution Press, Washington

Palomino, JC, Marrero GA, Nolan B, Rodríguez JG (2021) Wealth inequality, intergenerational transfers, and family background. Oxf Econ Pap 74(3):643–670

Pier PF, Manes F, Scardi M, Riccio A (2020) Modelling matter and energy flows in the biosphere and human economy. Ecol Model 422:108984

Piketty T (2014) Capital in the twenty-first century, translated by Goldhammer A. Harvard University Press, Cambridge

Piketty T (2020) Capital and ideology, translated by Goldhammer A. Harvard University Press, Cambridge

Piketty T, Saez E (2013) A theory of optimal inheritance taxation. Econometrica 81(5):1851–1886

Piketty T, Zucman G (2015) Wealth and inheritance in the long run. Handbook Income Distrib 2:1303–1368

Pushpam K (2010) The economics of ecosystems and biodiversity ecological and economic foundations. Earthscan, London and Washington

Ravallion M (2001) Growth, inequality and poverty: looking beyond averages. World Dev 29(11):1803–1815

Ravallion M (2005) Inequality is bad for the poor. World Bank Pol Res WP No. 3677

Rockström, J, Steffen W, Noone K et al. (2009) Planetary boundaries: exploring the safe operating space for humanity. Ecol. Soc 14(2):32

Rodrik D (2018) Populism and the economics of globalization. J Int Bus Policy 1:12–33

Roldan M, Unai P (2020) Ecological economics in the age of fear. Ecol Econ 169: 106498

Seo H-J, Kim H, Lee YS (2020) The dynamic relationship between inequality and sustainable economic growth. Sustainability 12:5740

Stiglitz JE (2016) New theoretical perspectives on the distribution of income and wealth among individuals. In: Basu K, Stiglitz JE (eds) Inequality and growth: patterns and policy. International economic association series. Palgrave Macmillan, London

Traeger C (2014) A 4-stated DICE: quantitatively addressing uncertainty effects in climate change. Environ Resour Econ 59(1):1–37

Verburg PH, Dearing JA, Dyke JG, van der Leeuw S, Seitzinger S, Steffen W, Syvitski J (2016) Methods and approaches to modelling the Anthropocene. Global Environ Change 39:328–340

Vosters K, Nybom M (2017) Intergenerational persistence in latent socioeconomic status: evidence from Sweden and the United States. J Lab Econ 35(3):869–901

Washington H, Maloney M (2020) The need for ecological ethics in a new ecological economics. Ecol Econ 169:106478

Wrigley E A (2010) Energy and the English industrial revolution. Cambridge University Press, Cambridge

PART II

Financial, Monetary, and Fiscal Policies

CHAPTER 5

Interest Rates, Financial Markets, and Macroeconomics

Capital is the engine of capitalism and profit its reward. How much does it reward and cost to invest capital in a capitalist economy? This chapter investigates the evolution of different interest rates, explains their causes, and also analyzes some of their consequences. For a government concerned with economic growth, and for firms producing and selling goods and services, the expected return is the rate of return on physical capital (the growth rate of real GDP is a proxy for such a return at the macroeconomic level). For corporations, the ROCE (return on capital employed) is the benchmark for value creation. For a financial investor, investing in several assets allows a diversification of risks: residential and commercial real estate, equity, loans, sovereign, and corporate bonds. It is therefore relevant to study the rates of return on real estate assets, stock markets, loan markets, or treasury bills. For agents who take on debt, interest rates also matter because they determine the cost and sustainability of their debt. A comprehensive historical study of all these interest rates in industrialized countries since 1870 was done by Jòrda et al. (2016). Other works on interest rates in the very long run include (Hamilton et al. 2016; Piketty 2014; Schmelzing 2020). We focus our attention on the "recent" period, that is, since the beginning of the 1990s.[1]

---

[1] The interest reader can also read Farhi and Gourio (2018) and the comments by Gertler in the same volume.

© The Author(s), under exclusive license to Springer Nature Switzerland AG 2023
G. Dufrénot, *New Challenges for Macroeconomic Policies*,
https://doi.org/10.1007/978-3-031-15754-7_5

195

Here are some stylized facts, based on the findings of the recent literature:

- the rates of return on lending markets (money and bond markets) have evolved on a downward path and are very low today;
- the rates of return on equity required by shareholders have remained stable;
- stock market and real estate asset prices have been on an upward trend. This has fueled financial instability;
- the industrialized economies' neutral (or natural) interest rates have also experienced an uninterrupted downward phase since the beginning of the 1990s.

Figures 5.1 through 5.3 show examples of interest rates. In Fig. 5.1, the long-term (nominal) interest rates are those of ten-year government bonds. The curves suggest the existence of one or more common factors behind the fall in rates and their stability around zero since 2016. We can see that the decline was particularly significant at the beginning of the period, between 1990 and 1998, that is, long before the adoption of unconventional monetary policies. Figure 5.2 shows the evolution of share prices. The upward phases have been bridged by downward phases

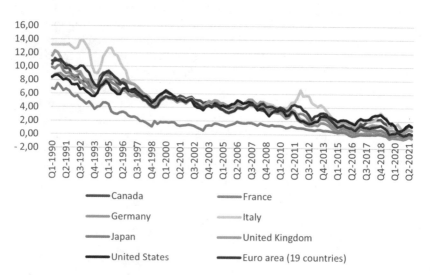

Fig. 5.1 Long-term interest rates. Source: OECD

Fig. 5.2   Equity price: selected industrialized countries. Source: OECD

corresponding to crises, one in the early 2000s and one corresponding to the Great Financial Crisis (GFC) of 2008. Prices evolve in phase, but the dispersion between countries fades after 2008. Figure 5.3 shows the neutral interest rate for some countries, estimated by the Holston-Laubach-Williams method. The authors define it as the real short-term interest rate expected to prevail when an economy is at full capacity and inflation is stable. The trend has been steadily decreasing since the early 1990s. We also observe a change in level since 2008, which can be attributed to unconventional monetary policies. Their influence has been added to that of more structural factors that we need to understand.

There are three ways of reading the evolution of interest rates. Firstly, some economists provide an explanation based on the role of real factors. Secondly, others consider that interest rates are primarily monetary and financial variables. Thirdly, for others their evolution reflects the influence of rent extraction activities.

Monetary and financial approaches to the interest rate do not conceive its evolution outside the functioning of capitalist economies for which money and finance are central. The trend decline in the market interest rates observed since 1990 is not an abnormal phenomenon. It started

Fig. 5.3 Natural interest rates. Source: Holston/Laubach/William, Fed. NY website

several centuries ago and has become more pronounced as monetary and financial assets became an alternative to physical assets and as financial liquidity became more abundant. This phenomenon was confirmed during financial globalization episodes, especially since the mid-1980s. International capital flows have been so large that they have mechanically crushed market interest rates. The real rates have fallen because nominal rates have fallen. Massive sovereign and private debt buybacks by central banks are therefore undoubtedly a factor in the observed decline in market rates in industrialized countries. This cannot be denied. But it is not the only one. We will see how the financial cycle has been another determining factor.

Alongside this conception, there is a voluminous literature devoted to analyses of the interest rate as a real variable. The vision is that of a vast market of financial funds where two types of agents meet. Some want to finance investment projects. Others are willing to lend their savings by depriving themselves of part of their present consumption.

Those who come to borrow money negotiate an interest rate according to the marginal rate of return on capital in the medium/long term. According to neoclassical theories, this rate depends on structural factors: potential growth, demographic changes, productivity gains, and so on.

Those who come to lend the money they have saved negotiate an interest rate according to the price they give to the sacrifice of postponing part of their consumption into the future and according to the uncertainty they perceive in lending this money. In neoclassical growth models, such elements are described by the rate of impatience, the degree of risk aversion, and so on. The fact that market rates are falling could therefore be linked to these different factors of a real nature.

A third view is that the interest rate is a rate of profit whose level results from the functional distribution of income among the factors of production. In an economy where, since the beginning of the 1990s, corporate governance has been based on shareholder value, firms' income is no longer divided solely between wages and profits, but between wages, interest payments to shareholders, interest payments to those with whom firms are indebted, and profits (self-financing of physical capital). There are therefore several interest rates, distinct from market rates. Some have not experienced a downward trend. For example, the returns required by shareholders have not decreased. Therefore, we cannot assert, for example, that the cost of capital has fallen (even if market rates have fallen). In such a context, there is a literature linking the evolution of interest rates to rents and inequality.

The reader needs to be aware that there is no consensus among economists on the interpretation of interest rate dynamics. There is no mainstream view, because not everyone has the same vision of the reality underlying these developments.

What is being debated today? What's new in the facts? We observe the following phenomena: potential growth rates are low and core inflation rates have been stable for several years at low levels.[2] And all this is happening though the cost of money is low and capitalist economies have abundant liquidity that could finance growth.

The great debate among macroeconomists in this twentieth century is the following. The paradox is that money is cheap, financial liquidity is abundant to finance growth, but industrialized countries seem stuck in a situation of underemployment. Can such an underemployment equilibrium last? And if so, how do we get out of it? Some economists answer

---

[2] This phenomenon has lasted for 25 years, but it is not yet clear whether this trend will continue given the recent resurgence of inflationary pressures following the end of the Covid-19 crisis and the 2022 war in Ukraine.

by showing that the equilibrium real interest rate corresponding to the level of full employment is not only low, but negative (this rate is the natural or neutral interest rate). It is so negative that, in a context of low inflation, central bankers are unable to adjust the nominal interest rate to the level that would be necessary to bring the observed real rate to its full employment level. Indeed, the nominal rate cannot fall below a zero lower bound (ZLB) because it is necessarily positive.

Those who focus on inequality argue that we need to look at the distribution of wealth and income to understand what causes this situation. First, falling market rates create financial rents. It is more profitable to borrow money cheaply and buy financial assets than to invest in physical capital. Savings is not the residual of income once consumed but financial savings. Second, since the richest tend to save more than the least rich, the concentration of wealth leads to an overabundance of financial savings.

In this chapter, we study these different approaches in detail.

5.1   What Are the Causes of the Downward Trend in Market Interest Rates?

We first look at the yield curve of sovereign bonds. We consider the United Kingdom as an illustration (our arguments also apply to the other industrialized countries). Sovereign bond yields serve as a basis for setting all market rates for short-, medium-, and long-term horizons. The yield curve (the hierarchy of rates according to maturities) provides indications of expected future returns at different horizons, generally from a few months to a long horizon of 10, 20, or even 30 years.

We consider the implied real spot curve from the Bank of England's (BOE) data between January 1990 and December 2020 (monthly frequency), with the following maturities: 2.5, 3, 4, 5, 6, 7, 8, 9, and 10 years. We conduct a principal component analysis to extract common factors to the different maturities. Table 5.1 shows that the first factor explains almost all the variance of the real yield matrix. Figure 5.4 shows its downward trend over time. This factor can be considered as an average interest rate that summarizes the trends of the different maturities.

A more sophisticated analysis is to look for common factors with economic interpretation.

Table 5.1 Principal components analysis. UK yield curve

Factor	Value	Proportion	Cumulative Proportion
1	8.882789	0.9870	0.9870
2	0.110977	0.0123	0.9993
3	0.004959	0.0006	0.9999
4	0.001028	0.0001	1.0000
5	0.000241	0.0000	1.0000
6	$5.47E{-}06$	0.0000	1.0000
7	$1.61E{-}07$	0.0000	1.0000
8	$4.81E{-}09$	0.0000	1.0000
9	$5.16E{-}11$	0.0000	1.0000

Source Author's estimates

First factor

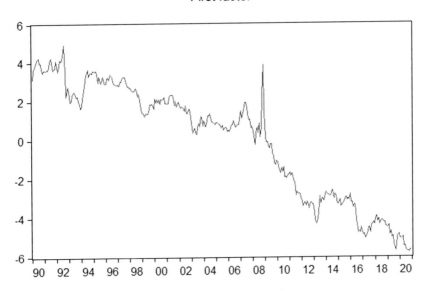

Fig. 5.4 First factor of the yield curve. United Kingdom

The market gross price at time t of a sovereign bond with a maturity $t + \tau$ is given by the following equation:

$$P_t^\tau = cpn \sum_{i=1}^{[\tau]+1} \frac{1}{[1 + y_t^i]^{\tau-[\tau]+i-1}} + \frac{Principal_{t+\tau}}{[1 + y_t^\tau]^\tau} \tag{5.1}$$

where cpn is the coupon, $Principal$ is the amount borrowed at time t and paid when the bond reaches maturity $(t + \tau)$, y_t^i are zero-coupon yields. $[\tau]$ is the integer part of τ. We consider Svensson's model to extract the short-, medium-, and long-term components of the yield curve:

$$\begin{aligned} y_t^\tau = \beta_{0t} + \beta_{1t} &\left[\frac{1 - exp(-\tau/\lambda_1)}{\tau/\lambda_1} \right] \\ &+ \beta_{2t} \left[\frac{1 - exp(-\tau/\lambda_1)}{\tau/\lambda_1} - exp(-\tau/\lambda_1) \right] \\ &+ \beta_{3t} \left[\frac{1 - exp(-\tau/\lambda_2)}{\tau/\lambda_2} - exp(-\tau/\lambda_2) \right]. \end{aligned} \tag{5.2}$$

The short-term rate is $y_t^{\tau=0} = \beta_{0t} + \beta_{1t}$. The long-term rate is $\lim_{\tau \to \infty} y_t^\tau = \beta_{0t}$. The slope of the yield curve is $(-\beta_{1t})$. λ_1 and λ_2 capture the speed of convergence to the short-term rate.

Figure 5.5 shows the estimates of long- and short-term components. The long rate has been decreasing regularly since the beginning of the observation period. The short rate also decreases by steps about every 100 observations (i.e., every ten years). Sovereign bond rates have had an influence on all real market interest rates. For example, Fig. 5.6 shows the 6-month and 12-month London Interbank Offered Rate (LIBOR). They, too, have been on a downward trend since 1990.

What factors explain these phenomena? Various hypotheses have been examined in the literature to explain the fall in rates: monetary and fiscal policies, structural supply factors influencing potential growth (demographics, productivity), demand factors influencing the ex-ante balance between desired savings and investment, and global financial factors (private sector deleveraging, financial cycles, excess global savings). We briefly review some of these explanations.

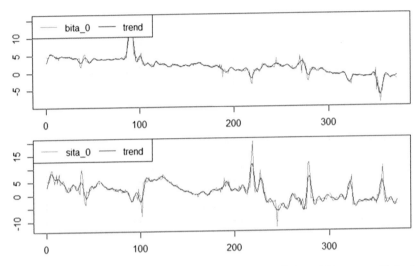

Fig. 5.5 Long-term and short-term components of the yield curve. United Kingdom

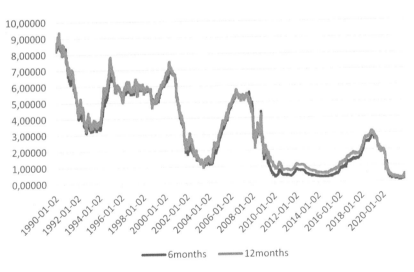

Fig. 5.6 LIBOR. United Kingdom

5.1.1   Do Monetary Policies Explain Negative Sovereign Bond Yields?

Since unconventional monetary policies were adopted by central banks from the GFC onward, they cannot explain the downward trend in interest rates observed in the years preceding the 2008 financial crisis. The following explanations are therefore valid for the developments observed *after the GFC*.

Massive purchases of sovereign debts in the bond markets have crushed term premiums to very low levels, driving down yields. Moreover, the massive buybacks have pushed up sovereign bond prices and driven down yields from the shortest to the longest maturities. Expansionary policies have led to a downward shift in the bond yield curves in both the primary and secondary markets. This phenomenon has been accentuated by a scarcity effect due to strong investor demand for safe assets to comply with the new prudential rules adopted after the crisis (a phenomenon called "safety trap"). Negative yields reflect the fact that purchases of sovereign bonds were more expensive than their nominal value (the present value of the payment flows have been higher than the nominal value of the bonds), which is symptomatic of a bubble situation in the markets.

In addition, central banks' actions have caused other investors to buy bonds at negative rates. First, expectations of currency appreciation in the countries where massive debt buybacks took place led to the hope that negative rates would be offset by exchange rate effects. Second, through self-fulfilling prophecies, it was attractive to buy securities at high prices and then sell them on secondary markets at even higher prices (investors expected that the bull market would last). This allowed them to expect capital gains that would offset the negative returns.

5.1.2   Do Low Market Interest Rates Reflect Low Natural Interest Rates?

Monetary policies have had little impact on the inflation rates observed over the last three decades (core inflation has remained low). Moreover, it seems that industrialized economies have experienced situations of persistent excess savings and a downward trend in investment. Some economists interpret these features as a situation in which the observed interest rates are moving along steady state equilibria. Such stationary equilibria, with stable inflation, allow us to estimate an interest rate that is considered as "natural" and influenced by structural factors that determine long-term growth. This interpretation is consistent with the vision of neoclassical growth models in which the long-term stationary equilibrium depends on real factors (for instance demographic factors, TFP and human capital, savings rates, the depreciation rate of capital, the share of production factors in national income). Neoclassical growth models of the Solow type, Phelps' optimal growth model, or Ramsey's growth model could be used here as a theoretical reference to define a natural interest rate interpreted as the long-run rate of return on capital. However, such models are unable to explain why the observed interest rates have become negative.

A great deal of empirical work has been devoted to estimating the natural rate of interest. The methodologies differ according to the interpretation given to it. Some economists interpret it as an equilibrium rate observed when there are no market friction or rigidity. DSGE models have been calibrated to estimate natural interest rates for the industrialized countries. The interested reader can refer to Brand et al. (2018), Cúrdia et al. (2015), Del Negro et al. (2017), Justiniano et al. (2014), Gerali and Neri (2019). These models allow us to study the influence of different shocks on the natural rate: preference shocks, productivity shocks affecting the marginal productivity of capital, and risk premium shocks. But they have a drawback in that they make the natural rate more volatile than the observed series would suggest. The reason is that the natural interest rate is defined as the rate for which the output gap is closed and inflation is stable.

An alternative interpretation is based on the Fisher relationship. The neutral interest rate is considered as a "pure" real rate (not influenced by monetary and financial variables), because it is a long-term rate. Its nominal value is simply the real interest rate plus inflation. The real rate is given by the Euler conditions of the intertemporal choice models between present and future consumption. It depends on households' discount rate, their degree of risk aversion, degree of impatience, or intertemporal elasticity of substitution. This approach has been used to see how changes in demography affect agents' intertemporal choices. See, for instance, Bielecki et al. (2020), Papetti (2021).

Another interpretation is Wicksell's neutral interest rate (see Wicksell 1898), that is, the rate that equals the real supply and demand of capital goods. In other words, it is the rate that equalizes, ex-ante, desired investment and savings. In models using this approach, the trend decline in the natural interest rate can be associated with the phenomenon of secular stagnation, an underemployment equilibrium characteristic of a situation of Keynesian unemployment with low aggregate demand (see, e.g., Eggertsson et al. 2016, 2019; Summers 2015).

All of these models point to a decline in the natural rate of interest over time and explain it by a multitude of factors:

- changes in demographic structure and the impacts on the labor market, savings, and investment choices;
- fall in the price of capital;
- consequences of deleveraging when the financial cycle turns around and causes major balance sheet losses and accentuates household over-indebtedness. Countries can then remain in a recession phase for a long time (see, e.g., Eggertsson and Krugman 2012, and the last section of this chapter);
- domestic and global saving glut, which can be explained by a flight to quality (strong demand for safe assets), or by some emerging countries' accumulation of current account surpluses in order to have precautionary foreign reserves);
- scarcity of risk-free assets (safety trap). See Caballero et al. (2017);
- slowdown in productivity gains;
- inequality (because the propensity to consume of those with higher incomes or wealth is lower than the rest of the population, which reduces aggregate demand); see Cynamon and Fazzali (2016).
- fiscal austerity policies.

Industrialized countries have been particularly affected by demographic changes, especially because of the effects on labor supply. Indeed, an aging population has two effects. First, as there are fewer people of working age, the supply of labor decreases, which reduces the demographic dividend, that is, the contribution of the labor factor to growth decreases. The second effect is a composition effect. Any change in the age structure of the population causes a slowdown in productivity gains (see the previous chapter). Moreover, the aging of the population reduces desired savings (which should raise the equilibrium rate). Another effect is intergenerational transfers. With the increase in life expectancy and the advanced periods of retirement, the older generations keep a high part of their wealth (for their own consumption) and transmit it late to the younger generations in activity who would need capital to invest.

The fall in the price of capital, at least since 1980, affects the natural rate, because it reduces desired investment. This is a cause of prolonged stagnation, as explained by Thwaites (2015). This author proposes overlapping generations models (OLG) model in which two mechanisms are at play. On the one hand, the decline in the relative price of investment goods allows more capital to be accumulated by drawing on available savings. On the other hand, the induced rise in the capital-output ratio reduces the marginal product. If capital and labor are complementary, the interest rate falls (this occurs in particular if the elasticity of investment with respect to the relative price of investment is less than 1). Here is an unsolved question: why have the prices of investment goods fallen? A usual answer is that new generations of capital incorporate less innovation and R&D. But are capital prices properly measured?

The current context of low inflation and zero lower bound accentuates the contribution of secular stagnation equilibria to the decline in natural interest rates. Indeed, the low level of aggregate demand can be explained by a combination of factors: a fall in public investment, concomitant with the policies of neutral fiscal policies, or even fiscal austerity adopted by governments before the Covid-19 crisis, excess savings, and weak private investment. This contributes to low effective growth rates and widens the gap in output gaps on a long-term basis. This also leads to a decline in potential growth (erosion of the productivity of human and physical capital). The strong post-Covid recoveries currently observed reflect a catch-up, and it is not clear whether they will lead to higher potential growth trajectories. Falls in potential growth lead to deflationary spirals that prevent real interest rates from falling sufficiently for a sustainable recovery.

We present here, for illustrative purpose, what can be considered as seminal models of the determination of natural interest rate that provide some explanations about the above stylized facts. We select Eggertsson and Mehrotra (2014)'s, Eggertsson et al. (2019)'s models, and Caballero et al. (2016)'s model.

The Determination of Interest Rates in Overlapping Generations Models á la Mehrotra and Summers

Overlapping generations models are an appropriate framework to test several hypotheses on the causes of downward pressure on the interest rate. First, they allow linking interest rates to population growth and to total factor productivity (TFP), which are two determinants of the productive capacity of economies. Second, they allow us to introduce the financial constraints faced by successive generations, which may explain the weakness of demand and the excess savings: forced deleveraging shocks or the accelerated aging of a population whose life expectancy is increasing.

We consider an economy composed of three generations of individuals whose life cycle is summarized by three periods. During the first part of their lives, they are young, then middle-aged (they enter the labor market), and finally old (in retirement). The young can only consume by borrowing from those who work (the middle-aged). To do this, they issue a bond. Those of working age must repay their debts incurred during the first period of their life cycle (interest and principal) and save for their retirement. In the model, it is assumed that the middle-aged receive an income endowment. Retirees consume from an income endowment and their savings income. Young people who borrow have a debt constraint, and working people cannot save all their income. The model is simple. There is no capital and no production function. There is only one homogeneous good that serves as a numeraire and whose price is normalized to 1. The population of the country consists of N_t individuals at each date, and it grows at a rate of n.

For an individual born at date t, the utility function and the budget constraints are written as follows:

$$U_t(C_t^y, C_{t+1}^m, C_{t+2}^o) = E_t \left\{ \log(C_t^y) + \beta \, \log(C_{t+1}^m) + \beta^2 \log(C_{t+2}^o) \right\},$$
(5.3)

s.t

$$C_t^y = B_t^y,$$
(5.4)

$$c_{t+1}^m = Y_{t+1}^m - (1 + r_t)B_t^y - (-B_{t+1}^m),$$
(5.5)

$$C_{t+2}^o = Y_{t+2}^o + (1 + r_{t+1})(-B_{t+1}^m),$$
(5.6)

$$(1 + r_t)B_t^i \le D_t, \ i = y, m,$$
(5.7)

with the following definitions of the variables:

C_t^j : consumption of generation $j = y, m, o$ at time t,
Y_t^m: endowment received by middle-aged agent at time t. It is assumed to be a proportional amount of productivity endowment : $Y_t = A_t \tilde{Y}$, where the ~means the variable is normalized by productivity,
Y_t^o: endowment received by old agent at time t,

r_t: interest rate,
B_t^i: bond issued by an agent of generation i,
β: discount factor,
D_t: debt ceiling. It is assumed to be a growing function of the middle-aged household's income: $D_t = A_t \tilde{D}$.

Equation (5.3) is a standard intertemporal utility function of an agent born at time t. Equation (5.4) says that a young agent consumes from her borrowing. Equation (5.5) says that the middle-aged reimburses her borrowing and saves $(-B_{t+1^m})$ for her retirement. The remainder of exogenous income Y_{t+1}^m is consumed. Then, when retired, the agent consumes on her savings (augmented with the interests) (Eq. 5.6). Equation (5.7) is the borrowing constraint.

Under the assumption of perfect foresight, by combining the agents' optimal choices and the loan market clearing conditions, the demand for and supply of loans are easily obtained:

$$\tilde{L}_t^d = \frac{(1 + n_t)(1 + g_t)}{1 + r_t} \tilde{D}, \tag{5.8}$$

$$\tilde{L}_t^s = \frac{\beta}{1 + \beta}(\tilde{Y}^m - \tilde{D}) - \left(\frac{1 + g_t}{1 + \beta}\right)\frac{\tilde{Y}^o}{1 + r_t}, \tag{5.9}$$

where n_t is the growth rate of population at time t, and g_t is the growth rate of productivity art time t. The equilibrium interest rate is

$$1 + r_t = \left(\frac{1 + \beta}{\beta}\right)\frac{(1 + n_t)D_t}{Y_t^m - D_{t-1}} + \left(\frac{1}{\beta}\right)\frac{Y_{t+1}^o}{Y_t^m - D_{t+1}}. \tag{5.10}$$

In this simple model, the demand for loanable funds is an increasing function of the growth rate of population and productivity, and a decreasing function of the interest rate. The supply of loanable funds increases with the interest rate.

If population growth slows, the interest rate falls because the proportion of young people in the population falls (the demand for loanable funds falls).

If productivity gains slow down, the interest rate also falls. Indeed, middle-aged households need to save more for their retirement because they expect their future income to fall. As a result, the supply of loanable funds increases (in Eq. (5.9) through $\tilde{Y}^m$). At the same time, the demand for loanable funds declines as the debt constraint on young people tightens. In Eq. (5.8) $(1 + g_t)\tilde{D}$ decreases). As can be seen in Eq. (5.10), there is nothing to prevent the interest rate from being negative, even if n_t and g_t are both positive.

A deleveraging shock hardens the debt constraint of young people. So the demand for loanable funds decreases, which lowers the interest rate.

We can also see that the relative endowment of young compared to old households has an influence on the equilibrium interest rate. In this type of model, intergenerational (not intra-generational) inequalities influence the interest rate.

What happens in the open economy model? Before answering, let's look at some intuitions about what we might expect. If we consider the imbalance between savings and desired investment in an open economy, capital flows can influence the adjustment of the interest rate. Countries with excess savings have current account surpluses and rising foreign exchange reserves. These can be invested abroad in countries with current account deficits. Thus, when a country's desired net savings are in surplus, it leads to capital outflows. Conversely, in countries where net investment is high, capital inflows can put downward pressure on interest rates. But capital inflows cause the exchange rate to appreciate, which can mitigate the decline.

To begin with, we neglect the role of the exchange rate. In the previous model, the impact on the interest rate can be studied by considering a world with two countries. In each country, in addition to households, we introduce a government. The latter starts date t with no debt arrears (public debt at time $t - 1$ equals 0: $B_{t-1}^g = 0$), issues new bonds to allocate lump sum transfers to the middle-aged households, and, in the next period, taxes the old households in such a way that the lump sum tax equals the principal of debt borrowed plus interests. We assume that neither young households are taxed nor they receive any transfers. Moreover, for simplification, it is assumed that there is no public expenditure and that the growth rate of population $n_t = 0$. We therefore have the following equations, for respectively the fiscal rule and government's budget constraint in the domestic country:

$$B_t^g = -T_t^m, \quad T_{t+1}^o = (1 + r_{t-1})B_{t-1}t^g, \tag{5.11}$$

and

$$B_t^g + T_t^o + T_t^m = (1 + r_{t-1})B_{t-1}^g. \tag{5.12}$$

where we assume for simplification purpose that the population growth rate $n_t = 0$.

In the foreign country, the government adopts the same behavior, and the same assumptions hold for the population growth rate ($n_t^* = 0$). But it also holds part of the public debt issued by the domestic country. This assumption is used to model the saving glut hypothesis. Indeed, one of the hypotheses to the fall in global interest rates is the current account surpluses of the emerging countries after the Mexican and Asian crises of the late 1990s. These countries have accumulated precautionary foreign exchange reserves and invested them in US Treasury bonds. We have:

$$B_t^{g*} + T_t^{o*} + (1 + r_{t-1})IR_{t-1} + T_t^{m*} = (1 + r_{t-1}^*)B_{t-1}^{g*} + IR_t. \tag{5.13}$$

International reserves (IR) are remunerated at the domestic interest rate.

In the open economy the households' constraints are defined by the following equations. For purpose of simplicity, we assume that only middle-aged households receive an endowment, denoted Y_t. They save by holding either domestic (A^D) or international (A^I):

$$C_t^y = B_t^y, \tag{5.14}$$

$$c_{t+1}^m = Y_{t+1} - (1 + r_t)B_t^y - A_{t+1}^D - A_{t+1}^I, \tag{5.15}$$

$$C_{t+2}^o = (1 + r_{t+1})A_{t+1}^D + (1 + r_{t+1}^*)A_{t+1}^I, \tag{5.16}$$

$$(1 + r_t)B_t^i \le D_t, \quad 0 \le A_{t+1}^I \le K_{t+1}, \quad i = y, m, \tag{5.17}$$

K_t denotes the upper bound of foreign capital held by domestic agents at time i.

The equilibrium of the securities market in each country implies the following expressions of the equilibrium interest rate:

$$1 + r_t = \left(\frac{1 + \beta}{\beta}\right) \frac{D_t}{(Y_t - D_{t-1}) + \left(\frac{1+\beta}{\beta}\right)\left(K_t^* - B_t^g + IR_t\right)}, \tag{5.18}$$

$$1 + r_t^* = \left(\frac{1+\beta}{\beta}\right) \frac{D_t + D_t^*}{Y_t + Y_t^* - D_{t-1} - D_{t-1}^* - B_t^g - B_t^{g*} - IR_t}, \quad (5.19)$$

An increase in K^* and IR lowers the domestic interest rate. Capital inflows from abroad or increased private sector indebtedness to foreigners exert the same downward pressure on the rate. The opening of the capital account allows the domestic interest rate to be lower than it would have been if the domestic sector (private and public) could borrow only in domestic markets. This is true provided that the degree of financial integration between the two countries is imperfect. Otherwise, public indebtedness in the single global market would raise the interest rate.

This analytical framework was extended by Summers and his co-authors to study other issues: the impacts of fiscal and monetary policies, the determination of the general price level by introducing an aggregate supply function. The model has also been calibrated on US data. One of the new points is that, without unrealistic assumptions, the equilibrium interest rate can be negative, which is usually impossible in many models considered in the literature. Its steady state value is around -1.5%, which is far below the Fed's policy rate.

Macroeconomic Impacts of Higher Equity Risk Premiums: An Illustration in the Model of Caballero, Farhi, and Gourinchas

We present the salient features of a model proposed by Caballero et al. (2016). In this type of model, heterogeneous risk-aversion behaviors explain the fall in interest rates. An interesting point of the model is to interpret the rise in the equity risk premium, that is, the difference between the return on risky and non-risky assets, as an endogenous phenomenon resulting from excess demand for non-risky assets, or—which has the same effect—from a lack of supply of non-risky assets. The mechanism is based on the existence of two types of investors. Some are risk-neutral, others have a high aversion toward risk. The latter hold their wealth in the form of non-risky assets. The former hold risky asset (equity). In case of a shortage of risk-free assets, their return falls. It then becomes more attractive to hold risky assets, which lowers the demand for risky assets, and the financial asset markets manage to balance.

In their model, the safe rate does not only depend on the supply and demand of safe assets. It is also influenced by the policy rate of the central bank, which may decide to change its interest rate target to support economic activity.

A decrease in the supply of safe assets causes production to fall. First, this is due to a wealth effect, since holders of safe assets determine their consumption in proportion to their financial wealth in risk-free assets (principal and interests). If production falls, this in turn reduces the dividends received by the holders of risky assets thereby implying a further decrease in the output. However, this decrease can be attenuated if the central bank decides to voluntarily lower down the target risk-free rate.

Some difficulties arise when risk-free interest rates reach the zero lower bound. In this case, a recession and a rise in risk premiums can be observed simultaneously. The economy then enters a safety trap with no way out, unless specific policies are implemented. We do not present the whole model, but some aspects that allow us to capture the main mechanisms. We consider the open economy version of the story.

We take the example of a world summarized as two economies with financial integration. This is a short-run model, where prices are assumed to be fixed. Aggregate demand is described by an IS curve augmented by risk-free interest rates, a Taylor rule, and an equation describing the equilibrium of the risk-free asset market. All variables in the model are described as deviations from their long-run values.

The IS curve depends on internal absorption and current account balance. For their productive capital expenditures, companies take on debt at the risky rate, but they can also issue, for example, assets that are sought after by investors because they are considered to be of good quality and safe (biotech startups, video game companies). Public investment can itself be financed at rates lower than the risky rate. Because the two economies are integrated, the risky and risk-free rates are the same in the domestic and foreign countries. y denotes the output, r the risky rate, and rs the risk-free rate. Locally produced and imported goods and services are substitutes for consumers. A stimulus in the foreign country improves domestic production. y_t^* denotes foreign production. A depreciation of the currency improves price competitiveness and increases domestic output. e denotes the exchange rate (a decrease indicates a depreciation). The bars on the variables indicate their long-run values. The domestic country (IS) curve is written:

$$y_t - \bar{y}_t = -\delta(r_t - \bar{r}_t) - \delta_s(r_t^s - \bar{r}_t^s)$$
$$-\eta_y(y_t - \bar{y}_t) + \eta_{y^*}(y_t^* - \bar{y}_t^*) \tag{5.20}$$
$$-\eta_e(e_t - \bar{e}_t).$$

Elasticities are assumed to be identical in the foreign country. A depreciation of the domestic currency lowers the foreign country output. Its (IS) curve is written:

$$(y_t^* - \bar{y}_t^*) = -\delta(r_t - \bar{r}_t) - \delta_s(r_t^s - \bar{r}_t^s)$$
$$-\eta_y(y_t^* - \bar{y}_t^*) + \eta_{y*}(y_t - \bar{y}_t) \tag{5.21}$$
$$+\eta_e(e_t - \bar{e}_t).$$

The long-term exchange rate $\bar{e}_t$ is reached when current account balances are at zero ($y_t = \bar{y}_t$ and $y_t^* = \bar{y}_t^*$).

The demand for safe assets in each country depends on the liquidity services provided by the assets (and thus varies positively with income) and the spread between their yield and the yield of money (zero). Supply is assumed to be exogenous. Safe asset markets are assumed to be unresponsive to the spread ($r_t - r_t^s$). In each country the equilibrium of safe asset markets is given by the following equations:

$$s_t = \phi_y y_t + \phi_s r_t^{sa}, \quad s_t^* = \phi_y y_t^* + \phi_s r_t^{sa*}. \tag{5.22}$$

where a means "financial autarky." When the two economies are financially integrated, we have one global market for safe assets and one for global interest rate. Instead of Eq. (5.22), we have:

$$e_t s_t + s_t^* = e_t(\phi_y y_t + \phi_s r_t^s) + (\phi_y y_t^* + \phi_s r_t^{s*}). \tag{5.23}$$

The world interest rate is a weighted average of the interest rates obtained at the autarkic equilibrium of the two countries. By substituting it in equations (IS), one obtains after some calculations the following two solutions of the risky interest rate and the exchange rate at their long-term equilibrium, which are both defined in terms of the financial autarky equilibrium):

$$\bar{r}_t = \frac{\bar{e}_t}{1 + \bar{e}_t}\bar{r}_t^a + \frac{1}{1 + \bar{e}_t}\bar{r}_t^{a*},$$
$$\bar{e}_t - \bar{e}_t^a = \frac{\delta(\bar{r}_t^a - \bar{r}_t^{a*}) + \delta_s(\bar{r}_t^{sa} - \bar{r}_t^{sa*})}{\eta_e(1 + \bar{e}_t)}, \tag{5.24}$$

where

$$\bar{r}_t^{sa} = (s_t - \phi_y \bar{y}_t)/\phi_s, \quad \bar{r}_t^{sa*} = (s_t^* - \phi_y \bar{y}_t^*)/\phi_s. \tag{5.25}$$

and $\bar{e}_t^a$ is the long-run exchange rate when $y_t = \bar{y}_t$ and $y_t^* = \bar{y}_t^*$.

If the domestic country has more risky or non-risky assets than the foreign country, then the autarkic equilibrium interest rates are higher there. Its currency is more appreciated than in autarky financial equilibrium. Indeed, in this situation, its current account must be in deficit to attract foreign capital.

From Eq. (5.23), we can see that if the supply of safe assets in the long-run equilibrium decreases, a new long-term equilibrium is reached, all else being equal, by a decrease in $\bar{r}_t^{sa}$, which lowers the equilibrium world interest rate in Eq. (5.24). At the same time, the country where the supply of safe assets decreases has its currency depreciate more than that in the steady state. This depreciation increases the downward pressure on the rate $\bar{r}_t$, as the supply of value decreases. Long-run output in turn declines and spreads to the foreign country via the trade balance. To counteract this effect, the central bank can lower its long-term target of the risk-free rate.

To investigate this, we can consider a simple Taylor rule where central banks only react to the output gap. The coefficient of the output gap is assumed to be identical in both countries:

$$r_t^{sa} = \hat{r}_t^{sa} + \phi(y_t - \bar{y}_t), \quad r_t^{sa*} = \hat{r}_t^{sa*} + \phi(y_t^* - \bar{y}_t^*). \tag{5.26}$$

$\hat{r}_t^{sa}$ and $\hat{r}_t^{sa*}$ are the central bank's interest rate targets in financial autarky.

From Eqs. (5.26) and (5.22) we see that

$$\frac{\partial r_t^{sa}}{\partial \hat{r}_t^{sa}} = 1, \quad \frac{\partial y_t}{\partial \hat{r}_t^{sa}} = -\left(\frac{\phi_s}{\phi_y}\right)\frac{\partial r_t^{sa}}{\partial \hat{r}_t^{sa}} < 0, \tag{5.27}$$

and from Eq. (5.21):

$$\frac{\partial r_t^a}{\partial \hat{r}_t^{sa}} = -\left(\frac{1}{\delta}\right)(1 + \eta_y)\frac{\partial y_t}{\hat{r}_t^{sa}} - \left(\frac{\delta_s}{\delta}\right)\frac{\partial y_t}{\partial \hat{r}_t^{sa}}. \tag{5.28}$$

The expression (5.28) is positive provided that δ_s) is small enough. Outside of a ZLB equilibrium, a drop in the risk-free rate target by the central bank lowers the interest rate, thereby stimulating output. Readers interested in an in-depth analysis of the case where the constraint is binding can refer to the authors' paper. The main purpose of the model is to show that anything that can contribute to widening the range of safe assets available in the world would be likely to relieve the downward pressure on world interest rates.

Which Factors Impact the Interest Rates in Great Britain? An Empirical Illustration

Following the presentation of these models, let us do an empirical exercise by investigating the factors explaining the evolution of British interest rates. We take as an endogenous variable the first estimated factor of the yield curve described in Fig. 5.4. We regress this variable on the trend component of the following variables:

- real fixed capital gross formation (Capital, quarterly),
- price of fixed capital (Price capital, annual),
- total share prices for all shares (Shares, monthly),
- total factor productivity (Productivity, annual),
- activity rate : aged 15 and over, all persons (Activity rate, quarterly),
- total credit to total non-financial sector (Credit, %GDP quarterly),
- real GDP growth rate (Growth, quarterly).

The data are from 1990 to 2020. The source of Data is FRED (Federal Reserve of St. Louis), except total factor productivity, which is taken from the Penn World Table 10.0. Quarterly data are converted into monthly data by replicating the annual/quarterly observations for the months in a given year. All variables are measured as index (2010M01=100) for purpose of comparability. We add two dummy variables corresponding respectively to 1992 and 2008. The model is estimated using Huber type MM-estimation, which is more robust than simple OLS to outliers in the endogenous variable and resistant to leverage points. We use Huber type I standard errors and covariance. The results are shown in Table 5.2. As can be seen, some of the variables mentioned above seem to have had a significant influence on the rates, that is, the participation rate, credit to the economy, total factor productivity, and investment.

Table 5.2 MM-estimation of the first component of the yield curve on different covariates. United Kingdom

Variable	Coefficient	Std. error	z-Statistic	Prob.
Intercept	−4.940286	3.021509	−1.63504	0.102
$F1(-1)$	0.953573	0.016237	58.72758	0.0
Activity	5.287636	3.015507	1.753482	0.0795
Productivity	0.559352	0.344241	1.624887	0.1042
Credit	−0.512113	0.233724	−2.191103	0.0284
Capital	−0.510749	0.219241	−2.329617	0.0198
Price capital	13.32978	17.56531	0.758869	0.4479
Growth	0.007898	0.035899	0.220007	0.8259
Share	−13.1106	17.49254	−0.749496	0.4536
Robust Statistics				
R-squared	0.836719	Adjusted R-squared		0.83311
Rw-squared	0.995228	Adjust Rw-squared		0.995228
Akaike info criterion	387.0763	Schwarz criterion		426.0975
Deviance	19.047	Scale		0.226019
Rn-squared statistic	58040.79	Prob(Rn-squared stat.)		0.00

5.2   Corporates' Return on Equity and Net Saving

The models described so far relate savings and investment through macroeconomic factors. We now investigate the role of microeconomic factors, reflecting the behavior and constraints of firms. Several interest rates and financial variables adjust and give rise to a savings-investment equilibrium. Several rates of return are important in explaining the evolution of corporate profit rates. The ROCE (return on capital employed, which can be considered as a proxy for their profit rate) depends on the risk-free rate, which determines part of the cost of debt, but also on the return on equity (ROE), and on the way in which value added is shared between factors of production.

5.2.1   A Decomposition of Corporates' Gross Value Added

One of the criticisms that can be made of some recent OLG-based models is that they consider the world to be a vast market of loanable funds in which the supply of savings from some sectors/actors meets the demand for investment from other sectors/actors. This is not true since the late 1980s for corporate investment. Firms' investment is financed by their own savings. According to Chen et al. (2017), it is today at least two-thirds. Since business investment supports the productive capacity of economies and thus potential growth, we need to understand how they influence the ex-ante balance between savings and investment. The macroeconomic literature has extensively discussed the saving glut hypothesis at the aggregate and country levels to explain downward pressure on market rates. There is also a corporate saving glut, reflecting a strong increase in corporate saving.

Very thorough studies by Armenter and Hnatkovska (2017), Bacchetta and Benhima (2015), and Chen et al. (2017) highlight the fact that a significant share of the increase in aggregate savings around the world is being driven by firms. How do we explain such an increase in corporate savings during the recent three decades? Does it tell us anything about the evolution of profit rates?

To understand the importance of firms' saving glut, it is necessary to recall the structure of sector accounts: income account, distribution of income account, and capital accounts.

Income account

Gross value added (GVA) − net taxes on production + subsidies

= gross operating surplus (GOS) + compensation to labor (WL).

GOS is considered by economists to be corporates' profits(Π).

Distribution of Income Account

This account describes the distribution of corporate profits.

Π = gross saving (S) + net dividends (Div : dividends paid

− dividends received from owned entities and subsidiaries)

+ interests (int) + taxes on profits (tprof)

− reinvested earnings in FDI (fdi)

+ other transfers (social contributions, rental payments on lands).

An alternative presentation of corporate sharing of gross value added is the following:

GVA − compensation to labor = $\left[\text{i.e., markup}\right]$

= corporate taxes[i.e net taxes on production

− subsidies + taxes on profits + other transfers]

+ payment to capital[i.e net dividends + interests

+ reinvested earnings]

+ gross saving (Sav).

Corporates' profits are therefore divided into three parts: one part is given to the government in the form of taxes on income of capital and production, the second part remunerates capital, and the third part is the savings of companies.

From the capital account and the financial account, we have the following relationships:

gross saving = net lending

+ gross fixed capital formation (GFCF) [i.e investment]

+ other[i.e changes in inventories

+ changes in non-financial produced assets].

Net lending = gross saving − investment = acquisition of financial assets

− accumulation of debt liabilities

− accumulation of equity liabilities.

A first stylized fact of the last three decades is that companies have increased the payment to capital and their savings. This has been possible by increasing the markup, that is, by reducing the payment to labor. This has been done by reducing the number of hours worked (by using labor-saving technologies that increase labor productivity) and by increasing the hourly wage at a lower rate than labor productivity.

A second stylized fact is that companies have massively increased their debt and bought back their own shares in order to maximize their return on equity. This has been facilitated by the drastic fall in market rates. The increase in interest payments thus reflects high leverage effects. To reduce labor costs, they have also relocated part of their production abroad, which has increased earnings in FDI.

A third stylized fact is that they have massively increased their savings and increased the share of cash held, while reducing their capital expenditures.

Declining Compensation to Labor

The secular decline in the wage share in industrialized countries is a stylized fact that is well documented in the literature. This raises a problem for macroeconomists, as this empirical observation contradicts one of the central assumptions of growth models (one of the stylized facts of Cobb, Douglass, and Kaldor), that is, the stability of the shares of labor and capital. This was true throughout the twentieth century but has not been the case since the early 1980s. There are currently several explanations for the decline in the labor share. A first explanation is that average wages have grown less than labor productivity, especially in those sectors where labor productivity has been the highest. A second explanation is that employment has grown faster in capital-intensive sectors, and these sectors have accounted for a growing share of the contribution to GDP growth (effect of technological progress). A third explanation is the globalization of labor markets, which has led to a crushing of labor costs at the global level. A fourth factor has been the reforms and structural changes in the labor markets that have modified the structure of jobs: job atomization in labor markets, multiplication of poorly paid part-time jobs, and dismantling of former regulations protecting employees seen as real rigidities (minimum wages, dismissal authorizations, etc.).

The reader interested in a detailed investigation of these facts can refer to the following papers among a vast literature. Aum and Shin (2020) suggest that the decline in labor share has coincided with the rapid rise in software and hardware investments, automation technology, and the lower share of manufacturing sector in the economy. According to the authors, these changes have accelerated the substitution of labor with capital. relate the fall in labor share to the elasticity of substitution between labor and capital that has become higher than 1. Some phenomena such as technology bias can influence the elasticity of substitution (see, for instance, Dao et al. 2019). Some papers point to the effect of monopoly and monopsony power and the weakening of bargaining power of the lowest paid workers (see De Loecker et al. 2020; Stansbury and Summers 2020). Piketty (2014)'s best-selling book also discusses the growing gap between wage earners and capital earners since 1970 in industrialized countries.

Saving Glut and Increasing Payments to Capital

Corporate saving glut is a situation where companies seek to increase their savings at the expense of productive investment. Several factors explain such a behavior, which has become more pronounced since the Great Financial Crisis. First of all, low potential growth rates and pessimistic expectations by firms about the medium-term ability of economies to recover have reduced investment opportunities. Second, strong balance sheet effects of the GFC have led firms to be more cautious and to accumulate precautionary savings by increasing their holdings of liquid assets. Another explanation is that the saving glut was caused by the difficulty of companies to use their intangible assets as collateral to obtain loans from the banking sector. Finally, companies, especially in the United States, have chosen to give priority to remunerating their shareholders through share buybacks rather than through dividend payments. This has increased their holding of cash. All these factors have led to an increase in corporate net lending. For the different explanations, the reader can refer to Alfaro et al. (2018), Bates et al. (2009), Begenau and Palazzo (2021), Caggese and Pérez Orive (2022), Chen (2008), Chen et al. (2017), Falato et al. (2020), Gruber and Kamin (2015), and Ozkan and Ozkan (2004).

To analyze the rise in payments to capital, it is important to complement the national accounting decomposition with a microeconomic decomposition of the corporate accounting framework. This is necessary because one of the constraints facing firms since the great wave of financial liberalization that began in the mid-1980s is the following. Governance by shareholder value has imposed minimum targets for the return on capital provided by shareholders.

The interesting relationship for us is the following:

$$AWCE = ROE \times \left(\frac{Equity}{Capital} \right) + i \times \left(\frac{Debt}{\text{Capital Employed}} \right), \qquad (5.29)$$

$$ROE = ROCE + (ROCE - i) \times \left(\frac{Debt}{Equity} \right), \qquad (5.30)$$

with the following definitions:

$AWCE$: weighted average cost of capital employed,
ROE: return on equity =

$$\frac{\text{Net Income}}{Equity} = \frac{Dividends + Savings}{Equity}, \qquad (5.31)$$

Leverage ratio

$$\frac{Debt}{Equity} = \frac{\text{Accumulation of financial liabilities}}{Equity}, \qquad (5.32)$$

ROCE : return on capital employed =

$$\frac{Profits}{Equity + Debt} = \frac{GVA - \text{Compensation to labor}}{Equity + Debt}, \qquad (5.33)$$

Interest rate =

$$i = \frac{\text{Interest payments}}{Debt}. \tag{5.34}$$

These equations show that in addition to market interest rates—which influence interest payments here—two other rates of return on capital are important. These are the ROCE (which is an economic rate of return, known in the literature as the rate of profit) and the ROE (which is a financial rate of return on capital).

A usual justification for dividend payments is based on principal-agent theory and asymmetric information. This constraint on firms' managers motivates the optimal allocation of resources by the stock markets. However, recent works highlight the influence of the pressure exerted by shareholders' short-term strategies. Large-scale companies, and to a lesser extend medium-scale corporates, choose to allocate a large part of the cash they hold to pay dividends rather than to invest. This pressure is motivated by the threat of absorption, the management by shareholder value (in particular the fact that directors receive a profit-sharing on the stock market value of the company), and a rapid turnover in the holding of bonds (high SOA—speed of returns—strategies). Over the last two decades, this has favored a focus not only on dividend payouts but also on strategies for companies to buy back their own assets. This has also increased debt—and therefore interest payments—as companies have used leverage to maximize returns on equity. See, for example, on these points (Acharya and Viswanathan 2011a; Acharya et al. 2011; Brochet et al. 2015; Driver et al. 2020; Gallagher et al. 2013), and (Lazonick 2018). Beyond the general framework, two models can be distinguished in practice.

Equation (5.29) shows that the cost of capital depends on the cost of debt and on the cost of equity. A decline in market rates does not imply that the cost of capital falls. This happens because companies have a constraint on ROE. Equation (5.30) shows which levers can be activated to maintain the ROE at the level required by the shareholders. They can increase the markup (the ROCE), by shrinking the labor costs. This is interesting when market rates are low, since the spread premium (difference between ROCE and i) increases. Companies can amplify the effect of the spread premium, by increasing the financial leverage through higher debt.

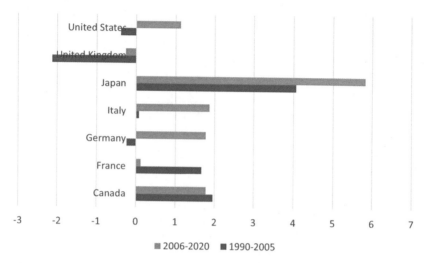

Fig. 5.7   Net lending in G7 countries. Source: OECD

5.2.2   Some Illustrations for Non-financial Corporations

Figure 5.7 shows the evolution of non-financial corporations' net lending position, over two sub-periods, from 1990 to 2005, and from 2006 to 2020 in the G7 countries. Net savings increase significantly in the second sub-period from 2006 onward in the United States, Germany, Italy, and Japan. In Canada, it remains positive in similar proportions between the two sub-periods. In the United Kingdom, it remains negative and decreases sharply in France between the two sub-periods. The evolution of net savings is similar in the United States and Germany. Indeed, until 2005 it is negative, then becomes very positive from 2006 onward.

In most countries, net lending positions have improved following the drastic fall in private investment (business gross capital formation). As we pointed out earlier, the fall in the relative price of productive capital (capital goods) is one of the causes of this fall. The rise in savings is also explained by greater wage moderation, lower potential growth rates, and lower interest rates on the debt markets.

Apart from these common factors, there are region- or country-specific factors. In Italy, Germany, and Japan, companies have been repairing their balance sheets in the years following financial crises (the Asian crisis of the

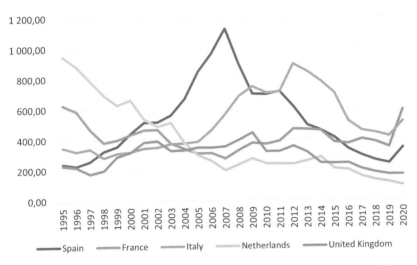

Fig. 5.8 Net debt-to-income ratio in selected European countries. Source: Eurostat

1900s, the financial crisis of 2008, and the European public debt crisis in 2010). This recovery of balance sheets has been helped by the evolution of corporate debt. For example, Fig. 5.8 shows that non-financial firms in Europe deleveraged sharply after the European public debt crisis.

The increase in US corporate savings must also be seen in the light of a change in their strategy since the early 2000s to remunerate shareholders through asset buybacks, and not just by paying them dividends. Therefore, they have accumulated cash and saved a lot. Figure 5.9 shows the earning yields (i.e., the inverse of the price earning ratio), the average dividend paid as a percentage of the share price (dividend yield) and the payout ratio (i.e., dividends minus preferred stock dividends divided by net income) for the companies in the S&P500. The difference between earning yields and dividend yields became more significant from 2004/2005 onward, when a shift from dividends to share repurchases was observed.

Figure 5.10 shows the spread between ROE and interest rates for non-financial corporations in some European countries, and Fig. 5.11 shows their profit share (defined as the ratio of gross operating surplus to gross value added). We see that they have remained constant since 1995 (it has even decreased slightly in Italy). According to the definition of GOS, this

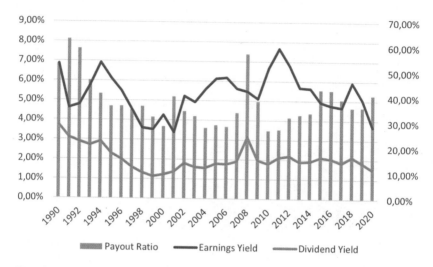

Fig. 5.9 Net debt-to-income ratio in selected European countries. Source: Eurostat

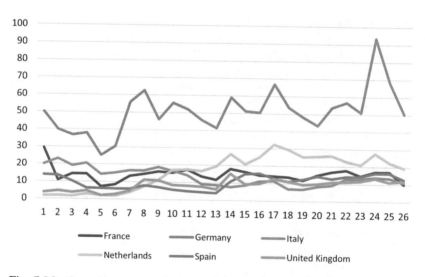

Fig. 5.10 Spread between ROE and interest rates in selected European countries. Source: Eurostat

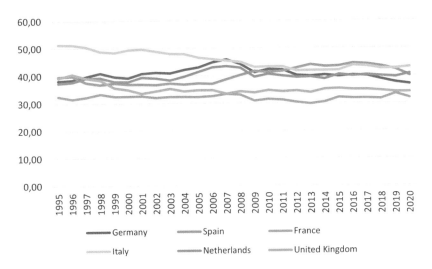

Fig. 5.11 Profit share in selected European countries. Source: Eurostat

includes gross savings and net dividends, in addition to interest, capital taxes, and so on. In some countries, such as Germany and Italy, net saving has increased significantly, compensating for the significant drop in interest rates paid on debt. The decrease in market interest rates has caused an increase in premiums reflected in a positive spread between ROE and interest rates. In Fig. 5.10, ROE is measured here by the ratio of net entrepreneurial income to equity and investment fund share (liability-assets). We note here the specific case of German companies where this premium was much higher than in other countries, due to the fact that they have a higher ROCE.

5.3   FINANCIAL MARKET DEVELOPMENTS AND MACROECONOMICS

A major fact of the last quarter of the twentieth century was the liberalization and globalization of financial markets from the mid-1980s onward. This changed the individual agents' behaviors in accessing financing for their activities and had major repercussions on the economies' real sector. Private and public debts have grown, wealth and balance sheet effects have become important following the greater financial volatility that amplified the rise and fall of stock and real estate prices. While during the years of Great Moderation, macroeconomists had focused their attention on the determinants of the business cycle, they finally came to the conclusion that financial cycles have amplitude and duration greater than those of the business cycle. They can therefore generate large-scale imbalances that can affect economic variables for very long time periods. Faced with this phenomenon, macroeconomists needed to think about new ways of analyzing macroeconomics in the twenty-first century.

The first important feature is that finance is not neutral for the real economy. It has strong effects on the real variables in both the short and long terms. The economist's job is to explain the determination of not only relative prices but also nominal (financial) prices.

A second feature is that the well-known maxim of the French chemist philosopher (and economist!) Lavoisier also applies to an economy: "nothing is lost, nothing is created, everything is transformed." If we have been deploring the apparent disappearance of inflation for at least two decades in the real economy, this phenomenon says nothing about the effectiveness of restrictive monetary policies, but it does indicate that inflation has moved from the real sector to the financial sector: very regularly for the past 30 years, financial asset prices have been experiencing bubbles.

A third implication of the development of finance is that spontaneous equilibria in any economy must be seen as an exception. The economic cycle is not only caused by exogenous shocks. It is also caused by a financial cycle resulting from permanent endogenous imbalances related to the functioning of financial markets. As a result, cyclical fluctuations can no longer be explained by the theory of real business cycles (or DSGE models without a financial sector). When they make optimal choices, households and firms do not only decide on the number of hours worked, their demand or supply of labor, or their consumption. They must also decide in what form to accumulate their wealth. They are not always free to decide how much they save, or how much they dis-save because of the imperfections of financial markets. The role of the constraints that hinge on financial intermediaries has become crucial.

Fourth, finance can thwart the recovery of economies when it triggers the following vicious circle. During financial euphoria (Minsky moment), private debt is run up, the value of collateral and net assets on the balance sheets of companies and households increase, and production is sustained by financial bubbles. When the cycle turns around, over-indebtedness appears, balance sheets weaken and consumption falls, causing output to fall. However, dis-saving or deleveraging (which purges the excesses of the bull phase) can be thwarted by the fact that incomes fall. In this case, the adjustment is made by a fall in investment, which plunges economies into prolonged stagnation (secular stagnation). This in turn can affect medium/long-term potential growth. A good indicator of this vicious circle is that the marginal rate of return on capital corresponding to the economy's level of full employment is steadily falling.

In the following paragraphs, we review these different features.

5.3.1   Defining the Financial Cycle

One of the reasons why financial cycles have long been absent from macroeconomic models is that they seemed quite modest in comparison with economic activity cycles, as long as the financial sector was highly regulated and capital markets had not yet become sufficiently internationalized. This changed in the mid-1980s, with the increasing degree of world financial integration. Not only did we have to admit that these cycles have very large amplitude. But it was also observed that they have both short and long durations.

How can we define a financial cycle? The simplest way is to look at the causes of financial crises. According to and Reinhart and Rogoff (2008), they are multi-faceted and combine crises of over-indebtedness, inflation rates, currency crises, bursting financial bubbles, and banking crises. All these crises correspond to changes in financial regimes between amplified upward phases of prices and financial volumes and brutal downward phases.

An important stylized fact of the last three decades has been the upward drift of private and public indebtedness. Private debt to the banking sector has increased, but even more so the debt of corporations, governments, and financial actors in capital markets. This increase has been facilitated by financial innovations (securitization) and by the generalization of the phenomenon of debt collateralization. Collaterals are physical or financial assets. The supply of and demand for loanable funds depends on expectations about the evolution of the valuation of assets. Credit booms and busts exacerbate the deleveraging phases and can amplify financial crises (see, Jòrda et al. 2016 for a history of credit-fueled crisis in the industrialized countries since 1870, coinciding with high public debt levels and financial crisis recessions).

As Borio (2012) explains, there are different ways to represent financial cycles. The most general approach is to take a large number of diverse financial asset prices and volumes and extract their common components. For example, Hatzius et al. (2010) propose a financial composite indicator. In addition to market rates and asset prices, it includes survey-based indicators. One can also focus on a few key financial indicators. For instance, one can define financial cycles by considering private debt and financial asset prices. Drehman et al. (2012) propose an empirical characterization of the financial cycle by filtering the short- and medium-term components of credit and property prices since the mid-1980s. They show that financial cycles have longer duration than the business cycle and that the depth of the latter is greater when its recession phases coincide with financial recession phases. Their empirical method is based on a multivariate representation that combines the cycles of individual financial series. One of the techniques proposed is to average the individual filtered series and to identify the peaks and troughs by Harding and Pagan's method.

We propose here several methods to highlight the existence of financial cycles of multiple durations (frequency approaches based on long-memory models and wavelet decomposition) by focusing on three series: private credit, stock market asset prices, and real estate prices.

Example of the United Kingdom

We consider the following three series taken from the Fed of St. Louis database. All data are taken at quarterly frequency from January 1990 to July 2021:

- Real residential property prices (index $2010 = 100$),
- Share prices for all shares − CPI (consumer price index of all items), index $2015 = 100$,
- Credit to private non-financial sector by banks (% of GDP).

A decomposition of the short- and long-term components can be obtained by modeling each series as a GARMA process (Gegenbauer ARMA):

$$\Pi_{i=1}^{k}(1 - 2u_i B + B^2)^{d_i} \Phi(B)(1 - B)^{id}(x_t - \mu) = \theta(B)\epsilon_t, \tag{5.35}$$

where:

ϵ_t is a random *iid* process,

$\Phi(B)$, $\Theta(B)$ are short-memory AR(p) and MA(q) processes,

$(1 - 2u_i B + B^2)^{d_i}$ is the long-memory Gegenbauer components (there can be k of them),

x_t is the observed time series,

id is the degree of integer differencing,

d_i is the long-memory parameter.

The coefficients are estimated by using a Whittle estimator which allows to capture the influence of frequencies close to zero in the spectral density of the series. We take up to three frequencies to characterize the long-term components of the series, while the short-term cyclical components are captured by an ARMA(1,1) model. To highlight the existence of multiple cycles, the estimation of GARMA models is completed by a wavelet analysis. Wavelet analysis is more general than Fourier-based transform and allows multiple time scale analysis. We perform a multi-resolution decomposition by applying J-level wavelet filters to the series of financial prices where $J = \{1, \ldots, 9\}$ (Mallat decomposition). Low values of J capture high-frequency components (short-term), while as J increases the decomposition filter low-frequency components (long term). The figures below show cycles of different lengths depending on the value of J (as an example, we have selected the graphs corresponding to $J = \{1, 4, 5, 6\}$).

Table 5.3 shows the estimates obtained. The existence of Gegenbauer frequencies close to zero whose spectral density "explodes" is indicated by the values of exponents d_i close to 0.5 (trend components corresponding to an infinite or very large periodicity) or significantly positive corresponding to cycles of long duration. For share prices, we detect a cycle corresponding to that of the business cycle (33 quarters, i.e., about eight years). For credit, we detect a longer cycle of 94 quarters, that is, 23 years, and for real estate prices a long cycle of 74 quarters, that is, 18 years.

Figure 5.12 shows the long-term (Gegenbauer) components of the three series. They represent the long waves of different components of the British financial cycle. The share prices show a faster "mean-reverting dynamics" than the other two series. There has been a very long upward phase in residential prices since 1990, barely interrupted by a downturn in prices that lasted only two years. In the case of the credit cycle, we observe long upward phases that follow long downward phases. The periodicities

Table 5.3 Estimation of Gegenbauer processes for financial series : United Kingdom

Share prices

	Intercept	u1	d1	u2	d2	AR1	MA1
Coeff.	0.67	0.99	0.50	0.98	0.33	0.486	−0.87
s.e	0.04	0.002	0.25	0.006	0.17	0.372	0.16

	Factor 1	Factor2
GG frequency	0.0009	0.03
GG period	1121.06	33.36

Credit

	Intercept	u1	d1	u2	d2	AR1	MA1
Coeff.	0.73	1.0	0.415	0.99	0.14	−0.52	0.73
s.e	0.01	0.0004	0.24	0.002	0.24	0.18	0.13

	Factor 1	Factor2
GG frequency	0.0	0.0106
GG period	∞	94.63

Property prices

	Intercept	u1	d1	u2	d2	u3	d3	AR1	MA1
Coeff.	0.58	1.0	0.5	0.99	0.40	0.83	0.15	0.35	−0.83
s.e	0.01	0.003	0.16	0.01	0.18	0.02	0.10	0.22	0.133

	Factor 1	Factor2	Factor3
GG frequency	0.00	0.01	0.09
GG period	∞	74.69	10.55

Fig. 5.12   Long-term
components of financial
series: United Kingdom

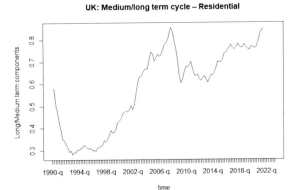

Wavelet

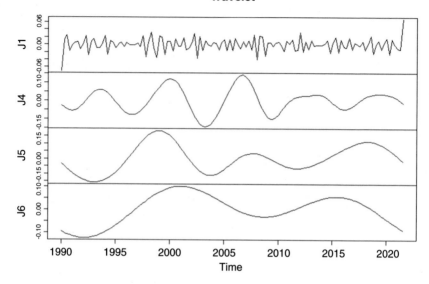

Fig. 5.13   Wavelet decomposition, share prices: United Kingdom

of the short-term cycles of the series can be obtained from the rational spectrum of the ARMA components. However, one can improve the decomposition by referring to a wavelet analysis instead.

Figures 5.13, 5.14, and 5.15 show this breakdown for the three series. It allows to understand that different cycles of different periodicities are nested in each other. The financial cycle is thus characterized by short, medium, and long waves. The figures clearly show that the duration of the bullish and bearish phases can be different depending on the series considered. The share prices have the shortest long cycle (i.e., ten years), compared to the other two series whose long cycles have multi-decade durations.

Based on these observations, we adapt the methodology proposed by Drehman, calculating a synthetic indicator of the three financial cycles of individual series. After normalizing the series so that the magnitudes are comparable, we compute their cycle by applying a Christiano-Fitzgerald filter with frequencies ranging from 6 to 96 quarters. The financial cycle is the average of the individual cycles (see Fig. 5.16). The reader should

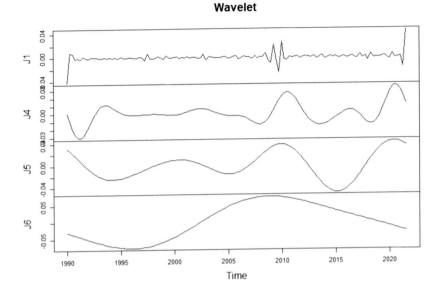

Fig. 5.14 Wavelet decomposition, credit: United Kingdom

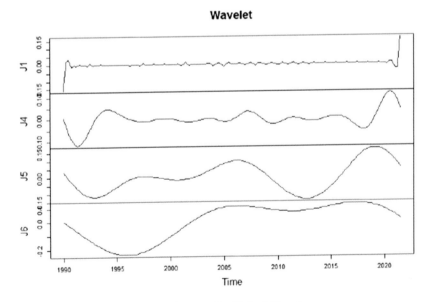

Fig. 5.15 Wavelet decomposition, credit: United Kingdom

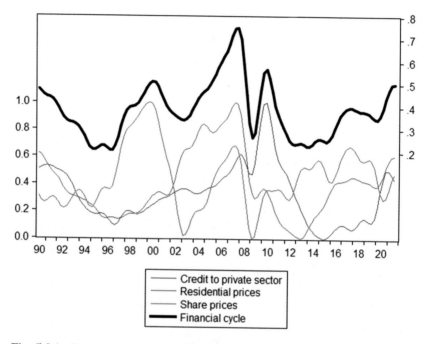

Fig. 5.16   Financial cycle: United Kingdom

notice that when using a filter, the cycle is defined in terms of gap, that is, each component is initially computed in deviation from its reference level (potential), before being normalized.

The amplitude and duration of the financial cycle depends on the degree of synchronicity of the individual cycles. For example, the bearish phase from 2000 to 2002 is explained by the dotcom bubble burst. But despite the sharp decline in equity prices, the fall is limited by the fact that during the same period residential prices and credit to the private sector are in an upward phase. On the contrary, between 2003 and 2009, the financial cycle has a stronger amplitude (high peak and very low trough) because the three individual cycles evolve in the same bullish and bearish phases.

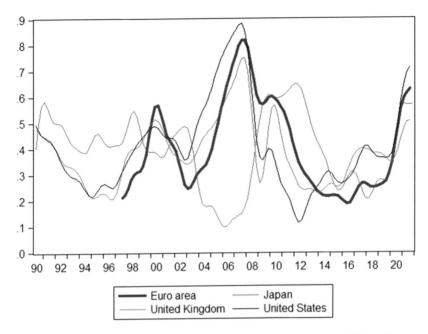

Fig. 5.17 Financial cycle: Euro area, Japan, United Kingdom, and United States

United States, Japan, and the Euro Area

We did the same exercise for Japan, the Eurozone, and the United States. Here we represent only their financial cycles, and that of the United Kingdom (see Fig. 5.17).

We see that, in all countries, financial cycles are slow-moving and suggest long-run cyclical persistent fluctuations. This is in line with the mechanism of accumulation of imbalances with overinflated prices and credit volumes followed by periods of corrections and downward adjustments. The synchronization of the other three cycles, and the fact that the amplitude of the cycles is almost identical, shows an interesting phenomenon. The Eurozone is characterized by a "bank-bias," while the Anglo-Saxon financial system relies more on capital markets. Contrary to a widespread idea in the literature, we do not see a situation here where the lesser diversification of funding sources would increase the vulnerability of the financial system in the Eurozone compared to that of the United Kingdom and the United States. One reason is that bank and non-bank capital flows have a common denominator, that is, the credit gap and leverage behavior. Another common point, highlighted in a large sample of advanced countries, is that equity prices are among the best leading indicators of financial cycles (see Chen and Svirydzenka 2021).

The Japanese cycle and the other three cycles have been highly asynchronous until 2009. The financial cycle shows a major trough corresponding to the years 2004–2008. This time frame has been characterized by important events in the credit cycle. Firstly, in 2004/2005 the banking and financial system experienced heavy losses when the regulators introduced new rules in the provisioning of bad loans. Secondly, Japan has been impacted by the 2008 subprime crisis. The trough of the cycle due to credit events appears to be much more important than the smaller troughs of lesser magnitude observed in the 1990s, which were rather explained by events that affected stock prices (collapse of an overvalued stock and real estate market and imposition of restrictive measures on lending to the real estate sector). Because of the bad events in the credit markets in the early 2000s, the bullish euphoria of the years preceding the subprime crisis was less important in Japan. The fact that there were fewer accumulated imbalances explains why the recovery toward a bullish phase after the Great Financial Crisis was earlier than in other countries.

5.3.2   Linking the Financial Cycle and the Real Economy: Empirical Evidence

Many works in the literature have empirically studied the responses of fluctuations in output, unemployment, factor productivity, and investment to shocks, to shocks from financial asset prices, bank lending activities, and intermediation spreads (see, e.g., Ajello 2016; Furlanetto et al. 2019; Gerali and Neri 2019). We present an illustration of a simple empirical model to explain the phases of major recessions in the business cycle by the reversal of the credit, real estate, and stock market cycles. We then study an aspect less investigated in the literature, which concerns the effects of the financial cycle on potential growth.

Can Fluctuations in Credit, Real Estate Prices, and Financial Assets Help Predict Major Recessions?

One way of studying the interaction between the financial cycles and the real economy is to understand how the former can be leading indicators of some deep recessions that economies experience. Financial cycles have been the epicenter of at least three deep recessions since the early 1990s.

First, the 1991–1991 crisis following the Gulf War and the subsequent surge in oil prices led to a severe recession which particularly hit the United States with a rise in unemployment. The exit from the crisis was slow because of the over-indebtedness of households in the previous years, a cut in bank credits due to the fact that they had to consolidate their balance sheets.

Second, there was the stock market crash of 2001 – 2002, which particularly affected the new information and communication technologies sector. The heavy indebtedness led to the formation of a bubble that finally burst after the rise in interest rates in March 2000. The bursting of the bubble led to a drop in orders in this sector, drastic cost-cutting strategies, bankruptcies, and balance sheet consolidation strategies. Among the countries whose economies suffered particularly from this crisis was Japan, where the growth of Internet companies played the most important role in the growth of the information and communication technology sector. This crisis came on the heels of two others, that is, the bursting of a bubble in 1992–1993 and the banking crisis of 1997–1998.

Another major event was the Great Financial Crisis of 2008 caused by the bursting of a mortgage bubble that had multiple facets: stock market, real estate, banking, and currency crisis for some countries. The financial bubble that preceded the crisis was fueled by excessive credit, leverage, and the diffusion of risk in financial markets.

A fourth event was a "prolonged" recession that set in from 2016 caused by a regime of self-sustaining low potential growth. This coincided with the worsening of phenomena that we have studied previously: a prolonged decline in investment following a trend decline in the rate of return on capital, excess savings, a decline in aggregate demand, and inflation rates that were too low to allow for a decline in real interest rates in a ZLB context. In this context of secular stagnation, the Covid-19 crisis of 2019/2020 has provoked another recession that coincides with the formation of bubbles in the financial and real estate markets.

These phenomena have led policymakers to consider that financial variables contain signals that provide information on the future state of the economy. By controlling the financial cycle, we can prevent or mitigate recessions. The subprime crisis has led to a proliferation of studies highlighting the leading nature of the housing market cycle with respect to the business cycle (for references, see Cesa-Bianchi 2013; Dufrénot and Malik 2012; Huang et al. 2020; Leamer 2015, and Liu et al. 2013). The empirical methods used are diverse. We provide here an illustration based on TVTPMS (time-varying transition probabilities Markov Switching) models. These models, which are widely used in the empirical macroeconomic literature, generalize Hamilton (1989)'s, Hamilton (1996)'s model. They were first proposed by Filardo (1994) and Filardo (1998), and have been further developed by Bazzi et al. (2017), Kim et al. (2008), and Diebold et al. (2021). We summarize here their methodological framework.

We investigate the cyclical phases of real GDP. Denote $(x_t)_{t=1,...T}$ the observations of real GDP growth (measured as the logarithmic first difference of GDP level). A typical TVTPMS model is as follows. We assume that $x_t \approx AR(1)$ process with regime-varying coefficient and heteroskedastic variance:

$$x_t(s_t) = \mu(s_t) + \phi_1(s_t)x_{t-1} + \sigma_t(s_t)\epsilon_t. \tag{5.36}$$

μ is a constant, σ is the variance of the noise $\epsilon_t \approx iid(0, 1)$. $s_t = 1, 2$ is a hidden first-order Markov chain with the following time-varying transition probability matrix:

$$P(s_t = i, s_{t-1} = j, t) = \begin{bmatrix} p(Z_t) & 1 - p(t) \\ 1 - q(Z_t) & q(Z_t) \end{bmatrix}, \tag{5.37}$$

where $Z_t = z_{t,t-1}, \dots$ is a vector of the history of conditioning variables leading real GDP growth. These variables are assumed to be informative with regard to detecting growth turning points. In our case, Z_t is a vector of financial variables. The functional forms of $p(s_t)$ and $q(s_t)$ are usually of logistic type. Suppose that we have only one informative variable. Then, the transition probabilities are given by

$$p(t) = \frac{\left[\theta_{p0} + \sum_{k=0}^{K_1} \theta_{pk} z_{t-k}\right]}{1 + \left[\theta_{p0} + \sum_{k=0}^{K_1} \theta_{pk} z_{t-k1}\right]}, \tag{5.38}$$

and

$$q(t) = \frac{\left[\theta_{q0} + \sum_{k=0}^{K_2} \theta_{qk} z_{t-k}\right]}{1 + \left[\theta_{q0} + \sum_{k=0}^{K_2} \theta_{qk} z_{t-k1}\right]}. \tag{5.39}$$

K_1 and K_2 are the maximum lag of the informative variable z_t. This model can be estimated using maximum likelihood, MCMC, Bayesian methods, and so on.

We estimate such a TVTPMS model for the United States, the United Kingdom, the Euro area, and Japan, and report the smoothed probabilities of being in a recession phase (see Figs. 5.18, 5.19, 5.20, and 5.21). In a preliminary step, both growth rates and financial variables are filtered using a Christiano-Fitzgerald filter. In the probability transition function we select the most significant lags. For the United States, we take the

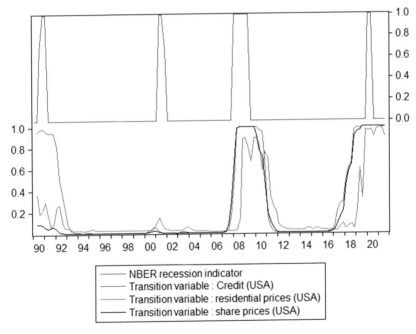

Fig. 5.18 Smoothed probability of a recession: United States

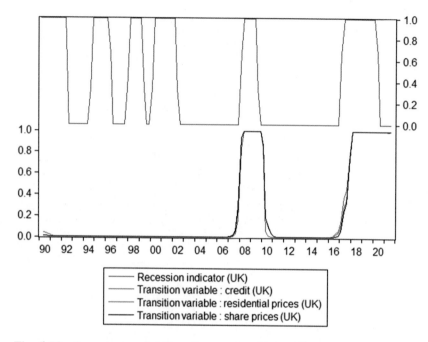

Fig. 5.19 Smoothed probability of a recession: United Kingdom

NBER recession indicators, while for the euro area, United Kingdom, and Japan, we consider the OECD recession indicator.

We see that the financial variables predict well some major recession episodes:

- United States : 1990–1991; 2008–2009;2019–2020,
- United Kingdom: 2008–2009; 2019–2020,
- Japan : 2001–2002; 2008–2014; 2018–2019,
- Euro area : 2008–2009; 2019–2020.

We see that the model captures not only the timing of recessions but also their varying duration across countries.

The Financial Cycle and Potential Growth

An idea that has long been accepted by economists is that potential growth depends on supply factors that define the production capacity of economies in the medium/long term, while shorter-term growth fluctuates according

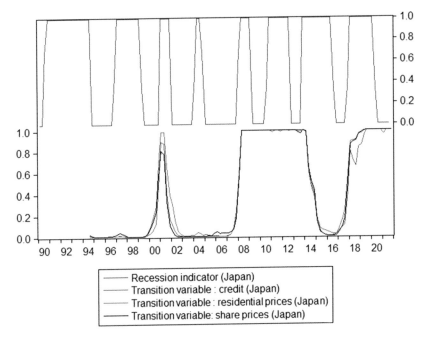

Fig. 5.20 Smoothed probability of a recession: Japan

to demand factors (including the financial cycle). The intuition behind this argument is that financial constraints play a role in aggregate demand, through the links between the credit cycle and household consumption, variations in asset prices and firm investment, and variations in risk premiums and public debt. The supposed neutrality of finance in the long run is based on the idea that the boom and bust phases explain above all the fluctuations of the business cycle. This idea is, however, not validated by empirical evidence. A simple way to show this is to check that there is a significant long-term relationship between growth rates and indicators of the financial cycle.

Starting with the example of the United States, we estimate an ARDL model with four maximum lags for the endogenous variable (GDP growth) and for the three variables representing the financial cycle (credit, share price, and real estate price). From this estimation, we deduce a level (long-run) relationship between these variables. We take the three components

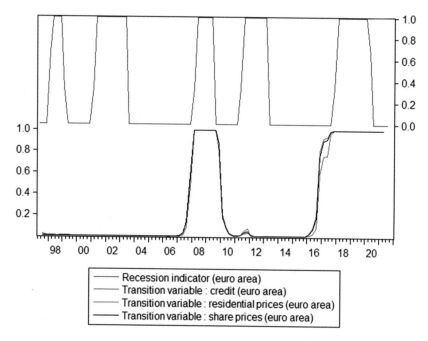

Fig. 5.21 Smoothed probability of a recession: Euro area

of the financial cycle described above as well as GDP growth series taken from the FRED database (growth rate of GDP by expenditure in constant prices). The frequency of the data is quarterly over the period 1990–2021.

The results in Table 5.4 show that there is a level relationship between the growth rate and all three components of the financial cycle. Indeed, the Fisher statistic for the test of non-existence of such a relationship is greater than the upper bound of the theoretical statistic (for a presentation of this test, see Pesaran et al. 2001). Moreover, we see that in the regression, the coefficients are all statistically significant at least at 10% level of confidence.

From the regression, we calculate the "financial" component of potential growth, that is, related to the financial cycle. To do this, we filter the exogenous variables by extracting the medium/long-term component using a Christiano-Fitzgerald filter for frequencies between 6 quarters and 64 quarters. The financial component of potential growth is obtained as the expected values of the long-run equation when the financial variables

Table 5.4 Long-run coefficients from ARDL model and bound tests: United States

Long-run coefficients from ARDL model and bound tests: United States				
Variable	Coefficient	Std. Error	t-Statistic	Prob.
Credit	−1.096461	0.252692	−4.339120	0.0000
Residential prices	0.738384	0.333909	2.211335	0.0290
Share prices	0.757381	0.282580	2.680230	0.0084
C	0.330917	0.182879	1.809483	0.0730
Null hypothesis: No long-run relationships exist				
Test statistic	Value	k		
F-statistic	29.00695	3		
Critical value bounds				
Significance	I0 Bound	I1 Bound		
10%	2.37	3.2		
5%	2.79	3.67		
2.5%	3.15	4.08		
1%	3.65	4.66		

Note The last column reports the P-values. The estimated coefficients are statistically significant when these values are lower than 1%, 5%, or 10%

move along their medium/long-run paths. In Fig. 5.22 (top), we compare it with the growth rate of potential GDP obtained as the one that would be observed if US firms were producing with high levels of capital and labor utilization rates (the series of potential GDP is taken from FRED database). In the figure, the data are annualized.

As we can see, the financial component of potential GDP is more volatile than the series measured by considering only capital and labor. In sum, the "true" potential growth is undoubtedly a weighted average of the two curves. For the weights, we attribute 34% to the financial component (which corresponds to the R2 of the estimated ARDL model) and 66% to the component obtained by taking into account capital and labor. Comparing the average curve with the one usually examined—omitting to weight by the influence of financial variables—we notice that the standard data of potential growth has led to underestimate potential growth during the boom phases of the financial cycle and on the contrary to overestimate it during the trough phases of the financial cycle.

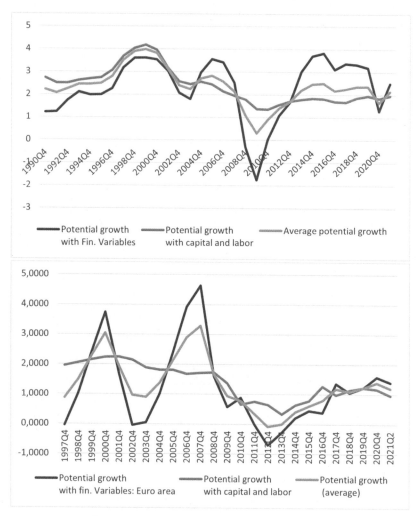

Top : United States, Bottom : Euro area

Fig. 5.22 Potential GDPs with and without Fin. Variables

Table 5.5 Long-run coefficients from ARDL model and bound tests: Euro area

Variable	Coefficient	Std. Error	t-Statistic	Prob.
Credit	−0.018529	0.373683	−0.049583	0.9606
Residential prices	0.669258	0.286976	2.332102	0.0222
Share prices	1.351923	0.295601	4.573472	0.0000
C	−0.468503	0.192103	−2.438808	0.0170
Null hypothesis: No long-run relationships exist				
Test statistic	Value	k		
F-statistic	30.19339	3		
Critical value bounds				
Significance	I0 Bound	I1 Bound		
10%	2.37	3.2		
5%	2.79	3.67		
2.5%	3.15	4.08		
1%	3.65	4.66		

Note The last column reports the P-values. The estimated coefficients are statistically significant when these values are lower than 1%, 5%, or 10%

Now let us look at the case of the Eurozone. The results of the long-term relationship can be found in Table 5.5. We see the greater sensitivity of growth to share prices and a weaker influence of the credit cycle compared to the United States. In the second graph—at the bottom of Fig. 5.22—we see that the financial component of potential growth has a higher variability than in the United States until the 2008 GFC. After 2008, there is a strong attenuation of the volatility. As before, we calculate potential growth as the average of the curve obtained by taking into account only capital and labor and the curve obtained from the financial variables. On the basis of the $R2$, the weighting coefficient of the latter is 0.54.[3]

It is interesting to compare both countries' potential growth rates The graphs in Fig. 5.23 show the curves when the usual estimation is used, omitting the financial variables (top) and when they are taken into account (bottom). Since 2014, the financial cycle has had two effects. On the one hand, it has raised the estimates of potential growth, both in the United

---

[3] The growth rate of potential GDP without the financial variables is the first difference of the annual potential GDP taken from the AMECO database.

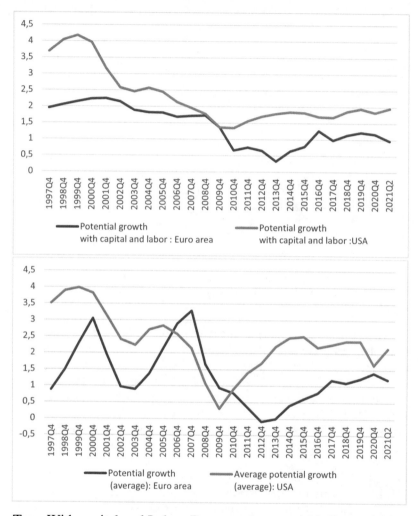

Top : With capital and Labor, Bottom : Average with fin. variables

Fig. 5.23 Comparing potential growths: United States and Euro area

States and in the euro area. On the other hand, it has increased the gaps between the two curves. This may suggest that long-term US growth is much more influenced by the direction of the financial cycle than in the euro area. Until 2014, we observe greater variability in potential growth—when financial variables are taken into account. Between 2005 and 2009, the financial cycle brought the trajectories of potential growth rates closer together (when European growth moved above US growth).

After 2009, the divergence in potential growth rates between the euro area and the United States is greater when the effects of the financial cycle are included.

5.3.3   Introducing the Financial Sector in Theoretical Models

In theoretical models, taking into account the financial cycle has had two implications. On the one hand, it has led to a reconsideration of the modeling of monetary policy, and on the other hand, it has made it possible to explain the role of financial intermediaries in the channels of transmission of shocks to the real economy.

The importance of the financial cycle leads to a serious questioning of the way monetary policy has been modeled so far, especially in the canonical macroeconomic models. A usual motivation for considering the LM curve was the following. A central bank targets a policy rate and reaches this target by intervening in the money market in such a way that the monetary base that coincides with the demand for money allows the target rate to be reached. However, this interpretation lacks realism. Indeed, monetary policy committees set the interest rate as a discretionary decision. They do so by taking into account developments in the economy (expected inflation, expected growth, capacity utilization rate, etc.). Moreover, the policy rate determines the interest rate spreads and has an impact on the difference between banks' lending and deposit rates. What is new in current thinking is that the state of the economy depends on the financial cycle. The credit cycle feeds consumption and investment. The real estate cycle determines the value of collateral and the level of financial wealth of banks, households, and firms. The same is true of the stock market cycle.

Several works have accordingly proposed "augmented" Taylor rules incorporating indicators of the financial cycle: credit growth rate (Christiano et al. 2014), fixed, counter-cyclical or procyclical debt ratio (Angeloni and Faia 2018), financial stress indicator. In general, the question raised is that of coordination between monetary policy and prudential policy (see the chapter on monetary policy).

There has also been a vast literature on the role of financial intermediaries since the early 2000s.

Compared to the DSGE models of the 1990s, which already integrated financing constraints into the behavior of agents (households and firms), notably via the role of the financial accelerator or interest rate spreads,[4] new generations of macro-financial models give a more active role to financial intermediaries. The latter determine the optimal structure of their balance sheets by deciding on the optimal composition of their asset portfolios (between bank loans, the holding of financial assets, and their reserves volume at the central bank). They also decide on the optimal structure of their liabilities (between equity and debt on the financial markets). Such strategies condition the distribution of credit and their leverage policy, which vary according to changes in net assets and their risk aversion. Their behaviors introduce new financial channels that explain macroeconomic and financial fluctuations. The solvency ratio, leverage, and collateral value of financial institutions are thus important determinants of business cycles. New channels are thus highlighted: the bank capital channel (Meh and Moran 2010), the interbank credit channel (Gertler 2010; Gertler and Kiyotaki 2010), and the risk-taking channel (Angeloni and Faia 2018; Faia and Karau 2021; Neuenkirch and Nöckel 2018). Financial intermediaries react to financial market shocks that induce losses in the value of their assets by adopting strategies to respect the non-bankruptcy constraint. Amplifying effects may result if they engage in fire sales, increase leverage, or change the liquidity of deposits.

Some alternative frameworks have been proposed to explain systemic financial risks. Brunnermeier and Sannikov (2014) study the role of adverse feedback loops and liquidity spirals (caused by overreaction of prices to changes in asset values and high leverage) that amplify the effects of financial frictions and endogenously drive economies toward equilibria far from steady states. The collateral principle accentuates financial leverage and is the source of the great amplitude of financial cycles. The effects on economic growth are amplified by balance sheet deflation, the role of the financial accelerator, and the credit supply channel.

---

[4] See Bernanke et al. (1999), Christensen and Dibb (2008), Christiano et al. (2014), and Kiyotaki and Moore (1997).

5.4   CONCLUSION

The crash in interest rates is undoubtedly one of the most striking facts about the functioning of financial markets over the past three decades. There is much debate about the causes of this phenomenon. One explanation that spontaneously comes to mind is that unconventional monetary policies are the main cause of this fall. But, with the exception of Japan, these policies have been triggered since the Great Financial Crisis of 2008. Furthermore, massive asset purchases by central bankers explain the crash in some specific asset class rates and explain the "safety trap" phenomenon: sovereign bond rates have reached a low floor.

But there are many interest rates in the economy. The transmission of the fall in sovereign bond and short rates to interbank market rates can be explained by corporates' saving glut in both financial and non-financial sectors. This explains why abundant idle savings, finding no borrowers, have helped keep market rates low. This phenomenon has also been aggravated by the accumulation of foreign exchange reserves by the emerging countries and by over-saving by households.

The fall in rates is therefore explained by a misalignment between savings and investment. The theoretical rate illustrating this gap is the natural interest rate. Theoretical models with heterogeneous agents provide explanations for the causes of the dizzying rise in savings rates, in a domestic and international environment. In this context, the puzzle is to know why low rates do not cause savings to fall and investment rates to rise. For the latter, one explanation is that market rates have certainly fallen, but the cost of capital has not experienced the same decline. In fact, the rate of return on equity required by shareholders has remained stable. However, the use of equity represents part of the financing of investments. Another explanation is that the rate of return on capital—the natural interest rate—has itself fallen. Explanations for this fall are usually attributed either to real causes (factor productivity, potential growth) or to monetary and financial factors (supply and demand of safe assets, monetary policy interest rates).

PIONEERS IN THE FIELD

Thomas Laubach and John C. Williams

These two authors have provided empirical support for the secular stagnation thesis by proposing a simple way of estimating the natural rate of interest of economies. In their model, the natural rate is based on an interpretation reminiscent of that of Knut Wicksell. It is a non-observable rate but one that can be estimated, which corresponds to the interest rate that would be observed if economies were operating close to a situation of full capacity utilization with a stable inflation rate. This is a real rate that can be used as a reference for setting the central bank's policy rate. Moreover, this rate is strongly influenced by the potential growth rate of the economies. Their approach has been extended in several directions (taking into account the financial cycle, extending the estimate to the entire term structure of interest rates, making aggregate demand dependent on inequality). Their estimates are publicly available and regularly updated.

Claudio Borio

This author is one of the economists who have drawn the attention of macroeconomists to the importance of the financial cycle on the macroeconomic system. He has provided empirical evidence that finance is not neutral for the economy. This is true, in the short term, as well as in the medium/long term. Borio and his co-authors have highlighted not only the existence of long-run financial cycles but also their importance for estimating output gaps. This leads to the conclusion that financial neutrality leads to an underestimation of economic expansions during periods of rising financial asset prices and, on the contrary, to an underestimation of the depth of recessions during the downturns of the financial cycle. The novelty of Borio's thinking consists in showing that the important thing is not what we think, that is, the inability of governments to prevent financial collapses and crises. We must pay attention to the rising phase of the financial cycle, because of momentum phenomena, and enormous leverage effects that destabilize the real economies. This is the well-known hypothesis of "excess financial elasticity."

(continued)

Pierre-Olivier Gourinchas

In contrast to analyses that point to the role of extraordinarily high global liquidity and saving glut in explaining the crash in interest rates on financial assets, Gourinchas and his co-authors put forward the hypothesis of a growing shortage of safe assets in the world. The originality of his contribution is to have pointed out the existence of a particular liquidity trap mechanism. While most of the literature refers to a ZLB for the central bank's policy rate, the author has shown that the same thing happens for particular classes of non-monetary assets. With H. Rey, he highlighted the phenomenon of "exorbitant privilege and duty" in the United States since the early 1950s with a positive excess return of net gross asset. This allows the United States, in turn, to play the role of insurer of last resort for the rest of the world in times of crises. Thus, an important mechanism is revealed, that is, the role of the financial cycle on the variation of the net international investment position of countries and the balance of payments.

REFERENCES

Acharya VV, Viswanathan S (2011a) Leverage, moral hazard, and liquidity. J Financ 66(1):99–138

Acharya VV, Myers SC, Raan RG (2011) The internal governance of firms. J Financ 66(3):689–720

Ajello (2016) Financial intermediation investment dynamics, and business cycle fluctuations. Am Econ Rev 106(8):2256–2303

Alfaro I, Bloom N, Liu X (2018) The finance uncertainty multiplier. Stand. Inst. for Econ. Pol. Res. (SIEPR), Working Paper n°18–020

Angeloni I, Faia E (2018) Capital regulation and monetary policy with fragile banks. J Mon Econ 60(3):311–324

Armenter R, Hnatkovska V (2017) Taxes and capital structure: understanding firms' savings. J Mon Econ 87(C):13–33

Aum S, Shin Y (2020) Why is the labor share declining? Fed Res B St. Louis 102(4):413–428

Bacchetta P, Benhima K (2015) The demand for liquid assets corporate saving, and global imbalances. J Eur Econ Assoc 13(6):1001–1035

Bates T, Kahle K, Stulz R (2009) Why do U.S. firms hold so much cash than they used to? J Financ 64(5):1985–2021

Bazzi M, Blasques F, Koopman SJ, Lucas A (2017) Time-varying transition probabilities for Markov regime switching models. JTSA 38(3):458–478

Begenau J, Palazzo B (2021) Firm selection and corporate cash holdings. J Financ Econ 139(3):697–718

Bernanke B, Gertler M, Gilchrist S (1999) The financial accelerator in a quantitative business cycle framework. In: Taylor JB, Woodford M (eds) Handbook of macroeconomics, vol 1, pp 1341–1393

Bielecki M., Brzoza-Brzezina M, Kolasa M (2020) Demographics, monetary policy and the zero lower bound. Eur Econ Rev 129

Borio C (2012) The financial cycle and macroeconomics: what have we learnt? BIS Working Papers, n0395

Brand C, Bielecki M, Penalver A (2018) The natural rate of interest: estimates, drivers, and challenges to monetary policy. ECB Occ. Pap. Ser. n°217

Brochet F, Loumioti M, Serafeim G (2015) Speaking of the short-term disclosure horizon and managerial myopia. Rev Acc Stud 20(3):1122–1163

Brunnermeier M, Sannikov Y (2014) A macroeconomic model with a financial sector. Am Econ Rev 104(2):379–421

Cúrdia V, Ferrero A, Ng GC, Tambalotti A (2015) Has U.S. monetary policy tracked the efficient interest rate? J Mon Econ 70:72–83

Caballero RJ, Farhi E, Gourinchas PO (2016) Safe asset scarcity and aggregate demand. Am Econ Rev 106(5):513–518

Caballero R, Farhi E, Gourinchas PO (2017) The safe assets shortage conundrum. J Econ Perspect 31(3):29–46

Caggese A, Pérez Orive A (2022) How stimulative are low real interest rates for intangible capital? Eur Econ Rev 142:103987

Cesa-Bianchi A (2013) Housing cycles and macroeconomic fluctuations: a global perspective. J Int Mon Financ 37:215–238

Chen YR (2008) Corporate governance and cash holdings: listed new economy versus old economy firms. Corporate Governance 16(5):430–442

Chen S., Svirydzenka K (2021) Financial cycles- Early warning indicators of banking crises? IMF Working Paper n°21/116

Chen P, Karabarbounis L, Neima B (2017) The global rise of corporate saving. NBER Working Paper n°23133

Christensen I, Dibb A (2008) The financial accelerator in an estimated new Keynesian model. Rev Econ Dyn 11:155–178

Christiano LJ, Mottto R, Rostagno M (2014) Risk shocks. Am Econ Rev 104(1):27–65

Cynamon B, Fazzali SM (2016) Inequality, the Gret Recession, and slow recovery Cam. J Econ 40(2):373–395

Dao MC, Das M, Koczan Z (2019) Why is labour receiving a smaller share of global income? Econ Policy 34(100):723–759

De Loecker J, Eeckhout J, Unger G (2020) The rise of market power and the macroeconomic implications. Q J Econ 135(2):561–644

Del Negro M, Giannone D, Giannoni MP, Tambalotti A (2017) Safety, liquidity and the natural rate of interest. Brook. Pap Econ Act 48(1):235–316

Diebold F, Lee J, Weinbach G (2021) Regime switching with time-varying transition probabilities, in Business cycles: durations, dynamics, and forecasting. Princeton University Press, Princeton, pp 144–166

Drehman M, Borio C, Tsasaronis K (2012) characterising the financial cycle: don't lose sight of the medium-term! BIS Working Paper n°380

Driver C, Grosman A, Scaramozzino P (2020) Dividend policy and investor pressure. Econ Mod 89:559–576

Dufrénot G, Malik S (2012) The changing role of house price over the business cycle. Econ Model 29(5):1960–1967.

Eggertsson GB, Krugman P (2012) Debt deleveraging, and the liquidity trap: a Fisher-Minsky-Koo approach. Q J Econ 127(3):1469–1513

Eggertsson GB, Mehrotra NR (2014) A model of secular stagnation. NBER Working Paper n°20574

Eggertsson GB, Mehrotra N, Singh S (2016) A contagious malady? Open economy dimension of secular stagnation. IMF Econ Rev 64(4):581–634

Eggertsson GB, Mehrotra NR, Robbins JA (2019) A model of secular stagnation: theory and quantitative evaluation. Am Econ J Macroecon 11(1):1–48

Faia E, Karau S (2021) Systemic bank risk and monetary policy. Int J Cent Banking December:131–176

Falato A, Kadyrzhanova D, Sim J, Steri R (2020) Rising intangible capital, shrinking debt capacity, and the U.S. corporate saving glut. J Financ 77(5):2799–2852

Farhi E, Gourio F (2018) Accounting for macro-finance trends: market power, intangibles, and risk premia. Brokk Pap Econ Act Fall

Filardo AJ (1994) Business-cycle phases and their transitional dynamics. J Bus Econ Stat 12(3):299–308

Filardo AJ (1998) Choosing information variables for transition probabilities in a time-varying transition probability Markov-switching model. Fed Res B: Kansas City. Rev Working Paper 98–09

Furlanetto E, Ravazzolo F, Sarferaz S (2019) Identification of financial factors in economic fluctuations. Econ J 129(617):311–337

Gallagher DR, Gardner PA, Swan PL (2013) Governance through trading: institutional swing trades and subsequent firm performance. J Financ Quant Anal 48(2):427–458

Gerali A, Neri S (2019) Natural rates across the Atlantic. J Macroecon 69(C):103019

Gertler M (2010) Banking crises and real activity: identifying the linkages. Int J Cent Bank 6(34):125–135

Gertler M, Kiyotaki N (2010) Financial intermediation and credit policy in Business cycle analysis, in Hand. Mon Econ 3:547–599

Gruber JW, Kamin SB (2015) The corporate saving glut in the aftermath of the global financial crises. Int Financ Dis Pap 1150

Hamilton JD (1989) A new approach to the economic analysis of nonstationary time series and the business cycle. Economics 57(2):357–384

Hamilton JD (1996) Specification testing in Markov-switching time-series models. J Econ 70:127–157

Hamilton JD, Harris ES, Hatzius J, West KD (2016) The equilibrium real funds rate: past, present, and future. IMF Econ Rev 64(4):660–707

Hatzius J, Mishkin F, Schoenholtz K, Watson M (2010) Financial conditions indexes: a fresh look after the financial crisis; NBER Working Paper n°16150

Huang Y, Li Q, Liow KH, Hou X (2020) Is housing the business cycle? A multiresolution analysis for OECD countries. J Hous Econ 49:101692

Jòrda O, Schularik M, Taylor AM (2016) Sovereign versus banks: credit, crises and consequences. J Eur Econ Assoc 14(1):45–79

Justiniano A, Primiceri GE, Tambalotti A (2014) The effects of the saving and banking glut on the U.S. economy. J Int Econ 92(1):S52–S67

Kaminsky GL, Reinhart C (1999) The twin crises: the causes of banking and balance-of-payments. Am Econ Rev 89(3):473–500

Karabounis L, Neiman B (2013) The global decline of the labor share. Q J Econ 129:61–103

Kim C-J, Piger J, Startz R (2008) Estimation of Markov regime-switching regressions with endogenous switching. J Econ 143(2):263–273

Kiyotaki N, Moore J (1997) Credit cycles. J Policy Econ 105(2):211–248

Lazonick W (2018) The functions of the stock market and the fallacies of shareholder value. In: Driver C, Thompson G (eds) Corporate governance in contention. Oxford University Press, Oxford

Leamer EE (2015) Housing really is the business cycle: what survives the lessons of 2008–09? J Mon Cred Bank 47:43–50

Liu Z, Wang P, Zha T (2013) Land-price dynamics and macroeconomic fluctuations. Economics 81(3):1147–1184

Meh C Moran K (2010) The role of bank capital in the propagation of shocks. J Econ Dyn Control 34(3):555–576

Neuenkirch M, Nöckel M (2018) The risk-taking channel of monetary policy transmission in the Euro area. J Bank Financ 93:71–91

Ozkan A, Ozkan N (2004) Corporate cash holdings: an empirical investigation of UK companies. J Bank Fin 28(9):2103–2134

Papetti A (2021) Demographics and the natural real interest rate: historical and prospected paths for the Euro area. J Econ Dyn Control 132(C):104209

Pesaran MH, Shin Y, Smith R (2001) Bound testing approaches to the analysis of level relationships. J Appl Econ 16:289–326

Piketty T (2014) Capital in the twenty-first century. The Belnap Press of Harvard University Press, Cambridge

Reinhart C, Rogoff KS (2008) This time is different: a panoramic view of eight centuries of financial crises. NBER Working Paper n013882

Schmelzing P (2020) Eight centuries of global real rates and the "suprasecular decline": 1311–2018. BOE Staff Working Paper n°845

Stansbury A, Summers LH (2020) The declining worker power hypothesis: an explanation for the recent evolution of the American economy. NBER Working Paper n°27193

Summers LH. (2015) Demand side secular stagnation. Am Econ Rev 105(5):60–65

Thwaites G (2015) Why are real interest rates so low? Secular stagnation and the relative price of investment goods. BOE Working Paper, n°564

Wicksell K (1898) Interest and prices. Macmillan, London

CHAPTER 6

New Challenges for Monetary Policy

The purpose of this chapter is to present some new challenges of monetary policy today. The goals have evolved over time as circumstances changed. We discuss some topics that have emerged in the debates between macroeconomists: Fischerian approaches to the interest rate suggesting a positive correlation between the level of interest rates and inflation rate, unconventional monetary policies, and helicopter money.

We investigate the following topics.

First Challenge: Monetary Policy Strategies Since the End of the Second World War Have Changed Drastically Over Time

During the 1950s, industrialized countries had two major concerns. On the one hand, they had to rebuild economies devastated by war. On the other hand, they had to find a way to liquidate the voluminous debts accumulated during the Second World War. Monetary policies helped to achieve these goals, based on financial repression. Massive repurchases of government debt securities, the building of a Treasury circuit in France, and regulations of the banking and financial sector helped to keep interest rates low, while inflation rates were high (see Reinhart and Sbrancia 2015).

In the early 1980s, fighting inflation became the priority in a context of an oil price shock and the active role of a price-wage loop when the bargaining power of unions was greater than today. The interest rate gradually became the main instrument of monetary policy.

© The Author(s), under exclusive license to Springer Nature
Switzerland AG 2023
G. Dufrénot, *New Challenges for Macroeconomic Policies*,
https://doi.org/10.1007/978-3-031-15754-7_6

From the mid-1980s onward, the context of financial liberalization favored the financing of economies by capital markets. Central banks gradually became independent of governments and chose to abandon the financial policies of leaning against the wind. Financial globalization has favored the evolution of short- and long-term rates below the growth rates of the economy. As a result, stock prices have risen sharply and private and public credits have surged.

The 2008 crisis was another period of change with the adoption of quantitative easing policies. This was the return of quantitative policies. These policies were described as "unconventional" compared to the interest rate policy that had prevailed since the period of Great moderation. Until then, the transmission of changes in the policy rate to other interest rates at all maturities had occurred through different channels (expectations, credit, etc.). In the wake of the 2008 GFC, central banks first lowered their interest rates until they reached the ZLB. To influence the whole interest rate structure, they then used the assets and liabilities of their balance sheet.

More recently, new strategies have complemented quantitative policies: yield curve control (keeping long-term interest rates at very low levels), equity purchases to reduce the cost of capital of corporates and to induce favorable wealth effects.

Second Challenge: Conflicting Objectives of Monetary Policies

What should central banks take care of? Many economists would spontaneously answer what they have learned from their economics courses over the last 30 years. Central banks control inflation, without causing damage to growth. They would also say that according to the Sargent and Wallace's monetary arithmetic (see Sargent and Wallace 1981), central banks' decisions cannot be subordinated to those of governments: fiscal dominance must be avoided. This independence of central banks serves to limit inflationary bias. In the short term, inflation is linked to imbalances in the goods and labor markets. There is a trade-off between inflation and activity. By using the interest rate, central banks can influence relative prices and thus economic activity, because nominal prices have some rigidity. In the long run, prices become flexible and there is a stable (equilibrium) relationship between the monetary base (the money supply) and GDP. Inflation is caused by an excess supply of money, compared to the volume needed to absorb the available production.

Several events have occurred that have changed this approach to monetary policy. The first change is the non-neutrality of the financial cycle on the real economy (see Chap. 4). The excess supply of money does not necessarily influence inflation in the real economy, but it does increase the prices of financial assets. By keeping interest rates at low levels, central banks have encouraged leverage effects that contributed to the upward phase of the credit cycle. Quantitative easing policies have fueled financial inflation even though inflation rates in the real sector remained very low.

Secondly, central banks now face additional challenges. The world is experiencing higher inflationary pressures caused by the disruption of global supply chains as a result of the Covid-19 crisis and the 2022 Ukraine war. Assuming that food and energy (oil and gas) price inflation persists, it could be transmitted to core inflation. This could happen if, for instance, many unfilled jobs in labor markets strengthens employees' bargaining power and leads to widespread wage increases). It is not clear how higher interest rates will help dealing with such an emerging inflation, as a too rapid exit from unconventional policies could cause a financial crisis by driving down financial asset prices.

A third aspect must be mentioned. Fighting inflation is now coming up against another objective, that of the sustainability of fiscal policies. Given the circumstances, the scale of public spending is high: all countries have had to absorb the Covid-19 shock, they have to finance the ecological transition, and adopt policies to fight inequality and poverty. This is only feasible if sovereign bond rates remain below potential growth rates (which are not that high).

In short, it is not certain that stabilizing inflation is enough to control other the macro-financial imbalances, or to reach a strong potential growth in the medium term.

Third Challenge: Debates on Helicopter Money

Helicopter money is money creation without any counterpart. For instance, this would be the case if central banks irreversibly buy back sovereign bonds A simple way to do this is to systematically buy back debts as their maturity is reached). This corresponds to a *de facto* cancellation of public debts. This money, "falling from the sky," could allow governments to finance their public spending (which includes subsidies to households and businesses).

What is the motivation for this? Money is first and foremost the only instrument that allows to create and extinguish debts (whatever its form, fiduciary, scriptural, electronic) as long as it is fiat money. Since making transactions in an economy is equivalent to contracting and settling debts with legal tender (and of which the central banks have the monopoly of creation), any individual in society should have access to it.

Unemployed people, for example, are excluded from access to fiat money, because they cannot offer their skills in the labor market in exchange for a debt that corresponds to the salary due for the tasks they perform. A high level of unemployment reduces the capacity to spend and thus reduces growth potential because aggregate demand is low. Nothing would therefore prevent a central bank from deciding, to discretionary create and give fiat money to the unemployed or to people not participating in the labor market in exchange for a fictitious asset or service. This is what happens, for example, when someone receives unemployment benefits larger than the social contributions he or she has paid, or when governments cover a large part of the financial costs of an expensive hospitalization. Such expenditures could be financed by perpetual buybacks of sovereign debt created to finance the budget deficit. Economists who advocate helicopter money see it as a way to combat prolonged recessions and high income inequality. Those who criticize it say that it has no theoretical basis (although we shall see that such a basis exists). They fear the "abuses" that it could cause: hyperinflation, explosion of public debts, and loss of confidence in money.

6.1   CHALLENGING THE THEORETICAL FOUNDATIONS OF MONETARY POLICY

Two issues are being questioned today. The first concerns the way in which monetary policy is conceived as an instrument for regulating the business cycle in the short term and for controlling inflation in the medium/long term. The second concerns the supposedly stabilizing character of Taylor rules.

6.1.1   Does the Quantity Theory of Money Still Hold?

How should the stabilization of the macroeconomic cycle unfold today according to the theories that underpinned monetary policies in industrialized countries until 2008? These theories are based on New-Keynesian approaches to inflation. Price rigidity in the short run allows monetary policy to have real effects. In the long run, money is neutral. It only affects nominal prices. Let's apply this reasoning to the current situation.

Inflation expectations and low potential growth rates in industrialized countries are creating deflationary pressures. To fight deflation, central banks have lowered their policy rates. As long as such a decrease is greater than the decrease in inflation, this stimulates activity. But as policy rates approach the zero lower bound, monetary policy has fewer effect on growth. As soon as policy rates hit the ZLB, interest rate policy becomes completely ineffective.

According to Quantity Theory of Money (QTM). By increasing the money supply, or by relying on forward guidance policies, central banks could expect to bypass the ZLB, bring back inflation and rise the output. This is what they have done through unconventional policies (but core inflation has remained low).

These arguments are invalidated by the empirical reality. First, the view that inflation is always a monetary phenomenon is not true. We saw in Part I that there are many other determinants of inflation. Second, Fisher's quantity theory of money must be reinterpreted in light of the central role of financial markets in the economy. Money (or liquid assets that are substitutes for it) is one asset among others (stocks, real estate, physical assets, bonds). Moreover, the monetary financing of the economy is only one channel of financing. What matters is liquidity and net lending/borrowing positions of financial and non-financial agents vis-à-vis each other.

These observations imply that there are at least two channels of transmission of monetary policy: one that explains the transmission of changes in the monetary base to the relative prices of financial assets, and another that explains the transmission of financial prices to real income. Moreover, the transmission of liquidity to all prices in an economy (physical and financial asset prices) depends on the rates of return on the different assets. The consequence is that the business cycle is regulated by wealth effects and not simply by inflation in the real sector.

A portfolio choice approach of monetarist theory would certainly explain the current situation better, because it takes into account the wide range of assets available in the financial markets. An increase in the supply of money changes the asset structure of economic agents' balance sheets. To restore their initial balance sheet structure, they use the additional money to buy financial assets, which changes their relative prices and creates wealth effects. The effect on real income is more or less small depending on the sensitivity of consumption and investment to these wealth effects.

Does the wealth effect channel work in reality? At the time of the 2008 subprime crisis, investment had fallen sharply because of balance-sheet effects. Firms and banks reduced their financial leverage to restore liquidity to their balance sheets, which had lost values given the fall in asset prices. Similarly, households had to reduce their debt. Then central banks adopted expansionary quantitative policies, the rise in asset prices was not transmitted to the real sector. This means that a significant part of the wealth created by portfolio revaluations continued to be saved. There is thus a paradox: we are simultaneously observing low nominal interest rates (or even negative rates, if we consider the shadow rates that reflect the expansionary quantitative policies) and low inflation rates. Monetary policies therefore have a cost, since they lead to the accumulation of "idle" financial wealth.

6.1.2   The Neo-Fischerian Interpretations of Monetary Policy

To explain the simultaneity of low interest rates and low inflation rates, The Neo-Fischerian theories propose the following relationship as a mechanism guiding inflation expectations(see, e.g., Cochrane 2016; Williamson 2016):

nominal interest rate = inflation expectations + real interest rate.

The real rate is assumed to be independent of monetary policy and determined exclusively by real variables (capital productivity, potential growth rate, rate of time preference, etc.). In Part I, we saw that this rate can be the natural rate of interest. If the real interest rate falls (e.g., because of a slowdown in productivity gains or potential growth), the central bank must lower the nominal rate. If the nominal rate hits the ZLB, the above equation holds only if inflation expectations rise. But if the latter are anchored at a very low level, the equation does no longer hold because:

nominal interest rate > expected inflation rate + real interest rate.

The nominal interest rate is too high and the economies are stuck in a recession.

The theoretical implications of the neo-Fisherian approaches can be presented by combining a Fisher equation and a Taylor rule. On this basis, Benhabib et al. (2001) and Schmitt-Grohé and Uribe (2009) were among the first to show that Taylor rules do not necessarily stabilizing rules. Indeed, they can generate multiple indeterminate equilibria. Among these equilibria, we find some for which monetary policy is passive, with the inflation rate remaining below its target without the central bank having the means to vary the interest rate more than proportionally to the inflation rate. To illustrate this phenomenon, we present the simplified version of

Benhabib et al. (2001)'s model with flexible prices (introducing rigid prices does not change the general conclusion).

The economy consists of a large number of infinitely-lived households with a utility function including both consumption, c, and real balance, m:

$$\int_0^\infty e^{-rt} u(c, m) dt. \qquad (6.1)$$

This function is maximized under the following constraint:

$$c + \dot{a} = (R - \pi)a - R\, m + y, \quad \lim_{t \to \infty} e^{-\int_0^t [R(s) - \pi(s)]} a(t) \geq 0. \qquad (6.2)$$

a is the real financial wealth, R is the risk-free nominal interest rate, π is the inflation rate, y is an exogenous endowment. $-Rm$ denotes the opportunity cost of holding money, $(R - \pi)$ is the real interest rate on the household's asset. $\dot{a}$ is the increase in the stock of real wealth. The limit condition in Eq. (6.2) is a transversality condition implying that the household does not engage into a Ponzi game.

The optimality condition and equilibrium of the goods market imply the following conditions:

$$y = c, \quad u_c(c, m) = \lambda, \quad u_m(c, m) = \lambda\, R,$$
$$\dot{\lambda} = \lambda\, [r + \pi - R(\pi)]. \qquad (6.3)$$

If $u_{cm} > 0$ and $u_{mm} < 0$, these conditions define a relationship linking the Lagrange multiplier λ to the nominal interest rate R: $\lambda = L(R), L' < 0$.

Now suppose that there exists a monetary policy rule linking the nominal interest rate to the inflation rate π, $R = R(\pi) > 0$, which is increasing, strictly convex and differentiable.

Finally, we suppose that there exists, at least, one equilibrium steady state at which the Fisher equation is satisfied:

$$R(\pi^*) = r + \pi^*, \qquad (6.4)$$

where r is the real interest rate and π^* is active when the policy is active. An active monetary policy rule is such that $R'(\pi) > 1$, when $\pi < \pi*$. A passive rule implies that $R'(\pi) < 1$, when $\pi < \pi^*$.

Combining the policy rule with the equilibrium and optimality conditions leads a first-order differential equation describing the dynamics of inflation:

$$\dot{\pi} = \frac{-L\,[R(\pi)]}{L'\,[R(\pi)]\,R'(\pi)}\,[R(\pi) - \pi - r].\tag{6.5}$$

Figure 6.1 provides an illustration of a situation with two equilibrium steady states: one which is unstable and corresponds to an active policy (B), and another which is stable and represents the passive policy (A).

The inflation rate π_1 is observed in a liquidity trap or ZLB context. The same result can be established in a discrete-time model by substituting a cash-in-advance economy for the utility function with real balances (see Schmitt-Grohé and Uribe 2000). Until recently, the equilibrium represented by A was considered a theoretical curiosity. However, the experience of the lost decades in Japan has shown that an economy can

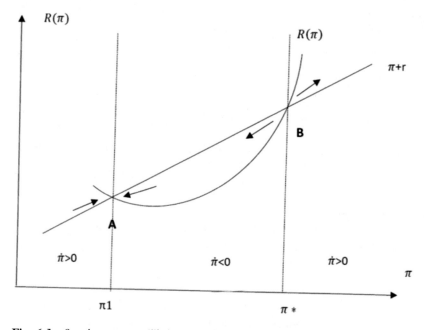

Fig. 6.1 Steady states equilibrium: passive and active policies

become trapped in a deflationary spiral with downward price expectations, especially if the potential growth rate is low.

A literature has rapidly expanded on the conditions of the existence of multiple equilibria around A. In particular, a ZLB constraint can make limit cycles and chaotic fluctuations appear from bifurcation processes. This illustrates the fact that around A there is a basin of attraction (see, e.g., Benhabib et al. 2002; Eusepi 2007; Schmitt-Grohé and Uribe 2009). Some works have shown the existence of low inflation equilibria associated with a ZLB situation based on empirical evidence. For example, the existence of a non-linear Taylor rule of the European Central Bank causing a liquidity trap steady state equilibrium is highlighted by Dufrénot and Khayat (2016). This equilibrium is locally determined in a New-Keynesian model for a large range of parameter values. Bullard (2010) compares the United States and Japan by showing a concentration of interest rate and inflation rate pairs corresponding to A in Fig. 6.1. When these equilibria are stable, only aggressive monetary or fiscal policies can move away from them (see, e.g., Chattopadhyay and Daniel 2018; Evans et al. 2008; Schmitt-Grohé and Uribe 2014).

According to the Neo-Fischerian approaches, unconventional monetary policies (forward guidance) have the opposite effects to what the standard theories predict. Expansive monetary policies do not induce higher inflation. Indeed, if a central bank adopts such a policy—especially if it announces that it will do so over a very long period of time—people think that it is doing so because inflation is structurally low and activity very sluggish. The Fisher equation therefore serves as a guideline for market expectations. Expected inflation rate is simply the difference between the nominal policy rate (the risk-free rate in Benhabib et al. 2001's model) and the natural interest rate.

Cochrane (2016) proposes the following theoretical foundation of the Fisher equation. He combines a standard intertemporal substitution equation of a consumption model with a simple formulation of the Phillips curve:

$$c_t = E_t c_{t+1} - \sigma(R_t - E_t \pi_{t+1}), \quad \pi_t = \kappa c_t, \tag{6.6}$$

and perfect foresight expectations: $\pi_{t+1} = E_t \pi_{t+1}$. the variables c and π are respectively consumption and inflation. $E_t x_{t+1}$ is the expectation made at time t of the variable x for time $t+1$. R is the nominal interest rate. π and σ are real parameters.

A substitution of π_t for c_t leads the following equation:

$$E_t \pi_{t+1} = \frac{1}{1 + \sigma\kappa} \pi_t + \frac{\sigma\kappa}{1 + \sigma\kappa} R_t. \tag{6.7}$$

A backward solution gives:

$$\pi_t = \frac{\sigma\kappa}{1 + \sigma\kappa} \sum_{j=0}^{\infty} \left(\frac{1}{1 + \sigma\kappa} \right)^j R_{t-j}. \tag{6.8}$$

If, to simplify, we set $\sigma = \pi = 1$, we see that

$$\pi_t = \frac{1}{2} \sum_{j=0}^{\infty} \left(\frac{1}{2} \right)^j R_{t-j}. \tag{6.9}$$

A permanent decrease in the nominal interest rate leads a decrease in π_t. A similar result can be obtained by considering a Phillips curve with adaptive expectations:

$$c_t = \kappa(\pi_t - \pi_{t-1}^e), \quad \pi_t^e = \lambda \pi_{t-1}^e + (1 - \lambda)\pi_t. \tag{6.10}$$

The new solution for inflation dynamics becomes

$$\pi_t = \frac{1}{1 + \sigma\kappa} (\pi_{t-1} + \pi_{t-1}^e - \pi_{t-2}^e) + \frac{\sigma\kappa}{1 + \sigma\kappa} R_{t-1}, \text{ or} \tag{6.11}$$

$$\pi_t = \frac{1}{1 + \sigma\kappa} [\pi_{t-1} + \gamma(1 - \lambda)] \sum_{j=0}^{\infty} \lambda^j \Delta\pi_{t-j-1} + \sigma\kappa R_{t-1}. \tag{6.12}$$

Again, inflation moves one for one with the interest rate. The usual Fisher equation $R_t = r_t + \pi_{t+1}^e$ is a special case of (6.8) and (6.12). If we apply this model to the current context, it is therefore normal for private agents to anticipate low inflation rates if the central bank rate is low. People consume more ahead of periods of low interest rates. Once the interest rate drops, they reduce their savings, receive less interest and then have to reduce their consumption. Lower consumption lowers inflation.

Some authors have found a positive correlation between the inflation rate and the policy rate of central banks (Lukmanova and Rabitsch 2018; Uribe 2017 for the United States and Japan). Others reject this relationship, either on the basis of the endogeneity of the interest rate with respect to the inflation rate (Crowder 2020) or by rejecting backward-looking expectations (Gobbi et al. 2019; Gabaix 2020).

6.1.3   Choosing Monetary Policy Targets

Inflation Target or Price Level Target?

Some macroeconomists remain concerned about the problem of avoiding excessive inflation in economies. This is the case even though core inflation has remained close to the central bank's target for the last three decades and inflationary expectations remain anchored at very low levels. For several years now, the economies of the industrialized countries have been suffering from disinflationary, or deflationary, pressures, which are holding back the decline in real interest rates.

The economic literature illustrates different approaches to inflation today.

On the one hand, papers study in depth the best inflation targeting strategies to limit the costs of inflation. The authors discuss the comparative beneficial effects of anchoring expectations with fixed targets, fluctuation bands or hybrid rules. They want to show that fluctuation bands around focal values, even if they serve to signal the existence of uncertainty about inflation control, reduce the anchoring of expectations (see, e.g., Ehrmann 2021; Grosse-Steffen 2021; Le Bihan et al. 2021).

On the other hand, work is being done on the important questions today: how can economies escape from deflationary traps? How can we get economic agents to start anticipating increases in inflation again? The debate is then moving in a different direction. Indeed, the choice to be made is a trade-off between targeting inflation and targeting the general price level. Inflation targeting has proven to be ineffective in changing inflationary expectations in a context of zero lower bound (see, for instance, Kiley and Roberts 2017). And we can understand why. Targeting an inflation rate of 2%, for example, implies that the reaction of central banks is not contingent on the history of past inflation rates. It does not matter whether economies have experienced high or low inflation in the past. What matters is that corrections are made to stay on target. The case of general price level targeting is different. The target is an average benchmark over a given period. This requires the central bank to adjust its interest rate, not to reach its inflation target immediately, but to return to the average. Let's say that the inflation target is 2% and that the inflation rate was 0.5 and 1% in the two previous periods. To get an average of 2% over, say, four periods, the cumulative inflation rate over the two future periods must be 6.5%. This means that the central bank leaves the inflation rate above its target for a few periods.

The proposal to adopt price level targeting in a ZLB regime was discussed by Ben Bernanke in 2017 at the Peterson Institute Rethinking Macroeconomic Policy conference. Although the author presents them as two alternative strategies, it has the same effects as temporarily raising the target in an inflation targeting framework. This author proposed a new target at 3 or 4%. This works provided that the measure is temporary, until inflationary expectations cause rates to rise on the markets and give interest rate policy more flexibility. The temporary nature of this measure makes its effects equivalent to those of a general price level control strategy. Readers interested in an in-depth analysis of price level targeting can refer to Ambler (2009) or Hatcher and Mindford (2014). Theoretical work shows that this strategy effectively modifies inflation expectations in New-Keynesian models. And the welfare losses when interest rates are at the ZLB are lower than with an inflation targeting strategy (see, e.g., Coibon et al. 2022; Covas and Zhang 2010).

An important aspect is to convince markets and private sector professional forecasters of the importance of changing central bank strategies. Economic actors need to be convinced that the reasons for this are not just technical, but make economic sense.

Let us take an example from the current situation. Why might it be inappropriate for central banks to respond to rising world prices by maintaining the standard monetary policy framework and choosing to raise interest rates? In the current context of soaring global energy and food prices, let us imagine the following scenarios: price increases accompanied by strong wage growth, a decline in household savings to finance spending that has been eroded by declining purchasing power, and a return of inflationary expectations. Such a chain of events would undoubtedly push structural inflation back above the central banks' usual target of 2%. The idea of raising policy rates sharply and permanently to curb this nascent inflation could prove counterproductive for several reasons.

First, due to the low interest rates of the past few years, private and public sector debt ratios have started to rise again. In the Eurozone, households' and non-financial corporates' debt ratios exceed 120% of GDP. In Japan and the United States, it is over 150% of GDP. Public debt in many industrialized countries is above 100% of GDP. Apart from the fact that a little inflation reduces the real value of debts, raising interest rates too quickly would increase vulnerability to debt crises. It would tighten the debt constraints of those who roll over the debt, weaken governments' fiscal support for growth, and cause financial asset prices to fall, leading to a sharp devaluation of balance sheets. All this would lead to a generalized phenomenon of forced deleveraging. The experience of the 2008 crisis has shown us that this type of scenario traps economies in prolonged stagnation.

Second, a rise in interest rates would trigger capital inflows from emerging and developing countries. Yet the current health crisis and geopolitical tensions have already increased their vulnerabilities to international capital markets. If the central banks of these countries respond to the capital outflows by raising their policy rates, these policies will cripple their growth and increase their financial distress. If they do nothing, capital outflows will lead to devaluations and greater exposure to global inflation. In either case, a rise in interest rates in the United States, Europe, or Japan would be a macro-financial shock for emerging countries.

Third, the current resurgence of inflationary pressures is not due to excess demand. It is quite the opposite. The low trajectories of potential growth rates, high global savings and low investment rates rather suggest a situation of stagnation. However, one does not fight stagflation (a combination of high inflation and low growth) by considering curbing an already sluggish aggregate demand. In this respect, raising the interest rate on the deposits that banks hold with central banks (on the grounds of preventing their reserves from fueling credit) would be ineffective. Indeed, these reserves are currently used to buy financial securities, and not exclusively to finance productive investment.

Should Monetary Policy Target the Natural Interest Rate?

Many economists agree that monetary policy should be based on an interest rate rule. In a simple case, the central bank's mandate is to target a nominal interest rate that allows output to be at its potential level. It is assumed that there is an inflation rate to target that meets this objective. Through its actions, the central bank is also supposed to converge inflation expectations to the inflation rate it targets. A formula that reflects this behavior is the following:

Target rate= natural rate+ core inflation+$\lambda_G(y_t - y_t^*) + \lambda_\pi(_t\pi_{t+\tau}^e - \pi_{t+\tau}^*)$,   (6.13)

where $(y_t - y_t^*)$ is output gap, $_t\pi_{t+\tau}^e$ is inflation expectation made at time t for time $t + \tau$ and $\pi_{t+\tau}^*$ is the inflation target for time $t + \tau$. There are several formulations of such a rule: the central bank can target a band, use average inflation targeting, and so on. And, instead of the output gap, we could consider the unemployment gap or the growth gap.

As we have seen, the natural rate is a real rate. If it were observable, things would be simple. All the central bank would have to do is adjust the nominal interest rate target according to expectations of the future rate of inflation. Since it is non-observable, there are debates among economists about how to interpret it. For many economists it is a long-term interest rate that prevails when the economy is at a steady state.

A first Fisherian approach considers that the natural interest rate depends on the subjective price of the future of economic agents and that it determines the trade-offs between consumption and savings. The interest rate determines the optimal level of consumption along the path of GDP. This idea is usually summarized by the following equation:

$$c_t^{-1/\sigma} = E_t \left[\frac{1 + r_{t+1}}{1 + \rho} c_{t+1}^{-1/\sigma} \right],$$ (6.14)

where c_t is current consumption, r_t is the real interest rate at time t, ρ is the discount rate, σ is the elasticity of intertemporal substitution rate.

A second interpretation is that of neoclassical growth models of the Solow or Ramsey type. In addition to psychological factors, the natural rate depends on real factors that are supposed to guide the economy toward its long-term stationary state: the savings rate, the population growth rate (n), the growth rate of per-capita consumption (g_c), and so on. A typical equation is the following:

$$r_t = \frac{1}{\sigma} g_{ct} + n + \rho.$$ (6.15)

Third, we have seen that in semi-structural models à la HLW (Holston-Lauback-William), the natural rate depends on the potential growth rate and on macro-financial imbalances (inflation, trade, output gap, capacity utilization rate, etc.).

Finally, there is an interpretation provided by the DSGE models. The natural rate is often defined as the rate that would allow full employment to be achieved when prices are perfectly flexible.

In all these interpretations, the natural rate is defined as a real variable. As a result, it is generally assumed to be positive. It can theoretically be negative, but under very specific assumptions that are usually considered to be unfeasible: demographic decline reflected by a fall in the size of the population, negative potential growth, a fall in per-capita consumption, dis-saving, and so on. However, empirical work has highlighted the possibility of negative natural rates with very plausible explanations: slowing productivity gains, excess savings and under-investment, or any phenomenon leading the economy into a self-sustaining low potential growth trap. We have seen that this kind of situation is very likely to occur when economies are subject to hysteresis phenomena with difficulties in recovering their pre-shock trajectories. This is what happens, for example, when a major crisis leads to capital losses (e.g., following a massive drop in investment as a result of forced deleveraging by companies).

When the natural rate of interest becomes negative, the central bank may no longer be able to lower the nominal interest rate to a level that would bring output up to its potential level. This is particularly true when inflation expectations are very low. Since it can no longer influence the economy through short rates, it has several options.

The first is to directly target medium-/long-term rates by buying assets directly at these maturities (see below, quantitative easing policies).

A second option is to influence agents' expectations. For example, if it announces that the short-term interest rate will be kept at zero for a long time, the private sector could deduce that this inflationary policy would raise prices. They may therefore anticipate price increases, which would lower real rates. But economic agents may think the opposite: if the central bank behaves in this way, it is because it thinks that the recession period will last a long time. This is all the more likely since we are dealing with a central bank that, in normal times, is very conservative by targeting inflation as a priority (whatever the cost to economic growth).

A third possibility is to flatten the yield curve.Indeed, by lowering its nominal short rate, the central bank hopes to lower expected future nominal short rates.

Beyond these possibilities, there is debate about whether it makes sense to target negative nominal interest rates in an environment where an upward trend in expected inflation rates cannot be counted on to drive down real interest rates. And if the answer is yes, how do we do it in reality?

Why do security buyers agree to hold securities that cost them money (negative rates of return)? To understand this, it is necessary to interpret negative rates according to financial logic. Indeed, holding an asset with a negative return can be interpreted as holding a hybrid asset. Let's take a bond, for example. The holder buys the security that provides a certain return until a given maturity. But, at the same time, he buys a put option to protect himself against events that could greatly affect the return on the asset (a sovereign default, a major recession). He must therefore pay a premium that guarantees him the possibility of recovering a good part of his capital. Therefore, there must be agents on the markets who sell put options, that is, who commit to repurchase the assets at a price defined in advance. In the case of sovereign bonds, central banks play this role by being buyers of last resort on the secondary markets for government debt. Therefore, the return can be defined as the coupon minus the option premium. Negative rates are accepted because they are the counterpart of a financial insurance (a buy-and-hold put option strategy).

It is interesting to note that this idea of negative nominal rates has been defended several economists (Kocherlakota, Mankiw, Rogoff, etc.). There are various ways of doing this: setting commercial banks' deposits with the central bank below zero, taxing the holding of cash, regulating the share of liquid assets in portfolios, buying huge volumes of outstanding debts (private and public). The markets would carry these negative rates, given the mass of cash that would seek to be invested.

But the point of view of economists is not necessarily that of the financial markets, nor of financial firms. One argument is that, below a certain interest rate, banks are averse to lending money because of the strong pressure on their financial profitability. Low returns on assets can significantly erode banks' interest margins and induce them to hold financial assets rather than lend to households and firms. For pension funds or insurance companies that guarantee fixed returns, the issue of balance sheet sustainability also arises. Either they are forced to take more risk to find higher-yielding assets or they impose higher contributions on households.

One of the important questions for central banks is therefore the trade-off between the effects of negative rates. On the one hand, they want to focus on the level of real rates that are negative. These rates give an indication of how well the real economy is doing. The objective of central banks in a liquidity trap situation is to bring the interest rate down below zero to stimulate investment and aggregate demand, and to bring inflation back. On the other hand, one cannot neglect the influence of such a policy on the financial markets (whose securities serve as a financial support for the savings of economic agents). For example, negative interest rates may be offset by significant wealth effects if the prices of financial assets rise. But this phenomenon can also increase inequality.

In the literature, work has been done to study the stabilization properties of the central bank's interest rate in tracking the neutral interest rate (see, e.g., Brand et al. 2018; Haavio and Laine 2021; Garadi and Neri 2019). The interpretation of DSGE models is that by bringing the policy rate to the level of the natural rate, the central bank achieves its inflation and output targets, provided that prices are flexible. In the presence of rigidity, there is a trade-off between inflation and output, and the interest rate instrument alone is not sufficient to stabilize the two variables. But the conclusions vary from one model to another, not so much because of econometric uncertainties as because of interpretations of the natural interest rate. For example, the rates calculated from HLW-type models are much smoother than those from DSGE models because the natural rate is assumed to be strongly influenced by the potential growth rate. In this context, the question of what is the right neutral rate to aim for seems difficult. On the other hand, one may wonder for which parameters of the Taylor rule the policy rate would converge to the calculated natural rate. Then compare these coefficients with those implied by the interest rates actually applied.

6.2   THE NEW CHALLENGES OF MONETARY POLICY

6.2.1   Unconventional Monetary Policies

Figures 6.2 and 6.3 show the evolution of policy rates and total assets of three major central banks: Federal Reserve (FED), European Central Bank (ECB) and Bank of Japan (BOJ). We see that interest rates have been

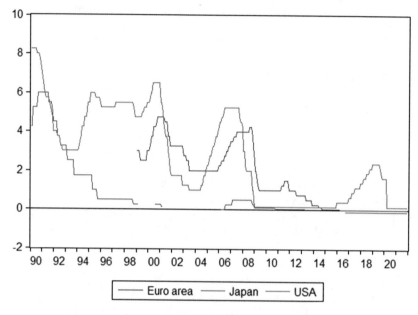

Fig. 6.2 Policy rates: Source Bank of International Settlements

falling steadily, and from 2008 onward have been around zero (in Japan, since 1999). Conversely, their balance sheet assets have grown strongly since 2008. These developments reflect a new way of conducting monetary policy since the 2008 GFC. The policy rate was no longer the preferred instrument of monetary policy, as the flexibility to change the interest rate has diminished as it has approached the ZLB. As the policy rate fell, all financial and debt market rates also fell. Financial markets were evolving in a liquidity trap.

Central bank's balance sheets have therefore been used as a counter-cyclical instrument to lower market rates by providing voluminous liquidity to financial markets. This was done in several ways:

- by purchases of assets of different categories (private bonds, sovereign bonds, stocks, gilts, commercial papers),
- by widening of maturities (e.g., for gilt purchases the duration was extended from 3–5 years to more than 25 years),
- by increasing of the monetary base.

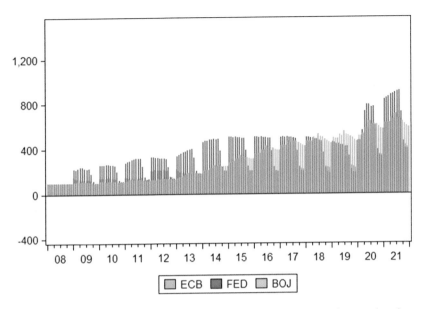

Fig. 6.3   Central bank assets: Index base 2008. Source Fred Database and author

As a result, central banks setting a target for their policy rate. What happened can be illustrated graphically.

In normal times the interest rate targeted by a central bank lies within a corridor, the upper bound of which corresponds to a penalty rate (collateralized lending) and the lower bound to a deposit rate. The monetary policy committee announces the policy rate and commercial banks determine the amount of reserves they want to hold at that rate. The policy rate is then used as a benchmark for all market rates (see Fig. 6.4).

The strategy for lowering the policy rate involves several steps.

The first step is to lower the corridor (by cutting all three rates). Then, the width of the corridor is narrowed. Imagine that the corridor is lowered until the deposit rate becomes zero, and then the central bank wants to bring its policy rate to the level of the deposit rate. At that point, the interest rate is set at its floor and the central bank targets commercial banks' reserves. It now has a quantitative target. As shown in Fig. 6.5, the central bank can increase the quantity of bank reserves, without limit, without

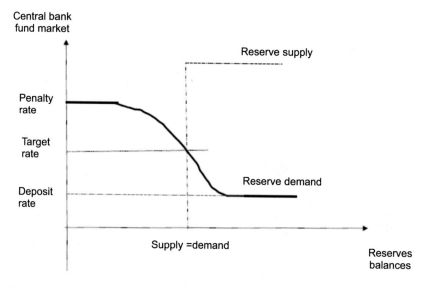

Fig. 6.4 Monetary policy when the policy rate is the main policy instrument

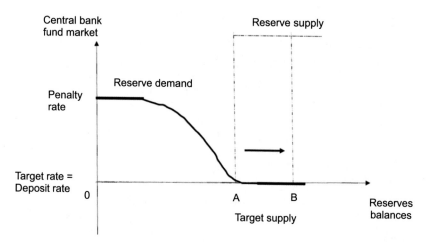

Fig. 6.5 Monetary policy with target supply = quantitative easing

Table 6.1   Central bank's balance sheet

Assets	Liabilities
Gold and currency reserves	Banknotes in circulation
Monetary policy securities	Bank current account (overnight balances)
Bank refinancing	Other residents and non residents in domestic currency
Other assets	Equity, reevaluation and other

changing the interest rate. The gap between points A and B corresponds to quantitative easing. In this case, the central bank leaves price targets and turns to quantity targets.

There are several forms of unconventional monetary policies that central banks in industrialized countries have used. They can be differentiated according to the quantitative instrument used. Let us briefly recall what a central bank's balance sheet looks like (see Table 6.1).

Unconventional monetary policies are distinguished according to whether the instruments used are on the liabilities or assets side of the central banks' balance sheet. Those on the assets side target the monetary base, in particular commercial bank reserves. They buy securities from the latter and in return increase their reserves. The use of asset-based instruments is aimed at influencing the structure of interest rates. The aim is to facilitate the refinancing of financial market players (amounts lent, widening of the range of collateral accepted, lengthening of maturities, etc.). These policies take place either at constant balance sheet size.AQPlease check the usage of 'either' in 'These policies take place either at constant balance sheet size' This implies a substitution between assets.

Three types of non-conventional measures have been adopted by the world's major central banks.

Quantitative easing measures aim to bypass the difficulties of the interest rate channel. The commercial banks are saturated with liquidity, in the hope that they will use the excess cash to extend credit to the economy. The idea is the following. Abundant liquidity crushes interest rates. Financial actors have excess cash to invest and have an incentive to do so by lending to the economy rather than investing in financial markets where returns are low. The reality has been different. They have preferred to buy financial assets despite low returns, relying on the valuation effects of high priced assets.

The credit easing measures aim to bypass the blockage of the credit channel. In this case, quantitative easing is concentrated on certain sectors of activity (sovereign bonds, corporate bonds).

Forward guidance consists of trying to influence market expectations by committing monetary policy to a given path in order to lower market rates.What is at stake here is the timing and duration of unconventional policies as perceived by the private sector and financial markets. The important aspect is the credibility of central banks. Theoretically, the ZLB can be circumvented and the economy stimulated by lowering real interest rates, if agents believe that the quantitative easing policy will be sustainable (see, e.g., Auerbach and Obstfeld 2005; Bernanke et al. 2004.

Unconventional policies have changed the transmission channels of monetary policy. Let us briefly recall what the conventional channels are when the interest rate is the main instrument of monetary policy.

First channel: the interest rate channel. When the central bank cuts its interest rate, the fall is passed on to the entire yield curve through expectations. The cost of credit falls and stimulates economic activity. Moreover, the fall in interest rates increases the price of financial assets and induces wealth effects that stimulate the economy.

Second channel: exchange rate channel. The drop in the key rate and market rates causes capital outflows, which leads to a monetary depreciation that favors exports and production.

Third channel: bank lending channel The refinancing cost of financial intermediaries decreases, allowing them to borrow more and lend more to the real economy.

Unconventional policies introduce other transmission channels.

Expectations Channel: Signal Effects

The interest rate R_t^T of an asset at a given maturity T is the average of expected future short-term rates between the current period and period T, $E_t\left(r_{t+j}\right)$, $j = 0, 1, \ldots, T$, plus a risk premium λ_t:

$$R_t^T = \frac{1}{T} \sum_{j=0}^{T} E_t\left(r_{t+j}\right) + \lambda_t. \tag{6.16}$$

By buying massively securities on the markets, the central bank sends a signal to the markets. Indeed, the greater the volume of securities purchased, the more costly it will be for the central bank to raise its interest rate quickly without lowering the value of the securities it has purchased in its asset portfolio (since interest rates and asset prices move in opposite directions). The markets conclude that the larger the volume of securities purchased, the longer it will take for the bank to change its policy.

This mechanism is supposed to lead to a decrease in expected nominal rates. This decrease is transmitted to the real economy, provided that agents anticipate an increase in inflation at the same time. The closer nominal rates are to zero, the more the effect on real rates depends on rising inflation expectations. If inflation expectations are anchored at low levels, then it is difficult to fully activate the expectations channel.

Risk Premium Channel

λ_t is the premium charged to cover several risks: liquidity risk, duration risk and default risk. The notion of liquidity means that the quantity of securities exchanged on a market must be high so that an investor feels that if he needs to sell his securities on the market, he will be able to do so easily (because there will be people on the market who are always willing to buy them). Duration risk refers to the fact that the potential losses incurred by the holder of a security depend on the length of the period between the date the security was purchased and its maturity. During this time, events can occur (prices can fluctuate, there can be inflation, the exchange rate can vary greatly. Finally, the risk of default corresponds to the case where the issuer of a debt security is unable to repay.

Unconventional policies reduce these risks. Indeed, the liquidity risk decreases because central banks become buyers of last resort, especially on asset markets that have suffered large devaluations at the time of the subprime crisis (MBS, ABCP,...). The duration risk decreases in markets where preferred habitat behavior is important. By buying securities of a given category, central banks reduce the supply on the financial markets. The risk of default decreases if the holder of a security is a central bank (which theoretically has very little likelihood of defaulting).

Portfolio Rebalancing Effect

Investors manage different asset classes. By drying up supply in some markets, the central bank is pushing them to buy securities in other segments if they want to maintain their desired portfolio structure. This leads to lower yields.

Anti-credit Rationing Effect

The subprime crisis has devalued the balance sheets of many financial intermediaries, reducing their lending activities to regain solvency. Credit constraints have tightened as a result of rationing by banks and financial institutions to households and businesses. Quantitative easing policies reduce credit rationing in two ways. First, central banks buy debt instruments directly from companies (Treasury securities, corporate debt). This improves the quality of corporate balance sheets by increasing their value. Secondly, by buying devalued assets from them, central banks increase their lending capacity to the traditional banking system.

Support for Fiscal Policies

Massive sovereign bond buyback policies allow governments to benefit from very low interest rates, and to reduce the liquidity and solvency risks of public debts.

To summarize, unconventional monetary policies affect the real economy and financial markets through channels that are indirect, compared to those of interest rate policies. Indeed, policy rates influence the overnight lending and borrowing rates of financial institutions on the capital markets and have an influence on the cost of credit granted to households and companies. They therefore have an influence on the short end of the yield curve. Unconventional policies affect medium- and long-term interest rates and activate monetary policy transmission channels that were much discussed in the 1960s and 1970s before interest rates became the main instrument of monetary policy. They induce more important wealth effects by modifying the prices of financial assets (as in the Modigliani-Miller or Mishkin theories). Moreover, the asset price channel becomes an important channel of monetary policy transmission, because of the effects of interest rate changes on stock valuations (as in Tobin's q analyses).

6.2.2   Experiences from Three Major Central Banks

Unconventional policies have been the new norm in monetary strategies over the last fifteen years. Below we summarize some examples of these policies in the Eurozone, Japan, and the United States. The interested reader will find detailed presentations in the literature (see, among many others, Acharya et al. 2019; Altavilla et al. 2022; Baumeister and Benati 2013; Berkmen 2012; Dell'Ariccia et al. 2018; Kuttner 2018; Lombardi

et al. 2018; Otsubo 2018; Pagliari 2021; Papadomou et al. 2020; Rudebusch 2018; Wang 2021; Westelius 2020.

Euro Area

Compared to other industrialized regions, the ECB's adoption of unconventional monetary policy came late, starting in 2014. Until then, the
strategy was first to lower long rates by easing the standard refinancing
terms for commercial banks at the central bank. The prevailing idea was
that it was necessary to first adopt measures complementary to those of the
interest rate policy which remained the reference. Between 2008 and 2011,
the ECB's balance sheet grew by only 50%, while it more than doubled for
the BOJ and the Fed.

The ECB's strategy remained anchored in the traditional approach. The
euro zone experienced a first deflationary phenomenon in 2009, that the
ECB tried to remedy by lowering the policy rate. And, as soon as signs of an
economic rebound appeared and deflation started to fade, monetary policy
turned to restrictive. The economic recession reappeared, and then turned
into an economic depression. Some observers have interpreted this as an
error in the steering of monetary policy. But the euro zone experienced
a severe public debt crisis between 2008 and 2012. Therefore, the ECB
wanted to safeguard the single currency. Figure 6.6 shows the evolution of
the ECB's interest rate corridor from August 2006 to March 2022. The
policy rate—which corresponds to the main refinancing operations rate—
moves between the deposit rate and the lending facility rate. We see that
rates rose in 2011, after an initial drop.

From 2008 onward, the corridor moved downward and narrowed.
Until 2012, the euro area gradually approached a liquidity trap situation,
after several measures were undertaken. Between 2007 and 2011, the
objective was to resolve the money market liquidity crisis and facilitate the
return of commercial banks to the money market through the following
measures:

- August–September 2007: 1-week to to 3-year LTRO (long-term
  refinancing operations) tenders,
- December 2007: exceptional call for tender and full allotment
  (resumed in October 2008),
- October 2008: extension of the list of eligible assets for refinancing
  operations,
- November 2008–April 2009: reduction of the policy rate from 3.25
  to 1.25%,

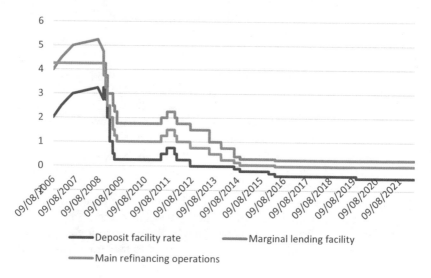

Fig. 6.6   ECB interest rates

- May 2009: policy rate reduced to 1% + CBPP (Covered Bond Purchase Programme) until June 2010,
- May 2010: public bond purchase plan (Securities Market Programme SMP) of 222 billion euros which replaces the CBPP, which was re-activated in 2011. This consisted in buying 220 billion euros of sovereign bonds in the secondary markets (Greek, Irish, Portuguese, Spanish). This bond buyback was interpreted by some economists as a circumvention of the rule of non-monetization of public debt. This led to the resignation of two German members of the Executive Board (Axel Weber, President of the Bundebank, and Jürgen Stark, Chief Economist of the ECB, who had been in office since 2006).
- August 2011: reactivation of the SMP + LTRO at 6 months, then at 1 year,
- 27 October 2011: 3-year VLTRO (very-long-term refinancing operations).
- February 2012; second LTRO to 800 European Banks;
- September 2012 the SMP is replaced by replaced by the OMT (Outright Monetary Transactions). Buyback programs continued (Spanish and Italian bonds) but with conditionalities. The aim was to lower

the risk premium of the most risky bonds to avoid public debt crises in some countries like Spain or Italy.

These initial measures were called non-standard (and not yet unconventional). This is one of the contrasts between the ECB's strategy and that of other central banks (Fed, BOE, BOJ, Bank of Canada), which from the outset of the 2008 financial crisis adopted policies that were intended as substitutes for interest rate policy. However, in the euro area, as the policy rate was approaching the ZLB policy-based strategies became ineffective. Unconventional policies thus started in earliest in 2014.

New TLTRO programs were adopted, between September and December 2014, and then from March 2015 to June 2016 on a quarterly basis. These were conditional loans to boost credit. For example, in September 2014 a TLTRO program of 400 billion euros was implemented with a 5-year maturity.

These programs differed from traditional LTROs in several ways:

- interest rate: for a classic LTRO, the rate was indexed to the refi rate, while for the new program the rate was set at 0.25
- amount borrowed: banks could borrow up to 3 times the amount of loans granted to the private sector (housing loans excluded to avoid bubbles),
- beyond a credit threshold, interest rates were negative at −0.40

In 2015, the ECB announced the adoption of a large-scale QE program. It is initially planned to last until March 2017 (the national central banks are the main executors). The ECB commits to buy 80 billion sovereign bonds (on secondary markets) every month, in addition to 10 billion of private securities. The purchases of sovereign bonds depend on the weight in the monetary zone: 40% German securities, 20% French securities, etc.).[1] In addition, it intervenes directly in the corporate credit market (eligibility of good quality assets issued by companies). These policies were complemented by a drop in deposit rates to below zero. The ECB was thus among the first central banks to adopt a negative interest rate starting in 2014.

Between June 2016 and December 2018, the ECB also implemented a Corporate Sector Purchase Programme. The reference programme today

---

[1] In fact, we have witnessed a phenomenon of re-nationalization of public debts, with German banks buying German securities, French banks buying French securities, etc.

for the implementation of its unconventional policy is the APP (Asset Purchase Programmes) and it includes several sub-programmes:

- CSPP: Corporate Sector Purchase Programme (since October 2014)
- PSPP: Public Sector Purchase Programme (since March 2015)
- ABSPP: Asset-Backed Securitized Purchase Programme (since November 2014)
- CBPP3: third covered bonds purchase programme (since october 2014)

These packages were used during the Covid-19 crisis and supplemented by two others, the PEPP (Pandemic Emergency Purchase Programme) and a package for the purchase of non-financial corporations' commercial paper.

The ABSPP and CBPP3 programmes are designed to diversify commercial bank funding sources. The CSPP program allows companies to obtain financing at an affordable cost, provided that the bonds issued are of good quality (investment grade). PSPP is a program for the purchase of public sector debt (nominal inflation-linked securities of Treasuries, domestic agencies, the European Stability Mechanism and multilateral development banks, securities issued by regions and municipalities).

The novelty of unconventional policies is how to combine them with the use of interest rates in a context where disinflationary shocks are persistent. There are two options. A central bank can choose either to adopt a prolonged negative interest rate policy or to use forward guidance to influence inflation expectations.

Regarding the first scenario, we saw in Fig. 6.6 that commercial bank deposit rates at the ECB have been negative since June 2014. These rates are passed on to the rates that commercial banks themselves charge their customers. On this point, we need to distinguish households from firms. With respect to households, leaving rates permanently in negative territory is likely to lead to infinite demand for holding cash (liquidity trap)—rather than leaving their income on deposits, because negative rates are equivalent to a tax. For companies this scenario is not at all obvious. A study of the Eurozone shows that commercial banks have applied negative rates to their customers' (corporate) deposits and have not experienced a decline in deposits (see Altavilla et al. 2022). On the contrary, on average, deposits have actually increased! By passing on the negative rates to their customers, commercial banks benefited from a decrease in the cost of collecting deposits, which allowed them to increase their lending even though lending rates were very low. The bank-lending channel has worked because negative rates did not affect banks' margin. Another channel was activated: the corporate finance channel. The companies most exposed to the negative rates have reduced the share of liquid and short maturity assets and have lengthened the maturity of their investments (e.g., by holding tangible and intangible assets). Therefore, contrary to conventional wisdom, a negative interest rate policy had a positive influence on the economy, because commercial banks were financially sound.

The interesting point in this first scenario is that the ZLB constraint is not effective if a negative interest rate policy is combined with prudential policies that ensure the financial soundness of the banking system.

An alternative approach is the forward guidance policy. The ECB's policy deserves specific attention.

The forward guidance strategy appears to be very useful in trying to prevent the deleterious effects of disinflationary shocks by fixing private sector expectations to the target set by the monetary authorities. In the case of the ECB, it has set a medium-term inflation rate target of 2%. Focusing on the medium term has several advantages: reducing the volatility of macroeconomic variables by letting shocks dissipate and being certain of their effects, and taking into account the time lags with which monetary policy affects the real economy. If medium-term inflation exceeds the target, then the central bank raises interest rates or reduces the use of its unconventional policies.

The new feature—compared to the inflation target rule adopted since 2003—concerns the situation where the medium-term inflation rate is below the target. There exists a de facto asymmetry in the changes in the interest rate. Indeed, if the target is exceeded, the ECB could raise its policy rate indefinitely (in theory). On the other hand, below the target, interest rate cuts are limited by a floor. The forward guidance policy consists of convincing the markets and the private sector that a credible monetary strategy to raise the inflation rate exists. In the event of a binding lower constraint, the ECB plans to leave rates at their current level or to lower them until the medium-term inflation rate becomes at least equal to the 2% target, before the end of the projection horizon and sustainably over the remainder of the horizon. The credibility of this strategy lies in ensuring that inflation converges to the target over time. Moreover, being on a medium-term path allows for transitory overshooting of the target. Finally, another condition imposed by the ECB is that core inflation must also converge toward the target.

Japan

The Japanese case is interesting. Indeed, the BOJ (Bank of Japan) has been forced to resort to unconventional monetary policies since 2001. Indeed, the Asian financial crisis of the late 1990s caused a recession that was accompanied by deflationary pressures. In February 1999, the BOJ began by lowering its policy rate to its lowest level. This was the beginning of a ZIRP (zero interest rate policy). To create inflationary expectations, it even announced that this policy would be maintained until it had overcome deflation. This policy was briefly interrupted in August 2000 and then reintroduced in early 2001. In the same year, the BOJ embarked on a quantitative easing (QE) policy, which was a credit easing policy coupled with a forward guidance strategy. Indeed, as the interest rate had reached the zero lower bound, it targeted the monetary base (composed largely of commercial banks' reserves at the BOJ). It bought massively JGB long-term bonds in order to lower long-term interest rates in the financial markets, and limits amounts of ABS (asset-backed securities).

At the same time, the central bank announced that it was considering leaving the policy rate at zero until core inflation started to rise again. At that time, there was no official numerical target for inflation. This strategy was maintained until 2006 when inflation re-started to rise. But it was not as successful as expected. Even though the country experienced a slight economic recovery, the growth rate remained low or even negative between 2001 and 2006. This was due to two impediments. On the one hand, the private sector continued to deleveraging in the wake of the financial crisis of a few years earlier. On the other hand, banks continued to have large non-performing loans and restricted credit to the economy.

In August 2010, the BOJ regained the use of its unconventional policy. It was forced to do so by two factors. First, because of the persistent deflation that followed the 2008 financial crisis, despite a policy rate at the ZLB. Second, in 2009, it embarked on a program of purchases of commercial bonds, corporate bonds and JGB bonds, which had little effect in stimulating economic activity.

QE was first characterized as CME (comprehensive monetary easing). This strategy was based on forward guidance and the pursuit of a policy of massive purchases of securities. To help anchor long-term inflation expectations and bring down real rates, the BOJ committed to keeping rates at zero until inflation returned to its medium-/long-term stable level. Officially, the inflation target had been 1% since 2006, but the central bank implied that it was interested in core inflation. Its securities purchases concerned a variety of assets (corporate bonds, commercial papers, real estate investment trusts). More than in 2001, its goal was to buy not only non-risky assets to bring down long-term rates, but also risky assets to bring down risk premiums and crush shorter-term rates.

April 2013 marked a new turning point. The inflation target was raised to 2% and the CME policy was strengthened in a new framework that was called QQE (quantitative and qualitative easing). In the absence of an improvement in the macroeconomic situation (inflation and growth remained low), the central bank introduced a policy of applying a negative interest rate to banks' excess reserves in 2016: NIRP (negative interest rate policy). By doing so, it sought to force short-term interest rates down and inflationary expectations up. This strategy had two effects. On the one hand, it shifted the yield curve downward. Indeed, rates up to a maturity of 20 years became negative. On the other hand, the part at the right end of the yield curve (at long maturities) became flatter. But this did not change the macro-financial situation: still low inflation, low demand, exchange rate appreciation, and inflation expectations still on the decline.

Against this background, the monetary policy framework was completed in September 2016 to yield curve control (YCC). This time, the aim was to target the JGB 10-year rates by bring it around 0.10%. Indeed, the expansion of the BOJ's balance sheet appeared unsustainable in the long run for the markets, which led the central bank to target its purchases on specific maturities.

The YCC policy in Japan is a long rate control policy. Unlike QE policies, its purpose is not to act on quantities in order to keep yields at zero, but to ensure that its target yield is adopted by the markets. Let's take an investor in the bond market who would like to sell a JGB. He would never agree to sell it to a buyer at a lower price than he would get by selling it to the central bank. Therefore, in the market the reference price is the one set by the central bank and corresponding to its target yield. This policy could be adopted by any central bank. It would be sufficient to set a target fluctuation band on an asset class of a given maturity. If the announced strategy is deemed credible (in the case of Japan, it is justified by the BOJ's desire to ensure the sustainability of the government's public debt, whose debt ratio is close to 260% of GDP). If the central bank's strategy is deemed credible, then it does not even need to actually buy government securities. This is what we are seeing in Japan, where massive JGB buybacks have been scaled back, without affecting 10-year interest rates.

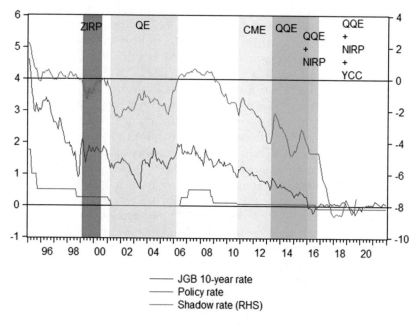

Fig. 6.7 Policy rate, JGB 10-year rate and shadow rate. Source: BIS, FRED and Central Bank of New Zealand

Figure 6.7 shows the evolution of three interest rates as unconventional monetary policies change. We see that the policy rate falls to the ZLB as early as 2000 and remains there constantly, except for the slight increase between 2006 and 2009. It becomes negative from 2016 onward. The JGB 10-year yield also becomes close to zero as soon as the QQE plus NIRP policy is adopted. We have superimposed on these two curves a third one that measures the stance of unconventional monetary policy when the interest rate hits zero, that is, the shadow interest rate. Several measures of have been proposed to capture the stance of balance sheet policy. We take here a measure provided by the New Zealand central bank based on the Krippner method.[2] This rate corresponds to the interest rate that would be in effect if the ZLB constraint was not binding. It is obtained using the information contained in the term structure of interest rates.

---

[2] An alternative method is Wu and Xia (2016).

Table 6.2 Sensitivity of shadow rate to BOJ's assets

	Average cumulative change in shadow rate Percentage point	Average cumulative change in BOJ's assets Percent	Sensitivity of shadow rate to changes in BOJ's assets
ZIRP	0.68	17%	4.00
QE	1.28	41%	3.12
CME	−1.12	65%	1.72
QQE	−2.44	144%	1.69
QQE+NIRP	−2.71	162%	1.67
QQE+NIRP+YCC	−6.04	207%	2.92

In Fig. 6.7 we observe that, as QE policies are adopted, this rate falls and remains in negative territory. Since the combination of QQE, NIRP and YCC, it has been around −8% and has remained stable around this level since 2018. Table 6.2 shows the average cumulative change in the shadow rate over the different monetary policy rounds and its sensitivity to cumulative changes in the BOJ' assets. It can be noticed that the sensitivity is high at the very beginning of unconventional policies, and also the most important at the time of the adoption of the YCC.

The United States

The switch in monetary policy strategy since the period of great moderation was first materialized by a change in the Fed's interest rate corridor in December 2008. They were set between 0 and 0.25%. The aim was to stop the credit crunch caused by the subprime crisis. This had degraded the balance sheets of banks and led to a fall in their capital-to-asset ratio. To maintain it at the level required by the prudential ratios, they had to reduce their loans to the private sector (increase in loan rates, refusal to roll over certain loans). This will lead to a deleveraging phenomenon. Companies could not finance themselves on the financial markets either because of the increase in interest rates compared to the Fed fund rate. The capital markets therefore became illiquid. When the Fed's rate cut proved insufficient (because it had hit the ZLB), quantitative monetary policies consisted of creating money by buying Treasury bonds and government-guaranteed securities. The goal was to lower medium- and long-term interest rates and to increase the price of financial assets.

The implementation of unconventional policies took place in several phases. Until 2014, its program consisted of using the assets of its balance sheet. This was characterized by several programs.

Quantitative easing I (QE I): from November 2008 to March 2009, the LSAP I (large-scale asset purchases) program consisted of buying debt issued by Fannie Mae, Freddie Mac, and agency-backed MBS, with the aim of subsidizing the rates on home loans to reduce the cost of credit. The amount of this program was 100 billion dollars of Treasury bills and 750 billion dollars of MBS.

Quantitative easing II (QE II): from November 2010 to June 2011, the LSAP II program consisted of purchasing Treasuries with extended maturities for a total amount of $600 billion.

Shortly after, a program called Operation Twist (between November 2011 and December 2012) consisted in buying Treasuries with maturities between 6 and 30 years and selling securities with shorter maturities of 1–3 years. The amount of this maturity extension program was $667 billion.

Quantitative easing III (QE III), an LSAP III program was conducted between September 2012 and October 2014. It consisted of buying MBS and Treasuries with longer maturities for an amount of $85 billion per month. Compared to the previous ones, this program was open-ended.

These three programs led to a sharp increase in the assets of the Fed's balance sheet. Its amount increased from 900 billion dollars to 4500 billion dollars between 2008 and 2015, an increase of 400%. They were accompanied by a forward guidance strategy between 2008 and 2012. The Fed committed to keeping interest rates low as long as the unemployment rate was below 65% and the inflation rate below 2.5%.

In 2017, the central bank started to reduce the size of its balance sheet by decreasing the volume of securities purchased (tapering). But it had to resume it at the time of the Covid-19 crisis. While its interest rates had started to rise again since 2015, it had to lower the target for Fed fund rates from March 2020 to between 0 and 0.25% (see Fig. 6.8). In September 2020, it reactivated its forward guidance policy by committing to keep rates close to zero until the economy returns to full employment and the inflation rate returns to its 2% target. In March 2020, it resumed its QE program by announcing the purchase of $500 billion in Treasury securities and $200 billion in government-guaranteed MBS over an open-ended horizon. In June 2020, the Fed announced a commitment to purchase

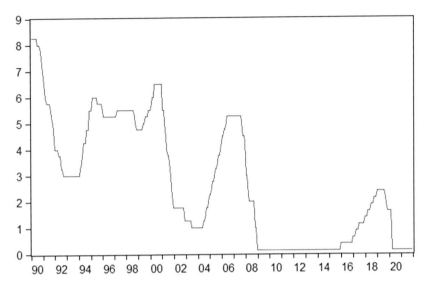

Fig. 6.8 Policy rate, United States. Source: BIS.

a minimum of $80 billion per month of Treasuries and $40 billion per month of residential and commercial MBS.

The QE program adopted during the Covid-19 crisis was as enormous in volume as during the 2008 crisis (see Milstein and Wessel 2021). The Fed created several facilities to ensure the continuity of financing for the private and public sectors in times of sanitary crisis. Here are a few examples:

- PDCF (Primary Dealer Credit Facility) from march 2020 to March 2021. This facility aimed at providing low interest loans to broker dealers (up to 3 months to 24 financial institutions against collateral (commercial paper, municipal bonds). The aim was to guarantee the proper functioning of the credit markets by avoiding cash hoarding.
- MMLF (Money Market Mutual Fund Facility) from March 2020 to March 2021. The Fed reactivated a program that existed at the time of the 2008 financial crisis. At the time of Covid-19, the economic recession led market participants to have doubts about the value of the securities they usually purchased from money market funds to serve as collateral for their refinancing operations, particularly short-term

corporate bonds. This triggered fire-sales by mutual funds. The Fed set up this facility to curb this phenomenon.

- PMCCF and SMCCF (Primary Market Corporate Credit Facility and Secondary Market Corporate Credit Facility), respectively from June 2020 to December 2020 and from May 2020 and December 2020. These were two programs to support large companies by facilitating their financing through the purchase of investment grade corporate bonds and the deferral of debt service payments for the first 6 months of the loan.
- CPFF (Commercial Paper Funding Facility) from April 2020 to March 2021. It was a program of purchases of commercial papers from companies (loans of up to three months at an interest rate of between 1 and 2% above overnight lending rates. The goal was to reduce the risk of illiquidity in the commercial paper market by allowing companies to roll over their debt.
- MSLF and PPPLF (Main Street Lending Facility and Psycheck Protection Program Liquidity Facility) respectively from July 2020 to January 2021 and from April 2020 to July 2021. These were financial support programs for small and medium-sized businesses. They received 5-year loans with an extension for the repayment period.
- TALF (Term Asset-Backed Securities Loan Facility) from June 2020 and December 2020. These are collateralized loans to households and small businesses holding the highest quality ABS, commercial MBS and collateralized loan obligations of the highest quality.
- MLF (Municipal Liquidity Facility) from May 2020 to December 2020. This is a novelty compared to the crisis of 2008 to relieve the municipal bond market from its stressful situation. indeed, the state and municipal governments had difficulty financing their anti-Covid-19 measures. The Fed allowed them to finance themselves on favorable terms. This facility was also designed for localities (airports, public transit, utilities).

These measures led the Fed to more than double its reserve balances between December 2009 and December 2011, increasing them by $4.62 trillion.

Readers interested in the effects of the unconventional policies of the BOJ, the ECB and the Fed on financial markets and the real economy can refer to the following articles (among a voluminous numbers of papers): Abassi and Linzert (2012), Altavilla et al. (2015), Anzuini and

Rossi (2022),Creel et al. (2016), De Peeter et al. (2018), Gagnon et al. (2011), Gambacorta et al. (2014), Gibson et al. (2016),Joyce et al. (2012), Kandrac and Schlusches (2021), Pagliari (2021), Wang (2021). For a more extensive presentation on other central banks, see Neely and Karson (2021) and Samarina and Apokoritis (2020). A common feature of all the studies is that these policies have had a strong influence on financial markets by easing financing conditions and raising asset prices. The empirical techniques used are based on "event studies" (in particular to study the effects of forward guidance), econometric methods (e.g., VAR or factor models), or the calibration and simulation of DSGE models. CGFS (2019), Fabo et al. (2020) and Gagnon et al. (2011) give a survey of empirical works for different countries and regions in the world.

6.2.3   Unconventional Monetary Policy in the New-Keynesian Model: Examples

Several theoretical models have been proposed in the literature to introduce unconventional monetary policies. Cúrdia and Woodford (2011) show in a New-Keynesian model that a credit easing policy (targeted asset purchases) is more efficient than a pure QE policy when an economy is at the ZLB. Gertler and Kaeadi (2011) shows that central bank intermediation to release financial constraints from the balance sheets of financial intermediaries is effective, especially when banks trade off between financing with debt or issuing short-term assets. Gertler and Karadi (2013) studies a model in which central banks buy Treasury bonds, but also risky corporate assets. They find that the latter have more macroeconomic effects than the former. A promising literature has recently developed on ways to model the communication policy of central banks, which is essential for guiding the expectations of economic agents (see, e.g., Bholat et al. 2019; Binder 2017.

We present two examples of how to account for unconventional monetary policies in a standard reduced-form macroeconomic model. The first example is based on the approach proposed by Wu and Zhang (2019) who show how long-term rates can substitute for short-term rates to influence households and firms'decisions. Monetary policy affects risk premiums, that is, the spreads between long and short rates. The second example is a small stylized model that describes the macroeconomic equilibrium when unconventional policies are constrained, namely when central banks are reluctant to lower long rates below a certain level.

6.2.3.1 The Wu–Xia Monetary Policy Rule

The reduced form of the standard New-Keynesian model consists of three main equations: (1) an IS curve in which the contemporaneous output gap depends on the expected short-term real interest rate and output gap and possibly on the past level of these variables; (2) a Philips curve in which current inflation depends on the expected—possibly past—inflation rate and output gap; (3) a Taylor curve in which the short-term interest rate is subject to a ZLB constraint. The IS and Taylor curves are modified to incorporate the effects of QE policies.

Consider an IS curve where the output gap depends on the expected future real interest rate for the following period:

$$y_t = -\alpha(r_t - E_t\pi_{t+1} - r^*), \tag{6.17}$$

where y_t is the output gap, r_t is the short-term rate, $E_t\pi_{t+1}$ is the expectation of inflation made at time t for time t+1, r^* is the natural interest rate. A forward iteration of this equation leads

$$y_t = -\alpha \sum_{i=1}^{T} E_t r_{t+i-1} + \alpha \sum_{i=1}^{T} E_t\pi_{t+1} + \alpha T r^*. \tag{6.18}$$

Assuming that the yield curve incorporates expectations of future short-term rates, the first term defines the medium-/long-term interest rate. Tr^* is the natural long-term interest rate. The model must therefore include an assumption about the central bank's behavior, whose actions influence the long-term rate. Define the long-term rate as r_t^B. The spread between long-term and short-term rates is the risk premium. It then becomes possible to link this risk to QE policies:

$$y_t = -\alpha\left(r_t^B - E_t\pi_{t+1} - r^{B*}\right), \quad r_t^B = \sum_{i=1}^{T} E_t r_{t+i-1} + pr_t, \tag{6.19}$$

where pr_t is the risk premium, $r^{B*} = \alpha T r^*$ is the natural long-term interest rate.

There are several possible specifications of the premium. For instance, based on the existing empirical literature, there is good reason to believe that there exists an inverse relationship between the quantity of government assets held by the central bank and this premium:

$$pr_t = pr_t^N - \kappa(b_t^{CB} - b_t^{CBN}), \quad \kappa > 0. \tag{6.20}$$

N refers to "normal times," that is, when the ZLB constraint on the short-term rate is not binding. It is assumed that the supply of bonds is held by households and the central bank. The monetary policy rule can therefore be defined as follows. The important equation is the long rate equation:

$$r_t^B = \sum_{i=1}^{T} E_t r_{t+i-1} + pr_t, \quad pr_t = pr_t^N - \kappa(b_t^{CB} - b_t^{CBN}). \tag{6.21}$$

In all cases, the central bank targets the long rate. But it does so in two different ways. It can do so by changing the short rate in such a way as to influence expectations of future short rates, provided that the ZLB is not binding. It uses its usual open-market policy. Its balance sheet assets are at the level b_t^{CBN} and the risk premium is at the level pr_t^N. If the short rate hits zero, then the central bank uses its balance sheet to try to lower long rates by crushing the risk premium; in this case, its instrument becomes its balance sheet and it increases its purchases above what they usually are, that is, to level $b_t^{CB} > b_t^{CBN}$. This causes the risk premium to fall below pr_t^N. Long-term rates are thus described by an hybrid rule. Aggregate demand in the New-Keynesian model with QE monetary policy is thus specified by Eqs. (6.19) and (6.21) and the following policy rule:

$$r_t^B = \begin{cases} s_t > 0, & b_t^{CB} = b_t^{CBN}, \\ s_t \leq 0, & b_t^{CB} > b_t^{CBN}, \end{cases} \tag{6.22}$$

where

$$s_t = r^* + \lambda s_{t-1} + (1-\lambda)\left[\phi_p(y_t - y^n) + \phi_\pi(\pi_t - \pi_t^*)\right]. \tag{6.23}$$

s_t is the shadow rate which can be negative even if r_t hits zero. QE can also be modeled by introducing credit lending facilities (see the authors' paper for more details).

6.2.3.2 Unconventional Policies When the Natural Interest Rate Is Low: An Illustration

In the Wu-Xia approach, it is assumed that the long rate is not constrained by a floor. The shadow rate can therefore be very negative, which does not pose a theoretical problem. However, this assumption may be restrictive with respect to what is observed in reality.

In the Wu-Xia approach, it is assumed that the long rate is not constrained by a floor. The shadow rate can therefore be highly negative, which does not pose a theoretical problem per se. However this assumption may be restrictive for several reasons. First, unconventional policies crush interest rates but raise financial asset prices. Central banks may wish to avoid the formation of bubbles, or to limit excessive increases in financial prices. Indeed, experience shows that the bursting of a financial bubble that has been forming for a long time creates recessions and triggers deflationary situations. A second reason why central banks should not lower long-term interest rates at too low levels is that deflationary episodes, in Japan as in the euro zone, have occurred in a context of weakened banking sector. To the extent that the fall in long-term rates is reflected in bank rates, this reduces the profitability of the banking sector. A problem may arise if the real long-term interest rate is prevented from falling to the level of the natural interest rate.

We propose a simplified model to study the consequences of such a situation. We assume that qualitative easing and quantitative easing are perfectly substitutable policies and that their effect on aggregate demand is described by several regimes. In a closed economy, we describe QE policy by a credit easing policy, an example being the TLTRO policy implemented by the ECB starting in July 2014: banks are encouraged to increase their financial support to the non-financial sector through targeted refinancing operations conditional on the growth rate of household and business credit volumes. The effect of this policy on demand is captured by the introduction of a Pigou effect (real balance effect) into the IS equation. In an extreme case, this effect would capture the influence of "helicopter money," that is, the direct creation of money distributed to the non-financial sector by central banks. The qualitative easing policy is described by the influence of purchases of risky securities on long rates. We assume that QE policy is triggered once QE policy reaches its limits. When it is no longer possible to lower long rates, the unconventional policy then acts directly on demand via credit easing. Our modeling of the effects of unconventional monetary policies therefore leads us to consider an aggregate demand function defined according to several regimes.

Taking into account the literature showing that the relationship between inflation and unemployment is unstable, we retain an aggregate supply function described by a Phillips curve that is "kinked." The responsiveness of inflation to the unemployment gap depends on the level of unemployment. When the unemployment rate is very high, the elasticity of inflation is lower than when it is low (we propose a Keynesian Phillips curve, where the responsiveness of prices to the unemployment rate depends on the share of wages in value added, the Okun coefficient and the degree of openness of economies).

Moreover, the central bank's forward guidance policy is described by the private sector's perception of the central bank's inflation target, and not of expected future short-term rates. This assumption is made for simplicity sake and therefore assumes that expected future short rates are equal to the ZLB short rate.

Extending the closed economy model to an open economy, we maintain the modeling of unconventional policy through domestic securities purchases. We add a foreign asset purchase policy to improve the net external asset position of the domestic country. These two policies affect the nominal exchange rate, either through the interest rate channel or through the risk premium channel. The open economy allows us to differentiate between different regimes of aggregate demand depending on whether the domestic currency is initially highly appreciated at the time the unconventional monetary policies are adopted.

The proposed model leads to several interesting results. In a closed economy, we highlight possible deflationary trap situations, as observed in Japan during the lost decade period, when the qualitative easing policy encounters a limit in its implementation. QE policy is ineffective when the economy is in a deflationary situation: it leads to a phenomenon known as "recession through deflation." Another interesting result is that QE policy is ineffective when private sector expectations are anchored. Paradoxically, it can only reduce unemployment if the inflationary effects of increased demand are countered by disinflationary factors on the aggregate supply side.

In the open economy, when the domestic currency is initially highly appreciated, the beneficial effects of unconventional monetary policies in lowering unemployment may be limited. In this case, an expansionary monetary policy coordinated with foreign countries may be useful. We also conclude that one way to improve the effectiveness of these policies, when there is a large price level differential between the domestic and the foreign country, would be to devalue the currency directly in order to get out of a deflationary trap with recession and an overvalued exchange rate.

Aggregate Demand and Supply

To facilitate understanding, we first present the model where supply and demand do not depend on different regimes. These will be introduced in a second step. The equations are written in log-linear form. The final objective of monetary policy is to stabilize the unemployment rate and the inflation rate around their targets. These objectives are achieved through an intermediate objective, which is the stabilization of output around its potential level.

The unconventional monetary policy is implemented by the central bank using its balance sheet. Its structure is in a very simplified form: A policy of qualitative easing is captured by an increase in the share of financial securities in total assets. Asset purchases increase the monetary base. M_t^A is the component of monetary base that is the counterpart of these purchases. Its influence on the economy operates through interest rates (by increasing liquidity in the monetary markets). A quantitative easing (QE) policy is supposed to increase the monetary base, through programs leading commercial banks to increase their supply of credit to the non-financial sector: M_t^0 is the counterpart of the increase in commercial banks' claims on the non-financial sector. They impact directly aggregate demand. In practice, M_t^0 and M_t^A are indistinguishable, but we differentiate them here for convenience of presentation (Table 6.3).

In the equations below, flows (rather than stocks) of assets and liabilities affect the output and inflation rate.

The demand side of the economy is described by an equation relating unemployment gap to and IS curve, and by a relationship linking short- and long-term interest rates.

$$u_t - \bar{u} = -(1/\varrho)(y_t - \bar{y}_t) + \varepsilon_t^u, \varrho > 0. \tag{6.24}$$

Table 6.3 Simplified structure of a central bank's balance sheet

Assets	Liabilities
Financial and government assets: A_t	Monetary base: $M_t^0 + M_t^A$

$$y_t - \bar{y} = -\alpha \max \left(\delta_r, i_t^L - \pi_t^e - \bar{r}r^L \right) + \phi(\Delta M_t^0 - \pi_t) - \Xi pb_t + \varepsilon_t^y, \quad (6.25)$$

$\alpha > 0, \phi > 0.$

$$i_t^L - \pi_t^e = \gamma(i_t^S - \pi_t) + (1 - \gamma)(i_t^{Se} - \pi_t^e) - \eta \Delta A_t + \varepsilon_t^L, \quad (6.26)$$

$0 < \gamma < 1, \eta > 0.$
The definitions of the variables are as follows:

- u_t and $\bar{u}$ are current and natural unemployment rates,
- y_t is GDP and $\bar{y}$ is potential GDP,
- i_t^L is the long-term nominal interest rate,
- π_t^e is the private sector's forecast of the inflation rate at time t, made at time t-1,
- π_t is current inflation,
- i^S is short-term rate,
- i_t^{Se} is expected short-term rate
- $\bar{r}r^L$ is the natural interest rate,
- pb_t is the primary balance as share of GDP.

$\varepsilon_t^u, \varepsilon_t^y, \varepsilon_t^L$ are demand and financial shocks. ε_t^u refers to shocks that affect the labor market, independent of economic activity. The unemployment rate is one of the final objectives of the central bank (with the inflation rate) and the output gap is an intermediate objective.

For simplicity, we assume that the effects of monetary policy are contemporaneous: the central bank chooses its policy at time t, and the economy reacts at the same time. The model can be easily extended by introducing time lags in the economy's reaction to policy changes, without changing the results. On the other hand, expectations of the inflation rate are made in the previous period. By the time monetary policy takes place (in period t), households have already negotiated with firms in period t-1 the wage they are paid in period t based on the expectations made in period t-1 of the inflation rate at date t. When the negotiations take place, the central bank announces in advance its inflation target for the next period. Households may or may not anchor their expectations to this target.

Equation (6.24) describes the reaction of unemployment gap to output gap. ϱ is the elasticity coefficient of a standard Okun Law.

Equation (6.25) is an (IS) curve where the output gap depends on the deviation of the long-term real interest rate from the natural real interest rate, which is assumed to be exogenous. If the natural rate is low, it may not be reached. The coefficient δ_r is the difference between the two rates. It indicates by how much the real long rate would have to adjust to the natural rate for output to be at its long-run level. pb_t is the primary balance at date t. Ξ is assumed to be positive, which implies that higher public deficits have Keynesian effects.

The impact of QE policy on aggregate demand is represented by a Pigou effect (real balance effect) $\Delta M_t^0 - \pi_t$. The central bank implements its policy at date t, which influences activity and inflation rate at the same date. In low inflation regimes, this policy has a significant effect on aggregate demand. When inflation is high, its impact is more limited.

Equation (6.26) describes how short- and long-term real interest rates are related. The expected real long rate is the average of actual and expected real short rate. In addition, we consider the effects on long-term rates of changes in the central bank's assets.

The aggregate supply curve is described by a Phillips curve augmented with inflation expectations:

$$\pi_t = b\,\pi_t^e - \varpi\,(u_t - \bar{u}) + \varepsilon_t^\pi, \quad \varpi > 0,\ 0 < b < 1. \tag{6.27}$$

In the literature, it is usually assumed that for monetary policy to have an effect on economic activity, it is necessary to have market imperfections. For example, in the case where the short-run Phillips curve is derived from a "New-Keynesian" model (NKPC), it is usually assumed that firms do not systematically adjust prices to changes in production costs or demand. We consider a Keynesian Phillips curve. Firms maximize their profit under market constraints, which leads to the equalization of the real wage rate and marginal labor productivity (what Keynes called the first classical postulate). But, unlike in a classical model, this relationship does not determine the level of employment. This is determined by the level of effective demand. In a closed economy, we assume for the moment that the degree of openness is zero. Prices react strongly to the unemployment rate as the income share of wages is high and employment is very reactive to economic activity. ε_t^π is a supply shock. It also captures the effects of fiscal policy (e.g., innovation policies that change firms' productivity).

Regime-Dependent Demand and Supply Curves

We now introduce regime-dependent aggregate demand and supply functions. We study the case of economies where the natural interest rate is low as well as inflation rates. We consider the simplest case where $\Xi = 0$.

On the demand side we consider a three-regime model (in each regime we have a trade-off between inflation and unemployment by combining Eqs. (6.24) and (6.25)):

$$
u_t - \bar{u} = \begin{cases} \left(\frac{\alpha}{\varrho}\right)\left(i_t^L - \pi_t^e - \bar{rr}^L\right) + v_{2t}, & \text{if } \delta_t > \delta_r, & \text{regime 2} \\ \left(\frac{\alpha}{\varrho}\right)\delta_r - \left(\frac{\phi}{\varrho}\right)(\Delta M_t^0 - \pi_t) + v_{1t}, & \text{if } \delta_t \leq \delta_r \text{ and } \pi_t < 0, & \text{regime 1} \\ \left(\frac{\alpha}{\varrho}\right)\delta_r + \left(\frac{\phi}{\varrho}\right)(\Delta M_t^0 - \pi_t) + v_{0t}, & \text{if } \delta_t \leq \delta_r \text{ and } \pi_t > 0, & \text{regime 0} \end{cases}
$$

$$(6.28)$$

$\delta_t = i_t^L - \pi_t^e - \bar{rr}^L$. v_{0t}, v_{1t}, v_{2t} are error terms that depend on ε_t^u and ε_t^y. i_t^L is given by Eq. (6.26).

Regime 2 is a deflationary regime. Indeed, the condition on the gap between the real rate and the natural rate $\delta_t > \delta_r$ can be written:

$$
\pi_t < -\delta_\pi = -\left(\frac{\delta_r}{\gamma}\right) - \left(\frac{1-\gamma}{\gamma}\right)\pi_t^e - \left(\frac{\eta}{\gamma}\right)\Delta A_t - \left(\frac{\bar{rr}^L}{\gamma}\right) + \left(\frac{\varepsilon_t^L}{\gamma}\right).
$$

$$(6.29)$$

When deflation is high, a policy of raising inflation and stimulating the economic activity through the long rate channel is possible provided that the central bank has sufficient room for maneuver, that is, if the real long rate is above the natural rate. Such a scenario corresponds to regime 2. Starting with a given initial inflation rate, below $-\delta_\pi$, to prevent deflation from worsening, unconventional monetary policy can cause the real long rate to fall, either through domestic asset purchases or through a policy of forward guidance that guides expectations on a higher level of inflation. This boosts activity and lowers the unemployment rate. In regime 2, inflation is therefore a decreasing function of the unemployment rate.

When the expected real long rate is "stuck" at the level $\bar{rr}^L + \delta_r$ (i.e., when the bottom floor $\delta_t = \delta_r$ is hit), another unconventional policy is activated. In regimes 0 and 1, it is described by credit easing (which leads real balance effects). We assume that a positive effect on consumption is only observed if the policy is activated in a deflationary regime (regime 1). When inflation is positive, wealth effects dominates: households save more. In this case, credit easing does not prevent the unemployment rate from increasing (regime 0).

On the supply side, we introduce a non-linearity into the Phillips curve. The inflation rate is less responsive to the unemployment rate gap when the latter is high than when it is low. The threshold is described by an exogenous parameter δ_u. The nonlinear Phillips curve is written:

$$\pi_t = \begin{cases} b\pi_t^e - \varpi_1 (u_t - \bar{u}) + \varepsilon_{1t}^\pi, & \text{if } u_t > \delta_u > 0, \\ b\pi_t^e - \varpi_2 (u_t - \bar{u}) + \varepsilon_{2t}^\pi, & \text{if } \bar{u} < u_t \le \delta_u, \end{cases} \tag{6.30}$$

where $\varpi_2 > \varpi_1 > 0$, $0 < b < 1$.

We now define the forward guidance policy. Inflation expectations are described by

$$\pi_t^e = \chi \pi_t^P + (1 - \chi) \pi_{t-1}, \quad \pi_t^P = \vartheta \pi_t^T + \xi_t. \tag{6.31}$$

They are defined as an average of the private sector's perception of the inflation target announced by the central bank for date t and the observed inflation at the time the central bank implements its monetary policy. $\xi_t \sim N(0, \sigma_\xi^2)$. If σ_ξ^2 is large, then the central bank's inflation target is poorly perceived by private sector agents (the information communicated by the central bank contains too much "noise" or uncertainty to be completely credible). If $\sigma_\xi^2 = 0$, the signal effect is considered credible by agents. They must then decide how much weight to give to public information and how much weight to give to their own observation of past inflation. A forward guidance policy that is effective is one that is judged to be credible $\sigma_x i^2 low$, ϑ close to 1, and which is accompanied by a situation in which expectations are as anchored on the central bank's announcements (captured by the coefficient χ).

Macroeconomic Equilibrium in a Closed Economy

Figure 6.9 presents an example of a short-run equilibrium describing the links between inflation and unemployment. The unemployment rate is assumed to be above its long-run level. The abscissa u_{At} is obtained by considering $\pi_t = -\delta_\pi$ in (6.28) in the equation corresponding to regime 2. In the deflationary regime 1 ($0 > \pi_t > -\delta_\pi < 0$), the unemployment

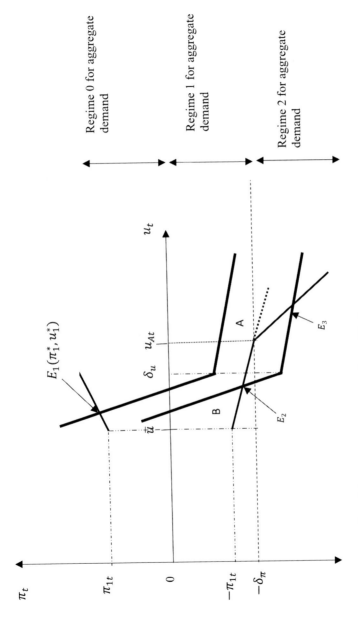

Fig. 6.9 Examples of short-run macroeconomic equilibria

rate is lower than in regime 2. Unemployment may eventually tend toward its long-term level and, in this case, the level of inflation is given by the ordinate $-\pi_{1t}$, where

$$\pi_{1t} = \Delta M_t^0 - \left(\frac{\alpha}{\phi}\right)\delta_r - \left(\frac{\varrho}{\phi}\right)v_{2t}. \tag{6.32}$$

The aggregate supply function is "kinked" at δ_u and has a negative slope. The figure shows two cases, one in which it intersects the aggregate demand function when inflation is positive (E_1), and others in a deflationary situation (E_2). The first case corresponds to an equilibrium with positive unemployment and inflation rates. In the second case, the equilibrium is characterized by a situation of unemployment with deflation.

Equilibrium with Anchored/Non-anchored Expectations

We use the expression "anchored expectations" to indicate that inflation expectations are not sensitive to announcements made by the central bank. Suppose that the economy is initially at an equilibrium where the aggregate supply and demand curves intersect at E_1. In this regime, there are both unemployment and positive inflation. A policy aimed at lowering the unemployment rate by influencing the real long rate is likely not to be effective, since this would imply that δ_t hits its floor level δ_r (E_1 is in regime 0 for aggregate demand). Assuming the unemployment rate is not too high ($u_t \leq \delta_u$), the equilibrium inflation and unemployment rates are given by

$$\pi_{1t}^* = \left\{\frac{\varrho}{\varrho - \varpi_2\phi}\right\}\left\{b\pi_t^e + \frac{\varpi_2\phi}{\varrho}\Delta M_t^0 - \varpi_2 v_{2t} + \varepsilon_{2t}^\pi\right\}, \; \varrho/2 > \varpi_2\phi. \tag{6.33}$$

$$u_{1t}^* = \bar{u} + \left(\frac{\alpha}{\phi}\right)\delta_r - \left(\frac{\phi}{\varrho}\right)\Delta M_t^0 + \left(\frac{\phi}{\varrho}\right)\pi_{1t}^* + v_{2t}. \tag{6.34}$$

In this regime, in order to lower the unemployment rate toward its long-run level $\bar{u}$, and to raise the inflation rate, the central bank can increase the monetary base through a QE policy ($\Delta(\Delta M_t^0) > 0$). This impacts both aggregate demand and aggregate supply (see Fig. 6.10).

During the period preceding the implementation of its monetary policy, the central bank announces its inflation target for date t. Since an increase in the monetary base usually has inflationary effects, this can credibly be interpreted as an increase in its inflation target ($\pi_t^T > \pi_{t-1}$) if we assume a

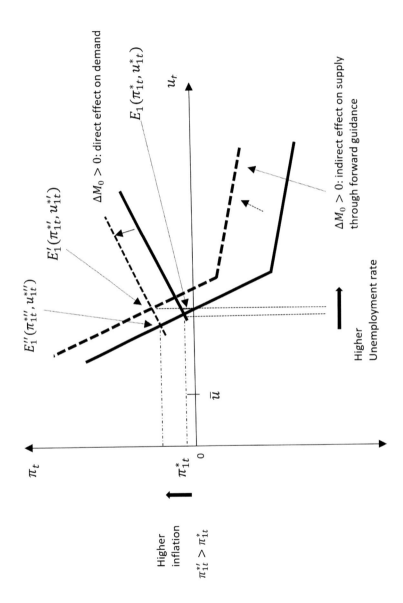

Fig. 6.10 Inefficient QE policy

relationship between π_t^T and ΔM_t^0 such as $\pi_t^T = \nu_\pi \Delta M_t^0$. Expanding the monetary base thus leads to expectations of higher inflation in period t by the private sector (see Eq. (6.31)).

The aggregate demand curve shift upward. Indeed, a positive change in ΔM_t^0 affects demand in regime 0, but also in regime 1 insofar as $-\delta_\pi$ (which depends on π_t^e) increases: this policy lowers demand side deflationary pressures by reducing the gap between the expected real interest rate and the natural rate). An increase in the monetary base impacts aggregate demand through two channels: (1) a direct channel (increase in available nominal cash) and (2) an inflationary effect that weighs on agents' purchasing power. The combination of both effects is captured here by a Pigou effect. An expansionary credit easing can have perverse effects on unemployment (via lower consumption) if it has too strong inflationary effects, that is, if inflation expectations are very reactive to monetary policy changes. We therefore obtain the following result, when expectations are anchored. If the economy is initially in regime 1, an expansive QE policy does *not* reduce the unemployment rate. The economy is then stuck in an equilibrium corresponding to $E_1'(\pi_{1t}^{*\prime}, u_{1t}^{*\prime})$ in Fig. 6.10, with a higher unemployment rate.

The effect on aggregate supply goes through the expected inflation channel. If expectations do *not* follow the central bank's target (χ and/or ϑ are small in Eq. (6.31), and/or σ_ξ^2 is large), the private sector agents do not revise their expectations. In the limit case, we have $\pi_t^e = \pi_{t-1}$. The credit easing policy is then fully effective. The new equilibrium corresponds to the $E_1'(\pi_{1t}^{*\prime}, u_{1t}^{*\prime})$ in Fig. 6.10 with a lower unemployment rate and a higher inflation rate than initially.

The beneficial effect on employment would then be high if there are strong real balance effects.

Equilibrium in a Deflationary Trap

Suppose that the economy is initially at E_3 in Fig. 6.9, which corresponds to an equilibrium with unemployment and deflation. Equating demand in regime 2 with supply when the slope of the Phillips curve is flattest, we obtain the coordinates of this point:

$$u_{3t}^* = \bar{u} + \left(\frac{\alpha}{\rho}\right)\left(i_t^{L*} - \pi_t^e - \bar{r}r_t^L\right) + v_{1t}, \quad i_t^{L*} = \gamma\left(\pi_t^e - \pi_{3t}^*\right) - \eta\Delta A_t + \varepsilon_t^L,$$

$$(6.35)$$

and

$$\pi^*_{3t} = \left\{\frac{\rho}{\rho-\varpi_1\alpha}\right\}\left\{\left[b+\varpi_1(1-\gamma)\left(\frac{\alpha}{\rho}\right)\right]\pi^e_t + \varpi_1\left(\frac{\alpha}{\rho}\right)\bar{r}\bar{r}^L_t\right\} \\ + \left\{\frac{\rho}{\rho-\varpi_1\alpha}\right\}\left\{\varpi_1(\frac{\alpha}{\rho})\eta(\Delta A_t) - \varpi_1(\frac{\alpha}{\rho})\epsilon^L_t\right\},\ \rho > \varpi_1\phi. \tag{6.36}$$

In this regime, to lower the unemployment rate, the central bank changes the structure of its balance sheet by purchasing financial assets $\Delta(\Delta A_t) > 0$ (policy of qualitative easing). The impacts on the economy are as follows.

Impact on Aggregate Demand According to Eq. (6.35), the nominal long rate decreases and lowers the unemployment rate. The magnitude of the decrease depends on $\left(\frac{\alpha}{\rho}\right)$. Unemployment decreases strongly if aggregate demand is sensitive to changes in the interest rate and as growth yields more jobs (low Okun coefficient). According to Eq. (6.36), the increase in aggregate demand reduces deflationary pressures. At the same time, according to Eq. (6.29), the line $(-\delta_\pi)$ moves downward (as the real interest rate falls, it approaches the natural interest rate). When ΔA_t increases, the economy thus gradually moves toward regime 1. This regime appears as soon as the gap between the real long rate and the natural rate equals to δ_r.

Impact on Aggregate Supply If the central bank's action drives the private sector expectations toward a lower rate of deflation ($\pi^T_t > \pi^*_{3t}$) the supply curve shifts upward. Employment increases, because we are in a deflationary situation and companies are hiring in a context where wages are falling.

The combination of demand and supply effects leads to an initial situation where unemployment has fallen, but the economy is still in deflation (E'_{3t} in Fig. 6.11). If the policy of qualitative easing continues, the economy moves toward regime 1 of aggregate demand. Suppose that from this regime, the central bank wants to further reduce the unemployment rate (starting from E_2 in Fig. 6.12). To do so, it must activate the QE policy (as we are in regime 1 of demand). This has the same effects on aggregate demand and supply as those studied in the previous paragraph. But this time, as the aggregate supply curve shifts to the right, the economy returns to regime 2, where the unemployment rate and the deflation rate are higher than at E_2. This case illustrates a typical situation of recession through deflation. One illustration is that of Japan from the early 2000s. The QE policy started in 2001 was conducted in a context where a number of factors contributed to maintaining disinflationary pressures:

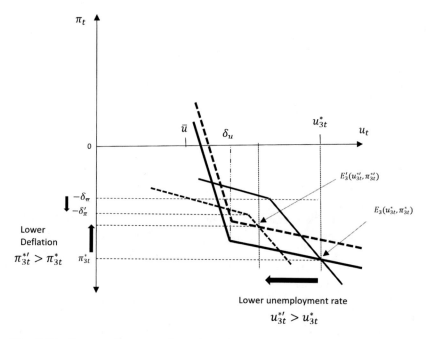

Fig. 6.11 Impact of asset purchases in regime 2

increased competition from emerging Asian countries, legislative measures that led to an increase in the number of large stores. These factors have contributed to exerting downward pressure on wages and have allowed the unemployment rate to remain close to its natural level of around 5% (even if the increase in employment has mainly concerned precarious jobs).

6.2.3.3   Unconventional Monetary Policy and the Open Economy

Unconventional monetary policies in an open economy stimulates external demand through changes in the real exchange rate. In our model, it also affects the aggregate supply function. The central bank's balance sheet is now as follows: Net foreign assets, NFA_t are the difference between foreign assets held by the domestic country and domestic securities held by the foreign country. They are expressed here in foreign currency. s_t is the nominal exchange rate and refers to the number of units of the domestic currency exchanged for one unit of the foreign currency (a depreciation is

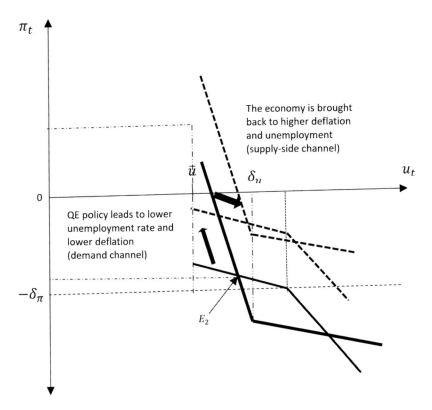

Fig. 6.12 Deflationary trap

Table 6.4 Structure of a central bank's balance sheet in an open economy

Assets	Liabilities
Financial and government assets: A_t	Monetary base: $M_t^0 + M_t^A$
Net foreign assets: NFA_t/s_t	

therefore reflected by an increase in s_t). NFA_t/s_t is therefore change in net foreign assets expressed in domestic currency (Table 6.4).

To boost net exports (and therefore aggregate demand), the central bank can cause a real depreciation of its currency in two ways. On the one hand, the policy of purchasing domestic assets, by lowering the domestic long rate, causes capital outflows that depreciate the domestic currency (for a given level of the foreign long-run rate and expectations of the future exchange rate). On the other hand, when this policy becomes ineffective (when the gap between the long-run rate and the natural interest rate reaches the floor threshold), the central bank can intervene in the foreign exchange market by buying foreign securities. These purchases improve its net international investment position, which reduces the risk premium associated with the exchange rate and leads to a depreciation of the domestic currency. We assume that this replaces the closed-economy policy of real balances when the interest rate policy becomes ineffective.

Main Equations

The capital market equilibrium is described by the uncovered interest rate parity condition linking the nominal exchange rates, s_t, to the foreign and domestic long interest rate differential, $i_t^{LF} - i_t^L$, to the expected nominal exchange rate, s_{t+1}^e, and to the risk premium, ρ_t:

$$s_t = i_t^{LF} - i_t^L + s_{t+1}^e - \rho_t, \quad \rho_t = -\psi[\Delta NFA_t - s_t],$$
$$i_t^L = \gamma(\pi_t^e - \pi_t) - \eta\Delta A_t + \varepsilon_t, \quad 0 < \gamma < 1, \quad \eta > 0. \tag{6.37}$$

A policy of asset purchases lowers the long-term rate, all things being equal, and leads to a depreciation of the nominal exchange rate. The depreciation of the domestic currency can also be achieved by purchasing foreign assets, which improves the country's net international investment position and lowers the risk premium ρ_t. The term $\Delta NFA_t - s_t$ represents the change in net foreign assets expressed in units of the domestic currency. This equation can therefore be written as:

$$s_t = \frac{1}{1 + \psi}\left[i_t^{LF} - i_t^L + s_{t+1}^e + \psi\Delta NFA_t\right] \tag{6.38}$$

We consider the following aggregate demand function in an open economy:

$$
y_t - \bar{y} = \begin{cases} -\alpha \left(i_t^L - \pi_t^e - \bar{r}r^L \right) + \check{\alpha} \left(y_t^F - \bar{y}^F \right) + \varepsilon_{2t}, & if \ \ \delta_t > \delta_r, \ \ \text{regime 2} \\ -(\frac{\alpha}{\rho})\delta_r + \tilde{\alpha}_{\varphi 1} e_t + \check{\alpha} \left(y_t^F - \bar{y}^F \right) + \varepsilon_{1t}, & if \ \delta_t \leq \delta_r, \ \ \text{regime 1} \end{cases}
$$

$$(6.39)$$

where $\alpha > \tilde{\alpha}_\varphi$ and $\delta_t = i_t^L - \pi_t^e - \bar{r}r^L$ is the gap between the real interest rate and the natural rate. e_t is the real exchange rate defined by $e_t = s_t + p_t^* - p_t$, where p_t^* and p_t denote the domestic and foreign price levels $\tilde{\alpha}_{\varphi 1}$ captures the effects of the real exchange rate on aggregate demand obtained by an unconventional monetary policy that activates the risk premium channel (foreign asset purchase policy). We assume here that the Marshall-Lerner-Robinson conditions on critical elasticities are satisfied, which implies that the real exchange rate is not the same as the real exchange rate. ε_{1t} and ε_{2t} are error terms capturing the demand shocks in each regime. We assume that an increase in activity in the foreign country benefits the domestic country ($\check{\alpha} > 0$). $y_t^F, \bar{y}^F$ denote the observed and long-run output of the foreign country.

Using the expression of the long-term rate and using the definition of the real exchange rate $e_t = s_t + p_t^F - p_t$ (where p_t^F, p_t are the foreign and domestic price levels), the condition $\delta_t > \delta_r$ is written:

$$
e_t > \tilde{e}_t = s_t - p_{t-1} + p_t^F + \left(\frac{1-\gamma}{\gamma} \right) \pi_t^e + \left(\frac{\eta}{\gamma} \right) \Delta A_t - \frac{\bar{r}r_L}{\gamma} - \frac{\varepsilon_t^L}{\gamma} + \frac{\delta_r}{\gamma}.
$$

$$(6.40)$$

The sign of $\tilde{e}_t$ depends on the model parameters. For example, it is possible for e_t to be negative (insofar as the variables in the model are expressed in logarithm). This situation is observed in particular when the domestic price level is higher than the foreign price level (according to the definition of e_t). Since the exchange rate designates the number of units of the domestic currency for one unit of the foreign currency, $\tilde{e}_t < 0$ can be interpreted as a situation where the currency is highly appreciated.

In regime 1, the currency is more appreciated than in regime 2 ($e_t \leq \tilde{e}_t$). We assume that the impact of a real depreciation on demand is less strong than in regime 2 ($\tilde{\alpha}_{\varphi 1} < \tilde{\alpha}_{\varphi 2}$).

In regime 2, the central bank causes a depreciation of its currency via the interest rate channel to increase demand. Indeed, purchases of domestic assets cause the long-term interest rate to fall, which depreciates the domestic currency (increase in s_t). This nominal depreciation leads to a real depreciation that stimulates external demand. In regime 1, the same effects are obtained by reducing the risk premium through the purchase of foreign assets.

In terms of unemployment rate gap, we have the following two regimes:
Regime 2: $\delta_t > \delta_r$

$$u_t - \bar{u} = \left(\frac{\alpha}{\rho}\right)\left(i_t^L - \pi_t^e - \bar{r}r^L\right) - \left(\frac{\tilde{\alpha}_{\varphi 2}}{\rho}\right)e_t - \left(\frac{\check{\alpha}}{\rho}\right)\left(y_t^F - \bar{y}^F\right) + v_{2t}.$$

(6.41)

Regime 1:$\delta_t \leq \delta_r$

$$u_t - \bar{u} = \left(\frac{\alpha}{\rho}\right)\delta_r - \left(\frac{\tilde{\alpha}_{\varphi 1}}{\rho}\right)e_t - \left(\frac{\check{\alpha}}{\rho}\right)\left(y_t^F - \bar{y}^F\right) + v_{1t}.$$

(6.42)

$\tilde{\alpha}_s$ measures the impact of the real exchange rate on prices set by firms (imported inflation). A depreciation of the real exchange rate leads firms to anticipate a rise in the price of imported inputs (or households to anticipate a rise in the price of imported consumer goods). In both cases, firms raise their prices. Under these assumptions, $\tilde{\alpha}_s > 0$. π_t^e is described by Eq. (6.31). For simplicity, we assume that b = 1 and that the foreign country is similar to the domestic country. In financial markets, the existence of a risk premium in the uncovered interest rate parity equation implies that domestic and foreign assets are imperfect substitutes. However, when one country increases its net credit position (or reduces its net debt position), the other's deteriorates (or improves).

Impact of Unconventional Monetary Policy on the Domestic Country

Figure 6.13 shows an example of a short-run macroeconomic equilibrium. It shows an equilibrium where the domestic currency is "highly" appreciated (E_1) and another where it is less so (E_2).

Suppose that the economy is initially at E_1. To stimulate demand and lower the unemployment rate, a depreciation of the currency is achieved by the central bank buying foreign assets, which lowers the risk premium. The economy moves along the demand curve to the left, for example, to the point E_1'. At this point, the unemployment rate falls. Moreover, the depreciation of the real exchange rate pushes firms to increase their

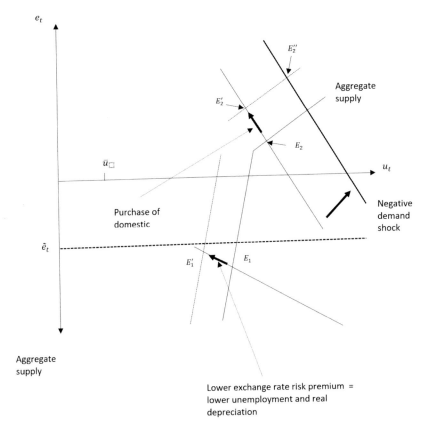

Fig. 6.13 Unconventional monetary policies in an open economy

prices, which leads an acceleration of inflation. This should lower the real long-term interest rate and stimulate domestic demand. But since we are in regime 1, the real interest rate is stuck at $E1'^L + \delta_r$. For $E_1\prime$ to be an equilibrium point, the supply curve must shift to the left. This is the case, provided that householders underestimate the acceleration of inflation ($\Delta \pi_t^e < \Delta \pi_t$).

Forward guidance is important here. If the initial equilibrium is a situation where the domestic currency is highly appreciated (overvalued) and inflation is low, then even if the unconventional monetary policy is expansionary and people think that this will generate upward pressure on prices, they will tend to underestimate the acceleration of inflation. In this case, it is attractive for the central bank to announce an inflation target that is lower than the inflation rate it actually anticipates. The optimal policy (the one that involves shifting the supply curve as far to the left as possible in Fig. 6.13) is to announce an acceleration of inflation close to that observed in the previous period.

Now suppose that the economy is initially at E_2. By buying domestic assets, the central bank lowers the nominal long rate, which leads to a nominal and real depreciation of money. The decline in the real long rate increases domestic demand and the depreciation stimulates external demand. The economy moves along the curve, for example, to E_2'. At the new equilibrium, aggregate supply corresponds to a situation where inflation rate is higher and expectations of higher inflation by the private sector are lower than the increase in actual inflation.

The two unconventional policies thus lead to the same result: currency depreciation, lower unemployment and higher inflation. But suppose that the foreign country also pursues a restrictive unconventional policy. For example, the foreign central bank may wish to exit quantitative easing by reducing the size of its balance sheet by selling part of its assets, or it may wish to deflate nascent financial bubbles by lowering financial asset prices. For the domestic country, this policy corresponds to a negative demand shock, reflected by a decrease in $\left(y_t^F - \bar{y}^F\right)$. Suppose the economy is at E_2'. The decline in foreign demand causes the demand curve to shift to the right. The unemployment rate rises and the domestic currency depreciates (E_2' in Fig. 6.13), negating the beneficial effects of the domestic country's unconventional monetary policy.

6.3   OTHER DEBATES ON MONETARY POLICIES: HELICOPTER MONEY, MACROPRUDENTIAL POLICIES

6.3.1   Helicopter Money

There are two ways of conceiving what is called helicopter money (an expression proposed by Friedman 1969). In the fiscal approach to helicopter money, public spending as transfers from government to households and businesses are financed by an increase in the monetary base. In the fiscal approach, the transfer may also correspond to fiscal spending or to a reduction in taxes.

In a purely monetary approach, the central bank provides direct monetary transfers to households and businesses. In both cases the monetary base increases are permanent in the sense that the money that has been created is not withdrawn in the future (either by tax increases or by repayment of the debt contracted by the private sector with the central bank).

Tables 6.5 and 6.6 provide a simple representation of the Statement of Government Operations and the central bank's balance sheet.

In the fiscal approach, the government increases subsidies and grants on the expenditure side and this increases its budget deficit. This additional deficit is financed by the issuance of new bonds purchased by the central bank. But, unlike in a standard open market policy, these bonds result in the issuance of perpetual debt. The grants that are paid by the government loosen the budget constraint of private agents by increasing their resources. This first option has a disadvantage. It increases the budget deficit. The second option is that central bank money be directly accessible by households and businesses—or transformed into a currency intended only for them. The counterpart is also a perpetual debt of the private sector to the central bank.

One of the theoretical justifications for this type of monetary policy is that the central bank changes its target to a nominal target: the growth rate or the level of nominal GDP. A given amount of money is permanently

Table 6.5 Statement of government operations

Revenue	Expenses and spending
Taxes (direct and indirect)	Wages and salaries
Social contributions	Uses of goods and services
Grants	Subsidies and grants
	investment
Financing	
Bonds	
Bought by private investors	
Bought by the central bank	

Table 6.6 Simplified central bank's balance sheet with helicopter money

Assets	Liabilities
Net Foreign assets	Banknotes
Perpetual IOU from the Government	Commercial banks reserves
Commercial banks assets	
	Private sector accounts (households and companies
Other assets	Government account
Perpetual IOU from the private sector	Capital and resources

paid to households so that consumption, investment and employment expenditures it generates increase nominal GDP. This can work, if there is no Ricardian equivalence behavior, especially in the case where the increase in the monetary base is the counterpart of the increase in budget deficits. Such a policy may be credible, for example, if there is no moral hazard behavior on the part of the government (since helicopter money can be interpreted as a form of monetary financing of budget deficits). Compared to an open market policy, there is no interest rate crowding out effect. This strategy is defended by economists who point out the risks associated with the financial instability of QE policies. Rather than money financing the purchase of securities and driving up their prices, then driving them down sharply at the end of expansionary policies, it directly finances economic activity.

Helicopter money is a form of QE policy, aimed at the non-financial private sector. Its assessment, beyond the actual effects on the economy, must be seen in the light of the question of whether central banks should adopt a nominal GDP level target, instead of the standard policy of inflation targeting.

One of the arguments that motivated central banks to target inflation during the Great Moderation was the theoretical result that in the long run there is always a trade-off between inflation and unemployment. We saw in the previous chapters that this link has not necessarily been empirically valid for at least the last 15 years. Before the recent surges in energy prices, the problem was that of low inflation rates, which even caused problems by preventing real rates from falling. However, many economists strongly believe that an inflation rate above a certain threshold destroys economic growth (what vertical Phillips curves mean).

In practice, things would work as follows. The central bank agrees with the government on a target growth rate for government spending (transfers to households and enterprises). It defines the growth rate of the monetary base necessary to achieve this target, based on the spending multipliers and with regard to its target nominal GDP growth rate. If the real growth rate is assumed to depend on forces independent of central bank policy, then the inflation rate target can serve as the adjustment variable for achieving the nominal GDP target. Inflation becomes a counter-cyclical variable. If the real GDP growth rate falls below its potential, then to keep the nominal growth rate on its target path, the central bank must raise its inflation rate target. This means that the monetary authorities have an expansionary policy (by increasing the monetary base). If the rule is deemed credible by the private sector, the money created increases consumption and investment because agents know that the central bank wants to move nominal GDP growth above its historical average (a necessary condition for it to return to the target path after having declined). The effectiveness of this policy is more important in a situation where money is given directly to the private sector, rather than by lowering the interest rate and passing through the transformation operations of the banking sector. This limits "leakage" from the credit channel. Such a policy policy, where the growth rate of real GDP and the inflation rate adjust to achieve the desired growth rate of nominal GDP, can be applied, for example, in a situation of general price level control.

One can provide at least two arguments in favor of helicopter money.

A first argument is that QE policies have had a limited effect on the real economy, especially on private sector consumption and investment spending. Rather, their influence is on the term structure of interest rates and asset prices. This implies that the channels likely to have the greatest influence on consumption and investment are the reduction in the cost of debt and wealth effects. In some regions (e.g., the euro area and Japan), these channels are less important than in the United States because of the structure of private agents' assets (households have much higher levels of savings and lower debt). Moreover, interest rate fluctuations have less effect on repayments (mortgage payment) if they are based on fixed rates that cannot be renegotiated frequently (the importance of bank financing compared to capital market financing makes repayment conditions more rigid). Moreover, empirical work shows that increases in equities or real estate prices lead to an increase in household savings—precautionary savings—and that interest rate cuts lead to a decrease in deposits without leading to an increase in spending (Chauvin and Muellbauer 2018; Muellbauer 2018; Aron et al. 2012).

A second argument is the following. Permanent income theory does not necessarily apply. Empirical work highlights a propensity to consume lower than 1 (Aron et al. 2012 find a nearby coefficient between 0.4 and 0.6 for the United States, Japan and the United Kingdom). This implies that a helicopter money giving $1000 to each household (corresponding to an unanticipated increase in current income) could lead to an increase in household consumption of between $400 and $600.

Other arguments for and against helicopter money have been the subject of several works in the literature. Buiter (2003) shows how The issuance of irredeemable fiat base money makes it possible to eliminate in theoretical models equilibria with liquidity traps in New-Keynesian models. Buiter (2014) proposes a simple model of helicopter money in the case that we retain a budgetary approach to this practice. He shows that it relaxes the government's budget constraint. Money creation corresponds to a transfer of wealth from the Government to households. It is obtained by adding the initial monetary base to the present value of all future net base money issues (net of any interest paid on the stock of base money in circulation). Reis and Tenreyo (2022) propose a taxonomy of channels through which helicopter money can influence an economy. Di Giogio and Traficante (2018) study the case of an open economy and shows the strong impact of financing an expansive fiscal policy with helicopter money than by issuing conventional public debt. In an open economy, the effect is increased thanks to the monetary depreciation caused by the money creation. The beneficial effect on economic growth is accompanied by a higher inflation rate. Drescher et al. (2020) show empirically that there is strong heterogeneity in the propensities to consume among European households (between 0.33 and 0.57) so that helicopter money would have unequal effects between countries and even within countries. van Rooij and de Haan (2019) show that the effects on Dutch households would also be ambiguous, with survey data showing that they would spend only one-third of the transfers allocated to them. Their study shows that the Dutch would make no difference whether the money was paid to them directly by the central bank or by the state. As a result, according to the authors, helicopter money would have little influence on inflation expectations.

6.3.2   Monetary and Macroprudential Policies

The multiplication of crises (financial, debt, health, geopolitical, social) has shown the limits of the approach that has prevailed for the last 20 years, which is a strategy of "compartmentalization" of policies: central banks focus on one major objective, which is price stability. Other entities deal with other problems. The limits of this approach have been demonstrated in several areas. For example, the idea that financial stability could be controlled by microprudential strategies alone (regulation of the behavior of banks, insurance companies and financial institutions by sectoral regulators acting at the micro level) was shattered by the systemic nature of the 2008 crisis and brought back into focus the importance of macroprudential policies conducted by central banks. Similarly, the sustained commitment of governments to support economies in times of acute crises (most recently the Covid-19 crisis) has highlighted the imperative for central banks to intervene in sovereign bond markets to prevent public debt from becoming unsustainable, which could trigger major sovereign debt crises. The need for a holistic approach is another form of monetary policy unconventionality. It is no longer just a matter of discussing the coordination of central banks' actions with those of other entities (government, micro-prudential supervisory agencies), but of making central banks themselves responsible for pursuing several macro-financial objectives that go beyond price stability alone. This is a novel aspect of a literature in full burgeoning.

Two areas in which these debates have gained momentum is coordination with financial stability policy and fiscal policy. On the latter, we provide some examples in the next chapter. On the former, we make a few observations.

Why should a central bank be concerned with financial stability issues? And how might it do so? The starting point is the question of the role of monetary policy. Many agree that it is to limit the variability of output and inflation. In this case, all macroeconomic variables that are likely to cause high volatility in these two variables should be taken into account. We have seen in previous chapters that the financial cycle is a determinant of growth, output gaps and price movements. Regardless of this, the response of output and prices to changes in monetary policy can be amplified or attenuated depending on the extent to which monetary policy affects the financial channel, such as the asset price channel or the financial gas pedal, the wealth and wealth effects. Since the early 1990s, empirical work has shown that financial asset prices are leading indicators of inflection points in the business cycle and has highlighted the predictive content of stock and real estate prices for future growth and inflation (see, e.g., the references in the chapter on interest rates, financial markets, and macroeconomics). Despite debates about the uncertainty surrounding the empirical studies because of the diversity of econometric tools, it is widely recognized that monetary policy is not neutral for the financial cycle, and that the financial cycle has an effect on real macroeconomic variables. The next question is therefore: should central bankers add a financial cycle stability objective to the two usual objectives of inflation deviation from its target and output gap? In practice, this is what we observe.

Reactions in terms of the policy mix (the combination of monetary and macroprudential policies) are heterogeneous across countries.

In 2010, the United States created a Financial Stability Oversight Council under the supervision of the Treasury secretary and independent from the Fed (such a decision was part of the Dodd-Franck Act). This illustrates the case of *de jure* independent monetary and macroprudential regulations.

In contrast, the United Kingdom created in 2013 a Financial Policy Committee within the Bank of England with the objective of maintaining financial stability. With a single institution coordinating macroprudential and monetary policies the United Kingdom illustrates the case of a "lean against the wind" de jure policy mix.

The Eurozone has established an "in-between" policy. In Europe, the ESRB was created in 2010 with a mandate to build a "risk dashboard," conduct stress tests, issue warnings and make recommendations, without having any decision-making power in terms of macroprudential policy. Although it is formally independent from the ECB, the ESRB's informational, administrative, and logistical support is provided by the national central banks. It therefore appears more as a pressure force to lead the ECB to take possible measures to stabilize the financial cycle.

Macroprudential policy in Japan is mainly under the supervision of two institutions, namely the Japanese Financial Services Agency (JFSA) (more specifically within it, the Macroprudential Policy Office) and the BOJ (notably, the Financial System and Bank Examination department). There is no formal coordination framework (such as a council or committee) to coordinate macroprudential policy outside of periods of financial crisis, with relations between the two institutions being regular and informal. The BOJ has been producing a Financial System Report twice a year since 2005. According to Article 1 of the BOJ Act, it must consider the macroprudential effects of its monetary policy.

On the theoretical and empirical level, a literature has developed on the addition of financial stability to the traditional output and inflation targets. The strategy is referred to as macroprudential policy. It does not aim to reduce the risks of individual institutions, but rather to monitor aggregate indicators of systemic risk.

The question regarding the choice of indicators is whether to aim directly at controlling excessive credit fluctuations at the aggregate level (since it is the cause of the leverage effects that destabilize the financial cycle), or whether to target the systemic risk factors at the origin of global macro-financial imbalances. In one case, the indicator to be followed is, for example, the ratio of credit to the economy (measured as a percentage of GDP), since periods of debt expansion and deflation are the driving force behind the phases of the financial cycle. The theoretical basis for this approach is the "Minsky moment" (see Dafermos 2018; Ferri 2019; Reissl 2020). Other indicators have also been proposed, for example, based on tracking changes in equity and real estate market prices (Borio 2014; Borio et al. 2020). On the other hand, when the choice is made for systemic risk targets, macroprudential policy seeks instead to prevent contagion phenomena by acting on interconnection channels (those related to the refinancing of financial institutions and which are likely to lead to liquidity crises, capital flows and changes in short-term interest rates, and the dynamics of refinancing on wholesale markets).

A typology of macroprudential regulation instruments exists. The "bottom-up" approach relies on regulation to impose standards on systemic financial institutions, for example, rules on provisioning levels, capital requirements, and credit limits at the individual level. They have counter-cyclical effects by weakening the link between the supply of credit and bank capital, and act all the more strongly the larger the institutions (see the recent work on 60 countries by Olszak et al. 2019). But, the recent literature also proposes instruments at the aggregate level, such as reserve requirements to mitigate asset price increases (see, e.g., Leduc and Natal 2018).

Some economists suggest including macroeconomic financial variables in the interest rate rules; these can be

- Stock market prices (Nisticò 2012),
- real estate prices (Gelain et al. 2013; Lambertini et al. 2013),

- credit (Cúrdia and Woodford 2016; Verona et al. 2017; Quint and Rabanal 2014),
- rate spreads (Carlstrom et al. 2017; Cúrdia and Woodford 2010; Gilchrist and Zakrajsek 2011).

This approach raises several interesting questions. The first is to be able to assess the risks of speculative bubbles. In the context of unconventional monetary policies, it has become impossible to find the equilibrium price of many financial assets. Indeed, since interest rates are very low, the present value does not exist (it tends to infinity) when the interest rates used for discounting tend to zero. A second question concerns the behavior to adopt in minimizing the macroeconomic volatility of inflation and activity when a central bank seeks to limit the occurrence of extreme events in the financial cycle. How can we avoid the risk that a strong reaction to inflation and output gaps will increase the volatility of these two variables? This may change the traditional way of conducting monetary policy. One can imagine that, rather than aiming to stabilize the financial cycle, the central banker sets limits that must not be exceeded on indicators of financial stress or extreme risks (these limits then become targets in the Taylor rules). This approach can be interesting when a financial crisis has high costs on the real economy, because, for example, the real estate or credit cycle generates imbalances and leverage effects that turn out to be catastrophic for balance sheets in the event of a reversal of the financial cycle (see on this point the papers by Ajello et al. 2019, Leduc and Natal 2018).

The literature on the trade-offs between monetary and macroprudential policies continues to be extensive, due to the changing context of monetary policy over the past decade. Recently, there has been interest in cost-benefit analyses of policies to combat macro-financial risks. For example, how to define the threshold of a credit target, knowing that it influences the depth of recessions, but also the duration of expansion phases? See papers by Gaeda Rivas et al. (2020), Chavleishvili et al. (2021). As another example, unconventional policies have reduced liquidity risk. But at the same time, low rates lead banks to take more risk to obtain higher returns, or increase systemic risk if they use assets issued by other banks as collateral (see Jasova et al. 2021; Mendicino et al. 2020). Readers interested in the question of the interactions between monetary and macroprudential policies can look at, for example, Cozzi et al. (2020), Martin et al. (2021) and Van der Ghote (2021).

6.4   CONCLUSION

Monetary policy in the industrialized countries has never been so much debated as in the current period. During the successive crises of the last decade, it has emerged as a pillar to avoid a collapse of the financial systems. To do this, it has been necessary to invent new ways of providing liquidity to the markets. Quantity-based policies were rediscovered, whereas the philosophy of the last 30 years had been to let prices regulate the adjustment between supply and demand of liquidity by banks and financial institutions. This change in strategy breaks with the vision of a neutral monetary policy and an approach that is too often exclusively "technical" (an issue for specialists). Many students have been trained over the last 3 decades to believe that central bankers have a primary mandate to stabilize inflation. They have been taught that central banks can eventually integrate other mandates in case of necessity (such as during a major crisis), but economists are waiting for a return to "normality": an exit from conventional policies, and above all an independence of monetary policy from political decisions that have an influence on the daily life of ordinary people: the reduction of inequalities, sustainable growth, private and public debts, stability of the financial cycle.

New debates will arise in the coming years. Indeed, over the last 30 years, the science of economic policy has been enriched by new theoretical and empirical tools of analysis. In a context that has been described as "great moderation," this has favored a certain "autonomy" of economic decisions in relation to political decisions. Monetary policy was conceived as a matter for central bankers, a "technical" discipline. The 2008 crisis, the Covid-19 crisis and the emerging geopolitical crises have reshuffled the deck. They have called into question something that had long seemed non-negotiable, that is, the independence of central bankers. In a context where inflation rates have been low for almost 25 years, the fight against inflation has become secondary to the threat that the crises have posed to economies, compared to the challenges of the twenty-first century: the financing of the ecological transition, the fight against inequality, and support for governments in their crisis mitigation strategies. One of the challenges ahead will be the political economy of monetary policy.

In this respect, we have not mentioned in this chapter the modern theory that aims to theoretically rebuild the analysis of money and monetary policy. This approach is still in its infancy, even if it is giving rise to a growing number of publications. Another important element concerns monetary policy in an international context and in an international monetary and payments system in which the dollar continues to play a predominant role, which gives the Federal Reserve a special status, notably that of being a lender of last resort at the global level by providing the markets with plenty of dollars in the event of a liquidity crisis. However, it is not certain that this system will last as the world's economic weight has shifted to Asia and China is playing a very active role. Can we imagine a payment system that is detached from the dollar and that would be supported by electronic currencies of central banks—new currencies, therefore—where the Renminbi would play a pivotal role? This would significantly change the conduct of monetary policies.

PIONEERS IN THE FIELD

Ben Bernanke

If you have not read it yet, do not hesitate to get the book by this former U.S. Fed governor who headed the Fed from 2008 to 2014 (the book is titled *The Courage to Act: A Memoir of a Crisis and Its Aftermath. W. W. Norton & Company*). This economist began working on unconventional monetary policies long before the 2008 crisis, when he was interested in the monetary policy of Japan in the context of the lost decades and the timid reactions of central banks during the 1929 crisis. In his numerous contributions to theoretical monetary analysis, we retain two ideas that may explain the Fed's choices at the time of the 2008 liquidity crisis created by the bursting of the subprime asset bubble. First, the economic collapse caused by a financial crisis is rooted in the fact that the transmission channels of monetary policy have seized up. This can come from the supply side (the tightening of credit lines by banks) or from the demand side (forced deleveraging); quantitative policies are perfectly justified to provide the private sector with the liquidity it lacks and activate the financial accelerator. Then, when an economy is threatened by deflation, or when deflationary pressures last, injecting money that allows to create inflation is, according to Bernanke, quite justified (it is the helicopter money.

(continued)

Mark Carney

He is one of the few people who has presided over two central banks in two different countries, The Bank of Canada between 2008 and 2013, and the Bank of England from 2013 to 2020. This economist is an advocate of a less "technocratic" monetary policy, which would be concerned with issues that go beyond the usual time horizon of policymakers and actors in the financial sector. He is one of the few bankers to associate monetary policy with the defense of the commons, for example, the fight against climate change, financial stability, or the fight against inequality. Carney will remain famous for having drawn the attention of economists to the tragedy of horizons, that is, the fact that economic actors have to make decisions whose results they will certainly not see in their lifetime. He also has a contribution to make on the redesign of the future international monetary system because of the asymmetric position of the dollar (half of world trade uses the dollar as an invoicing currency, which does not reflect the share of US imports and exports in world trade.

REFERENCES

Abassi P, Linzert T (2012) The effectiveness of monetary policy in steering money market rates during the financial crisis. J Macro 34(4):945–954

Acharya VV, Eisert T, Eufinger C, Hirsch C (2019) Whatever it takes: the real effects of unconventional monetary policy. Rev Fin St 32(9):3366–3411

Ajello A, Laubach WJ, López-Salido D, Nakata T (2019) Financial stability and optimal interest rate policy. Int J Cent Bank 15:279–326

Altavilla C, Carboni G, Mollo R (2015) Asset purchase programmes and financial markets: lessons from the euro area. ECB WP 1864

Altavilla C, Burlon L, Giannetti M, Holton S (2022) Is there a zero lower bound? The effects of negative policy rates on banks and firms. J Fin Econ 144(3):885–907

Ambler S (2009) Price-based targeting and stabilization policy: a survey. J Econ Surv 23(5):974–997

Anzuini A, Rossi L (2022) Unconventional monetary policies and expectations on economic variables. Emp Econ Forthcoming 63:3027–3043

Aron, J, Duca JV, Muelbauer J, Murata K, Murphy A (2012) Credit, housing collateral, and consumption: evidence from Japan, the UK, and the US. Rev Inc Wealth 58(3):397–423

Auerbach AJ, Obstfeld M (2005) The case for open-market purchases in a liquidity trap. Am Econ Rev 95(1):110–137

Baumeister C, Benati L (2013) Unconventional monetary policy and the great recession: estimating the macroeconomic effects of a spread compression at the zero lower bound. Int J Cent Bank June:165–182

Benhabib J, Schmitt-Grohé S, Uribe M (2001) The perils of Taylor rules. J Econ Th 96(11):40–69

Benhabib J, Schmitt-Grohé S, Uribe M (2002) Chaotic interest rate rules. Am Econ Rev 92(2):72–78

Berkmen P (2012) Bank of Japan's quantitative and credit easing: are they now more effective. IMF WP 12/2

Bernanke BS, Reinhart VR, Sach BP (2004) Monetary policy alternatives at the zero lower bound: an empirical assessment. Brook Pap Econ Act 2:1–100

Bholat D, Broughton N, Ter Meer J, Wolczak E (2019) Enhancing central bank communications using simple and relatable information. J Mon Econ 108(c):1–15

Binder C (2017) Fed speak on main street: central bank communication and household expectations. J Macr 52:238–51

Borio C (2014) The financial cycle and macroeconomics: what have we learnt? J Bank Fin 45:182–198

Borio C, Drehmann M, Xia FD (2020) Forecasting recessions: the importance of the financial cycle. J Macr 66:103258

Brand C, Bialecki M, Penalver A (2018) The natural rate of interest: estimates, drivers, and challenges to monetary policy. ECB Occasional Paper n°217

Buiter WH (2003) Helicopter money: irredeemable fiat money and the liquidity trap. NBER WP 10163

Buiter WH (2014) The simple analytics of helicopter money: why it works always. Econ 8:2014–28

Bullard J (2010) Seven faces of the "peril." Fed Res B S. Louis Rev Sept/Oct 92(5):339–52

Carlstrom C, Fuerst T, Paustian M (2017) Targeting long rates in a model with segmented markets. Am Econ J Macr 9(1):205–242

CGFS (2019) Unconventional monetary policy tools: a cross-country analysis. Committee on the global financial system, CGFS Paper n°63

Chattopadhyay S, Daniel BC (2018) Taylor rule exit policies for the zero lower bound. Int J Cent Bank 14(5):1–53

Chauvin V, Muellbauer J (2018) Consumption, household portfolios and the housing market in France. Econ Stat 500:157–178

Chavleishvili S, Engle RF, Fahr S, Kremer M, Manganelli S, Schwaab B (2021) The risk management approach to macroprudential policy. ECB WP 2565

Cochrane JM (2016) A very simple Neo-Fisherian model. The Grumpy Economist Blog

Coibon O, Gorodnichenko Y, Wielan J (2022) The optimal inflation rate in New Keynesian Models: should central banks raise their inflation target in light of zero lower bound? Rev Econ St 79:1371–1406

Covas F, Zhang Y (2010) Price-level inflation targeting with financial market imperfections. Can J Econ 43(4):1302–1332

Cozzi G, Darracq Pariès M, Karadi P, Korner J, Kok C, Mazelis F, Nikolov K, Rancoita E, Can Der Ghote A, Weber J (2020) Macroprudential policy measures: macroeconomic impact and interaction with monetary policy. ECB WP n°2376

Creel J, Hubert P, Viennot M (2016) The effect of ECB monetary policies on interest rates and volumes. Appl Econ 48(47):4477–4501

Crowder WJ (2020) The Neo-Fisher hypothesis: empirical implications and evidence. Emp Econ 58:2867–2888

Cúrdia V, Woodford M (2010) Credit spreads and monetary policy. J Mon Cred Bank 42:3–35

Cúrdia V, Woodford M (2011) The central bank balance sheet as an instrument of monetary policy. J Mon Econ 58(1):54–79

Cúrdia V, Woodford M (2016) Credit frictions and optimal monetary policy. J Mon Econ 84(C):30–65

Dafermos Y (2018) Debt cycles, instability and fiscal rules: a Godley-Minsky synthesis. Camb J Econ 42(5):1277–1313

De Peeter M, Martin R, Pruitt S (2018) The liquidity effects of official bod market intervention. J Fin Quant Anal 53(1):243–268

Dell'Ariccia G, Rabanel P, Sandri D (2018) Unconventional monetary policies in the euro area, Japan and the United Kingdom. J Econ Persp 32(4):147–172

Di Giogio, G, Traficante G (2018) Fiscal shocks and helicopter money in open economy. Econ Model 74:77–87

Drescher K, Fessler P, Lindner P (2020) Helicopter money in Europe: new evidence on the marginal propensity to consume across European households. Econ Lett 195:109416

Dufrénot G, Khayat G (2016) Monetary policy switching in the euro area and multiple steady states: an empirical investigation. Mac Dyn 21(5):1175–1188

Ehrmann M (2021) Point targets, tolerance bands or target rangers? Inflation target types and the anchoring of inflation expectations. J Int Econ 132:103514

Eusepi S (2007) Learnability and monetary policy: a global perspective. J Mon Econ 54(4):1115–1131

Evans GW, Guse E, Honkapohja S (2008) Liquidity traps, learning and stagnation. Eur Econ Rev 52(8):1438–1463

Fabo B, Jancokova M, Kempf E, Paster L (2020) fifty shades of QE: conflicts of interest in economic research. Becker Friedman Inst. WP n°2020-128

Ferri P (2019) Minsky's moment: an insider view on the economics of Hyman Minsky. Edward Elgar, Nprthampton

Friedman M (1969) The optimum quantity of money and other essays. Adline Publishng Company, Chicago

Gabaix X (2020) A behavioral new-Keynesian model. NBER WP n°22954

Gaeda Rivas DM, Laeven L, Peréz-Quirós G (2020) Growth and risk trade-off. ECB WP n°2593

Gagnon J, Raskin M, Remache J, Sack B (2011) The financial market effects of the Federal Reserve's large-scale asset purchases. Int J Cent Bank 7(1):3–43

Gambacorta L, Hofman B, Peerman G (2014) The effectiveness of unconventional monetary policy at the zero lower bound: a cross-country analysis. J Mon Cred Bank 46(4): 615–642

Garadi A, Neri S (2019) Natural rates across the Atlantic. J Macr 62:103019

Gelain P, Lasing K, Mendicino C (2013) House prices, credit growth, and excess volatility: implications for monetary and macroprudential policy. Int J Cent Bank 9(2):219–276

Gertler M, Kaeadi P (2011) A model of unconventional monetary policy. J Mon Econ 58(1):17–34

Gertler M, Karadi P (2013) Q1 vs 2 vs 3...: a framework for analyzing large-scale assets purchases as a monetary policy tool. Int J Centr Bank 9:5–53

Gibson H, Hall SG, Tavlas GS (2016) The effectiveness of the ECB's asset purchase programs of 2009 to 2012. J Macr 47:45–57

Gilchrist S, Zakrajsek E (2011) Monetary policy and credit supply shocks. IMF Econ Rev 59(2):195–232

Gobbi L, Mazzocchi R, Tamborini R (2019) Monetary policy, rational confidence, and Neo-Fisherian depressions. Univ. Deg. Stu. di. Trente, WP n°2019/19

Grosse-Steffen C (2021) Anchoring of inflation expectations: do inflation target formulations matter? Banque de France WP 852

Haavio M, Laine OM (2021) Monetary policy rules and the effective lower bound in the euro area. Bank of Finland Research Discussion Papers 5/2021

Hatcher M, Mindford P (2014) Stabilization policy, rational expectations and price level versus inflation targeting: a survey. CEPR Discussion Paper n° 9820

Jasova M, Mendicino C, Supera D (2021) Policy uncertainty, lender of last resort and the real economy. J Mon Econ 118:381–398

Joyce M, Miles D, Scott A, Vayanos D (2012) quantitative easing and unconventional monetary policy. An introduction. Econ J 122:F271–F288

Kandrac J, Schlusche B (2021) quantitative easing and bank risk taking: evidence from lending. J Mon Cred Bank 53(4):635–676

Kiley M, Roberts JM (2017) Monetary policy in a low interest rate world. Brookings Papers on Economic Activity. Spring, pp 317–396

Kuttner KM (2018) Outside the box: unconventional monetary policy in the great recession and beyond. J Econ Persp 32(4):121–146

Lambertini L, Mendicino C, Punzi M (2013) Leaning against the boo-bust cycles in credit and housing prices. J Econ Dyn Cont 37(8):1500–1522

Le Bihan H, Marx M, Matheron J (2021) Inflation tolerance ranges in the New-Keynesian models. Banco de Espagña, Doc. de Trab. n°2142

Leduc S, Natal JM (2018) Monetary and macroprudential policies in a leveraged economy. Econ J 128(609):797–826

Lombardi D, Siklos P, st. Armand S (2018) A survey of the international evidence and lessons learned about unconventional monetary policies: is a "new normal" in our future? J Econ Surv 32(5):1221–1250

Lukmanova E, Rabitsch K (2018) New VAR evidence on monetary transmission channels: temporary interest rate versus inflation target shocks. WP n°630040, KU Leuven, Department of Econ

Martin A, Mendicino C, van Der Ghote A (2021) Interaction between monetary and macroprudential policies. ECB WP Ser. n°2527

Mendicino C, Nikolov K, Suarez J, Supera D (2020) Bank capital in the short and in the long run. J Mon Econ 115:64–79

Milstein E, Wessel D (2021) What did the Fed do in response to the Covid-19 crisis? Brook. Post. Ser.: The Hutchins Center explains

Muellbauer J (2018) Housing, debt and the economy. Nat Inst Econ Rev 245:R20–R33

Neely CJ, Karson E (2021) More stories of unconventional monetary policy. Fed Res B St Louis Rev 103(2):207–270

Nisticò S (2012) Monetary policy and stock-price dynamics in a DSGE framework. J Macr 34(1):126–146

Olszak M, Roszkowska S, Kowalska I (2019) Do macroprudential policy instruments reduce the procyclical impact of capital ratio on bank lending? Cross-country evidence. Baltic J Econ 19(1):1–38

Otsubo KP (2018) How does unconventional monetary policy influence the economy in Japan? As Econ Fin Rev 8(3):308–330

Pagliari MS (2021) Does one (unconventional) size fit all? Effects of the ECB's unconventional monetary policies on the euro area economies. Banque de France WP n°829

Papadomou S, Siriopoulos C, Kyziaris NA (2020) A survey of empirical findings on unconventional central bank policies. J Econ Stud 47(7):1533–1577

Quint D, Rabanal P (2014) Monetary and macroprudential policy in an estimated DSGE model of the euro area. Int J Cent Bank 10(2):169–236

Reinhart C, Sbrancia MB (2015) The liquidation of government debt. Int. Mon. Fund Working Paper n°15/7

Reis R, Tenreyo S (2022) Helicopter money: what is it and what does it do? Ann Rev Econ 14:313–335

Reissl S (2020) Minsky from the bottom-up. Formalising the two-price model of investment in a simple agent-based framework. J Econ Beh Org 177:109–142

Rudebusch GD (2018) A review of the Fed's unconventional monetary policy. Fed Res B San Francisco Econ Lett 27:1–15

Samarina A, Apokoritis N (2020) Evolution of monetary policy framework in the post-crisis environment. DNB WP n°664

Sargent TJ, Wallace N (1981) Some unpleasant monetarist arithmetic. Fed Res B Minn Qu Rev Fall 5:1–17

Schmitt-Grohé S, Uribe M (2000) Price level determinacy and monetary policy under a balance-budget requirement. J Mon Econ 45:211–246

Schmitt-Grohé S, Uribe M (2009) Liquidity traps with global Taylor rules. Int J Econ Th 5:85–106

Schmitt-Grohé S, Uribe M (2014) Liquidity traps: an interest rate based exit strategy. The Man Sch 82(1):1–14

Uribe M (2017) The Neo-Fisher effect in the United States and Japan. NBER Working Paper n°23977

Van der Ghote A (2021) Interactions and coordination between monetary and macroprudential policies. Am Econ J Macr 13(1):1–34

van Rooij M, de Haan J (2019) Would helicopter money be spent? New evidence for the Netherlands. App Econ 51(58):6171–6189

Verona F, Martins M, Drumond I (2017) Financial shocks, financial stability, and optimal Taylor rules. J Macro 54:187–207

Wang R (2021) Evaluating the unconventional monetary of the Bank of Japan: a DSGE approach. J Risk Fin Mark 14(6):253

Westelius NJ (2020) Twenty years of unconventional monetary policy:lessons and way forward for the Bank of Japan, IMF WP 226

Williamson SD (2016) Neo-Fisherism: a radical idea, or the most obvious solution to the low-inflation problem. Reg Econ July:5–9

Wu JC, Xia FP (2016) Measuring the macroeconomic impact of monetary policy at the zero lower bound. J Mon Cred Bank 48(2–3):253–291

Wu CJ, Zhang J (2019) A shadow rate New-Keynesian model. J Econ Dyn Contr 107:103728

CHAPTER 7

Fiscal Policy Issues

The high level of debts in the world has revived debates and initiatives to try bringing them down and stabilize them before they get out of hand. In this chapter, our discussions focus on the developed countries.

Europe faced a violent sovereign debt crisis between 2009 and 2012 when financial markets decided to demand higher premiums on sovereign interest rates to compensate for the possible risks of default on public debts. This prospect, initially focused on Greece, generated a contagion effect to Spain, Italy, Portugal, and Ireland, countries perceived as being structurally more fragile than Germany, France, or the Netherlands. It took the intervention of the European Central Bank (ECB) in September 2012 and the announcement of its unlimited support to over-indebted countries benefiting from a program under the European Stability Mechanism for the crisis to stop.

Despite its dominant position that allows the United States to receive virtually unlimited amounts of international capital flows to finance government budget and current account deficits, US administrations have always faced situations where they have had to push back the legal debt ceiling. Every time there is a debate between Democrats and Republicans, the fear arises that a disagreement on the need for a budget extension will lead to fiscal austerity with a reduction in spending and a sharp increase in taxes (suspension of pensions, social security benefits, reduction in the budgets of federal agencies and departments, etc.). This would correspond to a situation of default on the sovereign debt.

© The Author(s), under exclusive license to Springer Nature
Switzerland AG 2023
G. Dufrénot, *New Challenges for Macroeconomic Policies*,
https://doi.org/10.1007/978-3-031-15754-7_7

Will Japan's debt soon get out of hand in a country where it will exceed 200% of GDP in 2022 and where spending related to the aging population and low taxes make it difficult to reduce budget deficits? It may be said that Japanese debt is held massively by domestic agents, but its accumulation is a burden bequeathed to future generations. Young people have to spend part of their income to pay for pensions and age-related expenses. Part of their income is also used to pay off the debt accumulated by past generations. The public debt may one day no longer be socially sustainable.

The Covid-19 health crisis has caused public debt ratios to rise. Even if it is not over from an epidemiological point of view, its economic effects are over: the massive support plans for the economies during the years 2020 and 2022 should generate higher economic growth rates. The massive sovereign bond buyback policies have crushed interest rates to unprecedented levels. By 2022, governments will be left with high debt ratios. But they should not have difficulties servicing their debt because they benefit from a very favorable refinancing situation for new debt. They will need it all the more as future budgetary policies will aim not only to stabilize the economic situation, but also to finance heavy infrastructures for the ecological and digital transition. Two questions seem to us to be at the heart of the debate among economists today. The first concerns the objective of fiscal policies. What is their purpose? The second question is that of the sustainability of public debts for the coming decades. The first question has the merit of challenging what generations of economics students have learned, namely that fiscal policy should be used primarily for cyclical macroeconomic stabilization and for redistributing wealth and income. In economic policy circles, the following idea has long seemed to prevail: fiscal policy should be neutral in normal times, that is, when there is no large shock. In the event of a serious crisis, it can support activity, but the objective is to very quickly rebuild fiscal buffers that can be used in future crises. A first corollary of this vision is that, in a financial world, the amounts of public debt depend on the constraints imposed by the financial markets. Default is avoided as long as debt service can be paid, that is, as long as risk premiums on sovereign rates do not rise to high levels. A second corollary is that structural spending that affects the potential growth of economies must come from the private sector (governments can eventually provide incentives to firms).

There are several criticisms of this line of reasoning. First, the time horizon of private sector agents is shorter than that of the rates of return on large infrastructure projects, which are only profitable after several decades.

It is not a question of financing the construction of roads or bridges, the costs of which can then be amortized by tolls or taxes. It is a question of making investments that have effects only in the medium term, but that require high amounts to have an impact on the factors of growth: research and development, technologies that accelerate the ecological transition, the development of the digital economy to modernize productive equipment, training to raise the level of human capital, and so on. Only the State, whose life horizon is infinite, can take charge of this type of expenditure. Moreover, the context in which fiscal policy is exercised has changed profoundly.

Debates on the rise of inequality have raised the issue of inclusive fiscal policies. The crisis of Covid-19 has added a function to states, that of being income insurers in case of economic collapse. Similarly, the growing evidence of the need to build common goods (and not only public goods and services) shows that the conception of state intervention in the economy has a political economy dimension that should not be overlooked.

Concerning the debates on fiscal sustainability, we have the distance to know where the important issues are and what are the false evidences that we should discard. One of them is the idea that there are fiscal expansionary consolidations. This idea was popular in Europe in the 1980s and 1990s and is based on the assumption that fiscal austerity policies increase economic growth. Several theoretical reasons were put forward. For example, lower public spending would lead agents to anticipate future tax cuts and thus higher growth. Non-Keynesian effects of fiscal policies have also been suggested when debt ratios are high (see, e.g., Blanchard 1990; Alesina and Perotti 1997; Feldstein 1982; Perotti 1999; Sutherland 1997). Empirical works have highlighted this phenomenon (for a recession, see Afonso 2006 for a survey). However, correlation should not be confused with causation. Fiscal consolidations reduce budget deficits when these policies are carried out in a context where economies are not in economic recession. This does not mean that the cyclical situation is the result of fiscal policies, but only that it conditions their success. It is well known that fiscal multipliers are very strong during a recession. Consolidating public finances in such times is counterproductive (see Blanchard and Leigh 2013). It is indeed the prior reduction of output gaps that allows the debt to stabilize, and not the other way around.

One novelty is the context in which fiscal policies have been played out over the last two decades. We have studied the phenomenon of secular stagnation in previous chapters. One of its characteristics is that the private sector does not want to invest, but saves a lot. This reduces the cost of expansionary fiscal policies, because the usual crowding-out effect that is mentioned in textbooks to explain the rise in borrowing rates on financial markets is not observed.

Moreover, the sharp decline in interest rates has given a new configuration to fiscal policy. If growth-adjusted interest rates are very low, this loosens the intertemporal budget constraint of governments. To stabilize the debt, they are no longer obliged to increase their primary surpluses for a long time. It is difficult to lower debt ratios if interest rates are not low. The difference with historical periods of very high public debt ratios (the postwar periods) is the following. During the period of the 30 glorious years, for example, the financial system was controlled by the states and there were controls on capital movements. Keeping interest rates low was done through financial repression (see Reinhart and Sbrancia 2015). Today, due to financial globalization, interest rates are determined by market mechanisms. But, as Kirkegaard and Reinhart (2012) point out, the return of financial repression has been taking place since 2008 through other channels. The first channel is that of macroprudential policies. Indeed, in order to reduce liquidity and solvency risks, the Basel III ratios increase the share of less risky securities in the portfolios of financial actors, which mechanically leads to an increase in the demand for sovereign bonds, and thus to a reduction in their yield. Moreover, as we have already pointed out, unconventional monetary policies have been a factor in keeping these yields at historically very low levels.

This chapter begins with a general discussion on the role of fiscal policy. It is necessary to broaden the usual frameworks of thought by approaching this question from a political economy perspective. Then, we devote lengthy developments to the question of the sustainability of public debts, which has become the major concern at the beginning of the twentieth century. To do this, we believe it is important to proceed as follows.

First, we need to understand the factors that contribute to increases and decreases in public debt ratios. There are two approaches to this. One is the academic textbook approach. We look at the implications of the debt dynamics equation. This highlights the contribution of factors such as real interest rates, economic growth and primary budget balances. The other approach is that of policy practitioners. We present the new framework proposed by the International Monetary Fund to study the risks of fiscal stress according to a granularity principle.

We then detail two examples. First, Japan. This country is the most indebted of the industrialized countries, with a debt ratio exceeding 200% of GDP. After having been dismissed for a long time, the hypothesis of a risk of unsustainability of public debt is resurfacing in the debates. The second example is that of the Eurozone countries, which have several particularities. To begin with, these countries constitute a monetary union without a fiscal union, which has forced them to adopt coordination by rules with numerical objectives for achieving various targets (debt and deficit ceilings). The other feature is that these countries have non-mutualized debts. This results in significant divergences in interest rate spreads in the event of a crisis in one of them. The sovereign debt crisis in 2011 showed the limits of this situation: when interest rates rose for Greek debt, this rise was mechanically transmitted to other countries, such as Portugal, whose macroeconomic fundamentals were not very bad. In order to limit the contagion, all countries had to initiate fiscal consolidation policies, which did not have the expected virtuous effects. The reduction of public deficits was carried out in a context of strong recession. The recovery of public finances has therefore had a very high social cost, with an increase in poverty rates in countries subject to fiscal austerity. The case of the Eurozone countries is being discussed in academic and economic policy circles. Should the rules be revised? Should numerical targets be maintained? Shouldn't we consider a fiscal union? We shall see that the points of view are very heterogeneous and that there is no consensus among economists.

7.1   NEW GOALS FOR FISCAL POLICIES

7.1.1   *What Political Economy of Fiscal Strategies in the Twenty-First Century?*

Any analysis of fiscal policies should begin with a discussion on the new role of governments at the center of economies that have undergone a metamorphosis over the last 30 years. What role will governments play in the coming years? The state is not an economic agent like any other, even if for reasons of convenience national accounting classifies public administrations among the institutional sectors that play a key role in the economy. Governments are the emanation of an institutionalized compromise in the way economies are regulated. The configuration of the role of governments is therefore naturally subject to change. Fiscal policy cannot be separated from political compromise and the social contract.

At one extreme, we find institutional forms where the state centralizes all economic activities, guiding market equilibria. In this type of compromise, order and social stability are favored, combined with an objective of sustainable growth. In this case, the state is a strong body operating on the model of a form of "enlightened" authoritarianism. This is authoritarian national capitalism. Hénin and Insel (2021) describe the main features of this mode of coordination: the combination of market economic capitalism and political authoritarianism. It is an organizational form that favors a top-down mode of coordination. We have many historical examples: for example, Japan at the beginning of the Meiji era from 1868 to 1939, the authoritarian and monarchical German Reich between 1871 and 1918, Chile between 1973 and 1990, and so on. Today we think of countries like China, India, Indonesia, Turkey, Vietnam.

At the other end of the spectrum, the market comes before the state in the hierarchy of institutional forms (except in times of crisis). The United Kingdom and the United States are two examples. The development of finance since the mid-1980s has played a decisive role. In industrialized countries, the wage relationship that had characterized the Fordist accumulation regime of the 30 glorious years was profoundly transformed by the rise and preponderance of financial logic. The shareholder value approach to corporate management—both public and private—has financialized the management of jobs and the wage relationship, and modified the trade-offs between investment and savings. Three phenomena have contributed to the spread of relatively "neutral" forms of state intervention in economies. There is their greater dependence on financial markets, but also the context of internationalization of economies and the emergence of new technological paradigms. These phenomena are behind the idea of the need for a certain moderation of fiscal policies, in a context of less volatility in macroeconomic variables (see, e.g., Davis and Kahn (2008)).

In-between these two extremes, there are various hybrid institutional forms. To understand the challenges of fiscal policies in the twenty-first century, their analysis must include political economy dimensions. We also need to move away from an exclusively domestic approach to fiscal policy making. This is important when it comes to discussing the consequences: the sustainability of public debts, fiscal consolidation strategies, the role of fiscal policy in responding to challenges such as ecological and digital

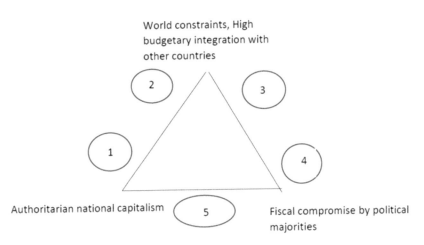

Fig. 7.1   The political constraints of fiscal policy

transitions. The choice of a given mode of regulation of economic activity by the state can be explained from Fig. 7.1.

First of all, any fiscal policy is subject to global constraints that can be summarized as globalization (of trade, finance, information flows, people, etc.) and the degree of integration with the fiscal policies of other countries. On the other hand, some nations may opt for authoritarian national capitalism. Finally, budgetary decisions may be subject to political majorities.

Most state institutions based on authoritarian nationalism reject multilateralism. Fiscal policies pursue primarily national objectives. But states cannot avoid international constraints (the financing of sovereign debts on international capital markets, the acceptance of bilateral or multilateral public financing in case of fiscal crisis, the investment of foreign exchange reserves in foreign assets. As a matter of principle, command capitalism is incompatible with fiscal democracy. Countries may be at point 1 or 2 depending on whether international constraints weigh more or less heavily on fiscal strategies. The integration of fiscal policies may be on the expenditure side, especially in the context of global hegemonic struggles. For example, increased military spending is the result of a global security race.

In countries where budgetary choices are based on political compromises, two situations must be distinguished. The first characterizes patrimonial capitalism, that is, budgetary choices based on connivance (which lead to confusion between private and public interests). This would be the case of a country located at point 5. The second case is that of democratic political regimes, with budgetary strategies more or less integrated with those of other countries. This is the case, for example, of the United States, the country that holds the monetary hegemony in the hierarchy of international means of payment. The other countries in the world can only save if the United States has current account deficits, a situation corresponding to point 3. The countries of the Eurozone would be more like point 4. They are composed of nations where budgetary choices are based on political majorities. Each nation is integrated with another not through fiscal policy coordination but through fiscal rules (i.e., a set of constraints on member countries, rather than choices). The important point here is that, very recently, the fiscal framework of the Eurozone has become more inclusive by including in its objectives the sustainability of growth characterized by a more inclusive social contract: reaffirmation of the protective state in the face of repeated crises, participation of civil society in debates about fiscal issues, intervention by states to correct the negative externalities of markets: poverty, inequality, and so on.

7.1.2   A Renewed Role of the State Favored by Repeated Crises: The Need for Inclusive Fiscal Policies

The story we have told since the mid-1980s about budgetary policy gives a primary role to market mechanisms as a mode of coordination and social regulation. Until very recently, the doctrine that prevailed was that of the greatest neutrality of government in the functioning of the economies: fulfilling above all regulatory missions, leaving, as far as possible, the economic cycle to regulate itself and the markets to decide on the optimal allocation of resources and relative prices. However, the repetition of large-scale global shocks, yesterday a serious financial crisis, today a global pandemic, is gradually calling this doctrine into question.

Well before the 2008 crisis, China had already begun to tell its own story, which it will gradually seek to internationalize. By showing high growth rates, by lifting millions of people out of poverty in just a few decades, and thanks to numerous technological innovations that have nothing to envy Europe or the United States, it has shown that state capitalism can have virtues. In a way, an enlightened authoritarism, like the indicative planning that guided post-Second World War industrial policies, when it was necessary to rebuild completely destroyed European economies. These policies were made possible by activating expansive fiscal policies supported in some countries by regular devaluations and a rise in public debt (as in France).

Since the financial crisis of 2008, another story has begun to emerge, which can be summarized as follows. States will have to intervene more and more to prevent market failures, because of the costs that these have generated: inequalities of wealth and income, forms of concentration of capital, an increase in the poverty of a fringe of society, hypertrophies linked to the financial boom or to the over-indebtedness of the private sector, over-exploitation of resources that modifies natural ecosystems, not to mention the environmental costs. The Covid-19 crisis has added a new dimension. It aggravates these symptoms and thus forces governments to play the role of income insurers in the face of unforeseen and large-scale health shocks.

Are we therefore witnessing the great return of states to the economy? We sometimes read that the market economy is the economic counterpart of political democracy. But capitalism is first and foremost the result of a historical and social construction. The form it takes depends on its interactions with the social order. Whether it is state or liberal, these forms reflect a systemic coherence. It is striking that in the United States, at the heart of economic liberalism, there is now a great deal of debate about the interventionism—desired or not—of the federal and state governments in areas that were once considered strictly within the private sector. Should digital companies be downsized? Should federal governments not assume part of the cost of health care for some of the poorest people? Should it privatize all production of goods and services?

It is likely that a new story about the role of the state will emerge in the coming years, this time not from economic or political interest groups, nor from intellectuals, nor from scientists, nor from international organizations, but from civil society. The awareness of the existence of increased vulnerabilities due to the multiplication of large-scale shocks (financial, health, security, natural) will lead populations to demand more State. But under democratic control. Social cohesion will then depend on the degree to which they respond to this demand. It is striking that, in a large number of countries, political elites are no longer adulated for their know-how or their competence (they are even sometimes decried), but that the key criteria for their acceptance are now ethical. It is not only a question of morality. But the state capitalism that seems to be gaining public acceptance, and that is taking shape today, has the following features. The state must show that it pursues objectives that are part of the "social welfare function."

Among these, common goods occupy an important place, including protection against unpredictable shocks. The definition of the commons varies from society to society, depending on its choices. In a number of Asian countries, for example, social order is a common good. It leads people to accept the deprivation of certain public freedoms. In Europe and the United States, the fight against inequality and poverty, and social injustice, are at the top of the list of what people consider to be essential common goods. In a large number of countries, the fight against global warming is also high on the list. Finally, for a growing number of citizens in European countries, governance is also a common good. They expect their governments to be coordinators of initiatives and ideas. Instead of hierarchy, civil societies increasingly prefer a minimum of horizontality: being consulted on important issues, in favor of transparency mechanisms on the decisions taken.

7.1.3   Rethinking Fiscal Policy Objectives in Times of Crisis: Insurance Against Large-Scale Shocks

The unexpectedly recurrent crises since 2008 have had surprises for economists and are leading to a thorough rethinking of economic policy strategies. In 2008, internal dysfunctions in the financial markets finally led to the irreversibility of unconventional monetary policies. In 2020, it is a health crisis, exogenous to the economy, which risks upsetting the steering of fiscal policy by the States for many decades to come. What is new compared to 2008 is that governments have had to make decisions in a context of radical uncertainty that cannot be reduced to probabilistic risks.

The role of the states, in the front line, was not thought of as in normal times. Governments were not able to fight the pandemic without imposing a (temporary) break in the productive capacity of economies and without depriving households and businesses of income because of the containment measures. This context is similar to what would be observed in a war situation, or a large-scale natural disaster. Resilience to such unpredictable shocks implies that states play a new role, that of revenue insurers. Nobel Prize-winning economist Edmund Phelps uses the term systemic insurance. Substitute revenues are of such a magnitude that markets alone could not cover them in full.

This type of strategy is justified by a new mission, namely that of insurer. The measures voted in the United States and those envisaged in European countries and the rest of the world at the time of the Covid-19 crisis were not simple Keynesian stimulus plans, nor were they supply-side policies. They were designed to compensate for the loss of income resulting from the containment measures needed to control the speed of the spread of the virus among the population: massive transfers to households, support funds for the unemployed and businesses, deferral of tax charges, and so on. These measures were added to the crisis' impact on the economy. These measures were added to its more traditional role: the State continued to pay its civil servants and to carry out its other missions, and contributions and taxes remained due even if their payment was postponed. On the other hand, new expenses were devoted to the fight against the pandemic, such as the purchase of medical equipment and materials, the financing of research and clinical trials, the construction of hospitals, the payment of the salaries of people who volunteered to help, and so on.

In the years following the 2008 financial crisis, the stimulus packages implemented during the crisis were followed a few years later by fiscal austerity programs (especially in the Eurozone countries). Since the multipliers were very high, this could have amplified the effects of the initial crisis, had it not been for the interventions of central banks. While voices are being raised to warn of the risks of budgetary slippage, we can emphasize that the budgetary doctrine will undoubtedly change. State intervention must be analyzed in terms of political economy.

Indeed, there is a broad consensus on the necessity and the validity of the role of governments as systemic insurers in times of crisis. For it is a question of safeguarding what societies consider to be common goods, that is, vital goods and services of which no one can be deprived, unless social cohesion, or even the very existence of individuals, is jeopardized: to feed oneself at a minimum, to avoid the cascade of business and household bankruptcies, to ensure that the partial shutdown of the productive apparatus does not lead to irreversible losses in the productivity of labor and capital, to ensure even at a minimum the usual public services: continuity of education, of public and national security missions, of justice services. This basic foundation, which allows us to continue to ensure social cohesion, comes on top of the massive expenditure devoted to the fight against the expansion of Covid-19.

Once societies agree with these principles, new ways of analyzing how these insurance expenditures are financed must be considered. For example, the money spent could be financed through perpetual borrowing from central banks. They would thus be recorded on the assets side of their balance sheet with infinite maturities. The States would therefore guarantee the revenues, and the central banks would be the payers of last resort. This could open a discussion on the role of money in times of crisis. Unlike in 2008, it is not a question of making up for a lack of liquidity in the financial system, nor of saving the banks. It is even less about over-indebted households and companies in the hope that they will be able to repay their loans once the crisis is over. When a natural or health catastrophe threatens the social and economic integration of societies, fiscal policy must retain its fundamental role: the right of everyone to access liquidity to ensure a minimum of subsistence.

7.2   Debt Sustainability

7.2.1   Theoretical Framework

The study of debt sustainability aims at understanding that a government has several ways to liquidate sovereign debt: (1) keep nominal interest rates low, (2) raise potential growth, (3) control primary budget deficits (i.e., excluding debt interest) to prevent them from exploding, and (4) default (by requesting debt rescheduling or debt forgiveness).

Let us start with the following equation. The government's primary expenditure (G_t) and interest expenditure (rD_{t-1}) are financed by tax revenues (R_t) and debt issued by the government and held by investors (public, capital markets, central banks,…). In the following equation Dt is the stock of debt at time t:

$$G_t + rD_{t-1} = D_t + R_t. \tag{7.1}$$

rD_{t-1} does not measure debt service, as a portion of the principal would have to be added. It is the interest expense that is recorded in the annual state budget.

By solving this equation recursively, we obtain the government's intertemporal budget:

$$D_t = \sum_{k=0}^{\infty} \frac{1}{(1+r)^{k+1}} P_{t+k+1} + lim_{k \leftarrow +\infty} \frac{1}{(1+r)^{k+1}} D_{t+k+1}. \qquad (7.2)$$

where $P_t = R_t - G_t$ is the primary balance at time t. From this expression, the debt sustainability condition is obtained by assuming a no-Ponzi game situation (transversality condition):

$$lim_{k \to +\infty} \frac{1}{(1+r)^{k+1}} E_t [D_{t+k+1}]. \qquad (7.3)$$

where E_t is the expectation made at time t for future periods.

The intertemporal budget constraint is then defined by

$$D_t = \sum_{k=0}^{\infty} \frac{1}{(1+r)^{k+1}} E_t [P_{t+k+1}]. \qquad (7.4)$$

Public debt must be paid back by the expected discounted future primary surpluses. This works if the transversality condition holds, that is, if the discounted expected value of debt is zero in the long run. Equations (7.3) and (7.4) define intertemporal solvency: initial debt plus discounted future primary spending must equal discounted future revenues.

If the interest rate varies over time, compound rates must be introduced and the debt can be defined at any horizon T starting from a given initial date t. To do this, we define

$$\kappa_{a,b} = \Pi_{j=b}^{a+1}(1+r_j), \quad \kappa_{bb} = 1, \qquad (7.5)$$

and we iterate the debt equation to obtain

$$D_T = \kappa_{t-1,T} D_{t-1} - \sum_{i=t}^{T} \kappa_{i,T} P_i. \qquad (7.6)$$

From this equation, we have

$$D_t = \kappa_{\tau_0,t} D_{\tau_0} + sum^t_{i=\tau_0+1} \kappa_{i,t} P_i, \tag{7.7}$$

which implies

$$D_{\tau_0} = \lim_{t \to \infty} \frac{D_t}{\kappa_{\tau_0,t}} + \sum_{i=\tau_0+1}^{\infty} \frac{P_i}{\kappa_{\tau_0,i}} \tag{7.8}$$

The no-Ponzi game condition implies that the first term on the right of the equality tends to 0. We then obtain the usual sustainability condition, that is, the stock of debt at a given time tau_0 must be equal to the sum of the discounted primary balances.

The main factors contributing to intertemporal debt solvency can be derived as follows. We consider a more detailed expression of debt dynamics:

$$D_t = D^d_{t-1}(1 + r^d_t) + S_{t-1} D^f_{t-1}(1 + r^f_t)(1 + s_t) - P_t. \tag{7.9}$$

with the following definitions of the variables:

- D_t: debt stock at the end of time period t,
- D^d_t: domestic debt; D^f_t: foreign debt,
- r^d_t: interest rate on domestic debt,
- r^f_t: interest rate on foreign debt,
- S_t: nominal exchange rate at time t,
- s_t: nominal exchange rate appreciation/depreciation (+ is depreciation),
- P_t: primary balance.

Dividing both sides of the equation by GDP, we obtain the following equation:

$$d_t = \frac{d^d_{t-1}(1 + r^d_t)}{1 + g_t} + \frac{d^f_{t-1}(1 + r^f_t)(1 + \sigma_t)}{1 + g_t} - p_t. \tag{7.10}$$

d_t, p_t respectively denote the public debt ratio and primary balance as share of GDP. g_t is GDP growth between time $t-1$ and t. r^d_t and r^f_t

are respectively the real domestic and foreign interest rate. σ_t is the real exchange rate appreciation/depreciation.

Defining $\Delta d_t = d_t - d_{t-1}1$, the equation can be rewritten:

$$\Delta d_t = \frac{\left[r_t^d d_{t-1}^d + r_t^f d_{t-1}^f \right] - g_t d_{t-1} + \sigma_t (1 + r_t^f) d_{t-1}^f}{1 + g_t} - p_t. \qquad (7.11)$$

We can see that some factors automatically contribute to the debt dynamics:

1. domestic and foreign interest rates,
2. the real GDP,
3. the real exchange rate depreciation.

These variables critically affect debt solvency. The primary ratio p_t results from discretionary fiscal policy.

Let us consider the simplified case where $r_t^d = r_t^f = r_t$, $d_t^d = d_t^f = d_t$, and $\sigma_t = 0$. Then, we can write

$$d_t = \theta_t d_{t-1} - p_t, \quad \theta_t = \frac{1 + rr_t}{1 + g_t}. \qquad (7.12)$$

rr_t is the real interest rate.

Equation (7.12) is a first-order difference equation with a time-varying coefficient. Sufficient conditions for the global asymptotic stability of its solution are the following:

Condition 1: $-p_t$ is bounded everywhere $t > 0$ and $\theta_t < 1$ nearly everywhere $t > 0$,

or

Condition 2: $\theta_t < 1$ everywhere $t > 0$ and $-p_t$ is bounded nearly everywhere $t > 0$.

These two conditions say that the debt does not explode in two configurations. In the first condition, governments set a limit on the budget deficit $(-p_t)$ that they never exceed. This limit can be achieved, for example, through budgetary rules on the primary balance or on variables that influence it (a ceiling on current expenditure, a minimum revenue threshold, a golden rule for capital expenditure). In this case, from time to time the real interest rate can be higher than the GDP growth rate without the debt exploding. An alternative configuration is that the growth rate remains above the real interest rate for a very long time. Then the budget deficit can increase sharply at certain times without causing the debt ratio to explode.

A case much studied in the literature is that where θ is constant. In this case, the conditions for debt solvency imply that $rr_t < g_t$, whatever t. The debt ratio will stabilize in any case, provided that the primary balance is stationary. Equation (7.12) with a constant coefficient θ has a general solution:

$$d_t = \theta^t(d_1 - l), \; l = \frac{-p_t^*}{1 - \theta}, \; |\theta| < 1, \; p^* = \frac{rr - g}{1 + g}d^*. \tag{7.13}$$

d^* is the debt-stabilizing primary surplus. The point is that even if the public debt ratio is high, and the growth-adjusted real interest rate is negative, governments do not need to continuously generate primary surpluses to stabilize it. If at some point the interest rate exceeds the growth rate, it becomes necessary to generate primary surpluses.

7.2.2   Debt Sustainability When Interest Rates Are Very Low

In practice, a public debt is sustainable if a government does not need to make large-scale fiscal adjustments to service the debt. if $rr > g$ for a long time, those who pay for the debt are 1/ the economic agents of the current generation (through tax increases or welfare decreases associated with spending cuts), and 2/ future generations who will have to repay the remaining stock when the debt matures.

When $rr < g$, not only can governments run primary deficits without encountering risks of debt unsustainability. But moreover, those who pay the debt are the holders of the sovereign bonds. It may seem surprising, but they are willing to hold securities that yield less than the return they would get by investing their money elsewhere in the economy to obtain the equivalent of g. So why do they do it? For a variety of reasons. First, they may be forced to do so because of macroprudential rules that require them to hold a minimum amount of non-risky securities in their securities portfolios. Second, when financial markets are volatile, there may be a race to safe assets.

When $rr < g$ for a long period of time (as is the case today in industrialized countries), the constraint of debt payment no longer weighs on governments but on those who buy the debt. This situation is frequently observed when inflation is high (which has not been the case in industrialized countries over the last three decades, until the price surge of 2022). This is also achieved by keeping nominal rates low (which is the case, in particular, because of the massive policies of buying up public debt by central banks). Given the very low level of interest rates, governments would not necessarily have an interest in playing a Ponzi game against the buyers of public debt (see, e.g., Abel et al. 1989; Blanchard and Weill 2001; Mehrotra and Sergeyev 2021).

This situation raises several questions.

Is There a Limit to Debt Accumulation?

Governments could take on debt without it costing them much. But is there a limit to what they can do? Imagine a case where, over the next 30 years, real interest rates are expected to remain well below growth rates. Would it be in the interest of governments to increase their debt levels sharply by making the debt rollover process systematic (i.e., increase the debt without increasing taxes)?

To answer these questions, economists usually look at the effect of public debt on welfare.

Neoclassical models with infinitely lived agents (e.g., Solow or Ramsey-type models) are of little help in answering this question, as their conclusions do not apply to the reality of the last three decades. What are these conclusions?

First, public debt is supposed to crowd out private investment. However, we have seen in the previous chapters that private investment has fallen for reasons other than the evolution of interest rates in the markets for loanable funds. In particular, the pessimistic outlook for market opportunities (secular stagnation) and the development of corporate shareholder value have highlighted other rationales for investment choices. Despite the high level of government indebtedness, interest rates have never been so low in the capital markets.

A second conclusion of these models is that when $rr* < g*$ the economy is assumed to be in a situation of over-accumulation of capital (dynamic inefficiency). It is usually in this configuration that debt is seen as a good thing. However, we have evolved over the last two decades in an environment where both the natural interest rate has been far below potential growth in industrialized countries, and where at the same time private investment rates have fallen sharply. What the current situation tells us is rather that the welfare cost of public debt is quite low in industrialized countries.

In overlapping generations models, the debt burden and the risks of over-indebtedness can be transferred to subsequent generations. The job of today's generations is then to adapt their consumption and savings trade-offs over their life cycle while ensuring that future generations are able to repay future debts. It is the degree of "altruism" of present generations toward future generations that conditions the transmission of the debt burden between generations. The economic literature is divided into two parts.

Political economy approaches to debt emphasize the short-sightedness of decision-makers, who pursue only self-interest for re-election or other political rewards. They do not necessarily take into account the intertemporal aspect of the government budget constraint and ignore the fact that more debt today may imply higher taxes and/or lower spending for future generations (see Alesina and Tabelini 1990; Alesina and Perotti 1995).

Another literature focuses on the redistributive effects of public debt. When generations have heterogeneous preferences, to an intergenerational Pareto improvement, because it allows for risk sharing between generations. Welfare is higher than that generated by private risk-sharing contracts (see, e.g., Gordon and Varian 1988; Shiller 1999). To prevent intergenerational conflict (young people are more inclined to fiscal discipline, while old people prefer to receive high amounts of pensions, paid out of debt incurred by younger generations), models emphasize the importance of bequest motive (see Fochman et al. 2018; Song et al. 2012).

Is Public Debt Harmful to Economic Growth?

This issue has fueled controversy around the idea of a "debt overhang." It is important to stress that the idea of a Laffer curve of debt has no theoretical basis. It is an empirical hypothesis for which one can find economic arguments to justify it, or to reject it. Reinhart et al. (2012) propose an empirical study since the early 1800s and show that negative effects on economic growth of an excessive accumulation of public debt appear when the debt ratio exceeds 90% of GDP. Above this threshold, additional debt leads to a loss of about 1.2% compared to periods with low debt. This type of effect is persistent over time and can last up to 23 years. Once the critical threshold on the debt ratio is crossed, perverse cumulative effects are triggered. Thresholds may differ across countries, regions, and time (see Panizza and Presbitero 2013; Eberhart 2017; Heimberger 2021). The assumed existence of a Laffer curve of debt suggests that the condition of a negative real interest rate adjusted for economic growth is not a sufficient criterion to stabilize the debt ratio. It would be necessary to add an equation linking g to d, which is not systematically done in the literature on debt sustainability. In a study of 28 European countries between 1995 and 2016, Vanlaer et al. (2021) show that a 10 pp increase in public debt reduces private investment by 18.32 trillion euros. The authors interpret this as the consequence of a crowding-out effect (mitigated by the degree of openness of countries to financial flows from international capital markets). The other explanation is that governments associate rising debt with tax increases that penalize the private sector.

7.2.3   An Illustration of Interest Rate Stabilization Effects on Debt: United States and United Kingdom

We consider the examples of the United States and of the United Kingdom to illustrate the stabilizing effect of the growth-adjusted interest rate on the public debt ratio. For g_t, we take the potential growth rate calculated from the Holston et al. (2017) (HLW) model and whose series are available on the New York Federal Reserve website.[1] For rr_t, we consider two rates. The first is the natural interest rate calculated by HLW. The second is the nominal 10-year Treasury bond rate adjusted for core inflation (all items less food and energy). The inflation rate and the 10-year Treasury bond rate are taken from the St. Louis FRED database.

Figure 7.2 shows the evolution of the $rr_t - g_t$ spread between 1980 and 2020 using quarterly series. When considering the spread calculated with the natural rate, the growth-adjusted interest rate was quite systematically negative over the entire period. The gap remains stable in the United Kingdom, but increases steadily in the United States.

When we measure the $rr_t - g_t$ spread using 10-year government bond yields (Fig. 7.3), we observe that for the United States rr_t evolves below g_t almost systematically from the mid-1990s. In the United Kingdom, it was not until the years following the 2008 financial crisis that the spread became systematically negative.

[1] See https://www.newyorkfed.org/research/policy/rstar.

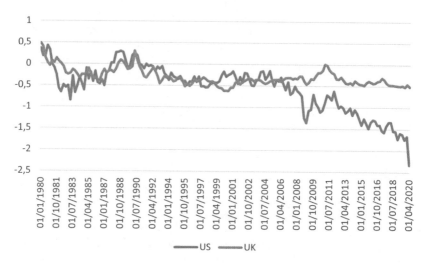

Fig. 7.2 $rr_t - g_t$ computed with HLW natural interest rate

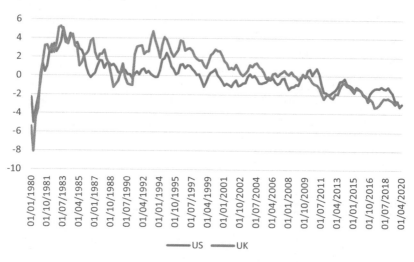

Fig. 7.3 $rr_t - g_t$ computed with 10-year government bond yield

To account for the interest rate received by holders of government debt, one would need to find an indicator that takes into account the maturity of sovereign debt portfolios of taxes on interest received (for an example, see Blanchard 2019; Hilscher et al. 2021). Looking at 10-year rates, there may be a bias in that we are capturing the effects of monetary policy on long rates, whereas central bank holdings of sovereign debt prior to the 2008 financial crisis were at shorter maturities. By considering weighted averages of short and long rates, we would probably find more periods during which $rr_t < g_t$.

Figure 7.4 shows the stabilizing effects on the dynamics of the debt ratio. We consider different initial values of d_t (1995, 2000, 2005, 2010) and look at what would have been the evolution of the debt ratio if the primary balance had been zero. We take rr_t equal to the natural interest rate. In order to make comparisons, we normalize the debt ratios by taking the starting year as the base year. We observe a trend decline in d_t, faster in the United States than in the United Kingdom.

7.3   A GRANULAR APPROACH TO DEBT VULNERABILITY

The theoretical approach to debt sustainability is interesting. However, from a policy point of view, a granular approach highlighting the progressivity of default risk, identifying very early on the liquidity and solvency risk factors that a government must face, is necessary. The most appropriate and comprehensive framework existing to date for industrialized countries is the one proposed by the IMF in its latest version of 2021, after several revisions since 2013. We will summarize here the main important things in this framework. The interested reader will find all the details on the IMF website dedicated to Debt sustainability analysis for market access countries.[2]

The starting point is that the sustainability of the debt is assessed with a forward-looking objective based on a risk-based approach. It consists in simulating the trajectory of two important indicators: the public debt ratio and the gross financing needs. Depending on whether or not these two variables exceed a threshold, an in-depth analysis is conducted to study the macro-fiscal risks and the debt profile. To explain the construction of the debt sustainability framework, we will take some examples.

---

[2] See https://www.imf.org/external/pubs/ft/dsa/mac.htm.

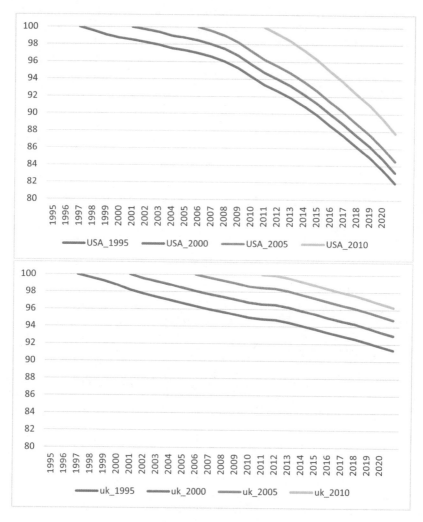

Fig. 7.4 Stabilizing effects of the growth-adjusted interest rate on the debt ratio

7.3.1   Debt Sustainability Analysis Under the Lower Scrutiny

The framework proposed by the IMF is based on an analysis that defines a first alert threshold for two variables. On the one hand, the observed public debt ratio must be less than or equal to 60%. On the other hand, the gross financing needs (GFN) must be below 15%. This second variable makes it possible to capture the liquidity risks of a government. Indeed, we have

GFN = primary deficit + debt service.

Other indicators may raise red flags, especially if a country needs to make significant adjustments to service its debt. One indicator is the adjustment of the cumulative structural primary balance over three years (it must remain below 3%). In addition, to take into account the risks associated with an unexpected reversal in budget revenues, the framework takes into account the volatility of economic growth (which must be less than 1). Finally, to take into account uncertainties due to the interest rate of the debt, bond yield spreads must be below 600 basis points.

If a country meets the first two criteria on debt ratio and GFN, then its public debt sustainability analysis takes place under the "lower scrutiny." This implies a "basic" sustainability exercise. This is done in the following way.

It is a prospective exercise that aims to do two things: first, to study the time profile of the ratio of gross nominal public debt and gross financing needs; second, to investigate the factors contributing to changes in the debt ratio.

Two scenarios are defined. The first one is a reference scenario called baseline. Assumptions are made about the forecasts of key macroeconomic variables (GDP growth rate, inflation rate, effective interest rate on the debt, real exchange rate, primary balance, current account balance, existing stock of debt, debt service of existing debt, new disbursements and their financing terms, etc.). The economic policies considered for the future correspond to those in the pipeline at the time the forecast is made. The government also has a complete view of the public debt portfolio and maturities. There are also indications of interest rates and ratings of the public debt by the rating agencies (S&P, Moody's, Fitch).

The second scenario is a stress scenario. It consists of studying how the trajectories of macroeconomic indicators change if negative shocks are considered: an economic slowdown, an increase in risk premiums that would raise the interest rate, a monetary depreciation, and so on. Stress cases are generally "customized" according to the structural characteristics of the economy of the countries studied. For example, for a country frequented by tourists, it will be important to consider the effects of a decline in tourist arrivals. One also simulates the effects of an increase in contingent debts (a deterioration in the situation of the financial sector, a shock suffered by several large public enterprises, the effects of a rapid decline in the birth rate, etc.).

We take a fictitious example to explain how the data usually look. The example, in Table 7.1, concerns a country for which the rating agencies consider the debt to be of very high quality (with a very low probability of default). The CDS spreads are very low (10 pp). In the projections, the public debt ratio is expected to decrease at the end of the projection, after having increased.

In 2021, 2022 the country experiences a drastic decline in its growth rate, but forecasts predict a rebound in activity in an environment where the inflation rate and the effective interest rate on public debt remain stable.

The first important piece of information in a debt sustainability analysis is to look at changes in the debt ratio and understand why it is falling or rising. In the example of our country, Fig. 7.5 shows a downward dynamic of this ratio, after a significant increase until 2022. This decline is due to an expected increase in the primary fiscal balance and a boost in real GDP growth. Table 7.2 corresponds to the figure. The line "Other debt creating flows" corresponds, for example, to one-off measures, such as privatizations, which increase budget revenues, but in a one-off manner.

Figure 7.6 shows an example for the country under consideration of the evolution of the gross nominal public debt (as a percentage of GDP) in the baseline scenario and under different stress assumptions. It can be seen that the public debt ratio would fall rapidly from 130 to 105% in 2029 in the baseline scenario. But the debt ratio would increase in the three years following an interest rate increase, before beginning to decline. The ratio would stabilize at a much higher level than in the baseline scenario (above 130% in 2029). The debt is also sensitive to other shocks (GDP growth rate and real exchange rate shocks), but in a different way, since the downward momentum would not be halted, but only slowed.

An important exercise in forecasting is its realism. One way to do this is to judge the forecasts made in the past. We look at the forecast errors that have been made. These errors are defined as the difference between the actual value of the variables in year t and the projection for that year made in year $t - 1$, or several years earlier. There are two cases. Either the difference is negative, which means that the forecast was too optimistic. Or it is positive, which means that they were too pessimistic. The country is compared with a group of other countries with the same structural characteristics and for which the same exercise is carried out. For each year,

Table 7.1 Example public debt sustainability analysis (DSA): baseline scenario

	Actual		Projections					
	2014 2020	2020	2021	2022	2023	2024	2025	2026
Nominal Gross public debt	100	113	122	130	128	125	122	118
Public GFN	20	22	24	22	21	24	22	19
Public debt (% on potential GDP)	98	115	119	125	123	121	118	115
Real GDP growth(%)	0.4	0.6	−2.2	−1.7	0.9	1.8	2.2	2.3
GDP deflator (%)	1.6	1.8	1.7	1.5	1.6	1.6	1.6	1.6
Nominal GDP growth(%)	2	2.4	−0.5	−0.2	2.5	3.4	3.8	3.9
Effective interest rate (%)	3.7	3.6	3.5	3.6	3.6	3.6	3.6	3.6
Sovereign spreads								
EMBIG	0.00							
5Y CDS	10							
Ratings	Foreign	Local						
Moody''s	Aa	Aa						
S&Ps	AA	AA						
Fitch	AAA	AAA						

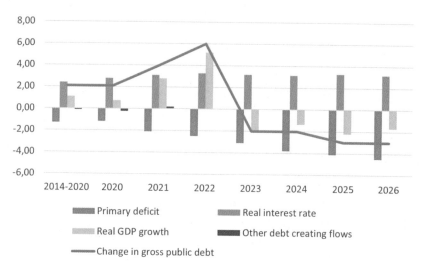

Fig. 7.5   Contribution to changes in public debt: illustration

we calculate the median of the forecast errors of the sample, as well as the first and third quantile Q3. Then one calculates the percentile rank of the country studied. For example, a percentile rank of 76% would indicate that the median forecast error of the sample is 76% close to the forecast error of the country, which would be an indication of a "good" forecast quality. The idea is to look at whether or not the forecast errors of a country are very far from what they should be (the "counterfactual" being a group of countries with the same macroeconomic characteristics as it). The example in Fig. 7.7 concerns the forecasts of the primary balance. We see that they have tended in the past to be too optimistic. Given the distance of the forecasts from the median, our country would have a low percentile rank.

7.3.2   Debt Sustainability Analysis Under the Higher Scrutiny

If the current or projected d_t exceeds 50% or if the gross financing needs is greater than 10%, then the DSA analysis takes place under the "higher scrutiny." This means that an in-depth analysis is carried out, beyond the basic DSA, on some warning indicators of stress on the debt. These

Table 7.2 Example contribution to changes in public debt

	Actual			Projections				
	2014 2020	2020	2021	2022	2023	2024	2025	2026
Change in gross public debt	2.1	2.1	4.0	6.0	−2.0	−2.0	−3.0	−3.0
Primary deficit	−1.3	−1.2	−2.1	−2.5	−3.1	−3.8	−4.1	−4.5
Real interest rate	2.4	2.8	3.1	3.3	3.2	3.15	3.3	3.2
Real GDP growth	1.1	0.75	2.8	5.2	−2.1	−1.35	−2.2	−1.7
Other debt creating flows	−0.1	−0.25	0.2	0.0	0.0	0.0	0.0	0.0

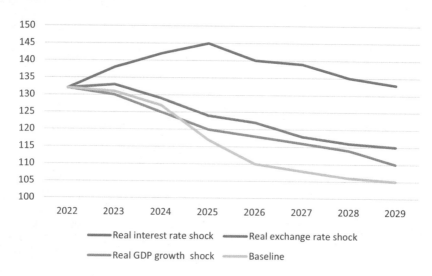

Fig. 7.6   Stress tests: illustration

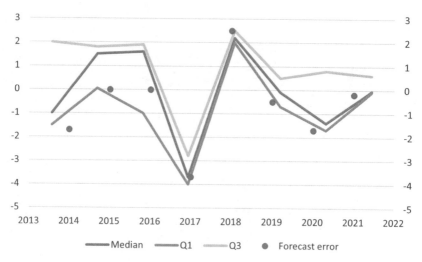

Fig. 7.7   Stress tests: illustration

indicators define the profile of public debt:

- sovereign bond or CDS spreads tend to increase before the onset of a debt crisis,
- external financing needs: they put pressure on a country's foreign exchange reserves and tend to increase before episodes of debt crisis,
- annual change in short-term debt: if it increases too quickly, it can be a source of liquidity stress,
- the share of government debt held by non-residents: this is very sensitive to market sentiment and can trigger self-fulfilling expectations,
- the share of public debt denominated in foreign currency: if it is large, it makes the debt vulnerable to currency depreciation.

For each indicator, there are minimum and maximum thresholds (see Table 7.3). From these, several levels of risk are defined for each indicator (identified by colors):

- the indicator is below the minimum threshold (green): low risk,
- the indicator is between the two thresholds (yellow): medium risk,
- the indicator is above the maximum threshold (red): high risk.

In addition to this analysis, particular attention is paid to the evolution of two key indicators (the public debt ratio and the gross financing needs). Three alert levels are defined (also identified by colors):

Table 7.3 Thresholds of the debt profile indicators

	Lower bound	Upper bound
Bond spreads (basis points)	400	600
External financing requirements (% GDP)	17	25
Annual change in short-term debt (% of total debt)	1	1.5
Public debt held by non-residents	30	45
Public debt held in foreign currency	20	60

Det level	Real GDP growth shock	Primary balance shock	Real interest rate shock	Exchange rate shock	Contingnent liability shock
Gross financing needs	Real GDP growth shock	Primary balance shock	Real interest rate shock	Exchange rate shock	Contingnent liability shock
Debt profile	Market perception	External financing requirements	change in the share of short-term debt	Public debt held by non-residents	Foreign currency debt

Fig. 7.8   Heat map: illustration

- if the thresholds on these variables are not breached (85% for dt and 20% for GFN), neither in the baseline scenario nor in a stress scenario, then the stress on the debt is low (green),
- if the thresholds are not breached in the baseline scenario, but in a stress scenario, the level of stress on the debt is medium (yellow),
- if the thresholds are breached in the baseline scenario, the stress level is high.

Figure 7.8 shows an example of what a "heat map" looks like, so called because it summarizes with colors the different risk levels for the different indicators. In the stress scenarios, negative shocks affecting the determinants of the debt ratio (real GDP growth rate, interest rates, etc.) are considered.

The approach we have just presented shows how, in concrete terms, one can assess the risks of future debt overhang for a government. Beyond the general theoretical definitions given in the previous section, it is fundamental to have a granular, progressive approach with benchmarks given by signals that "light up" and alert to liquidity problems, macroeconomic and financial vulnerabilities, a composition of the debt portfolio that needs to be readjusted, and so on. When we adopt this approach, the heat map of France was entirely red in 2021, except for the boxes corresponding to Market perceptions and foreign currency debt. 50% of the public debt was held by non-residents. The external financing requirement was 94%. For Germany, the line corresponding to debt vulnerability was green. But the GFN line was red for 4 out of 5 items. The debt profile indicators were red for debt held by non-residents (45%) and annual changes in short-term debt (4.5%, at least three times the maximum threshold). For the US, the heat map was entirely red except for Market perception and debt held by non-residents (only 30%, contrary to popular belief). In Japan, the debt profile indicators were fully green, while those related to the debt ratio and GFN were fully red.

7.4   IS THE JAPANESE PUBLIC DEBT UNSUSTAINABLE, OR HAS IT ALWAYS BEEN SUSTAINABLE?

Seen from Europe, and perhaps North America, a long-held sentiment among economists about Japanese public debt is this. While the country has one of the highest debt ratios in the world, it is not at major risk because of the small share of sovereign bonds held by non-residents (barely 13%), and because the holders of sovereign bonds bear the cost of the debt (nominal yields are low and when adjusted for economic growth the spread is negative). As we pointed out before, there is therefore no reason why a government faced with such conditions should not take advantage of them to take on debt. Figure 7.9 shows that the 10-year rate has been below the potential growth rate at least since 1996. In Fig. 7.10, we see the debt ratio rising continuously. Regularly, it reaches a plateau and stabilizes. Then it starts to rise again as soon as a crisis appears and requires counter-cyclical measures. This debt finances a budget deficit that has never turned positive since 1992.

The Japanese debt situation is beginning to worry economists in the country. It is interesting to go back in time to understand the circumstances

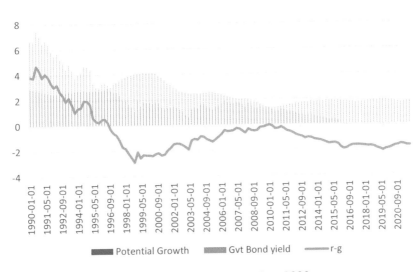

Fig. 7.9 Growth-adjusted interest rate in Japan since 1990

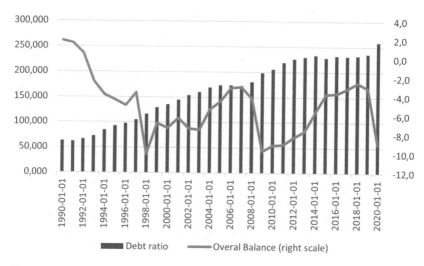

Fig. 7.10   Growth of debt ratio in Japan since 1990

in which a country can accumulate mountains of debt. We start in the early 1990s.

Japan's fiscal difficulties arose during the so-called lost decades, that is, from the early 1990s to the early 2010s. This period first started with the collapse of real estate and equity prices, ending a financial bubble that had been growing since the early 1980s. It was also the end of a credit bubble. The financial collapse led to a slowdown in economic growth. The central bank responded by lowering its policy rate. The central bank reacted by lowering its key interest rate, bringing it close to zero in 1995. And the government had to take counter-cyclical measures. Growth rebounded at first, until the Asian crisis. For much of this period, the r-g gap was positive. The expansionary fiscal policy was reflected in declining budget surpluses, followed by the emergence of deficits from 1993. Although potential growth continues to rise, the debt ratio experiences its first increases.

The government took advantage of the rebound to pursue a policy of fiscal consolidation, notably by increasing indirect taxes from April 1997 onward. However the fiscal austerity was implemented in the midst of the Asian crisis. The expected result was that growth became negative from 1998 to 1999. The financial crisis was reduced by a financial collapse (credit crunch, increase in non-performing loans). Potential growth in turn declined from the beginning of the 2000s. Despite the efforts made, the budget balance therefore remained negative during this period. In March 2000, the economy suffered a new shock, a global one this time, as Japan was hit by the bursting of the technology bubble. This shock had a lasting effect on economic conditions and marked the beginning of a period of declining potential growth for about ten years. all of this occurred at a time when the central bank was keeping its key rate at zero and beginning unconventional monetary policy measures.

There are good reasons why fiscal authorities have failed to rebalance their accounts during the two lost decades from 1990 to 2000. First, one of Japan's chronic problems has been low tax revenue growth, while spending (as a percentage of GDP) has steadily increased. Crises have regularly necessitated the introduction of corporate support packages (including tax exemptions). Second, fiscal multipliers have been low. One explanation that has been given is that the hesitation of fiscal policy (stop and go) has created uncertainty in the private sector. And that this was a source of Ricardian behavior when the government attempted to stimulate the economy. Another explanation comes from the composition of public spending. So-called "non-productive" expenditures have grown faster than productive expenditures (notably social security expenditures due to aging demographics). Public investment spending has grown less rapidly. For a summary of the history of public finance during the lost decade, see among many others Syed et al. 2009; Tukuoka 2010).

An important period was when the so-called Abenomics policy was retained, starting in late 2012. A stated objective of Prime Minister Shinzo Abe was to end the two lost decades and deflationary pressures, through a policy of forward guidance that could change the direction of private sector agents' expectations. This policy was based on three types of measures, of which we will only mention the fiscal policy here.[3] The fiscal strategy was described as flexible, meaning that the policy was expansionary and counter-cyclical in the short term, while aiming at fiscal sustainability in the medium/long term. From 2013 onward, public spending increased to 3% of GDP between 2013 and 2020. To reduce the budget deficit, which stood at 8.7% of GDP when Shinzo Abe took office, his government

---

[3] In addition to the fiscal measures, Abenomics was characterized by a very expansive monetary policy and an increase in the inflation target, as well as by structural reforms to raise potential growth.

adopted a plan to increase budget revenues over a five-year period. The VAT was gradually increased, as were social security contributions on the highest wages. This was a new strategy compared to previous ones, where direct taxes on households and companies had been lowered. The government was thus seeking to correct one of its structural weaknesses, that is, the low tax burden.

Analyses of the effects of this change in economic policy on budget deficits and public debt are controversial. Abenomics has not prevented the debt ratio from continuing to rise. We have seen budget deficits widen, but without success in returning to positive balances, despite intermittent periods of fiscal consolidation. One explanation is that government spending multipliers have been low, and tax multipliers have been higher. This may have prevented the onset of a growth acceleration phase (see on this point Auerbach and Gorodnichenko 2017; OECD 2000, although this argument is disputed by some authors, e.g., Goode et al. 2021; Miyamoto et al. 2018).

In Fig. 7.11, we have plotted the budgetary resources and primary expenditures (excluding interest) between 2005 and 2020. What can be seen very clearly is a reduction in the gap between the two curves, starting in 2011 and continuing continuously (if we set aside the exceptional increase in spending in 2020 due to the Covid-19 crisis). This is due to a

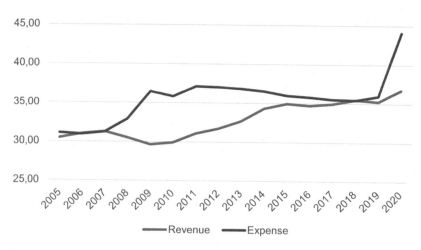

Fig. 7.11 Primary revenues and expenditure in Japan since 2005

continuous and steady increase in revenues and a decrease in expenditures as a percentage of GDP. The interesting point is that the downward trend in primary spending is occurring despite the demographic effects on spending related to the aging of the population (rising dependency ratio, longer life expectancy after age 65). Japan's fiscal problem is not that its debt ratio is not stabilizing. On the contrary, governments have benefited from a double effect. On the one hand, as we have just seen, primary deficits have been steadily decreasing. On the other hand, the interest rate adjusted for economic growth has been consistently negative.

Figure 7.12 shows that the problem in Japan is the level of the debt ratio. For comparison, we have represented the case of Germany. In this figure, the gross debt (in percent of GDP) is described on the abscissa and the primary balance is described on the ordinate. The data range from 2005 to 2020. The primary balances are taken from GFS (the IMF's public finance statistics database). The debt ratios are taken from the FRED database of the St. Louis Reserve. We see two diametrically opposed situations. On the left is Germany with a debt ratio that has never exceeded 100% and that has managed to transform negative deficits in some years into surpluses in others. On the right, Japan has a debt ratio of at least 150% (the 100% mark was passed in the mid-1990s) and has never been able to achieve

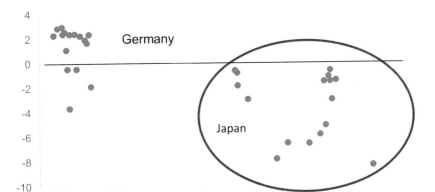

Fig. 7.12 Comparing Germany's and Japan's situations

Table 7.4   Population age structure: Japan (1960–2035)

	1960	1985	2010	2035
Population (millions)	93.42	121.05	128.06	112.12
Young (%)	28.07	26.03	16.84	11.29
0–14 years old				
Working age (%)	60	82.51	81.73	63.43
15–64 years old				
Elderly (%)	5.35	12.47	29.48	37.41
>65 years old				
Elderly (%)	1.63	4.71	14.19	22.78
>75 years old				
Elderly dependency ratio	8.9	15.1	26.1	59.0

surplus primary balances. The problem is therefore not the unsustainability of public debt but its "burden" on present and future generations. How to reduce the stock of debt (in percent of GDP). The answer seems to be that the key comes from a denominator effect and can be found in an increase in potential growth.

The burden of aging demographics is often cited as an aggravating factor for Japan's public finances. This also has an effect on potential growth and therefore also influences the denominator of the debt ratio. Indeed, if the debt is increasing, the debt ratio can be reduced if the trend growth rate of GDP increases at a higher rate than that of the public debt.

Table 7.4 shows Japan's age structure since 1960 and predictions through 2035. Data are taken from IPSS' population projections for Japan, the National Institute of Population, and Population Census of Japan. We see that the old-age dependency ratio has been steadily increasing, from less than 9% in 1960 to more than 50% projected in 2035. At the same time, the young and active population is expected to decline (people under 15 and 15–64 years old). These trends are primarily due to a combination of a decline in fertility rates that began in the 1960s and increased longevity. In addition, replacement migration is very low.

The long-term effects of Japan's demographic structure on the economy's medium-term productive capacity are unambiguous. Theoretically, the following consequences are expected. First, a decline in productivity for two reasons. The first is that labor productivity and human capital

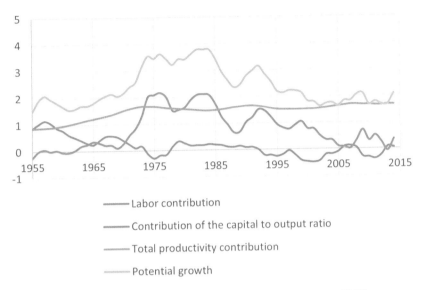

Fig. 7.13 Potential growth: production function approach since 1955

acquisition are age-specific. They decline progressively as workers age. Second, the contribution of aggregate labor supply to growth is likely to decline because the average number of hours worked per person tends to decrease with the old-age dependency ratio. These theoretical arguments are confirmed by the observed empirical stylized facts.

Figure 7.13 shows the growth of potential GDP estimated using the production function approach and its main contributing factors since the mid-1950s (left chart). It is obtained using the national account decomposition of GDP growth according to the production function approach. Data used comes from the Penn World Table (Pwt 9.0). Potential growth is computed as the sum of 3 components:

$$y^{pot} = (n + l) + \frac{\alpha}{1 - \alpha}(k - y) + \frac{tfp}{1 - \alpha}. \qquad (7.14)$$

All the variables are measured as growth rates. y^{pot} is potential growth, n is the number of population engaged, l is the average annual hours worked per person engaged, tfp is total factor productivity, k is capital, $1 - \alpha$ is the

Fig. 7.14   Growth rates of labor productivity, population employment since 1960

share of labor compensation in GDP. The growth rate of labor productivity is obtained as the sum of the growth rate of output per capital (in log) and capital-labor ratio (in log), where labor is the product of employment and average hours worked per person. The 3 components and the resulting potential growth are smoothed (4-quarter moving average).

We also show the evolution of labor productivity as well as employment and population growth rates (Fig. 7.14).

We find that potential growth has steadily declined since the mid-1980s, from a peak of 3.7% in 1984 to 2% in 2014. The decomposition shows that this decline is driven by a decrease in the contribution of the capital and labor coefficient. Specifically, starting in 1993, the contribution was often negative for labor. The factors behind the negative contribution of labor are twofold. First, labor productivity fell from 3% growth in 1990 to 0.11% in 2014. Second, the deceleration in population has become an "attractor" for the growth rate of employment. As a result, the latter evolved around a downward trend. The causes of the decline in employment are related to the decline in the working-age population and the average number of hours worked per worker (direct consequences of demographic changes).

In conclusion, to answer the question of this section, the Japanese public debt seems sustainable. But this is not the main point. Even if it is sustainable, the debt weighs heavily on the economy, since the larger the initial stock of debt, the longer it will take to pay off the principal. To try to bring down the ratio d_t (and not just stabilize it), several suggestions can be made. First, one should look at measures that would further reduce the primary deficit or even turn it into a surplus in future years. The first measures would be to rationalize expenditures by stabilizing the evolution of age-related expenditures and increasing expenditures that would facilitate the resumption of the birth rate. Examples include targeting modest elderly households, increasing free early childhood care. Other measures to increase revenues could include raising the consumption tax rate and expanding the income tax.

7.5   CAN PUBLIC DEBTS BE STABILIZED WHEN THERE IS NO FISCAL UNION? THE EUROZONE EXAMPLE

7.5.1   *The Institutional Context*

To study the evolution of public debts in the Eurozone countries, it is necessary to take into account the specific context in which fiscal policies are exercised. We have a group of countries sharing a common currency, but without a formal fiscal union. The policies of each country are governed by multilateral rules and a mechanism of surveillance and peer pressure. Yet countries have heterogeneous macroeconomic and financial structures. As a result, sovereign bond yields regularly diverge from one country to another. Governments are therefore also subject to the discipline of sovereign debt markets and thus face the difficulties of self-fulfilling expectations. Shocks affecting an economy can lead to a contagion phenomenon in the divergence of interest rate spreads. This is what happened at the time of the sovereign debt crises in 2010, and then at the time of the resumption of inflation in the post-Covid-19 period. This means that debt sustainability depends on several factors:

- the way in which governments apply community budgetary rules,
- changes in the interest rate premiums demanded by investors on the financial markets (and therefore in their behavior),
- macro-financial imbalances that affect economies and can spread between economies.

More so than in countries that are not members of a monetary union, the sustainability of public finances in Eurozone countries often calls into question the sustainability of the single currency. The difficulty is that debts must be sustainable in all countries in order not to risk monetary fragmentation of the zone.

The rules of the European Budget Pact (found in the TSCG: Treaty on Stability, Coordination, and Governance) consist of setting ceilings on different indicators:

- The overall budget deficit must be equal to no more than 3% of GDP.
- The public debt must not exceed 60% of GDP. if it does, countries must commit to reducing it at a rate of 1/20 of the difference with the target.
- In the event of a clear violation of the rules, countries are subject to an excessive deficit procedure and must undertake to improve their structural balance by more than 0.5% per year.
- The structural deficit cannot exceed 0.5% of GDP.
- If the debt ratio is below 60%, the structural balance may be in deficit up to a maximum of 1%.

Such numerical targets (difficult in practice to meet by all states) may seem strange. In fact, all Eurozone countries also have their debt sustainability assessed each year by the IMF according to the method described in the previous sections. Why not use this general framework, common to all industrialized countries? The reasons most often mentioned (by those who defend the use of the SGT) are the following.

The first is that we need to send a clear signal to the markets. Investors are familiar with a clause introduced from the outset between countries, that is, the no bailout clause. This means that no country can individually guarantee the debt of another country. Therefore, if a country defaults on its debt, investors cannot ask another member country to reimburse them. Another reason (fallen into disuse since the sovereign debt crisis of 2010/2011) was that by forcing countries to discipline themselves, one avoids the possibility of the ECB monetizing the debts.

A second reason is to avoid the negative externalities of monetary policy. For example, a country makes a stimulus financed by deficits and a higher public debt. This stimulus generates inflation that spreads to the whole area, forcing the ECB to raise its key rate. This would then penalize the economic activity of the entire zone.

A third reason is to avoid the sub-optimal nature of individual fiscal stimulus. The fourth reason, and perhaps the most significant, is a strong aversion among European leaders to budget deficits.

Several criticisms have arisen about the inappropriateness of these rules. The first criticism is that European multilateral budgetary surveillance forces the governments to have too many set of constraints that prevent them from arbitrating between cyclical stabilization policies and sustainability policies (fiscal policy is not flexible enough). Another criticism is that numerical targets on the structural balance prevent budgetary adjustments beyond the automatic stabilizers. A third criticism, which makes sense from a theoretical point of view, is the following. Imposing numerical targets does not guarantee that debts are sustainable. Similarly, exceeding thresholds does not necessarily lead to unsustainable debts. If numerical targets are to be retained, they must be contingent, that is, they should depend on the situation of each country.

The analysis of debt sustainability, for the countries of the Eurozone, can be done through three equations:

- an equation describing the dynamics of the debt ratio:

$$\Delta d_t = \frac{r_t - g_t}{1 + g_t} d_{t-1} - p_t, \qquad (7.15)$$

where d_t, r_t, g_t and p_t denote respectively the debt ratio, the real interest rate, the real GDP growth and the primary balance ratio. If we are interested in the dynamics of debt over the medium/long term, r_t, g_t can be the natural interest rate and the potential growth rate, and p_t the structural primary balance.

- a behavioral equation describing governments' response to debt and fiscal gaps:

$$\Delta p_t = \alpha(def_{t-1} - \tau_1) + \beta(d_{t-1} - \tau_2) + \epsilon_t^p, \quad \tau_1 = 3\%, \ \tau_2 = 60\%. \qquad (7.16)$$

α and β measure the speed of adjustment to the targets and ϵ_t^p is a noise component. This equation is usually called a fiscal reaction function. def_t is the overall deficit (revenues minus expenditure including interest expenses).

- a third equation describing the yield spread dynamics:

$$\Delta(r_t - r_t^*) = \beta_0(r_{t-1} - r_{t-1}^*) + \beta_1 d_{t-1} + \beta_2 \Delta X_t + \epsilon_t^r. \qquad (7.17)$$

where $X_t = (VIX_t, SP_t, SR_t, UNR_t, CAB_t,)$. There are empirical evidence in the literature that the following factors are determinants of the yield spreads in the developed countries: international risk captured by the VIX, monetary policy (represented by the short-term interest rate SR_t), the financial cycle (measured by housing prices, HP_t, stock prices, SP_t and credit to the private sector, $credit_t$) and macroeconomic imbalances (public debt ratio, current account balance, CAB_t, unemployment rate, UNR_t, the real effective exchange rate, $REER_t$, the debt ratio of the private sector, pd_t). $(r_t - r_t^*)$ is the yield spread defined as the difference between a country's interest rate and the yield of a riskless asset.

Dufrénot and Ulloa-Suarez (2022) study the conditions that guarantee the stability of the debt ratio in the long run (the authors interpret the stability of the steady state equilibrium as a case of sustainability in the sense that the debt does not explode when it deviates punctually from its trajectory following a violent shock) They show that these conditions are equivalent to imposing thresholds on the parameters of the equations. All the conditions are necessary conditions.

The first condition concerns the real interest rate adjusted for economic growth. It must not exceed a critical threshold. It is an indicator of liquidity that allows us to say whether a government is able to service its debt at any given time. At the steady state:

$$r - g < \alpha - \beta_0. \qquad (7.18)$$

The expression on the right of the inequality is not necessarily negative. The threshold for the size of the adjustment of the primary balance by a government in response to the deviation of the overall budget balance from the 3% deficit target. It also depends on the "momentum" dynamics that characterizes financial markets (captured here by the autoregressive coefficient β_0 that measures the degree of interest rate persistence).

A second set of conditions implies a minimum threshold on α and β:

$$\begin{cases} \alpha > \frac{\beta_0 \beta}{\beta_1(\alpha-1)-\beta_0(\pi-g)}, \\ \beta > \alpha(\beta_0 + \pi - g) + (\beta_1 - \beta_0). \end{cases} \qquad (7.19)$$

These inequalities say that the debt does not explode in the medium term provided that the fiscal authorities react sufficiently to the gaps that may appear between the debt ratio, as well as the primary balance, and their numerical targets. The variables to the right of the inequalities capture the macro-financial constraints that governments face (the rate of GDP growth, the rate of inflation, the way in which markets pass on changes in the debt ratio to risk premia, etc.). Dufrénot and Ulloa-Suarez (2022) show that these conditions have not been systematically verified for the Eurozone countries since 1999. They conclude that while governments have benefited from an $(r - g)$ below the upper bound, the constraints on α and β have often been invalidated by empirical observations.

The European Commission investigates the medium-term debt sustainability of Eurozone countries on the basis of two indicators, $S1$ and $S2$, respectively.

$S1$ measures the constant (and permanent) annual increase in the structural primary balance (say γ) from year $\tau_0 + 1$ to year τ_1, required to bring the debt ratio d_t to a given level (e.g., 60%) by year τ_2. τ_0 is the last year before starting fiscal adjustment, $\tau_0 + 1$ is the starting year of adjustment. τ_1 is the end of fiscal adjustment and τ_2 is the target debt for the debt ratio. By assumption $\tau_0 < \tau_1 < \tau_2$. For instance, $S1$ can measure the cumulative 5-year structural fiscal effort required for the debt ratio to reach 60% by 2033 if it were to be observed each year from 2025 onward after a decline from 2020 to 2025. Denoting sp_t the structural primary balance at time t, and p_t the primary balance, the adjustment of the primary balance is given by:

$$\begin{cases} p_t = sp_{\tau_0} + \gamma(t - \tau_0) - \Delta A_t + \Delta P I_t + CC_t, \text{ for } \tau_0 < t < \tau_1, \\ p_t = sp_{\tau_0} + \gamma(\tau_1 - \tau_0) - \Delta A_t + \Delta P I_t + CC_t, \text{ for } \tau_1 < t < \tau_2, \end{cases}$$
$$(7.20)$$

where $S_1 = \gamma(\tau_1 - \tau_0)$ (total fiscal adjustment) and $\Delta A_\tau = A_\tau - A_{\tau_0}$ denotes changes in age-related costs relative to the year τ_0. The adjustment effort therefore takes account of the fiscal pressure of population aging.

There is another indicator $S2$ defined by considering the intertemporal budget constraint. Using the same logic as in Eq. (7.8), we write

$$D_{\tau_0} = \sum_{i=\tau_0+1}^{\infty} \frac{p_{\tau_0} + S2 - \Delta A_i + \Delta P I_i + CC_i}{\kappa_{\tau_0,i}}.$$
$$(7.21)$$

It can be shown that $S2$ has two components, that is, the gap to the debt-stabilizing primary balance and the additional required adjustment due to the cost of aging. Il the interest rate is constant, then we have

$$S2 = A + B = \left[rD_{\tau_0} - sp_{\tau_0} - r \sum_{i=\tau_0+1}^{\infty} \frac{\Delta PI_i + CC_i}{\kappa_{\tau_0,i}} \right] + \left[r \sum_{i=\tau_0+1}^{\infty} \frac{\Delta A_i}{\kappa_{\tau_0,i}} \right].$$

(7.22)

$S2$ thus measures the primary balance adjustment required to stabilize the debt ratio over an infinite horizon. When $S1$ varies between 0 and 2.5, the sustainability risk is considered high. Above 0.25, it is considered low. For $S2$, sustainability is low when the indicator is above 6. Below 2, it is considered high. Between 2 and 6, the risk is moderate. The interested reader can find the derivation of both indicators in European Commission (2021).

7.5.2   Are the European Public Debts Sustainable?

Several empirical methods have been proposed in the literature to study the sustainability of public debts:

- cointegration techniques to investigate the joint dynamics of revenues and expenditures (see, e.g., the seminal paper by Bohn 2007),
- micro-based models (see Giammaridi et al. 2007),
- of signal extraction models (see Dufrénot et al. 2016; Savona and Vezzoli 2015),
- of stochastic debt sustainability models (see Consiglio and Zenios 2017; Goedl and Zwick 2017),
- of distributional models (see Dufrénot and Paret 2019; Medeiros 2012).

Work relying on systems of equations like what we have presented is rarer. Two exceptions are Collignon (2012) and Gosh et al. (2013). The former is in a framework where numerical targets on budget balance and debt ratios are ignored. They show that European public debts have been sustainable over the period from 1978 to 2009. The second shows that governments have become less responsive to debt increases since the debt is very high (around 90–100% of GDP).

One important concern is the influence of financial markets, beyond the discretionary policies of governments. Notably, in the case of the euro area, increases in bond spreads are regularly observed, without necessarily worsening macro-fiscal situations, which could be explained by self-fulfilling expectations phenomena (see, e.g., De Grauwe and Ji 2013; Dufrénot et al. 2016).

Regarding the role of fiscal policy response in promoting public debt sustainability, governments generally seek to avoid two pitfalls.

The first is the risk of unnecessarily restrictive fiscal policies. For example, excessive fiscal consolidation in response to rising deficits may ultimately prove ineffective in reducing the debt ratio. This can happen if multipliers are high and fiscal austerity lowers growth rates. This is what happened in the Eurozone during the sovereign debt crises in 2011. Economists had underestimated fiscal multipliers (see Blanchard and Leigh 2013; Fatás 2018).

The other risk is to adjust the primary balance insufficiently without succeeding in bringing down the debt ratio. This happens, for example, when there is a pro-cyclical fiscal bias, or when policies are not counter-cyclical enough (see Egert 2012; European Fiscal Board 2019).

In Europe, debt ratios are high in some countries and lower in others. The situations are therefore heterogeneous. Figures 7.15 and 7.16 show some examples. Countries such as Germany, Austria, and the Netherlands traditionally have lower debt ratios than France, Portugal, Italy, and Spain. With regard to indicators S1 and S2, the classification of countries in 2020 was as shown in Figs. 7.17 and 7.18. We consider here only the medium-/long-term sustainability indicators.

The absence of fiscal union between Eurozone countries is reflected by a heterogeneity of fiscal sustainability situations. For the countries we have selected as examples, here is what we observe.

The indicator of vulnerability to the risk of debt distress is low in Austria and Germany, medium in the Netherlands and Portugal, and high in Spain, France, and Italy. In these countries, the debt ratio falls slowly in the baseline scenario and stabilizes later than in Germany, Austria, and the Netherlands. Moreover, we see that in these countries there is a probability of having in 2025 a public debt ratio higher than in 2020 and higher than 90%. Unlike in Germany or Austria, a rise in interest rates on newly issued debt would lead to a high risk of unsustainability in Spain, France, Italy, and Portugal. The same conclusion is reached in the case of a negative shock to GDP, even when the shock is small (-0.5 PP). In the same way, a fiscal

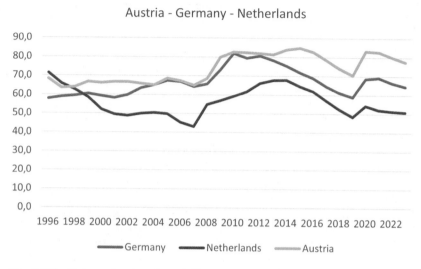

Fig. 7.15 Debt ratios in selected Eurozone countries: Austria, Germany, the Netherlands

loosening would have the same effect. The reasons for the heterogeneity of fiscal positions can be understood when one has a global picture of the macroeconomic imbalances of the countries.

Leaving aside the denominator effect (the fall in GDP following a major shock such as the Covid-19 crisis), these differences illustrate two growth patterns in the heart of Europe. In Germany and the Netherlands, the private sector is the engine of growth, and competitive pressures force companies that want to stay in business to increase labor productivity and reduce wages. The weakness of aggregate demand can be offset by two factors: either the credit cycle becomes the engine of growth, or foreign demand takes over from domestic demand to drive growth. Public spending is less of a burden, so tax rates do not peak at high levels. On the other hand, in other countries, such as France, public demand is the engine of growth, which explains why public spending ratios, fiscal pressure, and debt ratios, are very high there.

Dufrénot et al. (2021) find that up to the 2008 financial crisis, the saving of non-financial corporations was the main channel to the smoothing of idiosyncratic shocks on GDP, as well as international factor

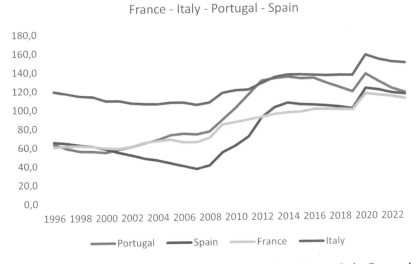

Fig. 7.16 Debt ratios in selected Eurozone countries: France, Italy, Portugal, Spain

income. For instance, 8% of the shocks were smoothed out in the short run and 11% in the long run by foreign direct investment. For the period after 2008, their work shows a different picture. Household and public saving contributed the most to the dampening of asymmetric shocks amounting to 38% of the smoothed shocks in the long run (largest contribution) and up to 54% in the short run. This means that national budgets, and debt, have been put to greater use to cushion asymmetric shocks.

7.5.3 *Should the Fiscal Rules in the Euro Area Be Reconsidered?*

The historical facts show that the governments of the Eurozone countries have always had difficulties in achieving the numerical targets set in the rules of the Stability Pacts over a long period. The Commission has often interpreted this as the consequence of a form of laxity on the part of countries, notably a tendency to favor pro-cyclical biases outside periods of crisis. This idea has been all the more accepted since one of the most important countries in the zone, Germany, has most often been the least far from the criteria. This can be explained by at least two phenomena:

S1 indicator

	Germany	Netherlands	Austria
S1 (baseline)	-1.1	0.1	-0.3
S1 (DSA overall risk)	Low	Medium	Low
Sovereign debt sustainability risk			
Baseline	Low	Medium	Medium
Debt peak year	2020	2025	2024
Struct. Prim. Bal. 2022-2031	52%	63%	57%
Negative shock on nominal GDP (-0.5pp)	Low	Medium	Medium
debt peak year	2020	2026	2025
Increase in the interest rate	Medium	Medium	Medium
Debt peak year	2020	2026	2025
S2 indicator			
Baseline	2.1	3.3	2.4
DSA overal risk	Low	Medium	Medium
Probability that d (2025>2020)	30%	94%	60%

Fig. 7.17 Fiscal sustainability risk in 2020: illustration for Germany, the Netherlands, and Austria

on the one hand, the extroverted growth model, which has led to a reduction in public spending, particularly the public wage bill. On the other hand, German surpluses have often led to a widening of the budget and current account deficits of other countries, notably Italy, Spain, Portugal, and Greece. There is therefore a real debate as to whether surpluses in some countries necessarily imply deficits in others, because the economic structures are heterogeneous. Or whether governments are not respecting the rules of the game, which they consider too restrictive. The German view, which is also shared by Austria, the Netherlands, and the northern European countries, has often prevailed: fiscal imbalances and debt are reduced by fiscal adjustments and numerical rules that constrain the values

S1 indicator				
	Portugal	Spain	France	Italy
S1 (baseline)	2.0	7.7	4.4	9.2
S1 (DSA overall risk)	Medium	High	High	High
Sovereign debt sustainability risk				
Baseline	High	High	High	High
Debt peak year	2020	2030	2026	2024
Struct. Prim. Bal. 2022-2031	27%	90%	82%	57%
Negative shock on nominal GDP (-0.5pp)	High	High	High	High
debt peak year	2020	2030	2027	2031
Increase in the interest rate	High	High	High	High
Debt peak year	2020	2030	2027	2031
S2 indicator				
Baseline	-1.5	0.2	-1.1	1.1
DSA overal risk	High	High	High	High
Probability that d (2025>2020)		24% Medium	Medium	Medium

Fig. 7.18 Fiscal sustainability risk in 2020: illustration for Portugal, Spain, France, and Italy

of fiscal balances. The arrival of Mario Draghi at the ECB has allowed for a relaxation of this vision, with the purchase of sovereign securities on the secondary public debt markets accompanying policies to support economies that had become moribund after the 2008 crisis (a context of secular stagnation studied in previous chapters). The core of the debate is the preservation of the euro. Whenever the markets discriminate against the debts of Eurozone countries by pushing up the interest rate spreads of the so-called peripheral countries, the ECB has no choice but to come to the rescue of the zone by sending signals to the market (one of the signals being to appear as a possible holder of last resort for the debts, which makes it possible to ward off the risk of defaults in the eyes of the markets). To preserve the euro, the ECB and governments cannot play the monetarist arithmetic of Sargent and Wallace (1981). In the current context, the opposite is true. Dufrénot et al. (2018) show that one way to liquidate part of the public debts when they are very high would be for the central bank to target an inflation rate (presumably well above the 2%

target) so as to stabilize the debt ratio. In this respect, too much debt is more easily disposed of through inflationary policies, rather than through deflationary measures such as fiscal consolidation. It is nominal growth that counts to prevent the debt from exploding, that is, a combination of high real growth and not too low inflation rates.

The current rules have several limitations. The first is probably that for a long time fiscal policy was thought of independently of its coordination with monetary policy, the latter being supposed to be confined to controlling inflation. Things are changing under the constraint of the events of successive crises (financial, debt, and health). Unconventional policies were used to buy up public debt, which allowed governments to benefit from low nominal interest rates. Dufrénot and Ulloa-Suarez (2022) show that Eurozone countries have shown little reaction to the gap between the debt ratio and its 60% target. One explanation is that the target is poorly chosen (it is too low) with respect to the data on potential growth rates and inflation rates of the countries (see also Francov'a et al. 2021). To study the implications for debt sustainability, the authors consider several regimes depending on the evolution of primary balances and the pressure exerted by the markets on the interest rate. This implies that the lack of reaction to the debt gap does not prevent the debt ratio from stabilizing, if the interest rate adjusted for the economic growth rate remains below a certain threshold.

There are now many proposals for reforming the rules of multilateral fiscal surveillance in the euro area. We review some of them.

A first solution would be to simplify the rules. There are no studies yet showing the coherence of a system that consists of simultaneously pursuing several numerical objectives on several rules: the budget balance (overall and structural), the debt ratio, the closing of the gap to the debt target. The global experiences of other monetary unions (e.g., the WAEMU countries, which proceed in the same way as the EU) show that targeting several rules makes it more difficult to achieve the targets effectively.

Moreover, it could be better to retain one rule and distinguish between the "good" debt that is accumulated in exchange for the construction of assets that are very useful for medium-/long-term growth (investment for the ecological and digital transition, investment for common public goods and services that allow for a sustainable reduction in inequalities and poverty). This means that a focus must be made on investment. Should we adopt a golden rule, excluding certain types of investment from the criteria (see, e.g., Darvas and Wolff 2021, who propose to exclude investment from the monetary indicators)?

An alternative approach, attractive in theory but difficult to envisage in practice, would be to retain differentiated targets between countries. This would make it possible to take account of heterogeneous macroeconomic situations, but would be tantamount to implicitly defining several equilibrium real exchange rate levels for the countries (implicitly reflecting the de facto existence of several euros within the zone). This is a recommendation that was made at the time of the sovereign debt crisis, and which was rejected.

Another approach would be to set a ceiling on the rate of increase in public spending (by making it conditional on the rate of economic growth). Whether or not to get rid of numerical targets is not clear. On the one hand, one can consider that the sustainability of European public finances can be studied within the common debt sustainability framework proposed by the IMF, which we presented earlier. Stochastic projections of public debt would give very credible warning levels, as is the case for many countries that do not have numerical targets (see on this point the very convincing analysis of Blanchard 2021). But, in practice, this would be tantamount to renouncing the very foundation of the euro, that is, to openly displaying to potential debt holders the no bailout clause (no country is a guarantor of the debts accumulated by others). Numerical targets make this credible and make the corrective measures adopted by governments, under the impetus of the Commission.

7.6   CONCLUSION

In this chapter, we have reviewed some important discussions about fiscal and debt policies. The reader can take away several ideas. The first is a likely shift in the horizon over which fiscal policy is conducted. For a long time, it has been customary to differentiate between two types of approaches. On the one hand, there are Keynesian approaches, focused on the short term, which assign the following objectives to fiscal policy: economic stabilization and redistribution. On the other hand, in the medium/long term, a sustainability objective based on a government's intertemporal budget constraint.

The reality is more complex than the theoretical approach. First, because the notion of sustainability or debt sustainability has several components, and it arises in practice, in the short term as well as in the long term. A state must service its debt. If to do so, it has to make significant budgetary adjustments, this is not a sign of good management, but rather a sign that it is facing liquidity stress. Debt sustainability is a granular phenomenon, which is assessed according to different thresholds crossed by the debt indicators under different scenarios. For the medium-/long-term analysis, solvency depends on several factors, including the potential growth rate and the evolution of interest rates on the debt. Having low adjusted rates does not imply that the debt ratio is low, but that it is stabilizing. There are therefore two issues that are not equivalent. First, there is the question of preventing the debt ratio from exploding. This is why we are trying to stabilize it thanks to the conditions of indebtedness of the states and of economic growth. The role of central banks is decisive here. Then there is the question of the amount or level of the debt. Interest rates do not affect the stock of debt that is accumulated. The debt is liquidated, either by borrowing less, or by bringing a denominator effect into play by increasing nominal GDP (through a little inflation and a rise in real potential growth).

The second idea is that the most indebted countries are not those with the highest risk of debt becoming unsustainable (Japan is a good example). Similarly, countries where fiscal policy is subject to very restrictive rules for public finances are not those where debt is most likely to be sustainable. The case of the Eurozone countries is a very good example. In a monetary union, without a fiscal union, there is no standard model because the countries are too heterogeneous.

PIONEERS IN THE FIELD

Carmen Reinhart

This macroeconomist, who is known to have worked on multiple topics related to macroeconomics and international finance, has taken a long interest in the issue of public debt liquidation from a historical perspective. With her co-authors, she has highlighted different ways in which governments have historically eliminated the mountains of accumulated debt. A typical way has been "financial repression," a term that refers to measures taken to keep interest rates much lower than if they were set directly by the markets. She has also been very

(continued)

interested in public debt crises and their links to financial crises. With Kenneth Rogoff, she is the originator of the idea of serial defaulters on public debt. This is an explanation for the fact that capital does not necessarily move easily from rich to poor countries. We recommend the following works to the interested reader, written with K. Rogoff "A decade on debt" published in 2011 (Columbia University Press).

Kenneth Rogoff

He is one of those economists who believe that excessive public debt has limits. His work on debt overhang and the existence of a threshold in the debt ratio beyond which the effects on growth are deleterious has been controversial. Whether or not the threshold is 90% is not the issue; the message is that above a threshold, governments are paying back too much of their revenues to repay debt and spending even less on investment. Rogoff also challenges a number of ideas that are gaining traction. For example, the fact that real interest rates are now below growth rates is not a guarantee that public debts are not vulnerable, when one looks at things over a long period of time. Another point concerns implicit debt. The pension systems in developed countries are such that it is as if the state borrows money from future pensioners and promises to pay them back when they stop working. But the share of income devoted to paying pensions today exceeds the repayment of current market debts, which poses a problem.

REFERENCES

Abel AB, Mankiw G, Summers LH, Zeckhauser RJ (1989) Assessing dynamic efficicency: theory and evidence. Rev Econ Stud 56(1):1–19

Afonso A (2006) Expansionary fiscal consolidations in Europe. New evidence. ECB Working Paper n°675

Alesina A, Perotti R (1995) The political economy of budget deficits. IMF Staff Pap 42(1):1–31

Alesina A, Perotti R (1997) The welfare state and competitiveness. Am Econ Rev 87(5):921–939

Alesina A, Tabelini G (1990) A positive theory of fiscal deficits and government debt. Rev Econ St 57(3):403–414

Auerbach AJ, Gorodnichenko Y (2017) Fiscal multipliers in Japan. Res Econ 71(3):411–421

Blanchard O (1990) Comment on Giavazzi ad Pagano (1990) In: Blanchard O, Fischer S (eds) NBER Macroeconomics Annual, 1990, pp111–116

Blanchard O (2019) Public debt and low interest rates. Am Econ Rev 109(4):1197–1229

Blanchard O, Álvaro L, Zetellmeyer J (2021) Redesigning EU fiscal rules: from rules to standards. PIIE WP 21-1

Blanchard O, Leigh D (2013) Growth forecast errors and fiscal multipliers. IMF Working Papers 13/1

Blanchard O, Weill P (2001) Dynamic efficiency, the riskless rate, and debt Ponzi games under uncertainty. The BE J Macr 1(2):art 3

Bohn H (2007) Are stationary and cointegration restrictions really necessary for the intertemporal budget constraint? J Mon Econ 54:1837–1847

Collignon S (2012) Fiscal policy rules and the sustainability of public debt in Europe. Int Econ Rev 53(21):539–567

Consiglio A, Zenios S (2017) Stochastic debt sustainability analysis for sovereigns and the scope for optimization modelling. Opt Eng 18(2):537–558

Darvas Z, Wolff G (2021) A green fiscal pact: climate investment in times of budget consolidation. Pol Cont, 18/2021, Bruegel

Davis SJ, Kahn JA (2008) Interpreting the great moderation: changes in the volatility of economic activity at the macro and micro levels. J Econ Persp 22(4):155–180

De Grauwe P, Ji Y (2013) Self-fulfilling crises in the Eurozone: an empirical test. J Int Mon Fin 34:15–36

Dufrénot G, Paret AC (2019) Power-law distribution in the external debt-to-fiscal revenue ratios: empirical evidence and a theoretical model. J Macr 60:341–359

Dufrénot G, Ulloa-Suarez C (2022) Public finance sustainability in Europe. A multicausal model. Unpublished WP

Dufrénot G, Gente K, Monsia F (2016) Macroeconomic imbalances, financial stress and fiscal vulnerability in the euro area before the debt crises: a market view. J Int Mon Fin 67(C):123–146

Dufrénot G, Jawadi F, Khayat G (2018) A model of fiscal dominance under the "Reinhart conjecture." J Econ Dyn Contrl 93(0):332–345

Dufrénot G, Gossé JB, Clerc C (2021) Risk sharing in Europe:new empirical evidence on the capital market channel. App Econ 53(2):262–276

Eberhart M (2017) Nonlinearities in the relationship between debt and growth: (no) evidence from over two centuries. Macr Dyn 23(4):1563–1585

Egert B (2012) Fiscal policy reaction function to the cycle in the OECD: pro or counter-cyclical, CEsifo Working Paper, 3772

European Commission (2021) Debt sustainability monitor 2020. Institutional Paper n°143

European Fiscal Board (2019) Assessment of EU fiscal rules with a focus on the six and two-pack legislation. European Fiscal Board Report

Fatás A (2018) Fiscal policy, potential output and the shifting goalposts. CEPR Disc Pap n°13149

Feldstein M (1982) Government deficits and aggregate demand. J Mon Econ 9(1):1–20

Fochman M, Sachs F, Sadrieh A, Weimann J (2018) The two sides of public debt: intergenerational altruism and burden shifting. Plos One 13(8):e0202963

Francov'a O, Hitaj E, Goosen J, Kraemer R, Lenarcic A, Palaiodimos G (2021) EU fiscal rules: reform reconsiderations, Disc Pap Ser n°17

Giammaridi N, Nickel C, Rother P, Vidal JP (2007) Assessing fiscal soundness theory and practice. Occ Pap n°56, ECB

Goedl M, Zwick C (2017) Assessing the stochastic stability of public debt: the case of Austria. Emp 45(3):559–585

Goode E, Liu Z, Nguyen TL (2021) Fiscal multiplier at the zero lower bound: evidence from Japan. FRBSF Econ Let n° 2021-14

Gordon RH, Varian HR (1988) Intergenerational risk sharing. J Pub Econ 37(2):185–202

Gosh A, Kim J, Mendoza E, Ostry J, Qureshi M (2013) Fiscal fatigue, fiscal space and debt sustainability in advanced economies. Econ J 123(56):F4–F30

Hénin PY, Insel A (2021) Le national-capitalisme autoritaire. Une menace pour la démocratie. Editions: Essais & Cie/ Bleu autour

Heimberger P (2021) Do higher public debt levels reduce economic growth? Vienna Inst for Int Eco St, Working Paper n° 211

Hilscher J, Raviv A, Reis R (2021) Inflation away the public debt? An empirical assessment. Rev Fin St 35(3):1553–1595

Holston K, Laubach T, Williams JC (2017) Measuring the natural rate of interest: international trends and determinants. J Int Econ 108, suppl 1(May): S39–S75

Kirkegaard JF, Reinhart CM (2012) Financial repression: then and now. PIIE Working Paper

Medeiros J (2012)Stochastic debt simulation using VAR models and a panel reaction function: results for a selected number of countries. Eur Econ Econ Pap n° 459

Mehrotra NR, Sergeyev D (2021) Debt sustainability in a low interest world. J Mon Econ 124:S1–S18

Miyamoto W, Nguyen TL, Sergeyev D (2018) Government spending multipliers under the zero lower bound: evidence from Japan. Am Econ J Macr 10(3):247–277

OECD (2000) OECD Econmic Surveys, 1999–2000: Japan

Panizza U, Presbitero A (2013) Public debt and economic growth in advanced economics: a survey. Swiss J Econ Stat 149:174–204

Perotti R (1999) Fiscal policy in good times and bad. Qu J Econ 114(4):1399–1436

Reinhart C, Sbrancia MB (2015) The liquidation of government debt. IMF Working Paper 15/7

Reinhart C, Reinhart V, Rogoff K (2012) Public debt overhang: advanced-economy episodes since 1900. J Econ Persp 26(3):69–86

Sargent TJ, Wallace N (1981) Some unpleasant monetarist arithmetic. FRBM Qu Rev 5(Fall):1–17

Savona R, Vezzoli M (2015) Fitting and forecasting sovereign defaults using multiple risks signals. Ox Bull Econ Stat 71(1):66–92

Shiller R (1999) Social security and institutions for intergenerational, intragenerational, and international risk-sharing. Carnegie-Roschester Conf Ser Pub Pol 50:165–204

Song Z, Storesletten AK, Zilibotti G (2012) Rotten parents and disciplined children: a politico-economic theory of public expenditure and debt. Econ 80(6):2785–2803

Sutherland A (1997) Fiscal crises and aggregate demand: can high public debt reverse the effects of fiscal policy? J Pub Econ 65(2):147–162

Syed M, Kang K, Tokuoka K (2009) "Lost decade" in translation: what Japan's crisis could portend about recovery from the Great Recession. IMF WP n° 09/282

Tukuoka K (2010) The outlook for financing Japan's public debt. IMF Working Paper n° 10/19

Vanlaer W, Picarelli M, Marneffe W (2021) Debt and private investment: does the EU suffer from a debt overhang. Op Econ Rev 32:789–820

CHAPTER 8

Beyond Mainstream Macroeconomics

The ideas and models we have presented so far do not provide all the answers to the challenges facing macroeconomics in the twenty-first century. What we have presented corresponds to a way of thinking that can be interpreted as mainstream macroeconomic theory. This is what many researchers in macroeconomics are working on in the fields we have investigated. We have presented the theoretical models and mechanisms taught to students in economics faculties around the world. To simplify, the intellectual framework of mainstream macroeconomics is still heavily influenced by the New-Keynesian synthesis. However, there are also many other macroeconomists who are critical of mainstream approaches. We will call them heterodox.

We do not include in the category of heterodox economics the "rebuilding macroeconomic theory" project, several contributions of which were published in the special issue of the Oxford Review of Economic Policy, issue 34(1–2) in 2020. The approach of the authors of the project consists in amending New-Keynesian and neoclassical-based models by changing some of its assumptions (for example, by integrating financial frictions, by weakening the assumption of rational expectations through heterogeneous agents' behavior, by strengthening some microeconomic foundations). Though the leaders of this project (David Wines and Samuel Wills) acknowledge changes that are intended to bring more pluralism, the approaches remain anchored in the neoclassical, New Classical, or New-Keynesian traditions.

G. Dufrénot, *New Challenges for Macroeconomic Policies*,
https://doi.org/10.1007/978-3-031-15754-7_8

389

For the topics discussed in this book, heterodox macroeconomics encompasses a variety of schools of thought: post-Keynesians, institutional economics and Regulationists, degrowth theorists, ecological economics, modern monetary theories, participatory economics, distributivism, and neo-Marxian economics. In this chapter, we present some arguments of heterodox macroeconomists on three topics that we discussed earlier, that is, the causes of inflation, the role of money and the way in which monetary policy (modern monetary theory) should be conducted, and the analysis of growth.

Before doing so, we would like to briefly mention some reasons why, despite the increasing body of work by heterodox macroeconomists, their theories are not systematically taught in all economics faculties around the world. As already mentioned in the introduction, macroeconomics is an experimental science. Theories should be constructed according to an inductive methodology. The process is as follows: (1) new facts appear that cannot be explained by current theories; (2) economists first try to understand what regularities hide these facts (by doing empirical studies or experiments); (3) they then formulate ideas about the underlying mechanisms, possibly using very simple models; (4) if the new facts persist and do not seem to contradict the intuitions, then further theoretical work can begin with more sophisticated models. A problem arises when we try to reverse this process in the following way: (1) in the face of new facts, we first try to amend the existing theoretical models, by enriching them with new hypotheses. In general, greater sophistication makes it possible to reproduce the new facts, but only after they have occurred; (2) if the new facts are repeated but invalidate the new assumptions, then (3) further work of changing assumptions and sophistication is considered until the new model reproduces reality. The second process led to the enrichment of New-Keynesian and neoclassical theoretical models (one of the culmination points being the DSGE models). One cannot blame mainstream macroeconomics for this. But the risk is to "lock oneself" into a theoretical framework, into an explanatory system that prevents the emergence of new and disruptive ways of reading the reality. On this point, see the stimulating paper by Gali (2018).

There are many historical illustrations of the processes by which new ideas that deviate from the dominant points of view generate paradigm shifts only after they have been embedded in the dominant paradigm for a longer or shorter time. Either the new ideas accommodate the dominant paradigm, and in this case we have "syntheses". Or they do not fit (because the reasoning framework of the dominant paradigm does not allow to bring out all the mechanisms to describe reality). In this case, alternative theories and frameworks are developed. Their scientific diffusion is more or less rapid and depends on non-economic factors (depending on whether some theorists want to push their ideas in order to keep the old models, despite their difficulties in explaining the observed reality).

Let us consider the first example. Keynes' detractors (notably Pigou and those who favored a Marshallian approach to describing macroeconomic equilibria) often criticized him for the lack of formal rigorous models to expose his main hypotheses (nominal rigidity, irrational expectations, non-clearing markets), which his literary formulation sometimes made confusing (they said). However, these ideas eventually became accepted, when the synthesis with neoclassical models were made by authors such as Samuelson and Hicks. The contribution of the so-called Classical-Keynesian synthesis was to bring the New-Keynesian ideas into the policy arena using the language of mainstream macroeconomics at that time. This is an illustration of the fact that heterodox ideas sometimes have needed to be brought to the corpus of the dominant system of thought before being considered by the scientific community. Apart from the synthesis models (Classical-Keynesian, or New-Keynesian), Keynesian ideas continued to spread by rejecting a certain number of assumptions of neoclassical theory (post-Keynesian, neo-Cambridgian models, etc.). Current events and the transformations of capitalism are giving renewed interest to post-Keynesian analyses.

To take the second example, there was a scientific "fashion" in growth analysis during the 1990s to incorporate institutional and governance variables into theoretical and empirical neoclassical models of growth. These analyses have been very useful. They have made it possible to integrate into reasoning the fact that economic growth is embedded in social, political, and cultural reality. This is an argument that has long been put forward in structuralist analyses of growth that associate growth with institutional regimes. Structuralist models have not regained interest, however (they are mainly used by development economists). The ideas have been taken up in neoclassical models of growth, but without the theoretical framework of institutional economics which are still considered as heterodox.

The third example is the following. During the 1960s, post-Keynesian and neoclassical economists had a different interpretation of what a production function is. For the former, it was a stylized representation of the technology of production. For the post-Keynesians, it was no more and no less than a rule for sharing value added between workers and employers. Until the 1990s, growth models based on the functional distribution of income were in the curriculum up to the PhD level. Then they were no longer studied in a systematic way. Neoclassical and New-Keynesian models of growth became mainstream, and many researchers started to work on endogenous growth. This is still the case today, though periods of fast growth have induced an explosion of inequalities (as suggested by the historical evidence provided by the works of Piketty, Stiglitz, and other authors).

An important question is whether growth theories should be primarily concerned with efficiency in the allocation of capital or with issues of wealth distribution, ex-ante or ex-post. Depending on what is chosen, the theoretical frameworks are not identical. The economic mechanisms for achieving each of these two objectives can be conflicting. Growth theorists believe, in good faith, that the best way to remedy inequality is to have the highest possible income flow and then redistribute it through, for example, taxation. Recent post-growth theories propose a radically different approach. To reduce income and wealth inequality, we need to change our objective. It is no longer a question of targeting economic growth but rather the satisfaction of basic needs—including immaterial needs—and access for all to common goods and services.

The fourth striking example concerns finance and two hypotheses that have been predominant in the works of financial macroeconomics, that of market efficiency and rational expectations of actors in the asset markets. The Great Financial Crisis and the inability of mainstream models to anticipate it led macroeconomists to once again take into consideration ideas previously formulated by Keynes (irrational exuberance) and Minsky (the financial instability hypothesis), and to focus on theoretical models in which the fundamental values of assets are formally indeterminate (they do not exist at all, because the multiple equilibria that result from transactions between agents correspond to equilibria of common conventions). This explains the existence of persistent dynamics in asset prices without mean-reverting phenomena. The economics of conventions has long emphasized this, and some recent areas of research analyze the role of Knightian Uncertainty Hypothesis (KUH) in macroeconomics. For instance, this hypothesis is proposed by a research program dedicated to imperfect knowledge economics, developed at the Institute for New Economic Thinking with authors such as Roman Frydman, Soren Johansen, Andreas

Rahbeh, Morten Tabor, and Michaël Golberg. Thus, since expectations can only result from subjective and changing psychological processes, economic behavior can only generate uncertainty that is impossible to foresee.

In this chapter, we choose to summarize some views of heterodox macroeconomists on three topics investigated in the previous chapters (inflation, monetary policy, and growth), focusing on an idea that is common to all heterodox economists. There is no such thing as "pure" economics, as introduced by neoclassical economists and abstracting from institutions. In our discussions, we present the details of neither the analytical frameworks nor the models. We expose the main principles. The interested reader can refer to several journals and websites where heterodox ideas on inflation, growth, and monetary policy have been discussed in recent years. This literature is rich, based on modern quantitative and qualitative tools of theoretical and empirical analysis. For example, one can look at the website of the INET (Institute for New Economic Thinking), a think tank founded after the 2008 financial crisis. Many journals offer heterodox views on macroeconomics confronted with recent real facts: among them, Journal of Post-Keynesian Economics, Review of Political Economy, Cambridge Journal of Economics, and Studies in Political Economy. A complete view of heterodox journals is provided by the Heterodox Economics Directory (general and field-specific journals). To use Kuhn's vocabulary, the views of the so-called orthodox economics, that of the dominant New-Keynesian model, can be considered as belonging to "normal" science, while the heterodox models belong to extraordinary science (i.e., they call for a paradigm revolution to go beyond existing paradigms).

8.1   INFLATION REGIMES AND MODES OF REGULATION OF CAPITALISM

A contribution of the structuralist approaches to the analysis of wages and inflation has been to emphasize that wages, prices, and the level of employment are not only indicators reflecting labor and good market imbalances. They are also linked to wage-setting institutions, to conflicts within firms, and to the bargaining power of unions. This reality can be incorporated into macroeconomic models of unemployment and inflation in two ways. The first approach was provided during the 1990s by labor market theories highlighting the strategic equilibria (see, for instance, the theories of implicit contracts or insiders-outsiders). An alternative approach is to consider that a labor market is first and foremost a social institution. Authors such as Aoki (1988) and Solow (1990)—who are not categorized as institutional economists—have shown that this is key to understanding how prices and wages evolve across time.

8.1.1 Inflation, Wages, and Competitive Market Capitalism from 1760 to 1913

Let us start with the period of the first industrial revolution, between the decades 1760–1770 and 1845, which was the period of the coal revolution and important innovations in the iron and steel industry, textiles, mining, the steam engine, and chemistry sector. It was also a period of triumph of a competitive mode of regulation (particularly in the United Kingdom and the United States), illustrated by several phenomena. First, wages and employment were sensitive to changes in industrial production. Nominal wages and prices were also highly correlated. The emergence of a working class of factory workers living in poverty was accompanied by an expansion—and concentration—of capital and labor in the colonized countries. This export of factors of production was equivalent to technical progress which saved capital and land in Europe. Second, economic growth was accompanied by a trend increase in prices. Nominal wages also rose—due to an increase in production prices—but less rapidly than inflation. This led to increases in "profit inflation" in several regions such as the United Kingdom, Castilla, and France (see Hamilton 1942). Rising wages and prices were caused by growing urbanization, migration from rural areas to urbanized regions, and high rates of investment. This resulted in higher production prices.

The following period between 1848 and 1873 was a continuation of the previous one. It was the apogee of the competitive mode of regulation of capitalism. At this time too, prices and wages rose sharply. But for other reasons than in the previous period. Indeed, although the dominant economic doctrine was liberalism, tensions and social struggles caused by the impoverishment of the working class and the harsh working conditions of the workforce led to institutional changes. Labor laws underwent important changes (minimum legal working age, reduction of daily working hours, laws on workers' associations, legalization of unions). Prices rose as a result of upward wage pressure.

Moreover, the excesses of speculation by banks in the real estate sector caused a great crisis that lasted from 1873 to 1896 and was characterized by a long period of disinflation and then prolonged deflation. In a context of recession, the productive sector saved its profits by proceeding to massive mergers through the absorption of companies weakened by the economic and financial crisis. This was a period of development of large industrial groups in the hegemonic nations at that time (konzern in Germany, trusts in the United States, zaïbatsu in Japan). The paradox of this period is therefore that it was a period of economic expansion and deflation. Changes in social legislation implied that wages fell less quickly than prices. And companies maintained their profits by increasing their substitution between capital and labor.

Declining trend inflation stopped between 1897 and 1913, with wholesale prices rising on average between 50% and 60%.

In summary, between the beginning of the first industrial revolution and the beginning of the First World War, the competitive market mode of regulation of capitalism in the hegemonic nations explained the dynamics of wages and prices. The forces at work were of several kinds: geography, which made it possible to exploit new technologies on a large scale in the colonies; capital flows, which allowed financial capitalism to flourish; and the lag between wage and price increases, which enabled the productive sector to maintain its profits.

8.1.2   Inflation, Wages, and Competitive Market Capitalism Since the Mid-1990s

Another period of competitive market regulation, with characteristics quite similar to those just mentioned, started in the mid-1980s. It has been a period characterized by a long downward trend in consumer prices.

This period corresponds to another era of globalization. Not only were financial capital flows multiplied across the planet, but so were trade flows. Markets were deregulated, balance of payments capital accounts were opened, and there was a great period of generalized tariff reduction. In this context, the forces that governed the dynamics of inflation and wages were linked to the evolution of production costs.

Since the mid-1990s, consumer price inflation has been correlated with changes in producer prices. The following factors have been at play: nominal wage growth, labor productivity gains, interest rate changes, capital productivity growth, changes in import costs, and taxes. Until very recently, the industrialized countries have evolved in a regime of falling inflation that has subsequently stabilized at low levels, in direct relation to the evolution of these components.

The deregulation of labor markets has led to a wage compression phenomenon through a decorrelation between nominal wage growth and labor productivity gains. This has accelerated with the weakening of the role of trade unions in wage negotiations. Downward pressures on wages were amplified by the structural transformation of labor markets (temporary and fixed-term contracts, proliferation of low-skilled jobs). Globalization has crushed production costs in international value chains. The participation of China and Asian countries to the WTO has had a strong impact, as have strategies to outsource tasks (offshoring, outsourcing). The cost of imports has therefore fallen. Finally, the greater integration of economies has led to tariff dismantling (lower taxes on imports) and encouraged tax incentives for foreign direct investment.

Since the end of the Covid-19 health crisis, these factors are now working in opposite directions and are likely to explain the emergence of a new long upward phase of inflation. Indeed, the rise in inequality and the increase in revolts and strikes among the middle classes are now leading to new societal compromises favoring higher wages (increase in minimum wages are an illustration). Moreover, the cost of imports is likely to rise sharply. "Slowbalisation" (slowdown of international trade flows) and the search for more sovereignty in the industrial and commercial policies will imply a resizing of international value chains. Geopolitical rivalries are accelerating these phenomena.

8.1.3 The Wage-Price Loop in Post-war Contractual Capitalism

The 30-year period following the end of the Second World War was characterized by contractual capitalism. This means that collective bargaining has been at the center of macroeconomic regulation. Wages and prices moved in tandem, as unions negotiated with company representatives the conditions for their progression. This was a time when economic growth was supported by counter-cyclical Keynesian policies (through transfers to households) and when the degree of financial openness of economies was low. The economies were financed through a repression of nominal interest rates in an inflationary context that allowed governments to borrow at low real interest rates). Massive investment by firms, and governments, to develop infrastructure and housing and to satisfy mass consumption was possible because of strong regulation of the banking and credit sectors and bargaining over working conditions. Inflation between 1950 and 1979 was mainly driven by the wage-price loop. The high inflation that occurred during this period was due to the "struggle" between different social groups (especially workers and business managers) to increase their real incomes (wages and profits) in a direction that was favorable to them. This was possible because several conditions were satisfied.

First, productivity gains, the low degree of internationalization, and the concentration of capital (consolidation of firms) made it possible to maintain profits at high levels and to meet workers' demands for wage increases. Such increases were possible because of a process of diffusion to all sectors of the economy. In a contractual regime, imbalances in the labor markets do not explain changes in prices and wages. The key factor is agents' expectations on productivity gains.

Second, strong state intervention, in Europe at least, with the aim of social progress, was a characteristic of the post-war period. It has contributed to increasing the bargaining power of employees by imposing standards (minimum wages, branch agreements to define pay progression, working conditions, and dismissal).

Finally, companies were able to rely on public demand, given the high level of government spending, financed by debt in a context of financial repression with capped interest rates.

A country that illustrates post-war contractual capitalism is Japan. Until the mid-1990s, the Japanese wage and employment system was determined by two rules: the life-long employment system (LES) and the seniority wage system (SWS). Once hired in a company, employees were guaranteed not to be fired until they retired. This was a way of keeping them loyal to an employer in a highly competitive environment where Japan was innovating and where the positive externalities associated with sector returns to scale were not yet being discussed. The SWS was introduced in 1920 and became widespread after the Second World War. Wages were indexed to the cost of living (to ensure that workers had a minimum standard of living) and increased regularly and automatically over the life cycle according to the grids set up within the firms. This corresponds to the so-called "Densan model". In addition to cost-of-living indexation, wages included a component linked to the characteristics of the workers (qualifications, region of residence) and to working conditions (hardship). The LES and the SWS operated through a system of consultation in the companies (in particular the setting up of Joint Consultation Committees). The governance model was that of stakeholder, taking into account the well-being of all the agents contributing to the activity of the companies. There were rounds of wage negotiations, in which trade unions and company managers played a leading role. For in-depth analyses of the Japanese system (and the transformations that have taken place since the mid-1990s), the interested reader can refer to Imai (2011), Nishimura (2017), Ogoshi (2006), Watanabe (2000).

8.1.4   Conflicts over the Sharing of Income at the Beginning of the Twenty-first Century

If we assume that negotiations on income sharing are the driving force behind price and wage variations, the beginning of the twenty-first century has several characteristics.

Since the deregulation of labor markets in most industrialized countries, the model that has prevailed is the result-based model for wages. In a highly competitive global context, companies have proceeded to organizational restructuring. In addition, the proportion of non-regular employment compared to regular employment has increased. Atypical work has developed and tends to become the norm in some activities. In the sectors at the cutting edge of innovation and where productivity gains are being made, there is a high concentration of capital (Internet, digital activities, information and communication technology, pharmaceutical industries). All this is likely to compress wages and increase profits. Until now, inflation rates have remained low, but exogenous shocks are causing them to rise.

Labor markets are characterized by an increasing fragmentation phenomenon. This has led to a change in the status of workers with the multiplication of self-employed workers. A priori, this is not likely to favor the role of negotiations between labor and employers on working conditions, wage progression, and so on. The new and emerging role of online work has also led to changes in labor market equilibrium and the determination of compensation rules. This has eroded solidarity among workers and weakened collective bargaining power.

There are forces pushing for a return to collaborative bargaining in wage setting. This is happening for several reasons.

(1) In the context of slowbalisation, changes in international value chains will stop to the strong compression of import prices that has resulted, so far, from globalization. The context of uncertainty accentuated by the succession of crises is pushing governments to encourage short circuits for the production and supply of goods and services.

(2) In companies, a stakeholder governance model is growing. In the shareholder value model, the purpose is to increase the stock market value of a firm in order to meet shareholders' financial return requirements. An alternative to shareholder capitalism is stakeholder capitalism. In Germany, for example, German labor law encourages a co-determination of the objectives of employees and companies. Firms that wish to do so can set up councils representing employees who participate in board decisions alongside the shareholders. This so-called "co-determination" system increases employee participation in management decisions. The objective is to maximize shareholder remuneration by satisfying the interests of the company's other stakeholders, particularly employees. In stakeholder capitalism, the transaction costs of achieving the shareholders' objective are minimized (e.g., there are fewer social conflicts). The conceptual differences between the two systems are summarized in Table 8.1 from Dennehy (2012).

It is difficult to say how long the current regime of competitive regulation by markets in financialized capitalism will last. The behavior of the younger generations toward work invites us to reconsider the determinants of labor supply. Some people refuse a job, even a well-paid one, because factors other than the division of time between leisure and labor play a role in the decision to work and in wage requirements. Some agents prefer work that is less well paid, but which generates less stress and allows them to have a balanced life between work and social activities (which are not leisure). Some companies face difficulty recruiting in some sectors, despite high wages. Moreover, social fractures and inequalities have led to the same phenomenon as that observed at the beginning of the industrial revolutions. The middle classes identify themselves as a socially "oppressed" social group and use other means than unionization to exert pressure on employers. In particular, in the era of social networks, the phenomenon of "reputation" is becoming crucial for companies seeking to maintain their brand profile. The working conditions in the package offered by recruiters are again becoming an argument to attract workers.

Table 8.1 Corporate governance: differences between shareholder and stakeholder contractual arrangement

	Shareholder	Stakeholder
Main objective	Maximize shareholder wealth	Multiple objectives of parties with different interests
Governance structure	Managers are agents of shareholders	Stakeholder-elected board of directors
Governance process	Control	Cooperation, coordination, and conflict resolution
Performance measures	Shareholder value enough to maintain investors' commitment	Fair distribution of value to maintain stakeholders' commitment
Risk holders	Shareholders	All stakeholders

8.2   Implication for the Theoretical Framework of Inflation Analysis

For an overview of theories of inflation among heterodox economists, including post-Keynesians, the reader can refer to chapter 8 in Lavoie (2015)'s book or Levy (2000). In what follows, we present just a few ideas about the approaches where the division of national income is a basis for discussing the determination of inflation.

8.2.1   National Account Framework

If inflation is the result of social relations in capitalism, then the analytical framework from which to start any analysis is national accounting. For an open economy with a government, we define the following variables:

T: taxes,
M: imports,
INV: private investment,
DIV: dividends,
G: public expenditure (current spending and public investment),
C: consumption,

X: exports,
P: GDP deflator,
Q: GDP in volume,
W: nominal wage rate,
L: labor (number of hours worked),
R: nominal interest rate,
K: volume of capital.

Profits are defined as the difference between GDP and wages plus property income (dividends). Considering the interest rate r as the return to capital, profits are also defined by the product of r and the volume of capital K. We therefore write

$$RK \equiv PQ - WL + DIV \Leftrightarrow PQ \equiv RK + WL - DIV. \qquad (8.1)$$

We can use this equation to define the balance between resources and uses. If we assume that there are two types of households in the economy, workers and owners of firms (shareholders or capitalists), they consume out of their wages and dividends. We write:

$$T + PQ + M \equiv RK + WL - DIV \equiv C + INV + G + X. \qquad (8.2)$$

Investment represents the value of non-financial assets. This corresponds to net investment taking into account the depreciation of capital stock and net changes in inventory stocks. This equation can also be rewritten as follows:

$$RK \equiv -(WL - C) + DIV + INV + (G - T) - (M - X). \qquad (8.3)$$

$(G - T)$ and $(M - T)$ are respectively the budget overall deficit and trade deficit. $(WL - C)$ is households' saving.

Price adjustments reflect the sharing of national income among different actors: domestic and foreign firms, the government, workers, and shareholders. Prices vary according to expansion and recession phases. According to post-Keynesian economists, profits are the driving force of the business cycle and inflation. There are two important points. First, firms do not have a production function and entrepreneurs are not agents who adopt an optimizing behavior to define their production level. Employees are not paid at their marginal productivity level. The reality is simpler.

Entrepreneurs face a technological constraint that is materialized by the capital/output ratio. Given such a constraint, they use profit strategies to produce value.

Income shares determine demand (the right-hand side of the equation) and sellers' base pricing determines supply (left-hand side of the equation). Prices adjust so that the above identity is always satisfied. Dividing each side by PQ, we obtain:

$$rv_K \equiv -\frac{1}{a_L}(\omega - ca_L) + div + inv + bdef - tdef, \qquad (8.4)$$

where

r and ω : real interest rate and real wage rate,
a_L: labor productivity,
div : ratio of dividends over nominal GDP,
c: propensity to consume,
$bdet$ and $tdef$: overall budget deficit and trade deficit (both as a ratio of GDP).

Firms' profit can be positive only if households' saving is negative (or equivalently if the wage rate is below labor productivity). If there are no banks, firms may hold claims on households (e.g., by selling them goods on credits). If there is a banking sector households can borrow from their bank. Households' debt keeps profits up. If the capital ratio is given, all else equal, for households to increase their debt (or dissave), the real interest rate must decrease, and therefore prices must rise.

There is a self-fulfilling phenomenon between investment rate and profit rate. Firms choose their investment level according to their expectations of future profits. As they extrapolate past trends into the present and future, expectations are bullish during economic expansions and bearish during recessions. An increase in investment increases production and thus profits. This mechanism works in the opposite direction during recessions. If expectations are too optimistic (which leads firms to invest and produce more than the level of demand), prices rise and cause real wages and the real interest rate to fall. On the contrary, if expectations are too pessimistic, excess production causes prices to fall and real wages and the real interest rate to rise.

Fiscal policy has counter-cyclical effects. During a recession, an increase in the budget deficit raises output and prices and cushions the decline in profits associated with the recession. The opposite phenomenon occurs during expansions. Budget deficits thus set a floor for profits and prices during downturns in the business cycle and a floor during expansions.

An increase in the trade deficit increases the profit of foreign forms at the expense of the domestic country.

The different variables on the right-hand side of the equation can be endogenized by proposing theories and mechanisms linking them to the inflation rate. By influencing prices, they should allow the real interest rate and the real wage rate to adjust so that the identity is always satisfied ex-post.

Any variable on the right-hand side of the equation can be made endogenous by proposing theories and mechanisms linking them to the inflation rate. By influencing prices, they should allow the real interest rate and the real wage rate to adjust so that the identity is always satisfied ex-post. The real wage ω can be related to agents' inflation expectations and to disequilibria in the labor and goods markets. The real interest rate may depend on portfolio arbitrage and shareholder governance. The trade balance may depend on the real exchange rate (and therefore on foreign prices). Labor productivity can be modeled according to Verdoorn's law relating it to the growth rate of output. Finally, we can even introduce a fiscal theory of inflation to model the effects of changes in the overall deficit on prices. Whatever the theories, the important feature is that the model must necessarily incorporate the previous identity. In empirical terms, this relationship could be considered, for example, as the cointegration or long-run relationship that constrains the different variables to evolve in accordance with the identity.

8.2.2   Heterodox Interpretation of the Phillips Curve: Example

A key assumption of the structuralist theories of inflation is that income distribution is the driver of inflation. We present here a simple example of a theory linking the inflation rate to the wage share. For a detailed presentation, the reader can refer to Aquanno and Brennan (2016), Bloch et al. (2007), Jany-Catrice (2020), Taylor and Barbosa Filho (2021), and Vera (2017).

Figure 8.1, taken from Taylor and Barbosa Filho (2021) shows an illustration of a structuralist reading of wage bargaining. The Y-axis shows the inflation rate set by firms. On the X-axis is the wage share, which is

Inflation rate

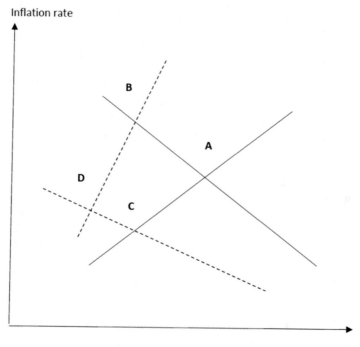

Wage share

Fig. 8.1 Structural approach to wage bargaining

negotiated between employees and employers. The lines with a positive slope describe the response of firms to the level of the wage share. If the wage share increases, they respond by raising prices to avoid a fall in profits. Nominal wages are assumed to adjust with a delay to inflation (nominal rigidities). The lines with negative slope represent the antagonism between wages and profits in the income distribution. Inflation determines the level of profits, while nominal wages determine the wage share. The antagonism between wages and profits explains the decreasing relationship between inflation and the wage share.

Point A corresponds to the initial point of agreement in the bargaining. It lies on a "stable share" line to indicate that it is an agreement situation. There are several such situations (described by all the points located on a decreasing line). Among them, the firm decides which one to select by setting the inflation rate that gives it a desired level of profit.

If a positive demand shock occurs, the initial positively sloped line shifts to the left, and the new trade-off point is point B. The mechanism is as follows. An expansionary policy leads, everything else constant, to an increase in demand. Firms therefore increase their level of production. Since production costs have risen, they must raise their prices. Profits rise and the wage share falls.

On the other hand, if the initial agreement between employees and employers is at point C, the expansionary policy reduces the wage share sharply and inflation increases slightly. Point C describes a situation where the bargaining power of employees is low. The position of the lines depends on market structures. As regards the lines describing the response of firms, those operating in oligopolistic markets have significant power to set their mark-up. For the stable share lines, the bargaining power of employees depends on the structure of the labor markets (nature of the jobs held, characteristics of the labor markets, wage levels, etc.).

8.3   MODERN MONETARY THEORY

What the public knows as modern monetary theory (MMT) is a theory that analyzes monetary policy and its links to fiscal policy in a counterfactual framework. What if, instead of the separation between governments and central banks that is enshrined in orthodox macroeconomics, the two entities were merged and their balance sheets consolidated into one? In this same counterfactual framework of thought, we must reason within a framework where money in the broad sense (which includes the enormous liquidity created in financial markets by issuers of securities and borrowers) is entirely controlled by the state. This is important to note to begin with. Indeed, some critics of this theory point to the unrealistic nature of its assumptions (see, e.g., Rochon and Vernengo 2003; Drumetz and Pfister 2021) or they make a confusion between the monetization of debt and the monetization of deficits (see for instance Prinz and Beck 2021). These are unfair criticisms, which overlooks the fact that MMT considers an institutional framework that is very different from the one that exists today and that MMT proponents want to change.

The success of MMT (with public opinion) is not surprising in a context where repeated economic crises call into question the foundations of the macro-financial governance on which economies have operated for several decades. This does not mean that we have to agree with all the proposals of the MMT. But if there are criticisms to be made, they should be directed at the internal inconsistency of the arguments being put forward. Moreover, it is a theory that still needs to be refined and to which several strands of economic thought are making contributions, in particular post-Keynesian, institutionalist, and Marxian economists.

In the next paragraphs, we discuss neither all the proposals of MMT nor its relations with other heterodox schools of thought. We limit ourselves to a few aspects, related to the issues discussed in the previous chapters. In particular, we will study the respective roles of fiscal and monetary policies in macroeconomic regulation. The analysis is based on a specific conception of the money circuit and money creation.

MMT suffers from the limitations of any nascent theory. Indeed, it remains poorly formalized, which leaves the door open to various interpretations. The lack of formalization introduces a certain "vagueness" into some proposals when one wants to know what exactly its contributions are in relation to other schools of thought—Keynesian and neo-Keynesian in particular. Another difficulty is that the ideas have spread very well among public opinion and in the media, and less so in academic circles, where it is criticized either for reformulating theories already put forward by others, or for being unrealistic, or for lacking scientific rigor.

Yet, there are innovative and interesting ideas in MMT, even if not all the measures it advocates would be feasible within the current institutional framework. For the most important ideas in the theory, see Ehnts and Höfgen (2019), Mitchell and Muysken (2008), Nersisyan and Wray (2016), Mitchell et al. (2019), Tymoigne and Wray (2015), Wray (1998), Wray (2012), Wray (2019), and the recent collective work by Wray et al. (2023). For examples of models, see Palley (2015), Prinz and Beck (2021). Some authors attempt to reconcile the ideas of MMT with certain principles of post-Keynesian macroeconomics (see Lavoie 2019, 2022).

To avoid considering that MMT conveys unrealistic ideas, we will consider it for what it is, that is, a normative theory that proposes a counterfactual theoretical framework to the existing ones in mainstream macroeconomics. It is based on several assumptions that do not always describe reality but rather what reality might be if the institutional framework of economic and financial governance were different from what it has been for the past 40 years. For example, it is difficult to understand MMT without reference to its proponents' vision of money. The latter, issued by the central bank, is a counterpart of the government's debt. Another example, its authors consider a world without involuntary unemployment, since the state offers every unemployed individual in the private sector a job in the public sector paid at a fixed wage rate. The economies studied are thus always at full employment.

Although MMT has weaknesses and limitations, some of the criticisms that have been made are not well motivated. They are explained either by a misunderstanding of the theses defended by its proponents or by formalized misrepresentations on the part of those who criticize this theory, because they reason outside the framework of MMT's thinking. Typical illustrations are Palley (2015), Palley (2019), Drumetz and Pfister (2021). For a few rare, formalized presentations of MMT, faithful to the theoretical frameworks of this school of thought, see Hannsgen (2014), Mitchell et al. (2019), and Tanaka (2021).

8.3.1 Some Contributions of MMT to the Analysis of Economic Policy

The success of MMT can be understood as the consequence of a reaction to what has been the backbone of the mainstream economists' vision of economic policy over the last 40 years: (1) a hierarchization of economic policy objectives with inflation at the forefront, sometimes sacrificing another objective that also affects people's standard of living, that is, unemployment and economic growth; (2) a resulting hierarchy of economic policies, that is, the central role of monetary policy in curbing inflation, the neutrality of fiscal policies in normal times; (3) the belief that the functioning of markets is sufficient to "naturally" regulate the growth and unemployment rates that economies need (which policymakers have emphasized by extolling the importance of so-called structural policies); (4) financial markets are sufficient to finance public debts and allow for an optimal allocation of resources by forcing governments to manage their budgets appropriately. Even countries that have tried to relax these principles have maintained the distinction between these three levers of economic policy. This is the case, for example, with the Abenomics policies in Japan. The euro zone is probably the example that most illustrates the separation between the three instruments of monetary policy, which has been enshrined in rules according to a strategy that can be described as ordoliberalism.

Criticisms of this way of thinking have led to a revision of the theoretical foundations of economic policy by putting forward theoretical approaches based on neo-chartalism and functional finance. The approach is motivated by the fact that MMT theorists consider that the main objectives of economic policy should be the achievement of full employment and the guarantee that each person can have access to common goods and services: access to health and education, access to decent jobs and wages, the right to live in an unpolluted natural environment, the right not to be subjected to a situation of poverty and precariousness in a sustainable way, the right for future generations to live in a world without global warming and with natural resources that are not depleted, and so on. These objectives cannot be fully achieved by the markets, which have their own objectives (notably profitability and short-term profitability). The achievement of these objectives is above all a matter of state power.

The first important question is that of money creation and the monetary circuit. With regard to the former, although MMT analyses often refer to the legacy of the chartalist theories of the early twentieth century, we can go further back in history to situate their approach, in particular to the theses put forward by the banking school in the nineteenth century. To put it simply, there is an opposition between those who think that the important issue is that of excessive money creation (for fear of inflation) and those who think that this is not the important issue: what matters is that the money and liquidity that circulates are intended to finance the needs of economic agents. In economic terms, what is fundamental is therefore the exogenous or endogenous character of money creation. Like the chartists, or the theorists of the Banking school, the theories of MMT are based on a conception of endogenous money. They are not the only ones (Keynesians and neo-Keynesians share this same vision). There is no reason for this system to generate inflation if money is issued in return for "real effects" and as long as the money issued grows at the same rate as output. There are several important points about MMT that differentiate it from other approaches to endogenous money.

Money Creation

According to MMT, money creation is the counterpart of the issuance of a public debt by the government to the central bank (i.e., to itself if the two institutions are not separated). This debt is equivalent to an expenditure on credit. This is an "extreme" situation, observed, for example, in a crisis. If commercial banks do not wish to hold government securities (e.g., because they fear default), then the central bank, which is not independent of the government, can buy these securities on the secondary bond market. This operation is equivalent to monetary financing of public debt. This proposal by MMT should be understood as a critique of the current functioning of central banks, which it criticizes for having self-imposed constraints: no authorized overdraft on their account and the existence of ceilings on the volumes of public debt that can be financed.

Contrary to what the loanable funds theory claims, an increase in government deficits lowers interest rates. It does not have crowding-out effects. Indeed, suppose that deficits are financed by government debt issues purchased by the central bank. By funding the government account with central bank money in exchange, this increases the supply of central bank money in the monetary system and lowers interest rates. This corresponds, for example, to what was observed during the purchase of government assets in secondary markets during quantitative easing policies. Moreover, monetary financing of budget deficits prevents private savings from being crowded out by public deficits.

Policy Mix

Another important issue is the way in which the state budget is conceived. Government deficits are indispensable in normal times, given the central role of governments in economies. MMT theories treat spending and taxes asymmetrically. Spending regulates the level of aggregate demand, while taxes regulate inflation by influencing the purchasing power of economic agents. Inflation has a fiscal origin—in addition to the influence of production costs that determine the evolution of relative prices. Moreover, in an economy where the private financial sector holds part of the securities issued by governments, central banks can curb inflation rates by buying and selling sovereign bonds through open market operations. Monetary policy thus appears as a substitute for taxes to finance public spending. Why this asymmetry between taxes and expenditures in a government's budget? The answer is that MMT has also inherited another approach, in addition to chartalism, which is functional finance. The principle was laid down in the 1940s and 1950s by Lerner (1943) and Lerner (1947).

The issue is identical to that of Keynesian theory, that is, how to achieve full employment and price stability. Lerner's influence lies in the fact that taxation is not considered as a budgetary phenomenon but as a monetary phenomenon. Indeed, the functional approach to finance refutes the idea that one should transpose to the state (an entity with a monopoly on money creation) the constraints encountered, at the microeconomic level, by firms and households that are obliged to balance their expenditures and resources. The concept of the state budget constraint comes from the microeconomics of individual behavior. Imposing a balancing rule or a target on deficits and debt makes no sense. On the contrary, both can fluctuate as long as they ensure full employment and avoid inflationary situations. When the economy is underemployed, the government must increase its own spending to stimulate aggregate demand. Conversely, it must contract its own spending when there is an inflationary risk. A government avoids the risk of overheating by raising taxes and reducing its debt, that is, by reducing the monetary financing of budget deficits.

MMT thus proposes a policy mix that is the opposite of that of mainstream economics. The regulation of the cycle and of inflation is the responsibility of fiscal policy. Monetary policy is subordinated to fiscal policy and must aim at the sustainability of public finances. In the MMT approach, the balance of public finances is therefore not an objective to be attained (for a more detailed analysis, see, e.g., Brady 2020; Rochon and Vernengo 2003).

Fighting Inflation

A third original topic of MMT concerns the stabilization of inflation (if we accept that it is caused in part by excessive wage increases) through a job guarantee mechanism. Indeed, in their analysis of wage and inflation dynamics, the government targets a steady state full-employment rate of unemployment. This is an alternative to trying to reduce the unemployment rate as much as possible to an incompressible level (the NAIRU). According to MMT theorists, the mechanism that allows an economy to be permanently at the level of full employment is the guarantee of employment by the state (this idea of an employer of last resort is already found in authors such as Kalecki or Minsky. For a detailed presentation of the so-called Job Guarantee program, see Tcherneva 2012). Any worker laid off in the private sector can find a job in the public sector at a fixed wage rate. The latter can correspond to a minimum wage corresponding to the subsistence minimum. One can imagine, for example, that this is a situation of "waiting unemployment". In order not to lose human capital, or simply to limit the social costs of unemployment (individual and collective costs), a worker can be offered training or an activity while being paid at a fixed rate, until the probability of finding a job in the private sector becomes more important. One can also imagine a system of unemployment benefits of a fixed amount, with an obligation to train or to take up public sector jobs in return. Public sector employment is thus described by MMT theorists as "buffer employment", and they define a quantity that is the BER (buffer employment rate) measured by the ratio between public sector employment and total employment (the latter is also full employment).

The BER is a counter-cyclical variable that acts as an inflation stabilizer. During recessions, instead of unemployment rising, BER rises. Aggregate demand from the private sector falls as the recession reduces demand for labor and lowers wage rates in that sector. As those laid off in the private sector migrate to the public sector and receive a fixed wage, this dampens the decline in aggregate demand in the economy. During expansions, the BER decreases the public wage bill, and some of the workers initially employed in the public sector migrate to the private sector. Wages rise in the private sector, as the demand for labor increases. But the increase is influenced by the level of the fixed wage in the public sector. The latter thus serves as an anchor for inflationary expectations and mark-up setting behavior of firms. According to MMT theory, a key concept for a government is the search for a NAIBER (non-accelerating-inflation buffer employment ratio), instead of the NAIRU. This implies setting the inflation target beyond which inflation should not accelerate by changing the composition of employment. Contrary to what is sometimes said, MMT does not claim that it is possible for a country to reach full employment with an inflation rate of zero. The authors call inflation a sustained rise or fall in prices. Thus, we should rather understand that there is a level of full employment for which there is neither acceleration nor deceleration of the inflation rate. This is the NAIBER that we mentioned earlier.

Let us assume that a government wishes to increase the level of full employment. In orthodox economics, this is not possible through cyclical policies (fiscal or monetary), but only through structural supply policies. According to MMT, the mechanism for achieving this is as follows. In order to reach a level of production corresponding to the target of full employment, the state increases public expenditure. This is financed in the following way. The central bank increases the monetary base, which increases the excess reserves of commercial banks. The interest rate in the interbank lending market falls. The lower cost of credit stimulates private demand. In addition, some of these excess reserves are lent to the government in exchange for the debt held by commercial banks. Government spending financed by this debt also stimulates activity. The demand for public sector labor increases, the BER decreases, private sector wages increase, and firms adjust their margins, which raises prices and generates inflation. What happens if inflation rises above the central bankers' desired target? Two types of measures are possible. One possibility is that the government reduces aggregate demand by raising taxes. The other possibility is for the central bank to increase the level of reserve requirements, so as to reduce the excess reserves of commercial banks and induce a rise in interest rates that increase the cost of credit. In both cases, the decline in part of aggregate demand implies that the BER increases. While remaining in a situation of full employment, the government chooses the BER that allows inflation to fluctuate around the target set by the central bank.

In this mechanism, it is fiscal policy (taxes and the public employment ratio) that allows the inflation target to be reached. The fixed-wage job guarantee mechanism also helps anchor private sector inflation expectations. Fiscal policy supports monetary policy. By modulating the amount of excess reserves held by commercial banks, it affects both the level of interest rates and the monetary financing of public debt.

8.3.2   Criticisms of MMT

One of the reasons why MMT is criticized by mainstream economics (and even by some heterodox schools of thought, such as the post-Keynesians) is that its counterfactual framework—the consolidation of government and central bank fiscal constraints—leads to policy proposals that seem unworkable and to theoretical inconsistencies. For recent criticisms, see Newman (2020), Palley (2019), Skousen (2020).

A Confusion of Money and Liquidity

MMT theorists reach several conclusions from their approach. The first is that there are no limits to money creation—apart from inflationary pressures—as long as it is used to finance public spending. The monetary financing of budget deficits is explained as a government going into debt in its own currency and borrowing from itself. Moreover, one of the reasons why the government does not have a budget constraint is that taxes are not used to finance public spending. They are considered as an instrument used to withdraw or, on the contrary, inject liquidity into the economy to curb inflation, by forcing economic agents to pay more taxes or, on the contrary, by reducing taxes. Money creation is "a credit" on public spending.

It is easy to see that one of the difficulties of MMT's reasoning is the confusion between money and the means of financing economic activities.

What matters is the liquidity that circulates in the economy. However, part of this liquidity is completely beyond the control of central banks, since it results from debts issued by some agents and purchased by other agents who have savings to invest. The engine of liquidity is credit, both that created by banks and that which emanates from lending and borrowing operations in the financial markets. According to the arguments of MMT, only central bank money is considered as a means of payment and reserve of value. Private currencies created by commercial banks, which account for a large part of money circulation, are neglected. The role of financial assets and liabilities, notably the bond market, in the financing of economies is not analyzed. One could say that for MMT theorists, the financing of public spending by taxes or through a public debt market is neutral for economic activity. MMT cannot therefore study the redistributive effects of the modes of financing budget deficits. This is one of the most important criticisms that can be made. The consolidation of the balance sheets of central banks and governments makes it impossible to grasp all the mechanisms of the monetary circuit in modern economies (see on this point the analyses of Lavoie 2014).

Government Budget Constraint in an Open Economy

Another very frequent criticism of MMT concerns one of its propositions, that is, there is no reason for a government to have a balanced budget constraint (even intertemporally), as long as a central bank is willing to buy public debt as a last resort. There is therefore no limit, in theory, to budget deficits. MMT theorists also say that the government must necessarily have a budget deficit in order for other agents to save. To examine these two propositions, we consider the case of an open economy. Indeed, a closed economy is of little interest given the high degree of financial integration between industrialized countries.

Considering the fiscal approach to the balance of payment, we have the following identity:

$$(G - T) = (Sp - Ip) - CA = (Sp - Ip) + CFA - RES \qquad (8.5)$$

where I and S stand for investment and savings, respectively, and the index p stands for private. G and T are, respectively, government expenditure and taxes. CA is the current account, and thus the negative sign indicates a deficit. CFA stands for capital and financial account, and RES stands for foreign exchange reserves. The difference in the left-hand side of the equality is the government's net dissaving, that is, the budget deficit (government expenditures minus budget revenues).

According to this equality, which is satisfied for any country in the world, the government deficit is constrained by the capital flows into the country to finance part of the current account deficit, by net savings of the domestic private sector and by the amount of foreign exchange reserves available. Let us assume an extreme case where net savings of the domestic private sector and the rest of the world equal zero. Under these conditions, we have $G = T$. The argument of MMT is that it is incorrect to consider that taxes T finance expenditures G. Indeed, their financing depends on money creation by the central bank. However, this identity says nothing about the financing operations, but simply allows for a comparison of resources and expenditures. They interpret this identity as a causal relationship. The government deficit triggers savings by other agents. According to this interpretation, there is indeed no limit to government deficits, because it is equivalent to saying that, whatever the deficit, the government will always find people willing to hold their savings in the form of sovereign bills and bonds. This is the case at least for domestic agents, since part of their savings is forced because they have to pay taxes.

Suppose that $(G - T) > (Sp - Ip) + CFA - RES$, assuming that CFA and RES are exogenous. If T increases, $(G - T)$ decreases, $(Sp - Ip)$ increases (people save more to pay taxes), and the equality is retrieved. This corresponds to a very specific case: money and sovereign debt are perfect substitutes. Money creation therefore depends on the amount of domestic public debt that the foreign private sector is willing to hold (through capital inflows). Depending on this amount, the central bank can force domestic agents to save by raising taxes. The rebalancing operation can only work if Sp increases faster than Ip (Ip increases because the budget deficit stimulates economic growth). But then, it is not necessary to raise taxes. Indeed, an increase in the budget deficit finances itself, because production increases faster than consumption, which increases Sp. If taxes are indexed to income, the government gets back some of the money it spent to finance its budget deficit. In this line of reasoning, money is not even necessary. It only plays a role if the behavior of the monetary sector is explicitly introduced. But a large budget deficit resulting in a large increase in taxes (or equivalently, in this case, an increase in central bank money) could lead to a fall in output, making the tax yield inefficient. The case of unlimited deficit described by MMT exists in reality, but it is certainly not related to monetary policy. One example is the United States, which issues

Table 8.2 Simplified balance sheet of the monetary sector

Assets	Liabilities
Foreign reserves: RES	Broad money: M
Net domestic assets	1.- Monetary base: M0
1.- Net domestic credits (private sector: Cp	1.1.-Currency (notes) = 0
2.- Net domestic credit (government: Cg	1.2.-Commercial banks reserves at the CB: CBR
3.-Sovereign bonds: 0	1.3.- Government account at the CB: G-T
4.-Other financial assets: 0	2.- Others = 0
	Quasi money: 0
Total: RES + Cp + Cg	Total: M = k M0 = k(CBR+G6T)

a currency that is the key currency in the international monetary system and for which world demand is strong. The other example is Japan, where net private savings are high because of demographic imbalances.

Let us now consider the consolidated balance sheet of the monetary sector, and let us assume, as MMT does, that the government is not independent of the central bank so that we can consolidate their balance sheets. For simplicity, we assume that budget deficits are financed by issuing money. A simplified balance sheet is as follows (in Table 8.2, CB means central bank). Moreover, we assume some components to be equal to zero, as they are not essential for the reasoning.

Let us assume that in an open economy the condition of purchasing power parity applies, that the money multiplier k equals 1, and that the demand for money depends on the national income PY, where P is the general price level and Y is the volume of production. We therefore have the following two relationships:

- PPP condition: $P = SP^*$ (S is the nominal exchange rate and $P*$ is the general price level abroad).
- Money demand: $Md = kPY$ (where k is a real number).

Monetary equilibrium implies the following relationship:

$$Cp + Cg + RES = kP^*SY \qquad (8.6)$$

The topic of the exchange rate regime is little discussed by MMT theorists. But it is important for the financing of budget deficits. Suppose that, in order to finance an increase in the budget deficit, the central bank decides to create central bank money equal to this deficit (an increase in Cg equivalent to an increase in $G - T$). The money supply becomes greater than the money demand. The implications are as follows.

Under a fixed exchange rate regime, the central bank must sell part of its reserves to prevent a depreciation of the domestic currency. For reserves to fall, there must be, all things being equal,

- less capital inflows,
- an increase in the current account deficit, or
- a mix of both situations.

Thus, with fixed exchange rates, the monetization of budget deficits offsets the decline in external financing. The monetary base does not increase. Money creation appears to be useful in the case of twin deficits (budgetary and external), and there is no reason for more inflation to appear. But a continuous decline in foreign exchange reserves may increase the probability of a balance of payments crisis.

In a regime of flexible exchange rate, money creation leads to a net excess supply of money and the rebalancing is done by a depreciation of the domestic currency (increase in S). Once again, this requires that one of the three previous situations occurs. This time the monetary base increases and the nominal depreciation may imply an increase in the general price level due to imported inflation. This time, money creation can be inflationary. Inflation can be high, if a high volume of money is created to finance budget deficits. To limit the inflationary effects, the central bank can decide to reduce private credit in order to reduce commercial banks' excess reserves. But in this case, the cost of monetary financing is a crowding-out effect on the private sector. If, as a result of this effect, output falls, the country can fall into a spiral of currency depreciation and eventually inflation.

With flexible exchange rates, there is therefore a limit to the monetary financing of public deficits, that is, the risks of recession and inflation.

Let us consider the more realistic case where economic agents hold their wealth, either in monetary form or in the form of financial assets. From the MMT point of view, money and domestic sovereign bonds are perfect substitutes. Under these conditions, the choice for agents is between holding money or foreign securities. Let us take the example of the floating exchange rate. Creating money to finance the budget deficit increases the monetary base. The central bank can, for example, buy part of the public debt through an open market operation. The increase in the money supply reduces the domestic interest rate and leads agents to prefer to hold more foreign assets (public debt of foreign countries). The national currency therefore depreciates, and we are faced with the inflationary risk mentioned above. In a fixed exchange rate regime, it is the foreign exchange reserves that decrease, and this can increase the risk of a balance of payments crisis.

Our conclusion is therefore as follows. Any central bank could decide at its own discretion how much central bank money it wants to create to finance public debts. But the practical limit to this creation is related to the costs it is willing to bear. This depends on the level of inflation it is willing to accept, its degree of aversion to the risks of economic recession, and the level of foreign exchange reserves needed to avoid a currency crisis. The argument that taxes can be raised to reduce inflationary pressures does not hold because inflation is not due to excess demand but to monetary depreciation directly linked to central bank policy. Money and taxes cannot therefore be considered as perfect substitutes.

Such aspects are little discussed by MMT, because it concentrates on another aspect, that is, the possibility that monetary financing of budget deficits removes the usual constraint stemming from the link between taxes and public spending. MMT rejects the idea of a budget constraint or balance. Money is not a resource for the state but corresponds to financing (unlike taxes). In the jargon of economists, monetary financing is recorded "below the line," while taxes and public spending are recorded "above the line" in the statement of government operations (see the chapter on fiscal policy). Writing a budget constraint in which money creation appears as a resource, in the same way as taxes, mixes concepts that are different in nature. According to MMT, the state can always close the gap between tax revenues and expenditures. It therefore has no constraints, as long as it can finance itself. Their view is to envisage a situation where, institutionally, the central bank is the holder of last resort of the public debt. There is thus a difference in approach from orthodox macroeconomics. The latter applies accounting concepts to the state that are only valid for private sector agents, who are indeed constrained in their financing.

A Concept of Fiscal Money

Let us assume that the proponents of MMT are right. Can a central bank acting as a buyer of last resort of public debt accept that it will never be repaid by a government? Indeed, the money that is created is the counterpart of the public debt, and this is shown by the fact that the central bank holds sovereign bonds on its balance sheet. MMT theorists go further. They consider that debt is not a problem in itself. In the hierarchy of macroeconomic imbalances, unemployment, inequality and poverty, inflation, and falling living standards are more important problems than debt. Can we conclude that a government could have a public debt ratio of 200%, 300%, 500% without this being a problem? MMT answers that this is not a problem because the government—which owns the central bank—is indebted to itself (because the debt is repaid in a currency of which it is the issuer and which it owns). Let's take this reasoning a step further. Since the state owes money to itself, it does not harm anyone. It could even decide to cancel part of its own debt. This point raises hot debates among economists, some of whom argue that a central bank cannot cancel public debts without risking bankruptcy, while others reply that a central bank does not function like a commercial bank.

We discuss these different aspects now, starting with the idea of a fiscal currency. The interesting idea is that through the monetary policy it conducts, a central bank can create additional resources for a government. We will show that this is true, but not necessarily for the reasons mentioned by MMT.

Let us consider an example. Suppose a situation where a government issues bonds to finance a budget deficit. The bonds issued have the following characteristics:

- loan: $L = \$10$ million = overall budget deficit (G-T), if initial debt is zero,
- maturity: $T = 10$ years,
- interest rate: $i = 2\%$
- discount rate to calculate the total repayment: $\beta = 0$ (to simplify the calculations). Taking a number other than zero would not change our arguments.

Let's assume that the government is not playing a Ponzi game and that it intends to pay off its debt when it matures. Under these conditions, the

Table 8.3 Loan payment schedules

Years	Interest	Principal	Unpaid balance
1	0.20	0.91	9.09
2	0.18	0.93	8.16
3	0.16	0.95	7.21
4	0.14	0.97	6.24
5	0.12	0.99	5.25
6	0.10	1.01	4.24
7	0.08	1.03	3.21
8	0.06	1.05	2.16
9	0.04	1.07	1.09
10	0.02	1.09	0.00
Total	1.13	10	

ten million plus interest must equal the sum of all (discounted) debt service payments:

$$10 + \sum_{k=1}^{10} \frac{Int_{t+k}}{(1+\beta)^k} = \frac{DS_{t+k}}{(1+\beta)^k} = \frac{DS_{t+1}}{1+\beta} + \frac{DS_{t+2}}{(1+\beta)^2} + \frac{DS_{t+3}}{(1+\beta)^3} + \cdots \tag{8.7}$$

where Int is the interest payments, DS is debt service (interest plus principal).

The calculation of debt service and its components is obtained from the loan payment schedules (see Table 8.3). The numbers are calculated as follows. The first step is to calculate the repayment annuities:

$$\text{Annuities} = \frac{L \times i \times (1+i)^T}{(1+i)^T - 1} = 1.11 \tag{8.8}$$

For the first year of repayment, we have the following:

- Interest: $2\% \times 10 = 0.2$,
- Principal: $1.11 - 0.2 = 0.91$,
- Unpaid balance: $10 - 0.91 = 9.09$.

For the second year of repayment, we have the following:

- Interest: $2\% \times 9.09 = 0.18$,
- Principal: $1.11 - 0.18 = 0.93$,
- Unpaid balance: $9.09 - 0.93 = 8.16$.

And so on for the following years.

To explain the principle of fiscal money, let us make a few assumptions:

- government debt issued on the primary market is initially purchased by commercial banks with their excess reserves, but they decide to resell the bonds they have purchased after five years,
- all items on the consolidated balance sheet of the monetary sector are initially equal to zero,
- the income in the SGO (statement of government operation) account (without grants) is initially equal to 10 and does not increase. Government expenditures are initially 40. Primary expenditures (excluding interest) do not increase.

Let us examine the SGO and the balance sheet of the monetary sector after five years (Tables 8.4 and 8.5).

Table 8.4 Simplified balance sheet of the monetary sector

Assets	Liabilities
Foreign reserves: 0	Broad money: $M = 0$
Net domestic assets	1.- Monetary base: $M0 = 0$
1.- Net domestic credits (private sector:0	1.1- Currency (notes) $= 0$
2.- Net domestic credit	1.2.-Commercial banks reserves at the CB:
(government: $1.13 - 4.75 - 0.81 + 10 - 4.75$)	$CBR = 0 + 10 - 4.75 = 5.25$
3.- Sovereign bonds: 0	1.3- Government account at the CB:
4.-Other financial assets	$G - T = 10 + 1.13 - 4.75 - 0.81 = 10 - 4.43$
(debt securities: commercial banks): 10	
5.- Other financial assets	2.- Others: 0
(debt securities: central bank): 0	
	Quasi money: 0
Total: $10 + 0.82$	Total: $10 + 0.82$

Table 8.5 Simplified statement of government operations

Revenue: 30	Expenditure: 40
1.- Taxes + social contributions: 2.- Non-tax revenue 3.-Grants	1.-Wages and salaries 2.-Use of goods and services + consumption of fixed capital 3.-Interest : 0.81 4.-Subsidies + grants + social benefits 5.-Capital spending (public investment)

Net lending/borrowing :
-10-0.81= −10.81

Financing : 10-4.75
1.-Foreign (loans and amortization)
2.-Currency deposit (loans and
amortization)
2.1.-Commercial banks : −4.75
2.2.-Central bank : 5.56
3.-Domestic securities
3.1-Debt securities (commercial banks)
: 10
3.2-Debt securities (central bank)
3.3.-Debt securities (others)

The government has a deficit of 10 (the difference between 30 in revenue and 40 in government spending). The deficit is financed by issuing securities held by commercial banks. Initially, in the balance sheet of the monetary sector, the item reserves of commercial banks is zero, because they can hold their wealth either in the form of central bank money or in the form of assets (in this case sovereign bonds). We add 1.13 million of interest that they will have to recover in ten years and which therefore appears as a claim on the state. This sum must therefore appear as a counterpart in the right-hand side of the government's account with the central bank.

After five years, the government will have repaid part of the principal (by adding the first five years, we obtain 4.75). If it pays this amount to the commercial banks, it reduces the net domestic claims of the commercial banks on the government.

The central bank purchases the debt from the commercial banks. It creates central bank money by paying them 10 minus the amount of principal already received (10-4.75). And they record this amount as a debt owed to them by the government.

In summary, in the monetary sector account the monetary base increased by 0.82, which is roughly the amount of interest paid by the government on its debt. What happens to the government account? Table 8.4 shows the SGO.

Initially, the government has a budget deficit of 10, which is financed by borrowing 10 million from the banking sector. After five years, the government will have paid interest (0.81 million) in addition to its current expenditures. The principal repayment (4.75 million) corresponds to the amortization of the debt and is recorded at the bottom of the line with a negative sign. The deficit (G-T) increases to 10.81, and the resources funding the deficit decrease to 10-4.75=5.25. Thus, there is a funding gap of 5.56.

Following the reasoning of the MMT, the central bank can create in the form of central bank money this missing 5.56 million dollars. To do this, it simply has to tax the private sector (in our example, the commercial banks). It is enough to enter this amount in the tax line (because the tax is paid in central bank money). We can easily see here the error of reasoning. Indeed, this operation has no consequence on the monetary base, since we take 5.56 from the banks' reserves to give them to the state. It is only the composition of the monetary base that has changed. Moreover, as this is a financing operation, 5.56 should not be entered under taxes, but below the line (in the financing resources).

If the central bank decides to finance more than the amount of the deficit gap (e.g., 7.56 instead of 5.56), the monetary base does not change. But in this case, there is a positive financing gap that can be filled, for example, by an increase in government spending. In the example we consider, changes in the composition of the monetary base create a crowding-out effect of private sector financing by the public sector. This is the case the monetary base is necessarily constant.

We will now see that there is a way for the central bank to generate resources for public finances. Suppose that from year 6 onward, the average interest rate on the debt decreases from 2% to 0.5%. Suppose also that a renegotiation takes place between the government and the central bank under the following conditions:

- loan: $L = \$5.25$ million (unpaid principal),
- maturity : $T = 5$ years,
- interest rate: $i = 0.5\%$,
- discount rate to calculate the total repayment: $\beta = 0$.

Using similar arguments as before the new monthly payment is 1.06 million. Table 8.6 shows the new loan payment schedule

With the new interest rate, the government saves \$0.24 million in interest payments on debt that it will not repay. In the SGO after the tenth year, this savings is recorded as a grant. Therefore, it is an additional resource that is independent of taxes. The interest expense from year 6 to year 7 is \$0.08 million (instead of \$0.32 million without the interest rate reduction). The government repays 5.25 million in capital. This time the financing gap has decreased to 5.09 million, instead of 5.56 million 5 years ago. The central bank can provide this money.

The monetary sector balance sheet is now as in Table 8.7.

The central bank must recover 0.08 million in interest and the remainder in capital, that is, 5.25 million. This is a claim on the state which allows the latter to finance part of its deficit. Therefore, the same amounts are recorded on the left and right sides of the balance sheet. The financing gap of 5.09 million is supposed to be taken from the commercial banks, so this amount is deducted from their reserves and added to those of the state. The important issue is the 0.24 million in grants that increase the state's resources. For the monetary sector, the only possibility is that the central bank takes this money in its equity.

The conclusion is that the grant element of a loan, which can be interpreted as fiscal money when, for example, it is linked to monetary policy (lowering of interest rates), has a counterpart because it reduces the equity of the central bank. The question of the limits of monetary policy to finance public spending is therefore the following. Can a central bank draw indefinitely on its equity to give additional resources to the state? MMT answers that this question is meaningless if the state and the central bank are the same entity. We can criticize this theory, saying that this case has not been seen in the last 40 years in the industrialized countries. MMT proponents can reply that this is an issue about institutions. Why not envisaging the suspension of the rule of independence of central banks from government in the coming years? Even if they are not nationalized, central banks could be assigned the task of providing the state with resources to finance essential public expenditures.

Table 8.6 New loan payment schedule

New loan contract				Grant element of the loan		
Years	Interest	Principal	Unpaid balance	Years	Interest	Principal
1	0.20	0.91	9.09	1	0.00	0.00
2	0.18	0.93	8.16	2	0.00	0.00
3	0.16	0.95	7.21	3	0.00	0.00
4	0.14	0.97	6.24	4	0.00	0.00
5	0.12	0.99	5.25	5	0.00	0.00
6	0.03	1.04	4.21	6	−0.08	0.03
7	0.02	1.04	3.17	7	−0.06	0.02
8	0.02	1.05	2.12	8	−0.05	0.00
9	0.01	1.06	1.06	9	−0.03	−0.01
10	0.01	1.06	0.00	10	−0.02	−0.03
Total	0.89	10.00		Total	−0.24	0.00

Table 8.7 Monetary sector balance sheet with the new loan schedule

Assets	Liabilities
Foreign reserves : 0	Broad money : M = 0
Net domestic assets	1.- Monetary base : M0 = 0
1.- Net domestic credits (private sector :0	1.1- Currency (notes) = 0
2.- Net domestic credit	1.2.-Commercial banks reserves at the CB:
(government :	0+10-4.75-5.56-5.09
1.13-4.75-0.81+10-4.75+0.08+5.25	1.3- Government account at the CB :
3.- Sovereign bonds : 0	10+1.13-4.75
	-0.81+5.56+0.08+5.25+5.09+0.24
4.-Other financial assets (debt securities : commercial banks): 10	2.- Others (equity): −0.24
5.- Other financial assets (debt securities : central bank) : 0	Quasi money : 0
Total : 10+0.81+0.08	Total : 10+0.81+0.08

As our example shows, there are two possibilities to achieve such a situation. First, if commercial banks keep sovereign bonds and do not sell them back to the government, then the grants that are added to the government's resources as a result of a reduction in interest rates can be interpreted as a tax (a transfer of financial resources from the banking sector to the government). This phenomenon has long been known in the economics literature as financial repression. If the state buys back its own debt in the secondary market (through a central bank that is subordinated to it), this is equivalent to a debt buyback. The condition for the government to have resources in the form of unpaid interest savings is that interest rates fall, which implies that the government buys back its debt at a higher price. And if bond prices rise, there is no reason why it should find commercial banks or investors willing to give up these bonds easily.

Is the debt buyback strategy an efficient way to reduce government debt? In general, it is interesting to buy back debt when interest payments are high and not the other way around. Otherwise, the net position of the sovereign (and thus of the central bank if government and central banks are one entity) may deteriorate. This question has already been studied in the literature for a long time, but it is still very much debated outside of MMT circles, with no consensus viewpoints (see, e.g., Bulow and Rogoff 1991; Eltrudis et al. 2019; Farazli 2003; Meideros et al. 2007).

8.4   Heterodox Views of Economic Growth

The most important contributions of heterodox macroeconomics over the last ten years have been in the area of economic growth. This can be explained by two phenomena about which we will say a few words before reviewing the scientific advances of the new approaches suggested.

8.4.1   Factors That Have Accelerated the Acceptance of Heterodox Ideas About Growth

The first phenomenon is the rejection of the idea of a global growth story for all countries in the world. Until the mid-1990s, for many cohorts of students and doctoral candidates, it was implicitly accepted that growth models they were studying were intended to serve as a reference for the entire planet. This education took place in a context that international political economists describe as one of hegemonic stability. This concept makes it possible to understand how the organization of international relations since the end of the empires has been based on the organization of a world-system with one or more very powerful nations, militarily, economically, and financially, at its heart, around which gravitate satellite countries that are committed to their vision of the world and to their cultural values. See, for example, the works of Gilpin (1987), Gilpin (2001), Keohane (2020), Wohlforth (2019). This vision has been criticized, and the criticisms have been reinforced during the last century by the rise of new regional economic, military, and financial powers challenging the hegemony of the United States and Europe (China, Turkey, Iran, Russia, Israel, etc.). For the critics, see, for example, Gavris (2021).

The existence of major cycles where the hegemon changes explains why visions of growth have evolved historically. The notion of economic progress since the eighteenth century has been associated with the European industrial revolutions, with the breakthrough of the United Kingdom and then of the United States as hegemon, but also with the historical role played by the Netherlands, France, and during the 30 glorious years by the extraordinary dynamic of economic catching up in Japan. According to the Western vision, progress is due to economic growth. This is linked to technological innovations, to the progress of new ideas, and to the adaptability of the market economy, which has given rise to the successive forms of capitalism that the world has known: commercial, industrial, and financial capitalism, and today e-capitalism based on the rise of digital technologies and the Internet. It was admitted in the policy circles that these different forms of capitalism would spread in a context of globalization. Countries have been encouraged to integrate into globalization as quickly as possible for their own benefit.

This reading of history is being challenged, since new nations wish to assert themselves as new powers and want to develop another narrative, breaking with a unilateral vision of history. New analyses insist on the fact that the economic organization of a country is structured by social relations, politics, and cultural values specific to each country, and not exclusively determined by the accumulation of capital with a global aim. These forces produce growth histories that are characterized by a great diversity across countries.

The second phenomenon that explains why heterodox approaches to growth have spread rapidly is people's awareness that the mechanisms of growth models (those presented in Chap. 2) have not worked as predicted by the theories. The lives of millions of people on our planet are still characterized by harsh working conditions leading to uprooted and poor workers, not to mention the effects of stress on mental health. Moreover, climate disruption has negative consequences that most people can now experience in real life: millions of climate migrants are a source of demographic and socioeconomic imbalances, and pollution raises public health problems and leads to the degradation of natural resources (pollution of water tables, damage to biodiversity, etc.). These difficulties are experienced by the younger generations, who are at the age to give birth to the next generation. They will be directly impacted by environmental changes, hence the strong demand for changes in thinking and actions.

Both phenomena suggest the importance of an interdisciplinary approach to macroeconomics. This attracts the younger generation of macroeconomists whose goal is not to rescue the models of mainstream macroeconomics by enriching them with new mechanisms, but rather to understand the complex mechanisms of growth using new tools and models.

8.4.2   The Main Ideas of Heterodox Approaches to Economic Growth

Social, political, economic, and geopolitical institutions change over time and are diverse across countries. Crises occur when their dynamics are asynchronous, while stability is observed when they are complementary. Huntington (1996) interpreted the break-up of the USSR in the early 1990s as a historical evidence that socialism and capitalism were not compatible with each other. According to him, productive processes are specific to civilizational areas. But unlike Fukuyama (1992), whose vision is anhistorical, he does not claim that the Western economic model is predominant over all others. Today, several types of capitalisms seem to coexist in the world: Chinese-style state capitalism, where the political domination of a party-state is the spur to entrepreneurial capitalism; and Anglo-Saxon liberal capitalism, where the concentration of capital in the new growth sectors (platform and e-economy) has been accompanied by an explosion of social inequalities and the social market capitalism of continental Europe.

China's success in terms of growth and the rise in the standard of living of its population since its entry into the WTO in the early 1970s has encouraged the emergence of a model of autocratic state capitalism which has been emulated throughout the world (Russia, Turkey, Indonesia, countries of the Middle East, Rwanda, etc.). This phenomenon is becoming more pronounced as states become less and less economically and financially dependent on the formerly dominant countries.

What should mobilize our attention is not the fact that China has had double-digit growth and that it has caught up technologically with the United States. The important question is whether autocratic capitalism is as sustainable as the liberal capitalism of the United States and some European countries. If we integrate institutions into our reading grid, then we immediately understand that growth in China is only an intermediate stage, a means to achieve a key objective, which is social order and stability (not growth per se). The growth models we have presented in the previous chapters do not allow us to understand or analyze this process. The sustainability of growth cannot be judged according to the usual criteria (optimality and efficiency in resource allocation). In the Chinese government's view, growth is sustainable if the rise in the standard of living allows for social cohesion that prevents China from being hit by centrifugal forces leading to the break-up of the country, as was the case in the former USSR. This is an important criterion for the authorities in a world of strong hegemonic rivalries between the leading industrialized countries and the emerging economies.

Moreover, there are other criteria for judging the efficiency of the productive system than productivity growth of the total productivity of factors, labor, or capital. According to some economists working on growth in Asian countries, the essential factors of economic growth, especially concerning the labor factor, are the following: social capital in companies (feeling of trust, social networks), certain cultural values (cohesion, family values), feelings toward others, and so on. The interested reader can refer to Yao (2002)'s stimulating book, Eiichi (2018)'s historical book on the drivers of Japanese growth during the Meiji era and the values of Confucianism, or Yu (2016)'s article.

Beyond the case of Asian countries, there is also a vast literature, both theoretical and quantitative history, in the field of comparative political economy that has emerged since the early 1970s on the socio-anthropological and political factors of African capitalism whose theories help to understand the slow growth dynamics of countries on that continent, and why some countries have more important growths than others: neopatrimonialism, traditional patterns of authority, pre-modern cultural norms, marginalism of domestic capitalists, ethnic coalitions, patronage systems, and the refusal to decolonize. For a survey, see Breckenridge (2021), Behuria (2019), Omeje (2021). What emerges from the literature is the idea that there are growth trajectories that are compatible with the sociopolitical and anthropological structures of countries, but that are "stifled" by the growth strategies chosen by countries and that correspond to the structures of dominant economies.

The same question arises when, instead of social order, we consider, for example, the sustainability of the climate, of the environment, of ecosystems as final objectives, and when growth is only a secondary objective. We have already mentioned this topic in a previous chapter. There is now a large body of literature belonging to the field of ecological economics (specifically New Macroeconomic Ecology, NME), which considers the modeling of growth in a very different way from that of the New-Keynesian or neoclassical models. The heterodox character of their approach stems from the fact that economic growth is no longer the focus of the analysis. It is analyzed from the point of view of its compatibility with objectives other than that of maximizing the standard of living of populations or making the most optimal use of scarce capital resources.

One of the questions raised by New Macroeconomic Ecology is whether economic growth should be curbed so that economies remain within ecological boundaries. What incentive mechanisms would guide the actions of entrepreneurs so that their prospects and capital accumulation are consistent with this goal? Proponents of the NME answer that there are none, for at least two reasons. The first reason is the so-called "tragedy of horizons", or in other words imperfect information. Indeed, since they cannot visualize medium/long-term time horizons, economic actors do not perceive ecological limits. The second reason is that economic actors ignore social returns. To take a trivial example, it is easier for an entrepreneur to accumulate capital and produce for private profit, than to accept the destruction of part of his or her carbon-rich capital in order to increase the availability of clean air in a country or to reduce public health problems linked to pollution.

NME growth theories fall into two categories.

The first group of models is based on the following idea. It is impossible to separate economic growth through capital accumulation from carbon energy needs. To lower the critical thresholds of pollution and climate disruption, a solution is therefore to change the objective (substitute collective well-being for growth) focusing on non-economic and collective goals. The reasoning is based on a standard approach in economics, that is, that of balanced growth. The criterion to be reached should be multidimensional, including both the evolution of GDP and that of environmental variables. On the one hand, economic models seek to bring growth to a level as high as possible and compatible with technological constraints (and possibly optimality criteria). On the other hand, it is important that the effects on the environment and natural environment do not exceed certain critical thresholds. But these two objectives are irreconcilable. According to the authors, instead of growth, it is thus necessary to identify activities and styles of life that increase collective well-being with low environmental costs.

This view is developed, for example, by economists of the Center for the Understanding of Sustainable Prosperity (CUSP). Theories of post-growth economics are proposed to deal with bio-geophysical limits. The idea is to focus on welfare state systems, as they exist, for example, in OECD countries, with a modification of the governance architecture. Instead of focusing on their redistributive role, states could have an active role as agents in providing and regulating vital goods and services. They could also play a more important role in protecting the assets on which tomorrow's world depends. Cosme et al. (2017), Corlet Walker et al. (2021), Jackson (2017), and Buchs and Koch (2017) propose several surveys on various aspects of the abundant literature on post-growth economics with the dilemmas that are posed to macroeconomists: how to build a welfare state without exaggerated GDP growth? How to manage the rising costs of such a system? How to reconcile individual preferences with the finite nature of available resources? What welfare criteria should be chosen that are not necessarily correlated with the satisfaction of material needs? An extreme version of post-growth theories is "Degrowth economics". The idea is about getting out of the productivist framework by voluntarily slowing down the rate of growth quantitatively (in particular by reducing activities that are harmful to the environment) and qualitatively (by changing the pace of work, e.g., by proposing a universal income). The objective is not to lower the macroeconomic standard of living, but simply to reduce the speed at which GDP grows, avoiding scenarios of economic collapse (rising unemployment, inflation, rising poverty, and financial collapse) while preserving the climate and the environment. One of the most original ideas is a reversal of perspective by giving priority to other forms of productivity than those put forward since the beginning of the industrial revolutions (material productivity, energy productivity): renouncing short-time and just-in-time flows, favoring slow fashion, preferring organic agriculture that is more labor-intensive than industrial agriculture. Supporters of the degrowth approach reject the catastrophic nature of the presentations that are sometimes made to the general public. Macro-socio-ecological models have been built to study the rates of degrowth compatible with low-carbon objectives while avoiding negative macroeconomic effects. See, in the very abundant literature, Alessandro et al. (2020), Borowy and Aillon (2017), O'Neill et al. (2018). Research on the same topic has also been conducted by the Post-Growth Economics Network (PEN) (see, e.g., Cohen-Fourot 2022; Hinton and Cornell 2022).

A second group of theories is based on green growth. The expression "Green New Deal" (GND) has even been used in reference to the new deal policy adopted under the Roosevelt administration between 1933 and 1938 in the United States. The proposal here is to redirect carbon resources toward decarbonized resources in order to generate a less polluting growth that preserves the environment. Although criticized by degrowth and post-growth economic theorists, GND propositions belong to heterodox approaches.

Degrowth economists criticize the macroeconomists in favor of green growth for keeping their reasoning within a productivist framework. One might think that more efficient technologies that internalize polluting emissions would make it possible to improve the energy efficiency of productive processes. In such a context, we simply have to move faster than in the past, accepting the possibility that some assets may be stranded, that is, that technologies and equipment using fossil fuels may be abandoned without reimbursing the opportunity costs to the actors who used them. But post-growth theorists respond that this is difficult to achieve because it is hard to separate productivist growth from the need for carbon resources and because GDP is growing faster than the technological discoveries that improve technological efficiency.

Proponents of a Green New Deal advocate the solution of a market for green bonds and a policy of taxing pollution: setting up incentives for market players to buy green bonds issued by firms actively engaged in the ecological transition, taxing more products manufactured with carbon assets, and prohibiting through regulations the use of carbon assets (diesel or gasoline-powered vehicles, e.g., in a future time horizon). From an economic policy perspective, the goal is for governments to make massive investments to accelerate the energy transition. This spending would be financed by an expansive monetary policy, in addition to the bond market. Some proponents of the Green New Deal put forward solutions that extend the proposals of the MMT. The first is that central banks should buy the green bonds issued by governments and keep these securities on their balance sheet forever, which is de facto equivalent to debt cancellation. The second proposal is that there can be no ecological transition without social justice. The guarantee of jobs to support the green transition is therefore a factor to be taken into consideration. The interested reader can consult the following books and articles on green growth, among a voluminous literature: Barbier (2010), Boyle et al. (2021), Davidson (2022), Fischer and Jacobsen (2021), Luke (2009), Mazzucato (2022), Pettifor (2020).

8.5   Conclusion

The views mentioned in this chapter suggest that heterodox macroeconomics conveys ideas that are useful in thinking about growth and its imbalances (inflation, unemployment, climate change), as well as the interdependence between monetary and fiscal policies. It seems to us that these ideas will spread rapidly in the scientific community during the forthcoming decades, if four pitfalls are avoided.

The first hindrance comes from the criticisms of orthodox economists, who often criticize the lack of rigor (in terms of theoretical models) of the proposed arguments. We should keep in mind that any new theory comes first with some principles, before the ideas are formalized. So, the debates should first focus on these principles.

The other two hindrances come from the heterodox schools of thought themselves. First of all, it is important to avoid unnecessary battles over whether a particular idea belongs to a particular school of thought. This is, for instance, what makes MMT currently distrustful, in our opinion (the fact that it does not clearly state what it revisits from old theories or from other theoretical schools of thought such as the post-Keynesians). Secondly, proposing new ideas while rejecting all economic formalization—on the pretext that reality is complex—is not a convincing argument. If there are criticisms to be made of orthodox macroeconomics, it is not because of the alleged hyper-mathematization of the discipline, but because some of the hypotheses, ideas, and mechanisms put forward in the models are false or invalidated by the empirical evidence. Mathematical models help a lot in the clarification of ideas.

The fourth obstacle is that it is not always possible to differentiate between scientific contributions and the political activism that takes place at the same time among some heterodox economists. Activism is a strategic—and useful—way of helping to disseminate ideas that may have difficulty penetrating the scientific community for reasons of conservatism or because of the slow pace of change in ideas among macroeconomists. This is the case of MMT which has become very popular in the public opinion following a book written by Stephanie Kelton's book (see Kelton 2020).

PIONEERS IN THE FIELD

Larry Randall Wray

Larry Randall Wray is one of the founders of modern monetary theory and of the Job Guarantee Buffer concept. It is difficult to

(continued)

pin him down to a particular school of thought, as his contributions are eclectic. The best way to define him is to say that he defends the ideas of Keynes and Minsky for the twenty-first century. He is also an advocate of neo-Chartalist approaches to monetary analysis. Wray has written and edited many books. We recommend two of them to the reader. The first is a thorough presentation of Minsky's approach to understanding financial instability but also to the issues of poverty and unemployment (Why Minsky Matters, Princeton University Press). The second book is a handbook he co-edited with Flavia Dantas on economic stagnation. The main thread of this book is to show how economic stagnation is caused by the instability intrinsic to financial markets and the fragilities that arise from the formation and bursting of logs (Handbook of Economic Stagnation, Academic Press).

Tim Jackson

If you know nothing about the theory of the post-growth economy, Tim Jackson's book summarizing its main ideas is to be recommended (Post-growth: Life After Capitalism, Polity Press). His work, devoted to the interactions between economics and ecology, illustrates the originality of the so-called multidimensional approaches to the ecological transition. He is one of those who have proposed an original approach to the concept of sustainable growth, leaving the field of neoclassical growth models. The notion of prosperity compatible with the well-being of individuals is put forward in front of GDP growth. The originality lies in the definition of the concept of well-being, which introduces non-material elements of satisfaction. Even if he does not claim to do so, Jackson's work has inspired the theorists of degrowth, because of a law of diminishing social returns beyond a certain growth threshold. In addition to the harmful effects of exponential growth on the environment, Jackson is also interested in the social effects (e.g., human exploitation, social inequalities). An interesting point, and one that differentiates him from neoclassical economists, is the fact that he substitutes the well-being of "communities" for that of strictly individual desires.

REFERENCES

Alessandro JD, Cieplinski A, Distefano T, Dittmer K (2020) Feasible alternatives to green growth. Nat Sustain 3:329–335

Aoki M (1988) Information, incentives and bargaining in the Japanese economy. Camb Univ Press, Cambridge

Aquanno S, Brennan J (2016) Some inflationary aspects of distribution conflict: reassessing Canadian inflation, Part I. J Econ Issues 50(1):217–244

Barbier EB (2010) A global green new deal. Rethinking the economic recovery. Camb Univ Press, Cambridge

Behuria P (2019) African Development and the marginalization of domestic capitalist. ESID WP n° 115, The Univ of Manchester

Bloch H, Dockery M, Morgan M, Sapword D (2007) Growth, commodity prices, inflation and the distribution of income. Metroeconomica 58(1):3–44

Borowy I, Aillon J-L (2017) sustainable health and degrowth: health, health care and society beyond the growth paradigm. Soc Theory Health 15(3):346–368

Boyle AD, Leggat G, Morikawa L, Pappas Y, Stephens JC (2021) Green new deal proposals: comparing emerging transformational climate policies at multiple scales. Energy Res Soc Sci 81:102259

Brady GL (2020) Modern monetary theory: some additional dimension. Atl Econ J 48(1):1–9

Breckenridge K (2021) What happened to the theory of African capitalism? Econ Soc 50(1):9–35

Buchs M, Koch M (2017) Post-growth and well-being. Challenges to sustainable welfare. Springer, Berlin

Bulow J, Rogoff K (1991) Sovereign debt repurchases : no cure for overhang. Q J Econ 106(4):1219–1235

Cohen-Fourot L (2022) Looking for growth imperatives under capitalism: money wage labour, and market exchange. WP Ser 01/2022, Post-growth Economics Network

Corlet Walker C, Druckman A, Jackson T (2021) Welfare systems without economic growth: a review of the challenges and next steps for the field. Ecol Econ 186:107066

Cosme I, Santos R, O'Neill DW (2017) Assessing degrowth discourse: a review analysis of academic degrowth policy proposals. J Clean Prod 149(15):321–334

Davidson EA (2022) Science for a green new deal. Connecting climate economics and social justice. John Hopkins Univ Press, Baltimore

Dennehy E (2012) Corporate governance: a stakeholder model. Int J Bus Governance Ethics 7(2):83–95

Drumetz F, Pfister C (2021) Modern monetary theory : a wrong compass for decision-making. Intereconomics 56(6):355–361

Ehnts DH, Höfgen M (2019) Modern monetary theory: a European perspective. RW Econ Rev 89:75–84

Eiichi S (2018) Confucian capitalism. Palgrave Macmillan

Eltrudis D, Bailey SJ, Monfardini P (2019) Sub-sovereign bond buyback: a way forward for debt-laden regions in austerity. Pub Mon Manag 39(8):571–580

Farazli JM (2003) Profitable buybacks in sovereign debt. Rev Int Econ 6(4):649–659

Fischer C, Jacobsen G (2021) The Green New Deal and the future of carbon pricing. J Policy Anal Manag 40(3):988–995

Fukuyama F (1992) The end of history and the last man. Free Press

Gali J (2018) The state of New-Keynesian economics: a partial assessment. J Econ Perspect 32(3):87–112

Gavris M (2021) Revisiting fallacies in hegemonic stability theory in light of the 2007–2008 crisis: the theory hollow conceptualization of hegemony. Rev Int Policy Econ 28(3):739–760

Gilpin R (1987) The political economy of international relations. Princeton Univ Press, Princeton

Gilpin R (2001) Global political economy: understanding the international order. Princeton Univ Press, Princeton

Hamilton EJ (1942) Profit inflation and the industrial revolution, 1751–1800. Q J Econ 56(2):256–273

Hannsgen G (2014) Fiscal policy, chartal money, markup dynamics, and unemployment insurance in a model of growth and distribution. Int Rev Econ 65(3):487–523

Hinton JB, Cornell SE (2022) Profit as a means or and end? A conceptual framework for an ecological economics approach to sustainable business. WP Ser 03/2022, Post-Growth Economics Network

Huntington S (1996) The clash of civilizations and the remaking of world order. Simon and Schuster, New York

Imai J (2011) The transformation of Japanese employment relations. Palgrave Macmillan

Jackson T (2017) Prosperity without growth: economics for the economy of tomorrow. Routledge, London

Jany-Catrice F (2020) A political economy measurement of inflation. The case of France, Springer, Berlin

Kelton S (2020) The deficit myth, 5th edn. John Murray

Keohane O (2020) Understanding multilateral institutions in easy and hard times. Ann Rev Policy Sci 23(1):1–18

Lavoie M (2014) The monetary and fiscal nexus of neo-chartalism: a friendly critique. J Econ Issues 47(1):1–32

Lavoie M (2015) Post-Keynesian economics: new foundation. Edward Elgar

Lavoie M (2019), Modern monetary theory and post-Keynesian economics. RW Econ Rev 89:197–108

Lavoie M (2022) MMT, sovereign currencies and the Eurozone. Rev Policy Econ 34(4):633–646

Lerner AP (1943) Functional finance and the federal debt. Soc Res 10:38–57

Lerner AP (1947) Money as a creature of the state. Am Econ Rev 37:312–317

Levy SJ (2000) Profits: the view of Jerome Levy and Michal Klecki. Jerome Levy Econ Inst WP n°309

Luke TW (2009) A green new deal: why green, how new, and what is the deal? Crit Pol Rev 3(1):14–28

Mazzucato M (2022) Financing the Green New Deal. Nat Sustain 5:93–94

Meideros C, Polan M, Ramlogan P (2007) A primer on sovereign debts buybacks and swaps, IMF Working Papers, n°07/58

Mitchell W, Muysken (2008) Full employment abandoned : shifting sounds and policy failures. Edward Elgar

Mitchell W, Wray LR, Watts M (2019) Macroeconomics. Red Global Press, London

Nersisyan Y, Wray L R (2016) Modern money theory and the facts of experience. Camb J Econ 40(5):1297–1316

Newman PJ (2020) Modern monetary theory: an Austrian interpretation of recrudescent keynesianism. Atl Econ J 48(1):23–31

Nishimura I (2017) Changes in the wage system in Japan: circumstances and background. Jpn Labor Issues 1(3):21–32

O'Neill DW, Fanning AL, Lamb W, Steinberger JK (2018) a good life for all within planetary boundaries. Nat Sustain 1:88–95

Ogoshi Y (2006) Current Japanese employment practices and industrial relations: the transformation of permanent employment and seniority-based wage system. Asian Bus Manag 5(4):469–485

Omeje K (2021) The failure and feasibility of capitalism in Africa. Palgrave Macmillan

Palley TI (2015) Money, fiscal policy and interest rates: a critique of modern monetary theory. Rev Policy Econ 27(1):1–23

Palley TI (2019) Macroeconomics vs. modern money theory: some unpleasant Keynesian arithmetic and monetary dynamics. RW Econ Rev 89:148–155

Pettifor A (2020) The case for the Green New Deal. Verso, London

Prinz AL, Beck H (2021) Modern monetary theory: a solid theoretical foundation of economic policy? Atl Econ J 49(2):173–186

Rochon LP, Vernengo M (2003) State money and the real world: or chartalism and its discontents. J Post-Keyn Econ 26:57–67

Skousen M (2020) Pouring new wine into old bottles: can modern monetary theory work? Atl Econ J 48(1):11–21

Solow RM (1990) The labor market as a social institution. Basil Blackwell, Cambridge

Tanaka, Y (2021) Very simple mathematical model of MMT. Business and economic research. Macrothink Institute, pp 77–87

Taylor L, Barbosa Filho NH (2021) Inflation? It's import prices and the labor share. Int J Pol Econ 50(2):116–142

Tcherneva PR (2012) Beyond full employment. The Employer of last resort as an institution for Change. Levy Econ Inst of Bard College

Tymoigne E, Wray LR (2015) Modern monetary theory: a reply to Palley. Rev Policy Econ 27(1):24–44

Vera L (2017) The distribution of power and the inflation-unemployment relationship in the United States: a Post-Keynesian approach. Review Radical Political Econ 49(2):265–285

Watanabe S (2000) The Japan model and the future of employment and wage systems. Int Lab Rev 139(3):307–331

Wohlforth W (2019) The stability of unipolar world. Int Sec 24(1):5–41

Wray LR (1998) Understanding modern money: the key to full employment price stability. Edward Elgar

Wray LR (2012) Modern monetary theory: a primer on macroeconomics for sovereign money systems. Palgrave Macmillan

Wray LR (2019) Alternative paths to modern money theory. RW Econ Rev 89:5–22

Wray LR, Armstrong P, Holland S, Jacjson-Prior C, Plumridge P, Wilson N (2023) Modern monetary theory. Edward Elgar

Yao S (2002) Confucian capitalism: discourse, practice and the myth of Chinese enterprise. RoutledgeCurzon, London

Yu Y-S (2016) Confucian ethics and capitalism. In Duke MS (ed) Chinese history and culture: sixth century B.C.E. to seventh century. Columbia Univ. Press, New York, pp 208–221

CHAPTER 9

Conclusion

The challenges facing macroeconomics in the first quarter of the twenty-first century are very different from those of the last century. Just 75 years ago, barely industrialized countries faced the challenges of rebuilding after two world wars that had devastated and ruined economies. European countries had vast colonial empires. The United States, the great victors of the war, had only one military rival, that is, Russia, which had also extended its zone of influence in Eastern Europe and in several developing countries where it exported communism. The hegemonic stability of the world was based on a geostrategic balance built around the Cold War concept. The entire United Nations system was designed so that the economic model would be the reference in the major institutions. During this period, theoretical macroeconomics had great success. The reconstruction of post-war states, the need to build a social consensus, and the demographic challenge led to a proliferation of ideas. Most of the growth models taught to today's students began to be thought of during the period of the 30 glorious years. Then, gradually, the world was transformed. Despite independence, the influence of the former colonial powers remained important and was a bridge to globalization, a system of world economies built around central and so-called peripheral states. The revolution of information and communication technologies has occurred, and finance has profoundly transformed the morphology of economies. Poverty and inequality, which had initially faded, returned. So much so that globalization has led to a downgrading of the middle classes (in the

© The Author(s), under exclusive license to Springer Nature
Switzerland AG 2023
G. Dufrénot, *New Challenges for Macroeconomic Policies*,
https://doi.org/10.1007/978-3-031-15754-7_9

United States, the United Kingdom, Japan, and in a number of European countries). In addition, there has been a greater degradation of natural and environmental ecosystems. Social crises have become more important. The level of private and public debt has increased (in times of peace). The hegemonic stability of the past is being challenged. After the miracle of the Asian Tigers in the 1980s, China has become the new hegemonic power of the twentieth century. It competes with the United States and Europe on all levels: economic, military, technological. It provides its own narrative and reading grid on the transformation of the world. As at the beginning of the last century, the world needs macroeconomists to provide a framework for reading the transformations we are experiencing, and to suggest strategies for economic policies.

Macroeconomists are not magicians. They cannot change a complex world. Nor can they predict what will happen in the next decade, or in the next century. Many who have ventured to make predictions have been wrong. Think of the crisis of 2008, which we did not anticipate except for a very small minority. The future is not entirely in the past. It has its share of newness. The best strategy is to better understand what is going on to help societies adopt the best behaviors to live through the transformations, build resilience in the face of shocks, and enable people to live as well as possible.

The task is difficult because macroeconomists are interested in global phenomena that cannot be reduced to the aggregation of individual microeconomic phenomena. Several fields of macroeconomics have adopted this choice of deducing aggregate phenomena from individual behavior. This methodology has been the basis of simulation and calibration models, and of rational expectations models. It has also guided economic policy recommendations based on randomized methods (experimental economics). All these techniques have improved our knowledge of certain economic mechanisms. But they have not solved all the problems. How can we explain the return of piecework in our economies (uberization), after a long era of wage employment in industrialized countries? Why do highly qualified labor suppliers in certain sectors of activity refuse to work, even if they are offered high wages? Why have interest rates been falling steadily for several decades? Why, in the age of highly advanced technologies, has a pandemic like Covid-19 killed so many people in the United States, while the number of deaths in China and Japan has been much lower? How can we explain the fact that finance always rises from its ashes, even after serious financial crises? Why, contrary to popular belief, is the digital transition not the most efficient way to fight global warming and the imbalance of natural ecosystems? How can we explain the slowdown of potential growth processes in industrialized countries? Why do new economies manage to reach the supposed technological frontier of the Western countries so easily? The phenomenon is so astonishing that it is a source of geopolitical tension. China and other emerging nations are shown to be strategic rivals. Answering that it is because they are stealing technology from the industrialized countries is an insufficient response.

What we have done in this book is something very modest. We aimed to review a few key areas where macroeconomists' thinking is changing and certainly opening up new paradigms. There are two important areas. The first area is growth. There are many issues at stake here. The crucial question of this century is not the efficiency of resource allocation. It is the question of sustainability in the medium/long term. Will we succeed in guaranteeing future generations a satisfactory standard of living and quality of life? First, we need to choose a trajectory for potential growth. Second, we need to think about our production and consumption patterns. Are they compatible with maintaining the productivity of human capital at a satisfactory level? Third, are we leaving enough resources for future generations to choose the growth trajectories that will best suit them? In this book, we have explained how economists approach the question of growth when the economy is based on the new technologies of the twenty-first century: automatic and digital. This profoundly changes the production relationships between labor and the different forms of capital: intangible services, natural and ecological resources, human capital, and so on. We have traced the doubts that are currently in the minds of macroeconomists, who are trying to analyze the causes of the slowdown in productivity gains, the fall in investment rates, the degree of substitution between labor and robots, and the role of the aging population. These doubts also stem from the multiplication of shocks that threaten the resilience of productive systems that are subject to super-hysteresis phenomena: Each new shock further lowers potential growth trajectories. In this context, the debates on secular stagnation and its interpretations are interesting. They highlight contradictions in capitalism: We have also underlined the interest of Schumpeterian analyses that put forward the latency periods inherent in the phenomena of creative destruction, and the metamorphosis of professions and therefore of qualifications. Sustainability also concerns questions of well-being, which cannot be separated from questions of social justice. What is the point of having high growth rates and high GDP levels if many people are victims of poverty and inequality?

One of the serious avenues for sustainable growth in the years to come will be a comprehensive approach. This approach considers the determination of production and growth in conjunction with the other balances of living and natural ecosystems. This makes the modeling and the tools used more complex. But it is more realistic to take into account the concept of capitalocene: human activities modify the cycles of natural elements and these have feedback effects on human activities. The second area that is being reconsidered is that of economic policy (fiscal and monetary policies). We have reviewed the many aspects that are changing. In terms of monetary policy, in addition to the return of quantitative policies, the issue of targets is being debated. The natural rate of interest has become a central concept. In addition, we must consider the new challenges of monetary policy. Central bankers will no longer seek only to control inflation, but are also increasingly called upon to finance the ecological transition, to support fiscal policies by crushing interest rates to prevent debt servicing from increasing too much, and possibly to extend quantitative policies to households (helicopter money). On the fiscal policy side, the role of governments has evolved. The recent health crisis has revealed their role as income insurers. And they must finance new innovations to support potential growth, while at the same time conducting counter-cyclical policies. But the major constraint is that of debt and over-indebtedness. We have reviewed different scenarios. In the eurozone, the problem of common fiscal rules for macroeconomically heterogeneous economies remains. In Japan, the world's most indebted country, the aging of the population is one of the greatest threats to the possible unsustainability of the debt. In the United States and the United Kingdom, interest rates have been kept very low, thus avoiding a snowball effect and stabilizing debt ratios, even if potential growth rates are not very high.

In recent months, inflation has made a comeback. It has been caused by two shocks that have occurred in quick succession. First, there was the decision by policymakers to lift health restrictions related to the Covid-19 crisis. This was a counter-shock to demand. After falling during the containment periods, aggregate demand rose again, causing bottlenecks. Then, rising energy prices and the Ukraine war in Europe triggered a supply shock caused by grain supply restrictions and an increase in all production costs. The mechanisms for indexing wages to prices will perhaps cause a price-wage loop to reappear and will once again drive up inflation expectations. Is this the end of the structural phenomena that have been in place for several decades? Will the Phillips curve reappear? Is this the end of the secular stagnation that was characterized by weakening potential growth rates, low inflation rates, and falling interest rates? Will the financial cycle see the end of its long upward phase? Will prices fall as a corollary to the likely rise in interest rates? Will monetary policy once again be based on interest rate rules? It is too early to answer.

INDEX

Printed in the United States
by Baker & Taylor Publisher Services